1977

The Supreme Court Review

1977
The

"Judges as persons, or courts as institutions, are entitled to
no greater immunity from criticism than other persons
or institutions . . . [J]udges must be kept mindful of their limitations and
of their ultimate public responsibility by a vigorous
stream of criticism expressed with candor however blunt."
–*Felix Frankfurter*

". . . while it is proper that people should find fault when
their judges fail, it is only reasonable that they should recognize the
difficulties. . . . Let them be severely brought to book,
when they go wrong, but by those who will take the trouble
to understand them."
–*Learned Hand*

THE LAW SCHOOL

THE UNIVERSITY OF CHICAGO

Supreme Court Review

EDITED BY

PHILIP B. KURLAND

AND GERHARD CASPER

THE UNIVERSITY OF CHICAGO PRESS
CHICAGO AND LONDON

INTERNATIONAL STANDARD BOOK NUMBER: 0-226-46429-6
LIBRARY OF CONGRESS CATALOG CARD NUMBER: 60-14353
THE UNIVERSITY OF CHICAGO PRESS, CHICAGO 60637
THE UNIVERSITY OF CHICAGO PRESS, LTD., LONDON

PRINTED IN THE UNITED STATES OF AMERICA

FOR

MARY JANE AND REGINA

Die guten Leute erkennt man daran
Dass sie besser werden
Wenn man sie erkennt.

—Bertolt Brecht

CONTENTS

BARRY D. KARL

EXECUTIVE REORGANIZATION AND PRESIDENTIAL POWER

I

The attention paid in recent years to the question of legislative veto, rather than the problem of executive reorganization from which the issue of legislative veto derives, is a curious transformation of perspective. The opening sentence of Joseph and Ann Cooper's study of the constitutionality of the legislative veto makes the point for us. "Over the past several decades Congress increasingly has become concerned with and put emphasis on its role as overseer of the executive branch."[1] To a historian, the statement itself is an oddity. The battle over the president's power to reorganize the executive agencies and departments goes back into the nineteenth century. The issue has always been that of congressional oversight. The power of reorganization has been grudgingly and reluctantly given, on short-term grants, and renewed only when the president has requested it and has been willing to fight his way past

Barry D. Karl is Professor and Chairman of the Department of History, The University of Chicago.

[1] Cooper & Cooper, *The Legislative Veto and the Constitution*, 30 Geo. Wash. L. Rev. 467 (1962); see also Miller & Knapp, *The Congressional Veto: Preserving the Constitutional Framework*, 52 Ind. L. J. 367 (1977).

0-226-46429-6/78/1977-1000$02.84

a suspicious Congress. The Coopers' proposition has a Rip Van Winkle quality about it, as though a Congress were awakening from some decades of sleep. The fault, if it can be called a fault, is in the perspective. The issue is not the legislative veto, at least not in itself, but the power of the presidency. Edward S. Corwin made the point almost forty years ago, when he reluctantly accepted some of the New Deal presidency and announced that the Lockean doctrine that "the legislature may not delegate its power" had gone the way of laissez-faire.[2] A cautious critic of administrative reorganization, he nonetheless viewed the historical transformation as a necessary one and stood, like Strauss's aging Marschallin, with one dry eye and one wet one, giving an intellectually satisfying aesthetic shape to something he could not change.

What one can say about the last decade is that, for the first time in over forty years, the debate over the power of the presidency has shifted ground. Corwin's position in 1940 was essentially a conservative one. It opposed the liberal acceptance of the strong presidency as the center of American government. In the academic community, Corwin stood almost alone in his questioning of the President's Committee on Administrative Management and its assertion of historical and constitutional support for the strong presidency. Theirs was a "Jacksonian" position, he argued, not one the framers of the Constitution would have acknowledged.[3] Nonetheless, he countered a whole generation that had focused its youthful energies on admiration of Theodore Roosevelt and Wilson and celebrated the rebirth of its youth in Franklin Roosevelt. Their literature evoked a history of Arthurian returns to Camelot, interspersed with sluggish episodes of what one of their favorite analysts, Wilfred Binkley, called "Congressional hegemony."[4] Such legislative eras were at worst corrupt and irresponsible, at best the source of political character sketches replete with humor and professional savvy. That perspective changed gradually through the Lyndon Johnson presidency and abruptly in the Nixon presidency. But the basic conflict over executive organization is old enough and rich enough to deserve more historical speculation than it is presently receiving.

The president's power to restructure the executive branch is a

---

[2] CORWIN, THE PRESIDENT: OFFICE AND POWERS 115, 153, and notes (1940).

[3] *Id.* at 96–110.

[4] BINKLEY, THE PRESIDENT AND CONGRESS (1962 ed.)

great power if, in some respects, a new one. It is possible to say precisely when it began, although the precision is deceptive. In May of 1918 the Overman Act authorized the president "to coordinate or consolidate executive bureaus, agencies, and offices, . . . in the interest of economy and the more efficient concentration of the Government."[5] The president was specifically forbidden to abolish any agency without congressional approval. Money could be spent only for purposes Congress had already specified. The power would lapse six months after the end of the war. "Upon the termination of this Act all executive or administrative agencies, departments, commissions, bureaus, offices, or officers shall exercise the same functions, duties, and powers as heretofore or as hereafter by law may be provided, any authorization of the President under this Act to the contrary notwithstanding."[6] Because it was confined to wartime agencies alone, the act is a fragile hook on which to hang the history of executive reorganization, but there it is.

In June of 1932, under the pressure of the growing emergency of the depression, President Hoover was given the authority to reorganize, this time by executive orders which would be subject to veto by either house of Congress within sixty days of their submission by the president. The section, contained in the legislative appropriation bill, specifically stated that its purpose was to carry out "the policy of Congress."[7] Hoover had requested the authority some time earlier, but Congress had been reluctant to grant it. In any case, his efforts at reorganization were vetoed.

On March 3, 1933, the day before Franklin Roosevelt's inauguration as president, Congress provided him with reorganization authority. The authorization appears in a section of an act making appropriations for the Treasury and Post Office Departments and was to lapse in two years.[8] The language of the act is an expression of congressional hysteria, invoking the urgency of the crisis and pressing on the new president the need to act effectively—but only for two years. Nonetheless, this statute remains the only instance of legislative authorization without the need for extensive presidential arm-twisting.

---

[5] Pub. L. 152, 40 Stat. 556 (1918).

[6] *Id.* at 557.

[7] Pub. L. 212, 47 Stat. 382, 413 (1932).

[8] Pub. L. 428, 47 Stat. 1489, 1517 (1933).

Still, it is clear that to this point Congress considered the reorganization power temporary, a product of emergency circumstances of either war or depression. The mood which propelled the legislation through Congress was the mood of crisis, along a pathway smoothed by the older assumption that curtailing the power of government was a good thing at any time and greased by the purported ease with which executive orders could be vetoed by a suspicious and watchful legislature.

By 1935, with the reorganization authority due to lapse, Roosevelt was more acutely aware of the distinction between the crisis that had brought him to power and the expansion his administration had already begun to accept as a new standard of national government. While a certain amount of New Deal administration had been planned as temporary, the bulk of newly asserted authority involved permanent administrative change to be absorbed into the routines of the executive branch. His decision to appoint a committee to examine the problem and to recommend changes was an important step in the process of transforming emergency power to government routine.[9] Yet in 1937, when Roosevelt requested the authority to reorganize the executive branch, he was castigated as a would-be dictator, and the power was refused by a Congress dominated by one of the largest Democratic majorities in history. The sense of emergency had diminished, partly under assurances from the president himself, who continued to announce the end of the depression in spite of the realities of economic conditions. While the 1936 landslide election suggested overwhelming public approval of the New Deal, a sequence of legislative defeats for the New Deal over the next two years revealed a distinctly defiant Congress, one to be sustained in the last analysis by a public that opinion polls showed to be curiously ambivalent.

If the emergency was over, the power was excessive. With examples of European dictatorships flashing from every newsreel screen, the concern was real enough. By 1939, however, as the new war approached, Congress was inclined to view the incipient emergency as sufficient ground for a new grant of authority to reorganize the executive branch. This time, however, the method was changed. Although the constitutionality of the old legislative veto had not been seriously challenged, an understandable touchiness about con-

---

[9] See Brownlow, A Passion for Anonymity cc. 18, 30, 31 (1958).

stitutionality in the wake of the Supreme Court's behavior led to the idea that both houses be required to veto in parallel of the normal legislative process. The concept of a reorganization plan to be submitted in place of the old executive order was a critically important change.[10] Louis Brownlow, one of the architects of Roosevelt's reorganization program and the former chairman of the Committee on Administrative Management, was inclined to see the new method as one which made the president an "agent" of the legislature. He seemed to see no constitutional issue and no violation of checks and balances, despite the fact that the new method complicated the veto process enough to give the president more power than Brownlow had dreamed possible in his earlier reorganization proposal.[11]

The war made emergency normal once again. But by 1946 Congress appeared to be no more willing to relinquish its control over an authority it could not exercise itself than it had been in 1932. What had changed was its recognition of the fact that the problem had not been solved and would not go away. Truman's genius lay in his calling Herbert Hoover out of his virtual banishment to head the new reorganization committee that Congress had authorized, thus bringing to the task a man who symbolized for critics and admirers alike the skills of professional administration. That and the administrative complexities of managing the new foreign policy mark 1949 as a year of crucial transition in congressional awareness of the relation between Congress and the executive branch.

The Reorganization Act of 1949 followed the most extensive review of the executive departments undertaken up to that time, dwarfing in its detail the work of the Brownlow committee, on whose precedents, nonetheless, it rested.[12] The presence of Don K. Price, Brownlow's leading protégé, helped. The restrictions in the act, however, are significant. The legislative veto could now be exercised by a majority of the full membership of either house. The president was forbidden to abolish or transfer an executive department or to consolidate two departments, an old restriction but one

---

10 For an account of the development of the new form, see POLENBERG, REORGANIZING ROOSEVELT'S GOVERNMENT (1966). Polenberg argued that Brownlow and his committee had very little to do with the reformulation of the legislation, although Roosevelt did in fact call on Brownlow to help plan the reorganization.

11 BROWNLOW, note 9 *supra,* at 414.

12 Pub. L. 109, 63 Stat. 203 (1949).

soon to be violated by Truman's successor in office. An older note was struck by the provision that the reorganization plan "shall specify the reduction of expenditures (itemized so far as practicable)."[13] In the last six months of 1949, Truman submitted eight reorganization plans, two of which were vetoed. The next year twenty-seven plans were submitted, seven of which were vetoed. In the remaining two years of his administration, he submitted six plans, three of which were vetoed.

Eisenhower's use of reorganization plans during the first two years of his presidency was spectacular. The creation of the Department of Health, Education, and Welfare by reorganization plan violated the spirit of the authorization but was condoned by an enthusiastic Congress which supported him with a joint resolution enabling the plan to go into effect ten days after presidential signature rather than being delayed through the sixty-day waiting period.[14] Successive plans in 1953 strengthened the management of several of the executive departments, most notably Defense, where Truman's difficulties in maintaining civilian control seemed to Eisenhower a matter of serious concern. Although it would be several years before Eisenhower would ask Congress for legislative authority to reshape Defense, he moved immediately to increase civilian management and reduce the administrative authority of the Joint Chiefs of Staff. He dealt with congressional opposition by the simple assertion that he, as a former general, obviously knew better.[15]

In a remarkable sense, the Eisenhower years were peak years for the idea of executive reorganization. State governments throughout the country adopted various versions of the method. The debates and subsequent state legislative and court battles suggest that the sense of danger was still there, but without the precisely defined shape it had had in the 1930s. Sunset provisions assured legislatures an opportunity to rethink the matter, but little of the old ideological concern troubled the disputes.[16] Congress provided Kennedy with a two-year extension in April of 1961.[17] He apparently con-

---

[13] *Id.* at 204.

[14] H. J. Res. 223, 67 Stat. 18 (1953).

[15] Rovere, Affairs of State: The Eisenhower Years c. 31 (1956).

[16] Eley, The Executive Reorganization Plan: A Survey of State Experience (1967).

[17] Pub. L. 87–18, 75 Stat. 41 (1961).

sidered using it to create a Department of Urban Affairs but feared that the attempt would backfire and went the legislative route instead, and his strategy backfired.[18] The renewal of the authority in 1964 expressly forbade the creation of new executive departments or the abolition or consolidation of old ones.[19]

Lyndon Johnson sought and received extensions of the authority, as did Nixon. The only new restriction Congress chose to add was in 1971. Instead of a simple extension, Congress restated its aims—the search for better, cheaper government, the hope for less government—but now added the insistence that no more than one plan be submitted in any thirty-day period.[20] The pressure to understand was apparently upon them. The record beyond that is unclear. The authority lapsed and was not requested by Ford during his brief administration.

The Carter administration's insistence that there really is nobody in the White House but efficiency and economy lovers brings us back full circle. But, in a peculiar way, the center of the circle is still out of view. Indeed, one can argue that the center of the circle was visible only once in the history of the reorganization issue: in 1937, when the so-called dictator bill was under attack. For better or for worse, the problem was then spelled out for what it is: presidential power versus congressional power in the management of the nation's basic resources. Until that point, only emergencies justified the relinquishing of congressional authority over resource distribution, and then only under the guise of the utterly fraudulent claim that less government would be the result. That a transfer of power was at issue could not be faced. That such a transfer, however necessary it might prove to be, required a review of constitutional principles was equally unacceptable. The argument that Congress was gradually awakening to some new understanding of its responsibilities is perhaps not the best way of looking at the problem. A

18 The story is interestingly complex. According to Theodore Sorensen, the president wanted to combine in a sequence of actions the creation of the new department, naming a black to the new cabinet post, and the executive order ending discrimination in federally financed housing. SORENSEN, KENNEDY 481 (1965). When the bill was killed in committee, Kennedy asked Sorensen to draft a reorganization plan, not because he thought he could get it through, but because the required roll call would reveal the opposition. He later acknowledged that his tactics had been too tricky in any case. SCHLESINGER, A THOUSAND DAYS 711 (1965).

19 Pub. L. 88–351, 78 Stat. 240 (1964).

20 Pub. L. 92–179, 85 Stat. 574 (1971).

recurring nightmare in which reality unexpectedly intrudes seems a better description.

We are dealing with a problem of expanded executive authority reluctantly authorized by a frightened legislature which sees no alternative and mistrusts, rightly, as its experiences seem to point out, the only methods of oversight it has evolved. Presidents seem all too soon to master a kind of legerdemain in which methods acceptable in one context seem suddenly and unexpectedly useful in another. One fairly recent example may suffice. In January of 1955, Eisenhower requested a congressional resolution empowering him to act in the national interest with regard to the protection of Formosa. It was a move designed to placate the warlike Senator Knowland without actually doing anything warlike. But congressional internationalists, still smarting from the persistent attacks on Franklin Roosevelt's international leadership, saw it as a sellout of presidential control of foreign policy, a step back from the independence Roosevelt had sought and Truman seemed to them to have won.[21] Actually the vagueness of the mandate provided a model for a new kind of freedom. The lesson was apparently not wasted on Senator Lyndon Johnson, who as president used it in the Gulf of Tonkin episode, but with results quite different from those intended by Eisenhower or feared by his critics.

In the aftermath of the so-called imperial presidency, Congress has looked for legislative devices for controlling presidential authority to engage in military activities. Even there, however, the issues remain obscure, tied to time clauses and to threats which, under the pressures of fast-moving circumstances and fragmented information, are likely to result in paralysis. What is clear is that the choice between administrative power and legislative direction is not better for the experience of the past sixty years. The point is dramatically underscored by the Nixon presidency, which once again obscures the fundamental issue with a highly colored historical bumble. Watergate enables specialized observers and the public alike to center attention on flawed character or charlatanism rather than on the problem of presidential power itself. Nixon's efforts to create within the White House a command center for administrative policy management extends to its ultimate conclusion the logic of systematic administrative control in twentieth-century American gov-

---

21 Rovere, note 15 *supra*, at 250–52.

ernment. At the same time, those efforts violate one of the essential principles of the Brownlow report: that advice and command be separated in the White House, with the power to command the exclusive power of the president. By combining the offices of national security adviser and secretary of state and making the secretary of the treasury a White House economic adviser, Nixon sought to obliterate the distinction between advice and command. However meaningless—even disruptive—that distinction may be in the field of industrial management, it is a crucial distinction in politics. The problem of acknowledging it is as great as the problem of respecting it once it is acknowledged. Richard Neustadt's *Presidential Power* provides an elegant statement of the dilemma on the eve of the Kennedy administration; but it, too, presents it a bit wryly, caught between touches of humor and a tragic vision.[22] Watergate is the raw, crude representation of the conflict between the administrative presidency, designed to accomplish effectively whatever the president believes he was elected to accomplish, and the political presidency, the need to use the full partisan range of the political system to achieve the managerial authority that comes only from election to office. The conflict between the two is at the heart of the problem of reorganization.

This bare historical outline distorts the matter somewhat, chiefly because the language of the immediate historical outline is deceptive. Executive reorganization is not the large historical issue. It is a term introduced quite deliberately to avoid historical confrontation with the problem of the presidency itself. Indeed, one could argue that the entire history of the American use of the term "public administration" is an effort to find a vocabulary capable of removing partisan politics from debates about policy. It is an elaborate charade that has given us such terms as "administrative management," "policy science," and, more recently, "public policy," as well as the now legendary backfires that occur when the nonpartisan purists get caught lobbying for their reforms, end up in crestfallen rejection, or, perhaps worse, find their names and reputations attached to programs so drastically altered that they bear only an embarrassing resemblance to the original idea. This is not to deny the utility of the method. Like the surgical sheets that focus the surgeon's attention on the mechanism of human physiology he is

22 (1960).

trained to affect, to the exclusion of everything else, it is a way of focusing on technical concerns. Thus the mechanism here may be administrative; but the animal is political.

Such reluctance to confront the structural issues was not always the case. Americans in the 1880s were not so shy about making suggestions for major restructuring of the presidential office and its relation to the other branches of government. Indeed, until World War I, many writers of a wide range of political persuasions were perfectly willing to consider this the only route to governmental reform. By 1920 such arguments were moribund. By 1930 they were deemed threatening in a world beset by revolution. By 1940, to Americans beginning to be optimistic about the role the United States was to play in reshaping world politics, the issue was changing. Party responsibility was revived, and the possibility of party realignment was suggested by no less a participant than Franklin Roosevelt.[23] By 1950 Americans had begun to consider their governmental form part of a natural evolutionary process that worked, despite irrationalities or even because of them. They were prepared to recommend that emerging nations emulate as much as they could of the American system.[24] By 1960 there were questions again, suggestions of deadlock, and the dramatic concern with presidential succession.[25] Still, the last two decades have unleashed a series of historically unprecedented events which have led to suspicion and befuddlement, along with sporadic announcement of revolutionary agendas by a minority so impotent that its only outlet has tended to be violent rage.

II

The American presidency as it stands today probably violates—or renders irrelevant—many of the intentions of the framers

[23] Samuel Rosenman asserted that Roosevelt had sent him to discuss the possibility of party realignment with Wendell Willkie after the 1940 election. ROSENMAN, WORKING WITH ROOSEVELT c. xxiv (1952).

[24] A movement in political science under way since the end of World War II is illustrated by works such as CHAMBERS, POLITICAL PARTIES IN A NEW NATION (1963).

[25] The immediate reference here is BURNS, THE DEADLOCK OF DEMOCRACY (1963). FINER, THE PRESIDENCY: CRISIS AND REGENERATION (1960), and TUGWELL, THE ENLARGEMENT OF THE PRESIDENCY (1960), were politely received but practically ignored when they appeared. Despite its dramatic title, REEDY, THE TWILIGHT OF THE PRESIDENCY (1970), was quickly forgotten.

of the Constitution. Although much can be said about the colonial experience with monarchy, royal governors, and the like, the conditions of national life at the beginning and through much of the nineteenth century simply did not raise the issues of management on the dynamic and shifting scale that followed the Civil War. The framers had no reason to envisage the management of an industrial nation as the essential function of the office. Whatever managerial insights Hamilton had were confined to commerce, banking, and monetary policy, certainly among the central elements in such management but by no means the only ones. Nor did the framers forecast the development of extensive managerial bureaucracies to tend to social policy and related problems. Quite to the contrary, they assumed local communities to be adequate to that charge. Nor did they conceive of the presidency as an institutionalized representation of popular will distinct from, let alone capable of opposition to, the will expressed by the legislature. Even Hamilton's most strenuous defenses of executive authority emphasized the president's role as the managerial agent for the legislature, not his popular independence in reflection of some other popular will. Finally, the framers of the Constitution had no reason to envisage the vast development of national resources for federal distribution or the gravitation of the power to distribute those resources to the executive branch.

The Jacksonian era was a major period in the redistribution of national resources. The Jacksonian presidency and the Supreme Court were at the center of a movement to limit exclusive rights. Jackson's exercise of the theretofore little used veto power was, in effect, the assertion of the authority of the president to control national monetary policy and thereby to affect the distribution of national wealth. The very use of the veto itself transformed it from an instrument for checking legislative unconstitutionality into an instrument for asserting alternative presidential policymaking. Rotation in office, better known as "the spoils system," utilized the party system to shift control over personnel from one group to another. Jackson faced the issue whether the president or the Congress would control national policy in banking and patronage, establishing clearly the rhetorical base for the concept of the independent executive. From an administrative perspective, it is significant that Jackson's opposition to the Supreme Court's view of treaties with the Indian nations eventuated in the creation of the

Bureau of Indian Affairs in 1836, the first step in a major administrative reshaping of the issue, but again in the interest of redistribution of resources, the Indian lands.

Of the earlier departments—State, Treasury, War, the Attorney General's, and the Post Office—only the last had significant patronage to distribute. Although one of the motives for the creation of a national government had been the need to adjudicate differences about boundaries and the control of the resources they reflected, not until 1848 and the creation of the Department of the Interior could one begin to see real acknowledgment of the economic, political, and hence managerial realities of continental expansion. The department seemed initially an afterthought, jokingly referred to as the "Department of Everythingelse." It took over the function of dealing with the Indian tribes from the Department of State, as well as the management of public lands, in administrative acknowledgment of the brutal fact that the tribes were to be considered no longer national interests to be negotiated with but, rather, occupants of "public" property. From that point on, the management and distribution of the country's basic resources for expansion and growth shifted from the states as represented in Congress to a kind of uncomfortable joint custody with the executive branch. Territorial government was federal, and territorial resources were managed, militarily defended, and scientifically explored by the federal compromises that grew increasingly shaky as the slavery issue came to dominate and inevitably to distort, in its own peculiar form, all of the issues of national management. The Civil War did not resolve the issues; rather, it expanded them largely through the administrative structures generated by the consequences of Reconstruction. Concern with veterans' affairs covered a wide range of interests, from public health and pensions to scientific agriculture, to create issues for national debate for the next three decades. Congress's attempts to manage such problems—railroad expansion is one of the prime examples—helped to establish the basic managerial reform image which viewed Congress and its politics as essentially corrupt and generated the search for executive leadership.

The battles between successive presidents and the Congress finally eventuated in the creation of the independent commission, the quasi-executive, quasi-judicial, quasi-legislative body that seemed, at times, to have cast the opposition in some permanently rigid form, a tug-of-war in bronze. Yet that seemed an improvement over the older conflict. Glorified as "fact finding," objective, and scientific, commissions were intended as a means of removing disputes from the political firing line without surrendering all control to the White House. Embedded in that formulation—as it was indeed in the rhetoric of the dispute—was the belief that congressional control would always be political, while the president, above politics, would reflect the national interest in its purest form.

The commissions, however, were part of the resolution of a drama that had been stated in much harsher constitutional terms in the immediate post–Civil War period. Andrew Johnson battled a Congress so determined to take control over executive policymaking and administration that they effectively deprived him of command of the army. And that was only the opening step in a battle that culminated in his impeachment for firing a cabinet officer in violation of the legislative will. The fact that conviction failed by only one vote did not encourage faith in a reemergence of leadership in the presidency. The history of legislative oversight of administrative action begins there, in a test no one wanted to try again.

From 1870 until the eve of World War I, writers on American government seemed confirmed in their belief that the mechanisms of executive leadership were inadequate. That confirmation, however, is expressed in two phases, both of which avoid the issue of constitutional reformation. The first phase looked to heroic leadership, first in Grant, whom even as shrewd an observer as Henry Adams viewed with hope.[26] Adam's youthful observations of the Grant administration all point to the need for a strong executive to manage a chaotic and corrupt legislative process. Adams's discussions of the methods of establishing monetary policy all involve distinctions between technical economics and politics, as he surveys the gold crisis of 1869 and the *Legal Tender Cases* of 1870 and 1871. His recurrent calls for knowledgeable executive action are important in that they recognize a distinction between the moral man—he had no question about Grant's morality—and the selection of experienced and trained personnel. His concern with civil service developed out of the same awareness. While many of his contemporaries saw corruption entirely in moral terms, Adams was capable of seeing a technical issue which transcended simple virtues, even if it raised continuing questions about democracy.

Adams's resistance to seeing the problem in structural terms sur-

---

26 See Adams, The Great Secession Winter of 1860–61 (Hochfield ed. 1958), a collection of essays.

faced clearly in the review he and his friend, Henry Cabot Lodge, wrote of Herman von Holst's magisterial treatise on American government.[27] Von Holst asserted that the problem was structural, the indivisibility of sovereignty. While he did not single out the presidency as the source of the problem, he did raise for Adams and Lodge the question of whether their criticisms would best be resolved by constitutional revision. Their answer was no. The Constitution remained beyond criticism. They continued to criticize governmental practice, and Adams grew more disillusioned year by year. To be sure, part of his problem can be ascribed to the dispossession of the Adams family in politics. For the man who, as Henry James put it, "was not in politics, though politics were much in him,"[28] did not achieve the career his family tradition seemed to have planned for him. There is a still more modern dimension to it. His awareness of the role of technical knowledge in executive management can be found in his writings several decades before it shows up in the growing literature of administrative management in public service.

The second phase is represented by a kind of evolutionary constitutionalism which is as difficult to describe as the evolutionary socialism of a later generation of American reformers. The evolutionary constitutionalist appears as eager to deny that constitutional revision is really ahead as the evolutionary socialist is to deny that any kind of revolutionary change in government will occur. The denials are usually not explicit but take the form of refusing candidly to describe the end of the process. Wilson's prepresidential writings make the question clear. *Congressional Government*, published in 1885, suggests that the presidency is at best a ceremonial and symbolic office in need of executive and administrative support from a reorganized Congress. Wilson's leanings toward British cabinet government and his admiration of Bagehot are obvious, though only as leanings. Like his contemporary A. Lawrence Lowell, he sees the bullet but refuses to bite it. Both men continued to teach the virtues of cabinet government, suggesting that American government might be evolving in that direction but insisting that the evolutionary process would not be complete or in any event identical with the British process—except that it, too, would be evolution-

[27] Adams & Lodge, *Book Review*, 123 N. Am. Rev. 328 (1876), reprinted in Adams, note 26 *supra*, at 255.

[28] The Notebooks of Henry James 57 (Matthiessen & Murdock eds. 1947).

ary. Wilson's chapter on the executive opened with the Bagehot-like statement, "It is at once curious and instructive to note how we have been forced into practically amending the Constitution without constitutionally amending it."[29] And he concluded,[30]

> The Constitution is not honored by blind worship. The more open-eyed we become, as a nation, to its defects, and the prompter we grow in applying with the unhesitating courage of conviction all thoroughly-tested or well-considered expedients necessary to make self-government among us a straightforward thing of simple method, single, unstinted power, and clear responsibility, the nearer will we approach to the sound sense and practical genius of the great and honorable statesmen of 1787.

Yet he prescribed no remedies, indeed proudly refused to do so. His function, he insisted, was critical description.

By 1908 at the latest, however, as the publication of *Constitutional Government in the United States* revealed, he had changed his mind. The practice of the presidency since Cleveland had demonstrated greater potential power than Wilson had thought possible. His own presidency suggests, at least initially, some of the routes of compromise he had selected. As a minority president, he chose to strengthen his own party's power rather than to realign progressives of both parties on ideological lines. He selected William Jennings Bryan as secretary of state, thus providing himself with a prime mover whose congressional constituency was strong enough to help press legislation through. And his first steps, calling Congress into session immediately, rather than waiting the customary ten months, and addressing them in person, were both steps designed to take advantage of the charismatic potential of the office in the wake of a dramatic election rather than allowing a year to pass between victory at the polls and the transformation of that victory into policy.

Journalist and reformer E. L. Godkin took many positions similar to those suggested by the young Wilson. In *Unforeseen Tendencies of Democracy*,[31] he was even more willing to enunciate

---

29 Wilson, Congressional Government, A Study in American Politics 163 (Meridian ed. 1963).

30 *Id.* at 215.

31 (1898).

the defects of democracy in dealing with problems of urbanization and industrialization. Democracy was not an industrial concept, he pointed out, but it could be adjusted to deal with industrial problems. English-born himself, he admired the Australian system. Unlike Wilson, however, whose admiration for American business led him to see entrepreneurial idealism as the model for government, Godkin saw the acquisition of money as the one element that had most changed democracy. In an interesting parallel to some of the ideals Thorstein Veblen was beginning to argue, Godkin attacked business acquisitiveness on similar moral grounds.

Other progressive reformers found their administrative ideals satisfied by German government more than British, in what at times became a hostile reaction to the British system. Herbert Croly's *Promise of American Life* was the bible of Progressivism, but it was also clear in its admiration of the German system and the managerial staff organizations developed there.[32] American political scientist John W. Burgess was another exponent of similar arguments. Wilson's critical review of Burgess's *Political Science and Comparative Constitutional Law* illustrates the sharpness of the distinction.[33] Indeed, although later historians have been inclined to see them as tightly related positions, the arguments for greater administrative efficiency came from two different and not always compatible points of view. One, the business and industrial community, had for some time been arguing the need for greater executive control over governmental expenditures at all levels. Part of a Victorian Anglo-American community, they exchanged reform ideas as an inherent part of the trade baggage on which the relationship rested. The other, the internationally ambitious community of young Roosevelt and Lodge, saw the need for greater executive independence in the management of the country's growing international power, a power becoming more competitive with and necessarily imitative of the power of a unified Germany. They saw Britain and British methods in an inevitable state of decline. While "pro-German" would be the wrong term to use for most of them, they saw the need to acknowledge German leadership in the development of methods of

---

32 (1909). See particularly c. 8.

33 Wilson, *Book Review*, 67 ATLANTIC 694 (1891), reprinted in 7 PAPERS OF WOODROW WILSON 195 (Link ed. 1969). In his correspondence with the *Atlantic*'s editor, Wilson makes even clearer his belief that he and Burgess represented two distinctly different schools of thought.

competition in science and technology, the base of the new industrialism. From the point of view of the presidency, the two positions took different perspectives, one seeking greater interdependence of the executive and legislative branches, the other seeking greater separation. One saw the need to make legislative government more efficient and effective, while the other saw legislative government as possibly the outmoded method of a preindustrial era.

During the Progressive era, the successes of executive reform movements in the revision of state constitutions and city charters seemed to point toward ultimate acceptance of the idea that effective executive leadership was a constitutional problem rather than one to be solved by traditional methods in new frameworks. For many analysts, the key to structural change was some method of giving the executive and the legislature more effective controls over one another. Various modifications of cabinet government were explored. The two "PRs," party responsibility and proportional representation, were thus part of the debate. The basic aim was clear: discipline. Let the executive call upon the voting public to discipline a legislature unwilling to enact proposals the executive deemed necessary. Let the public express its disapproval of either executive or legislature by recalling its choices and proposing legislation of its own, if necessary. As any formulation of the possibilities makes clear, the mood was generally antilegislature in its intention. Legislatures were linked with politics in the most pejorative sense of the term, whereas, again, executives were presumed to be—or at least more capable of being—free of the taint of politics. Bosses were not considered true executives, because they were responsible to political machines rather than to represented publics.

The transformation in Wilson's thinking between 1885 and 1908 is a transformation only in the focus of his thought, from legislative reform to executive reform, but not in the commitment to evolutionary change rather than revolutionary restructuring of the federal government. To be sure, the early volume implies greater structural change than the later volume, but only by implication. Although Walter Lippmann believed that Wilson's admiration for Cleveland was what turned him toward the presidency as the center of governmental power,[34] it was the presidency of Theodore Roosevelt which established the modern model of the new power. Cleve-

---

[34] Lippmann, *Introduction,* in WILSON, note 29 *supra,* at 13–14.

land's use of the veto turned it into an instrument of executive discipline, to be sure, rather than the alternative method of asserting constitutional protection it had previously been thought to be. But the second Cleveland administration in particular is more a model for the obstructive presidency than executive independence. The impasse caused by a president who makes himself an enemy in his own party without necessarily gaining any support from the opposition brings Cleveland closer, say, to Herbert Hoover than to the image of the strong president. A president who sets himself up as a nonpartisan opponent of the Congress is a president bent on political suicide, which is precisely what happened to both Cleveland and Hoover. The whole history of Progressive reform was based on that sin of political innocence. Theodore Roosevelt fell into it only during the messianic fervor of 1912, and even he seemed to know what the consequences of Armageddon were supposed to be. Neither his presidency nor his behavior toward his party after 1912 suggests that political innocence was a norm for him.

In his *Autobiography* Roosevelt insisted that he had greatly enlarged the power of the president,[35] a claim later critics tended to see as puffery. That he "stretched" the power might have stated it more precisely, because that kind of constitutional stretching was the new quality Roosevelt seems in fact to have introduced. To be sure, presidents had stretched the constitutional structure of the office before Roosevelt and had aroused controversy by doing so. But with the possible exception of Jackson, questionably constitutional action had been limited to emergencies in foreign affairs or civil war. Jefferson's purchase of Louisiana was not a domestic event, despite the fact that some history makes it appear so. As secretary of state, Buchanan stood nervously by as President Polk maneuvered the Oregon and Mexican crises. Then as president, Buchanan himself reiterated the logical paradox that characterized his entire administration: secession was unconstitutional, but there was not anything constitutional to do about it. Presented with that tightly tied Gordian knot, Lincoln solved it the only possible way, wielding the sword of presidential unconstitutionality in the process.

---

[35] (1913). Roosevelt announces proudly, "In a number of instances the legality of executive acts . . . was brought before the courts. They were uniformly sustained. . . . There was a great clamor that I was usurping legislative power. . . ." P. 393. And there is his famous statement, "I did not usurp power, but I did greatly broaden the use of executive power." P. 389.

As secretary of war, William Howard Taft stood by uncomfortably as Theodore Roosevelt enlarged the power of the presidency in foreign affairs by methods designed to avoid his constitutional obligation to include the Senate in the making of treaties. Executive agreements and plainly effective meddling both served to involve the United States in relationships with Latin America and Japan as well as the islands of the Caribbean.

Despite the fact that Roosevelt had chosen Taft as his successor, their disagreements on the constitutional power of the office were profound and underlay the ultimate opposition between them. Taft simply did not believe that the president could intervene in economic affairs to the extent that Roosevelt did. While Roosevelt's view of the presidency does not appear adventurous to us today, the anthracite coal strike of 1902 and the panic of 1907 both revealed to him his dependence on private powers whose impact on national policy could be greater than his own. Yet even his search for agencies to provide him basic information—the Bureau of Corporations was one—ran into opposition from Congress. To the extent that Congress reflected major national industrial interests, it was unwilling to allow a rambunctious president powers that those interests considered threatening. At the same time, to the extent that Congress represented its own interest as an independent policy-making body, such powers in the presidency were even more threatening. The creation of new executive agencies to deal with the problem, even to the extent of simply gathering and transmitting information, increased the power of the president to compete in the arena of interest representation. Congress forced Taft to sacrifice a great deal in order to obtain the Tariff Commission he believed would give him the control he wanted. His public praise of the Payne-Aldrich tariff may have been the crucial element in his downfall.

The creation of executive agencies to aid the president in the management of national interests that Congress feels it represents is the heart of the problem and the beginning of the battle over executive reorganization. The Progressive era is the richest source of examples; but Progressive language badly confuses understanding of them. Each agency and commission of the period was an effort on the part of reformers to get control through the executive branch of an interest they believed that a partisan Congress was misrepresenting. Thus one can describe Taft's desire for a Tariff Commission as a way of making tariff determination "scientific" or, in Progressive language, making it more "efficient" or, in later administrative language, "rationalizing" it. One can also describe it as a means of ending congressional "logrolling" or stopping the insidious influence of "the interests" on government policy. None of the languages really touches the basic issue itself, however, because each denies the political reality of the opposition by claiming either that politics cannot be responsible or that science and efficiency cannot be irresponsible.

Put simply, the problem can be described in this fashion. As administrative involvement in the control of resources for national distribution increases, congressional influence with the administrative agencies charged with that distribution must also increase if congressmen are to sustain their state or district political bases by satisfying constituents. Designated "pork barreling" by critics of the process, the relationship is nonetheless necessary to the maintenance of a career in politics. Some of that distribution obviously involves so-called special interests. But to the extent that those interests create jobs, roads, water resources, military bases, loans and mortgages, and the full range of opportunities the federal government oversees, those interests also represent local citizens seeking their rightful share of the pie. The power to create and abolish offices, to shift and consolidate functions, to increase or decrease personnel in the management of those functions, is a great power indeed. It is also the power to transfer citizen interest from the legislature as the distributor of its share to citizen dependence upon the administrative bureaucracy. It is the power to limit congressional control over national resources and their distribution, the economic base of political power itself.

To ask whether presidential control of that bureaucracy is constitutional requires us to ask whether congressional control of it is possible. For the Frankenstein monster of modern government is not that either question could be answered but that neither would be answered and that an uncontrolled and uncontrollable bureaucracy would govern American life. At the same time, putting the argument in constitutional form begs the issue in some crucial historical respects. It seems more than likely that, had the framers of the Constitution of 1787 envisaged the development of modern bureaucracy, they would have provided some constitutional check or balance capable of subjecting bureaucracy to political management. In that respect civil service has become a major constitutional anomaly. But it may be difficult to predict where that argument can lead. Recent attempts to revive agrarian Jacksonianism may be pointing in some direction, but where?

Executive reorganization thus belongs among a new tradition of executive inventions designed to cope with difficulties in adjusting the Constitution to the needs of modern government without revising the structure. In many respects the methods are directly traceable to Theodore Roosevelt and can be described. The elements include a strong sense of pragmatism, the term variously used to describe objection to restrictive principles, a capacity to act opportunistically where cautious executives might be shy, and a talent for using popular media to project a personality consonant with contemporary standards of acceptable leadership. All three elements have to be there at the same time. The pragmatism provides the capacity to see in existing methods of management instruments available for use in solving immediate problems, no matter how different these uses may be from those originally intended by the creators of the instruments. The instruments must be available for immediate action in such a way as to make the question of legality irrelevant, at least temporarily.

Opportunism involves the selection of the problems themselves rather than the instruments. It is the ability to select among the available issues those which, it can be argued, are so crucial as to require an unorthodox use of methods. Timing is critical, and support rests on a kind of popular agreement which makes it possible to believe that a search for new methods would be damaging. Franklin Roosevelt's handling of the Supreme Court fight rested on the belief that a sense of urgency and ripeness gave him the opportunity to use legislation rather than constitutional amendment in reforming the Court. His insistence afterward that he had lost the battle but won the war is further indication of the belief, at least, that legislative instruments had become irrelevant under the circumstances and had been replaced by some kind of persuasive impact. Justice Roberts's misunderstood "switch" seemed to support such beliefs. Successful uses of opportunistic advantage, however, make the leader appear to be brilliant, prescient in some mystical way, even though that aura may disappear in time, either because later critics, armed with the consequences of judgments and decisions, find reason to question, or because time gives successful solutions and failures alike the appearance of historical inevitability.

The distinction between existing instruments and new ones is crucial. New instruments require legislative action, and legislative action tends to limit executive independence. In recent years in particular, presidents have manipulated military authority to avoid legislative interference. Attempts on the part of the legislature to establish effective instruments have not been promising. One could argue from historical perspective that the refusal to reconsider the treaty-making provisions of the Constitution and to adapt them to the conditions of a modern world power is itself at the center of presidential adventurism, encouraging the search for extratreaty and therefore extracongressional (extraconstitutional?) methods of conducting foreign policy.

Finally, the president must have the personality to generate the public confidence which makes the use of the first two elements possible. He must be able to avoid arousing the sense of threat, unconstitutionality, or wrongdoing that could be present in the situation if someone were to see them and point them out. Franklin Roosevelt's wartime assurances that the powers he was requesting could be dangerous in the hand of another man are an example. But so was his disastrous relation to the Supreme Court. The three elements exist in delicate balance. They constitute the power and the weakness of the modern presidency.

While Theodore Roosevelt can probably be described as the first modern formulator of the method, the confirmation of it as an alternative to constitutional revision was the product of the era of the New Deal. The willingness to discuss constitutional revision of the executive-congressional relationship ended with World War I. Throughout the 1920s and 1930s, the launching of a worldwide attack on nineteenth-century liberal democracy established an era which could be called, in an adaptation of historian R. R. Palmer's description of the era of our own revolution,[36] "the age of the anti-democratic revolutions." The postwar pattern seemed clear enough: establish first a liberal constitutional democracy with legislative bodies to represent and to reflect public interest; let the deadlocks emerge; then replace them with some form of decisive leadership capable of solving problems—by force, if necessary. Russia's revolution appeared to be on such a course. Mussolini's Italy, Hitler's Germany, Franco's Spain, and similar transformations in Japan and China were on such a course.

---

[36] Palmer, The Age of the Democratic Revolution (1959).

Americans considered themselves protected from such misjudgment. William Yandell Elliott had published a book in 1928, *The Pragmatic Revolt in Politics.* The title was the term Americans considered themselves to have defined to describe the movement.[37] American writers on Fascism quoted Mussolini's suggestion that the greatest influences on his thought had been Nietzsche, Sorel, and William James.[38] Nonetheless, Americans dissociated themselves from the world revolution. In the depths of their depression, they prided themselves on the tranquillity of the election of 1932, joked their way through the brief drama of the bank closings, and went to see a movie called *Gabriel over the White House*, which depicted a crass politician who successfully sought the presidency and then, once in office, proceeded to go through a moral transformation of his character.

On April 30, 1933, comedian Will Rogers welcomed the new president in a radio broadcast. His drawling monologue is worth quoting at length as a revelation of the national mood:[39]

> Now Mr. Hoover didn't get results because he asked Congress to do something. There's where he made a mistake. . . . This fellow Mr. Roosevelt, he just sends a thing up every morning, says, "Here, here's your menu, you guys, sign it, you know what I mean, right here." Now Mr. Roosevelt, he never, you know, he never scolds them. Congress is really just children that never grew up, that's all they are. . . . Now Mr. Roosevelt, we've turned everything over to you. We've given you more power than we've ever given any man . . . in the history of the world. We don't know what it's all about. We tried to run the country individually and along democratic lines, but boy, we gummed it up, so you take it and run it as you want to, you know. And deflate or inflate or complicate or, you know, insulate. Do anything, just so you get us a dollar or two every now and then. . . . We don't know what it's all about, but God bless you.

Roosevelt's inaugural address had alluded to the possible necessity of action beyond constitutional authority. The "hundred days,"

---

37 Elliott's argument was well received, except among those who spotted his identification of American pragmatism with European movements.

38 Stewart, *The Mentors of Mussolini*, 22 AM. POL. SCI. REV. 843 (1928).

39 Taken from a phonograph record published by *American Heritage*. I am grateful to Patrick McCallig for calling this to my attention.

reaching its climax as Rogers joked about it, followed a pattern that looked much as Rogers described it. Later historians would trouble at the seeming sense of freedom, finding underneath much of the apparent haste a more complex order of political planning than appeared on the surface.[40] At the same time, significant portions of the legislation of that period were indeed declared unconstitutional by the Supreme Court.

Nor was humor the only form the expression of such ideas took. Many of those who were later to become Roosevelt's chief critics heralded what Roger Babson appreciatively entitled "the Roosevelt Revolution."[41] For a brief but significant moment, Roosevelt appeared to have precisely the managerial authority Rogers suggested. Ernest M. Hopkins, president of Dartmouth and one of the country's leading educators, had put it more precisely in a letter to a student:[42]

> Personally, I don't believe that we can go on much longer without a very major change in our form of government, and I think that we must either look forward to modifications toward a parliamentary system, which will make government more responsive to immediate need or else accept the opposite thesis and go back in theory but forward in method to the point of picking our best people and delegating authority to them rather than having them street-runners to whom we signal our will and from whom we expect immediate obedience.

It is interesting to note that Hopkins's comments were elicited by a letter congratulating him on a public stand he had taken against the veterans' bonus, an issue that then divided those who saw the political advantage to be gained by supporting the powerful veterans' lobby from those who, like Walter Lippmann and Hopkins, saw the fiscal dangers in continued expansion of benefits not warranted by genuine national interest.

Early in his administration, Roosevelt expressed admiration for Mussolini's handling of issues similar to those he was himself facing.

---

[40] See Freidel, Franklin D. Roosevelt: Launching the New Deal (1973); Rosen, Hoover, Roosevelt, and the Brains Trust (1977); but see Tugwell, Roosevelt's Revolution (1977).

[41] Babson, Washington and the Revolutionists (1934).

[42] Ernest M. Hopkins to Nelson A. Rockefeller, 26 Sept. 1932. Rockefeller Family Archive.

Mussolini responded similarly but with a subtler sense of caution to Roosevelt's *Looking Forward*, published at the outset of his presidency. Mussolini saw comparisons between what he was doing and what Roosevelt seemed to him to be trying to accomplish. But he pushed his questions beyond those Roosevelt was willing to ask. Did America's president see the crisis as being "in the system" or "of the system"? the Duce wondered.[43] The consequences of that distinction could be crucial.

Roosevelt's decision by 1936 was virtually to deny the existence of a crisis at all. At the same time, the rhetorical stance of the election campaign was distinctly radical, both on the left and the right, with Father Coughlin ripping off his clerical collar to dramatize his castigation of the administration and Roosevelt haranguing "economic royalists" in tones designed to arouse audiences to fury. The assassin's bullet that removed Huey Long from the fray provided little moderation in an atmosphere heated by revolutionary rhetoric on all sides save that of the Republican party, whose candidate breathed an older Progressive air that seemed, in context, strangely conservative.

In the academic community, few were considering anything even as radical as a constitutional convention, although, again, William Yandell Elliott provides an enlightening exception. His *Need for Constitutional Reform* appeared in 1935 but carried little weight in a group which had already decided that the New Deal was a genuine alternative to structural change.[44] Others had been persuaded by Roosevelt himself that constitutional revision, if by the amendment process, would be too slow; that a constitutional convention could not be relied upon to draw the same kind of intellectual support and participation that the country of 1787 had been fortunate enough to have. Indeed, that was precisely the point, though few besides Ernest Hopkins came close to articulating it. The democratic pro-

[43] *Roosevelt and the System,* Bolletino del R. Ministero degli Affari Esteri, 715 (1933). Ambassador Long sent Roosevelt a translation. Franklin D. Roosevelt Library, PPF 434. "The atmosphere in which the whole theoretical and practical system moves is akin to that of Fascism, but it would be an exaggeration to say anything more," the Duce decided.

[44] Elliott, The Need for Constitutional Reform, A Program for National Security (1935). He called for a constitutional convention to be held in 1937. Interestingly, one of his strongest recommendations involved changing the treaty-making power to enable treaties to be approved by joint resolution of both houses. P. 207.

cess could not any longer be depended upon to produce the kind of highly rational restructuring of the fundamental political design required to modernize the system. Both Mussolini and Hitler could argue such a position to publics already inclined to be suspicious of democratic politics and prepared to return to fundamental systems of authority remembered, if only in fancy, from some Roman or Nibelungen past. The only American past capable of useful romanticization was the frontier, where the distinction between rugged individualism and anarchy was best ignored.

Roosevelt interpreted his precedent-shattering victory in the election of 1936 as a mandate to take the actions he thought necessary to modernize American government. He was wrong. His defeats in judicial reform and executive reorganization, to name only the most prominent ones of his critical second term, were indeed fueled by public reaction against the power of his presidency. But the drama of those defeats conceals a crucial change Roosevelt had already discovered, as if by accident. The power of the presidency would not lie in dramatic legislative victories or constitutional revision, both of which had become chimerical in American politics. Administrative successes could proceed by bits and pieces of legislation turned to more effective use than the imagination of any legislator might have perceived. The planning of legislation from 1935 on is marked by the introduction of the young lawyers dubbed "Frankfurter's boys" to suit legislation as much to congressional will as to public need or at least to discover in advance the bargains that could be struck. If the older Progressives, with their sharp distinctions between politics and administration, resented the process, the younger New Dealers reveled in it. The older administrative dictum, "on tap but not on top," the idea that technicians should carefully refrain from confusing advice with command, began to crumble as Roosevelt sent the new technicians to the Hill to lobby for their plans.

Similar successes would come through the courts, again bit by bit, accumulating ultimate victories out of incremental changes in the habits and attitudes of those who involved themselves in the daily processes of government. Administrative law was destined to become a kind of ongoing reform, the rational restructuring in the reality of the courts of the compromises and battered idealism of legislative democracy. The *Schechter* rule,[45] that Congress could

[45] Schechter Poultry Co. v. United States, 295 U.S. 495 (1935).

not delegate its authority to legislate, gradually disappeared under the deluge of decisions supporting administrative redefinition of the law.

The universalism of the first flush of the New Deal, as represented by the massive industrial and agricultural legislative programs, became the pragmatic particularism which was the Roosevelt method at its best, its most effective, and, one might argue, its most questionable. At the very beginning of his first term, he had used the Trading with the Enemy Act[46] from World War I to control sales of gold abroad, a device Hoover had been trying, to no avail, to get legal sanction to use.[47] The act was an enormous catchall covering everything from trade to censorship of the press. But it was clearly the intention of Congress that the authority be only a wartime authority and that it expire with the signing of treaties ending the war. One has to rely on legislative intent, since the act defines "end of the war" in its preamble but does not specifically state the relevance of the phrase.

At other points Roosevelt followed the practice of using authorizations intended to provide one service in order to obtain other services Congress might not have been willing to provide, a practice long used by presidents accustomed to such borrowing in the executive branch. The various forms of the group that ultimately became the National Resources Planning Board were funded by piecing together the authorizations from the Employment Stabilization Act of 1931,[48] the National Industrial Recovery Act of 1933,[49] and private funding from the Rockefeller Foundation. It did not come out of the closet until the Reorganization Act of 1939. But when Congress abolished the board in 1943, declaring it both socialist and fascist, it was its failure to live up to the provisions of the act of 1931 that most of its critics cited as the reason. Congress also tried to make certain that none of the board's functions or its functionaries would be transferred elsewhere in government. But Roosevelt easily got around that. By 1946 Congress was willing to create the Council of Economic Advisers,[50] partly, it thought, to fulfill the promise of 1931.

Roosevelt's most dramatic use of these tactics came in his involvement of the country in World War II. The pressure for prepara-

---

46 Pub. L. 91, 40 Stat. 411 (1917).

47 FREIDEL, note 40 *supra*, at 190–1.

48 Pub. L. 616, 46 Stat. 1084 (1931).

49 Pub. L. 67, 48 Stat. 195 (1933).

50 Pub. L. 304, 60 Stat. 23 (1946).

tion in the face of isolationist, antimilitarist sentiments in Congress seemed to require the kind of manipulation he used to maintain a national posture commensurate with the clearly approaching international responsibility. One need not be critical of his purposes—it is hard to see an array of options where the Axis alliance was concerned—in order to puzzle about a method that made the declaration of war an almost irrelevant afterthought in a process that had been underway for almost two years. Our naval engagements in the North Atlantic, our supportive commitments to the Allies, and our financial pressures on a Japanese government backed to the wall all spelled a powerful war stance on the part of a nation no longer even claiming neutrality, in fact specifically denying it.

It would take historians a generation before they could begin serious questioning of the method. Indeed, another war managed on a far greater scale by the same basic method would serve as the background for what promises to be a new wave of revisionism. One can dispute the ultimate utility of that kind of history without touching the rich sense of tragedy that gives the shock of recent experience a startling and not altogether realistic hold on our understanding of the past. Nixon was not the first president to feel that his special understanding of the national interest required him to take action others might consider illegal. The great presidential gamble, that in the long run public understanding would come to approve actions a contemporary public might have rebelled against, is the basis of that mystical prescience used to define "greatness in the presidency." The constitutionality of that gamble tends to be raised only if the president craps out.

III

Up to this point, I have emphasized the historical ironies and paradoxes of the process called executive reorganization. My main point has been that the evolution of the presidency since 1900 has changed the constitutional character of the office by placing upon the president administrative responsibilities he does not have the clear-cut authority to manage. The Brownlow committee said that in 1937, and it has been repeated like a litany by presidential-management authorities ever since. Putting the problem in managerial terms, however, seriously misstates it by ignoring—for very good reason—its political dimensions. In some respects, the older generation of hard-line Progressives had their finger on the problem when they defined it as a confrontation between executive government and legislative government. But they confused their own perceptions by seeing it as a showdown between good and evil, honest management and corruption. While the generation of the 1930s was more sophisticated, to be sure, it still rested its case on a historical mystery that seemed to prove a point. No dishonest man had ever reached the presidency. Brownlow liked to quote James Fenimore Cooper's contention: "As a rule, there is far more danger that the President of the United States will render the office less efficient than was intended, than that he will exercise an authority dangerous to the liberties of the country.[51] But he quoted it in contexts that suggested less reliance on the cautious "as a rule."

In recent years, it has become even clearer that the legislative route to reform is slow and cumbersome. Changing the law to meet needs unforeseen when the law was passed or apparent only as a consequence of the passage of the law is a process even experienced legislators have come to see as inefficient, if not downright ineffective. The gradually increasing role of the courts in stepping in to interpret legislation to meet changing circumstances has paralleled and aided the development of independence on the part of managers throughout the bureaucracy in interpreting regulations to fit their understanding of the conditions with which they cope. Public reaction against seeming inequities in the system has led to anti-bureaucratic moods and, if one can take some interpretations of the Carter victory at face value, the election of a president with a mandate to bring the bureaucracy to task. The problem, of course, is that both Carter's rhetoric and the general public belief are based on the clearly stated assumption that taking the bureaucracy to task means abolishing it, not managing it. The fight against bureaucracy is built on the same misperception that made the old economy and efficiency arguments so useful and ultimately so useless. Modern society is bureaucratically managed. It will become more so. In the faceless anonymity of a society so managed, the smile of the president may be the only symbol of humanity in the system the public has. There are many reasons to predict Carter's failure. The public ambivalence will seem even to support that, too.

The dispute over the power of any president to reorganize the executive branch of government to meet his sense of administrative

[51] Brownlow, The President and the Presidency 136 (1949).

need is by now old enough to be seen as continuing, probably unresolvable, and therefore possibly more serious than even the most vociferous critics or supporters of the process have yet acknowledged. Yet it rests on some simple points. Simplest of all is the fact that the executive branch of government is something quite different from the managerial system controlled by the president. The tendency to see the two as the same is part of the irrational game plan the dispute often follows. The desire to create some ongoing conception of "the Presidency" is part of a recurrent subterfuge designed to get around the fact that the president is a partisan politician eager to control his own election. Again, and not unrelated to that fact, presidents may be among the shortest-lived careerists in American politics. Although the Twenty-second Amendment limits elected presidential terms to two, no president before Franklin Roosevelt, with the exception of Washington, had serious opportunity even to consider otherwise, and Eisenhower is the only president since Roosevelt who has filled the "normal" presidential span of eight years. Two Senate terms, in contrast, constitute a twelve-year stretch (the equivalent of three presidential terms), without limit on reelection, while membership in the House depends solely on the safety of the district and the stamina of the incumbent. There are no retirement rules, either. Other executives serve longer, even indefinite terms—mayors of major cities, governors who succeed themselves where state constitutions permit or rest for a term or two and then return—but not the president.

At the same time, civil service reform, that double-edged triumph of Progressivism, insures continuity at levels of protected coverage which makes change of administration in some areas irrelevant. Between them, Congress and civil servants of the executive branch sustain a going governmental enterprise that effectively outlives flashes of executive reform in the presidency. "Getting America moving," "bringing us together," "New Frontier," the sentiments of "the silent majority" all reflect rhetorical stances that appear and reappear against the background of an extraordinarily stable system of political administration. Any president who considers himself elected by the people to accomplish certain ends he believes he made clear in his campaign is virtually certain to find sizable majorities in agencies, bureaus, and departments who disagree with him, significant groups in Congress who will support their disagreement, and a puzzling confusion of opinion in the public mind when differences emerge in newspaper columns or headlines. Roosevelt after the landslide of 1936, Johnson after the landslide of 1964, and Nixon after the landslide of 1972 all assumed that they now had publicly backed powers they were not certain they had had before, plus a range of new experience that led them to think they knew what they needed to do. Yet each of them discovered that such an interpretation still seriously limited actions in ways they could not predict but ways that nonetheless rested on political powers shared among the effective triumvirate of continuing government in the United States: Congress, the bureaucracy, and public opinion.

Wilson had seen that alliance between Congress and the governmental agencies as the source of modern corruption over ninety years ago, and much of the administrative reform movement that followed was based on one or another of the attempts to break up the alliance, to get around it, or even to join it. The possibilities in just that order mark the history of executive reorganization at all levels of American government. The search for the strong executive with new power to control disruptive legislatures was based on replacement of the popular election of administrators by new processes of executive selection. While that was not a direct assault on legislatures, it was a frontal attack on the political process and the partisan selection system from which the new executive was supposed to be immune. That method was augmented even before the end of the Progressive era by a second echelon of methods having to do with systems of budgeting and accounting through which the executive would get around the legislative-bureaucratic alliance by forcing the bureaucracy to make its pleas for funds through a central budget controlled by the executive rather than through individual requests to relevant committees of the legislature. The New Deal reflects a complex of compromises with the two methods, to which Roosevelt ultimately added a third, namely, the pragmatic adjustment whereby the executive does what can be done to control systematic distribution of funds and programs at the same time that local political needs are given due consideration, usually in accordance with the power of the representative of those needs to influence the total legislative program sought by the executive. This kind of power brokering, often mislabeled "pluralist," ultimately becomes the dominant "theory" of executive-legislative relations. The relation between Eisenhower as president and Lyndon Johnson as majority leader in the Senate (with his fellow Texan, Sam Rayburn, as

Speaker of the House) confirms the new model. When Johnson became president, the system was raised to extraordinary heights of political effectiveness as the President who had helped create the new managerial politics took over its control. It is perhaps an irony of administrative history that the Johnson years exemplify the triumph and the disaster of the method. Highly systematized programs by teams of sophisticated experts are reshaped by political negotiations into programs with which no one can very assuredly identify, glorified in public relations terms by a president eager to sell them as broadly as possible, expanded by his successor using many of the same chaotic methods, and then served up as horror stories in the emotional antibureaucratic environment of the post-Vietnam era. In a sense the problem, historically speaking, has grown larger without changing its basic character. That character grows out of some historical realities that can be stated with what is perhaps deceptive simplicity.

Modern American nationalism to the contrary notwithstanding, the United States is a complex landmass of regional differences reflected in many governing bodies that do in fact represent local interests. That those interests are narrowly conceived and selfish is part of the very human nature that makes one interest cry "interest" as it points an accusing finger at another interest competing with it for resources deemed important for the survival of both. Madison saw the problem and provided a statement of it in the tenth *Federalist* that generations of Americans have quoted in justification of pluralism. The Congress of the United States represents the accumulated power of those interests in a long-lived and continuing body of career politicians whose success depends upon an ability to project to local citizens the belief that their interests (the ubiquitous utility of the term is mind boggling at election times) are being satisfied. A president who believes he has been elected to serve something called "the national interest" has only to look at the cacophonous noises emitted by Congress to turn for definition to those areas where he thinks he can be sure such a thing exists. For many years now, foreign policy has served such a purpose. Since the end of World War II, "national defense" has provided American reform with its most serviceable umbrella, generating revolutions in education, race relations, transportation, and indeed a whole panoply of programs once considered the protected province of local communities. Although the term "pork barrel" is not as much in use to describe projects like the race to the moon or Model Cities, the fact remains that the distribution of federal resources nationally is the essential nourishment of the lifetime careers of politicians elected to serve their fellow citizens. The president is not one of them, regardless of how securely he may have sat among them at a previous stage of his career. Like the Aztec young men chosen for sacrifice, his utility may lie in the public belief that he reflects them at their very best, a fact that makes him the perfect victim to honor virtues they suspect they do not have. Those virtues make him a threat; but the knowledge that they will be able to provide him a period of glorified existence, along with the assurance that his career will come to an end before he has an opportunity to be dangerously virtuous, reduces the threat.

The fact that the power to reorganize the executive branch of the government is therefore the power to control the distribution of national resources is thus the single most powerful threat to political careerism in American politics. This is equally true where social policy is concerned. Candidate Kennedy could attack President Eisenhower for his unwillingness to end segregation in public housing when he could do so by a "stroke of the pen," but that stroke was harder for the president of the United States than it was for the Senator from Massachusetts, at least in 1960. After all, *Profiles in Courage* was a study of people who sacrificed careers for the sake of political principle and was not, therefore, as much of a guide to professional success as the post–World War II generation was coming to conceive of it.

The history of executive reorganization thus has a tendency to obscure the basic purpose of reorganization: to secure power over a bureaucracy whose real source of independence is congressional funding. Congress has reason to protect that independence, and the bureaucracy has reason to respect the loose political oversight Congress is able to provide. The president who seeks the power to reorganize must obtain it from a legislature that sees clear benefit in his not having the power. The grounds for compromise are narrow, therefore, and depend upon couching the issue in language that conceals the no-win game actually being played. While the arguments do tend to emphasize the gains in power the executive will achieve, the loss in power to the legislature is rarely, if ever, defined with any clarity. Indeed, the terms used to describe that loss usually take the form of pejoratives no ambitious legislator would wish to use: logrolling, spoils, patronage, satisfaction of interest-group lobbyists, and the like. Legislative manipulation of the policies of the executive branch is seen as corrupt whenever it can be shown that the purpose of the manipulation was the gratification of a special request rather than the objective effectiveness of the program involved. That it is not always easy to distinguish the two from one another is the torment of an honest politician trying to please a constituent. Presidents with high-level managerial skills can find themselves victims of a political-bureaucratic alliance far more powerful than the rational considerations of executive management. Herbert Hoover's efforts to bring order to the Veterans' Administration ended up in what was perhaps the biggest debacle of his presidency, the bonus march of 1932. But recent research indicates that that event, while built on a series of misperceptions and misjudgments on the part of the president, nonetheless was the culmination of a battle between an executive searching for administrative order and a powerful bureaucrat with a sizable congressional constituency.[52]

We are far from an effective system of executive-legislative managerial relationships, as we have been in the entirety of the twentieth century. As one of the most far-reaching attempts to gain managerial control over government programs, the Nixon presidency threatens to become the most striking setback to necessary modern leadership in the entire history of the presidency. Fears have been raised on the basis of real, not imaginary, usurpations of power. But they have been raised in a fashion that does nothing to meet the question of leadership itself, its necessity in an increasingly complex society, its power for good and, above all, its absolutely unique ability to invoke public confidence. As theorists of popular democracy have pointed out for over 2,000 years, size, distance, and complexity can seriously limit the function of democracy. As this essay has tried to point out, that fact has served as the basis for antidemocratic movements recently enough to suggest that it will remain a factor to cope with whenever emergencies threaten the efficiency of government and whenever scientific and technological perceptions run counter to popular will.

The same holds for political perceptions of leaders convinced

---

[52] Lisio, The President and Protest: Hoover, Conspiracy, and the Bonus Riot (1974).

that they represent majority will, silent or otherwise. In that sense we need to know much more about the Nixon presidency than Watergate encourages us to see, for the problem was there long before the exaggerated hunger for reelection turned it into a travesty. Nixon's efforts to gain control over a bureaucracy that, as one recent study has shown, disapproved of his intentions,[53] ought to become a case study in the organizational problems of a president who believes he was elected to bring about something the federal bureaucracy does not approve. His attempts to infiltrate, to impound, to bring command control into the White House all point to efforts to be managerially effective through one of the most complex and massive reorganization programs of the century. Yet we know remarkably little beyond "the plumbers."

Although Americans have at several points in their history seriously believed otherwise, it is hard to see less presidential leadership as preferable to more presidential leadership. Congress cannot remake itself into an effective managerial body, and there is much reason to argue that that is precisely what it ought not to do. Even more problematic is the gradual usurpation of managerial responsibility by the courts, given the even greater limitation on their responsiveness to public will. What seems most needed is a clearer historical rationale for the power of the president, one that could provide better understanding of the changes that have taken place in the role of that office for more than three-quarters of a century now. Executive management or administrative reorganization, by whatever name, is a response to changes in the basic historical condition of American government. It is our alternative to revolution, but in a curious sense. It carries within it the threat of revolution, as we ought to know better than any other generation that thought it perceived the threat. That was its transformed role in the 1930s, the era of antidemocratic revolutions. It may be time now to see it more clearly for what it is as well as for what it must continue to be.

While it is not the function of a historical essay to suggest remedies, any survey of the literature on American government makes clear that they exist. Unfortunately, the only efforts to change the presidency constitutionally tend to be punitive rather than constructive, the two-term limitation being perhaps the most recent.

---

53 Aberbach & Rockman, *Clashing Beliefs within the Executive Branch: The Nixon Administration Bureaucracy*, 70 Am. Pol. Sci. Rev. 456 (1976).

In the wide-ranging concern for the effectiveness of the office, analysts have suggested them all, from item veto to personality tests. What history can provide, however, is a suggestion that, to put it bluntly, times have changed. That is not so obvious as it seems, particularly if it is taken to mean that modern managerial necessity must limit the traditional conception of American democracy, the most recurrent fear of all. Walter Lippmann pointed it out in 1922, when he suggested that modern Americans were too busy, too preoccupied with self to be able to oversee their government, and that more technical specialization and less meddling would be a good thing.[54] John Dewey in 1927 reached the opposite conclusion and called for more systematic organization of public opinion to give it greater effect in the operation of governmental problem solving.[55] Both books were written at a time when mass communication was, by our standards, primitive.

It is perhaps one of the greatest paradoxes in the history of democratic thought that, as the available methods of rational communication have expanded, faith in democratic government seems to have diminished. Greater education in the process of government and more constant perception of its daily operation produces disillusionment and cynicism. Yet those who govern today are better educated in general and better trained to govern than they have ever been. If one looks at the history of southern politics, for example, one would expect to find the hard-drinking, loud-talking Billy Carter as the successful politician in the Carter family, not Jimmy—even as recently as twenty years ago. American society is as ready for the tests of participatory democracy as any society has ever been, yet "populism" still is looked upon suspiciously in intellectual circles. Nonetheless, to argue that a highly technological society cannot be a highly democratic one is to argue that knowledge cannot produce self-government, that knowing thyself is no longer the place to begin.

What this essay has tried to suggest is that a clearer, more realistic understanding of the problems of executive power in American government might help. Current concerns with the moral dimensions of power may not be altogether amiss, even when they reach some of the levels of revelatory absurdity they have in their discus-

---

[54] Lippmann, Public Opinion (1922).

[55] Dewey, The Public and Its Problems (1927).

sions of such matters as sexual behavior. But if that concern becomes a device for concealing the more cogent realities of politics, we will be in serious trouble indeed. No political system has yet succeeded in legislating morality; but all political systems use power to distribute available resources to those entitled to benefit from the system. Protecting that process can no more eliminate the temptations produced by greed than bedroom revelations eliminate the temptations produced by lust. For a society which has undergone such revolutionary social change over the last few decades as American society has, a new view of the political system, one less inclined to see it in consensual terms, might be important.

DAVID P. CURRIE

CONGRESS, THE COURT, AND WATER POLLUTION

Section 301(a) of the Federal Water Pollution Control Act provides that, "except as in compliance with" specified sections of the law, "the discharge of any pollutant by any person shall be unlawful."[1] Prominent among the exceptions referred to is § 402, which authorizes the Administrator of the Environmental Protection Agency (or, upon his approval, a State) to "issue a permit for the discharge of any pollutant . . . , notwithstanding section 301(a)."[2] Permits may be issued, however, only "upon condition that such discharge will meet . . . all applicable requirements under sections 301, 302, 306, 307, 308, and 403 of this Act." Among the bewildering array of requirements imposed by these sections are three whose interpretation secured the attention of the Supreme Court during the 1976 Term.

One of these was § 301(b)(1)(A), which provides that by July 1, 1977, "there shall be achieved . . . effluent limitations for point

---

David P. Currie is Harry N. Wyatt Professor of Law, The University of Chicago. He is indebted to Mark Reinhardt of the class of 1978 for an informative paper on this subject, and especially for his analysis of the issues discussed in footnote 21.

[1] 33 U.S.C. § 1311(a).

[2] 33 U.S.C. § 1342(a)(1).

0-226-46429-6/78/1977-2000$01.93

sources, other than publicly owned treatment works, . . . which shall require the application of the best practicable control technology currently available as defined by the Administrator pursuant to section 304(b)."[3] A second, § 301(b)(2)(A), provides that by July 1, 1983, "there shall be achieved . . . effluent limitations for categories and classes of [nonpublic] point sources, . . . which . . . shall require application of the best available technology economically achievable for such category or class, . . . as determined in accordance with regulations issued by the Administrator pursuant to section 304(b)(2)."[4] Finally, § 306 provides for the adoption of "Federal standards of performance for new sources," which are to reflect "the greatest degree of effluent reduction . . . achievable through application of the best available demonstrated control technology."[5]

In *E.I. duPont de Nemours & Co. v. Train*,[6] the Supreme Court held without dissent that the Administrator may adopt 1977 and 1983 effluent limitations by regulation and that there is no require-

---

[3] 33 U.S.C. § 1311(b)(1)(A).

"Effluent limitation" is defined as "any restriction established by a State or the Administrator on quantities, rates, and concentrations of chemical, physical, biological, and other constituents which are discharged from point sources into navigable waters, the waters of the contiguous zone, or the ocean, including schedules of compliance." 33 U.S.C. § 1362(11).

"Point source" is defined as "any discernible, confined and discrete conveyance." 33 U.S.C. § 1362(14). Wastewater discharged from a pipe, for example, is included; water draining across a cornfield is not. See Appalachian Power Co. v. Train, 545 F.2d 1351, 1373–74 (4th Cir. 1976).

Federal construction subsidies are available for publicly owned, but not for privately owned, treatment works. 33 U.S.C. § 1281(g). Publicly owned facilities are required to achieve "secondary treatment" by 1977 and to utilize "the best practicable waste treatment technology" by 1983. 33 U.S.C. §§ 1311(b)(1)(B), and (2)(B), 1281(g)(2)(A). Since public and private works may be identical, there is no adequate basis for subjecting them to differing limitations. Since most public plants principally treat domestic sewage and most private plants do not, presumably Congress meant to distinguish domestic from industrial wastes. See Legislative History of the Federal Water Pollution Control Act Amendments of 1972 788 (Printed for Senate Comm. on Public Works, 93d Cong., 1st Sess. [1973]) (hereafter "Leg. Hist."), arguing that the "secondary treatment" standard required of public plants for 1977 was "generally concerned with suspended solids and biologically degradable, oxygen demanding materials" and might be thought "an empty standard" if applied to effluents containing other contaminants.

[4] 33 U.S.C. § 1311(b)(2)(A).

The 1983 standards must "result in reasonable further progress toward the national goal of eliminating the discharge of all pollutants"—a goal ludicrous on its face—and "shall require the elimination of discharges of all pollutants if the Administrator finds . . . that such elimination is technologically and economically achievable for a category or class of point sources as determined in accordance with regulations issued by the Administrator pursuant to section 304(b)(2)." *Ibid.*

[5] 33 U.S.C. § 1316.

[6] 430 U.S. 112 (1977).

ment that he provide for variances from the new-source standards. The latter holding is obvious from the face of the statute and need not be discussed at length.[7] The former, which had been the subject of fierce litigation in seven circuits, is of virtually no practical significance.

I

Industry had loudly contended that the effluent limitations that § 301 ambiguously said "shall be achieved" were to be set not

---

[7] 33 U.S.C. § 1316(e) provides flatly that "it shall be unlawful for any owner or operator of any new source to operate such source in violation of any standard of performance." Contrast the explicit variance provision in 33 U.S.C. § 1311(c), respecting the 1983 limitations: "The Administrator may modify the requirements of subsection (b)(2)(A) of this section with respect to any point source for which a permit application is filed after July 1, 1977, upon a showing by the owner or operator of such point source satisfactory to the Administrator that such modified requirements (1) will represent the maximum use of technology within the economic capability of the owner or operator; and (2) will result in reasonable further progress toward the elimination of the discharge of pollutants."

The House and Senate bills, as reported from committee, both contained provisions for variances from section 306 upon a finding that "the economic, social, and environmental costs of implementing such standard bear no reasonable relationship to the economic, social, and environmental benefits . . . to be obtained." Leg. Hist. at 993; 1626. Even this, the House Committee explained, "can apply only in the case of new sources resulting from modifications to existing plants," *id.* at 798. It was dropped along with the applicability of the section to modifications to existing plants.

In the face of the statute and its history the Fourth Circuit in *duPont II* ordered the EPA to adopt "some limited escape mechanism for new sources," arguing in support only the irrelevant truth that "[p]rovisions for variances, modifications, and exceptions are appropriate to the regulatory process." 541 F.2d 1018, 1028 (1976). Industry was more sophisticated before the Supreme Court, arguing that because "compliance with a permit . . . shall be deemed compliance . . . with sections 301, 302, 306, 307, and 403," 33 U.S.C. § 1342(k), "permit proceedings may result in limitations in a permit for a new source which are different from . . . and which override the new source standard." Brief for Petitioners in Nos. 75-1473 and 75-1705, at p. 8. The Court's reply is compelling: "[A]fter standards of performance are promulgated, the permit can only be issued 'upon condition that such discharge will meet . . . all applicable requirements under sectio[n] . . . 306 . . ." § 402(a)(1); and one of the requirements of § 306 is that no new source may operate in violation of any standard of performance. § 306(e). The purpose of § 402(k) seems to be to insulate permit holders from changes in various regulations during the period of a permit and to relieve them of having to litigate in an enforcement action the question whether their permits are sufficiently strict. In short, § 402(k) serves the purpose of giving permits finality." 430 U.S. at 138 n.28. See Leg. Hist. at 815, where the House Report states the purpose of this provision is "to assure that the mere promulgation of any effluent limitation . . . by itself will not subject a person holding a valid permit to prosecution. However, once such a requirement is actually made a condition of the permit, then the permittee will be held to comply with the terms thereof."

The total absence of any standards in § 402(k) suggests the unlikelihood that it was meant to allow variances from § 306; Congress can scarcely be presumed to have authorized permit issuers to nullify that section at will.

by regulation but in the course of issuing individual permits. Lying behind this position was the highly practical question whether all steel mills, for example, would be required to meet the same standard, or whether requirements were to vary according to the characteristics of the individual plant—in other words, whether "best practicable" or "best available" technology was to be determined on a nationally uniform or a plant-by-plant basis.[8] But this important question does not depend upon whether the Administrator may adopt effluent limitations by regulation. If he may, the question remains how much flexibility those regulations may or must allow at the individual permit stage.[9] If he may not, he may nevertheless adopt general "guideline" regulations defining "best practicable" and "best available" under § 304(b); and the question again is the degree to which those guidelines must allow for case-by-case variation.[10]

---

[8] See Brief for Petitioners, No. 75-978, at p. 27: "EPA's insistence on prescribing permit terms from Washington has eliminated the benefit which Congress intended to secure by having permit-issuing authorities in States or in EPA regional offices make factual findings based upon the particular circumstances at individual plants."

[9] See, *e.g.*, American Iron & Steel Inst. v. EPA, 526 F.2d 1027 (3d Cir. 1975), holding that limitations might be adopted by regulation but that they must provide "ranges" of permissible discharges and specify factors to be considered in determining the figures applicable to each plant; *duPont II*, 541 F.2d at 1028: Effluent limitations promulgated by regulation are "presumptively applicable to permit applications" subject to rebuttal on the basis of individual circumstances.

[10] 33 U.S.C. § 1314(b): "For the purpose of adopting or revising effluent limitations under this Act the Administrator shall . . . publish within one year of enactment of this title, regulations, providing guidelines for effluent limitations. . . . Such regulations shall—(1)(A) identify, in terms of amounts of constituents and chemical, physical, and biological characteristics of pollutants, the degree of effluent reduction attainable through the application of the best practicable control technology currently available for classes and categories of point sources . . . ; and

(B) specify factors to be taken into account in determining the control measures and practices to be applicable to point sources . . . within such categories or classes. Factors relating to the assessment of best practicable control technology currently available to comply with subsection (b)(1) of section 301 of this Act shall include consideration of the total cost of application of technology in relation to the effluent reduction benefits to be achieved from such application, and shall also take into account the age of equipment and facilities involved, the process employed, the engineering aspects of the application of various types of control techniques, process changes, non-water quality environmental impact (including energy requirements), and such other factors as the Administrator deems appropriate. . . ." Subparagraph (2) makes similar provision for 1983 guidelines.

See CPC International, Inc. v. Train, 515 F.2d 1032, 1037 n.11 (8th Cir. 1975), stating that, though the actual "limitations" were to be set in each permit, "[t]he guidelines are to be as precise as possible to assure uniformity of permits for industry categories." The same court later acknowledged that the question of limitation regulations had no substantive significance: "The only practical difference . . . is that the § 304(b) guidelines for *existing* sources must be reviewed first in the District Court." CPC International, Inc. v. Train, 540 F.2d 1329, 1332 n.1 (8th Cir. 1976).

Several courts have thought the question whether § 301 authorizes the adoption of regulations determines whether jurisdiction to review the Administrator's general regulations concerning effluent limitations lies in a district court or a court of appeals, for § 509(b) gives the latter jurisdiction to review "the Administrator's action . . . in approving or promulgating any effluent limitation . . . under section 301," while saying nothing of § 304.[11] However, the whole purpose of the § 304 guidelines is to define the limitations prescribed by § 301. The statutory language itself so indicates,[12] and the Senate Report could not be clearer: "[T]hese guidelines would define the effluent limitations required by the first and second phases of the program established under section 301."[13] To hold that guidelines defining effluent limitations are not themselves "effluent limitation[s]" within the judicial-review provision may be to split hairs without sufficient evidence that Congress so intended.[14] Moreover, § 304 guidelines and § 306 new-source standards are generally closely related and sometimes identical. To review them in different courts would be so absurdly inefficient that Congress can hardly have intended it.[15] It is thus easy to agree with the Fourth Circuit

---

[11] 33 U.S.C. § 1369(b).

See CPC International, Inc. v. Train, 515 F.2d 1032 (8th Cir. 1975), refusing jurisdiction because § 301 gave no authority to adopt limitations by regulation; American Frozen Food Inst. v. Train, 539 F.2d 107 (D.C. Cir. 1976); Hooker Chems. & Plastics Corp. v. Train, 537 F.2d 620 (2d Cir. 1976); American Meat Inst. v. EPA, 526 F.2d 442 (7th Cir. 1975), all *contra*. The Tenth Circuit in American Petroleum Inst. v. EPA, 526 F.2d 1343 (1975), avoided the problem by holding jurisdiction satisfied because the Administrator had purported to act under § 301; the Third Circuit in the *Iron & Steel* case, note 9 *supra*, did not discuss jurisdiction.

[12] See, *e.g.*, § 301(b)(1)(A), requiring the achievement of "effluent limitations . . . which shall require . . . the best practicable control technology currently available as defined by the Administrator pursuant to section 304(b)."

[13] Leg. Hist. at 1469.

[14] I find the statutory definition of "effluent limitation," note 3 *supra*, no help. One Congressman did argue that § 304 guidelines were not but should be reviewable under § 509. See Leg. Hist. at 892. He can scarcely have been speaking for all Congressmen and he did not suggest that the guidelines were reviewable in the district courts.

[15] The court of appeals in *CPC*, note 11 *supra*, conceded that § 304 guidelines were subject to nonstatutory review in the district courts, 515 F.2d at 1038, and the guidelines in issue in *CPC* were later so reviewed. Grain Processing Corp. v. Train, 407 F. Supp. 96 (S.D. Iowa 1976).

See Currie, *Judicial Review under Federal Pollution Laws*, 62 Iowa L. Rev. 1221, 1239–42 (1977), where the jurisdictional issue is discussed in greater detail. In the *CPC* case, note 11 *supra*, "the corn milling standard for new plants, which the court did review, was identical to the 1983 guideline for existing plants, which it refused to review." 62 Iowa L. Rev. at 1241. I argued in this earlier article that § 509's reference to approval or promulgation of § 301 limitations would be essentially redundant if it did not include

in *duPont I* that "any action taken by the Administrator under § 304(b) should properly be considered to be pursuant to the provisions of § 301 and, therefore, reviewable by this court under § 509."[16] Thus the Supreme Court's decision that § 301 limitations may be adopted by regulation was not necessary to assure court of appeals review of § 304 guidelines.[17] Indeed, it leaves open the question of review of those guidelines when adopted, as future guidelines well may be, in advance of § 301 regulations.[18]

What the Supreme Court termed "the critical question" was therefore of virtually no importance.[19]

II

Since the question that so agitated the courts of appeals and the Supreme Court is of no moment, I shall not go into it in customary

§ 304 guidelines, since § 509 independently provides for review of EPA action "in issuing or denying any permit." As industry argued in *duPont*, however, this latter provision does not cover permits administered by States, see Brief for Petitioners in No. 75-978, at p. 87; and the word "promulgation" in § 509(b) may refer to listed sections other than § 301. While "approving" is an inapt term for the failure to veto, I see nothing else in the cited sections to which it might refer.

[16] 528 F.2d 1136, 1142 (1975).

[17] A conclusion more plausible than district-court review would have been that § 304 guidelines were omitted from § 309 review because Congress did not consider them ripe for review in any forum. *Cf.* Bethlehem Steel Corp. v. EPA, 536 F.2d 156 (7th Cir. 1976) (designation of Air Quality Maintenance Areas under the Clean Air Act not ripe for review). On this view, § 509 should be held to preclude review in the district courts by implication. Such a conclusion would imply—or would be based upon the understanding—that § 304 guidelines have little immediate impact on the individual discharger, that is, that they are to leave considerable latitude for plant-by-plant variation. On this view jurisdiction would depend upon the power to issue regulations under § 301. This possibility, however, was never suggested by industry, by the EPA, or by any court. Once it is assumed that the regulations are reviewable somewhere, as it was throughout this controversy, the only rational conclusion is that "effluent limitations" includes the § 304 guidelines.

[18] See 430 U.S. at 124, explaining that it was only "[b]ecause the process proved more time consuming than Congress assumed when it established this two-stage process" that the EPA "condensed the two stages into a single regulation."

[19] It has been suggested that the real issue in these cases was one of federalism: whether the States or the Administrator would set the § 301 limitations. See Note, 10 GA. L. REV. 983, 1019 (1976); Comment, 125 U. PA. L. REV. 120, 123 (1976). But the latter commentator concedes that "apart from practical considerations" there may be little difference, since the EPA can promulgate "de facto" limitations in the guise of § 304 guidelines. *Id.* at 164–65. The "practical" consideration mentioned is the practical limitation of the Administrator's § 402 power to veto state permits that deviate from the guidelines. Yet the same facts of life limit his ability to veto state permits that violate effluent-limitation regulations adopted under § 301.

hideous detail.[20] Handfuls of obscure provisions of this disorganized statute were invoked by one side or the other for the indirect light they—in most cases probably to the surprise of those who drafted them—might cast on the question.[21] To the Supreme Court the issue was as clear as glass: § 301 requires 1983 limitations to be set "for categories and classes of point sources"; "[n]ormally, such class-wide determinations would be made by regulation, not in the course of issuing a permit to one member of the class"; and although the "categories and classes" terminology does not appear in connection with 1977 limitations, "[n]othing elsewhere in the Act . . . suggests

---

[20] See, *e.g.*, Comment, note 19 *supra*; Note, note 19 *supra*; Parenteau & Tauman, *The Effluent Limitations Controversy*, 6 Ecol. L.Q. 1 (1976); Comment, 10 Suff. L. Rev. 1225 (1976); Note, 45 Fordham L. Rev. 625 (1976). Only the last of these exhibits any sympathy for the view of the Eighth Circuit, note 11 *supra*, that § 301 limitations may not be set by regulation.

[21] §§ 303, 306, and 307 explicitly use the word "standards" with regard to effluent limitations; § 301 does not. 33 U.S.C. §§ 1313, 1316, 1317. Section 316(b), 33 U.S.C. § 1326(b), on the other hand, refers to "any standard established pursuant to section 301." § 402(d)(2), 33 U.S.C. § 1342(d)(2), provides for EPA veto of state permits outside the "guidelines." But it also refers to "requirements," which could include regulations under § 301. § 515(b)(1), 33 U.S.C. § 1374(b)(1), requires notice to an advisory committee of the proposed adoption of specified regulations but makes no mention of § 301. It also omits, however, pretreatment regulations under § 307. §§ 302(a), 303(d)(1)(A), and 316(c), 33 U.S.C. §§ 1312(a), 1313(d)(1)(A), 1326(c), refer to "effluent limitations established [or required] under [or by] section 301," but do not say how those limitations are to be established. § 301(e), 33 U.S.C. § 1311(e), recites that "effluent limitations established pursuant to this section . . . shall be applied to all point sources of discharge of pollutants in accordance with the provisions of this Act"; this may imply that "establish[ment]" and "appli[cation]" are discrete steps, or merely that all point sources are to be included, or that other sections of the statute must be consulted. § 309, 33 U.S.C. § 1319, speaks of violations both of § 301 and of any permit condition. But § 301, in addition to the 1977 and 1983 limitations, forbids discharge without a permit. § 505, 33 U.S.C. § 1365, allows citizen enforcement of any "effluent standard or limitation," defined to include both "an effluent limitation or other limitation under section 301 or 302" and "a permit on condition thereof." But § 301(f) flatly bars the discharge of "any radiological, chemical, or biological warfare agent or high-level radioactive waste" independently of permit conditions. § 509(b), 33 U.S.C. § 1369(b), authorizes court of appeals review both of EPA issuance or denial of a permit and of EPA action "approving or promulgating any effluent limitation or other limitation under section 301, 302, or 306." But "promulgating" may refer to §§ 302 and 306, and "approving" to EPA veto or refusal to veto a state-issued permit, which is not otherwise reviewable under § 509. § 401, 33 U.S.C. § 1341, requires an applicant for a "Federal license or permit" to provide a certification from the appropriate State either that any discharge will comply with, among others, § 301, or that "there is not an applicable effluent limitation or other limitation under sections 301(b) and 302." But such limitations could nevertheless be adopted in the § 402 permit process, since § 401 was meant to include licenses issued by such agencies as the AEC, FPC, and the Corps of Engineers. See Leg. Hist. at 1487.

any radical difference in the mechanism used to impose limitations for the 1977 and 1983 deadlines."[22]

It certainly would be odd to hold that the omission of the word "categories" for 1977 limitations meant the procedure for adopting them differed from that prescribed by the otherwise parallel 1983 provision. But the Court brushed rather too lightly over the question whether the reference to "categories" has any procedural significance at all. If the discrepancy is not mere accident, it seems to suggest that the 1983 limitations are to be substantively less flexible than the 1977 limitations in respect to individual circumstances, and the requisite inflexibility could as well be achieved by uniform § 304 guidelines as by regulations under § 301 itself.

The Court attempted to buttress its position with § 501(a)'s delegation of authority to adopt "such regulations as are necessary to carry out" EPA functions under the Act,[23] with § 101(d)'s provision that, except as otherwise provided, "the Administrator . . . shall administer this Act,"[24] and with the argument that Congress could not have intended to impose an "impossible burden" by requiring "individual consideration to the circumstances of each of the more than 42,000 dischargers who have applied for permits."[25] Even assuming that, notwithstanding the numerous specifically circumscribed grants of substantive rule-making power elsewhere in the Act, the boilerplate language of § 501 was intended to authorize anything more than the ordinary organizational or procedural arrangements incidental to the execution of any program,[26] it can scarcely have been designed to resolve the important question of uniformity which the Court seems to have thought depended upon whether effluent limitations could be adopted by regulation. All that § 101(d) means is that it is the Administrator, not anyone else, who administers the statute. It says nothing about how he is to do it. The "impossible burden" argument is again relevant not to the procedural question of § 301 regulations but to the substantive one of case-by-case variation.

I shall not further attempt to resolve the burning question of the

[22] 430 U.S. at 127.

[23] 33 U.S.C. § 1361(a).

[24] 33 U.S.C. § 1251(d).

[25] 430 U.S. at 132.

[26] But see National Petroleum Refiners Ass'n v. FTC, 482 F.2d 672 (D.C. Cir. 1973), construing a similarly bland authorization in the Federal Trade Commission Act to confer substantive rule-making power in the teeth of contrary legislative history. That statute, however, contained no specific rulemaking authorizations when it was adopted.

propriety of effluent-limitation regulations. There may be a more appropriate metaphor than angels and pin heads, but I cannot think of it.

III

The important question in the *duPont* litigation was the degree to which effluent limitations under § 301 are to vary according to individual circumstances.

At times the Court appeared to be resolving this question. It began by emphasizing that the statute provides for "class-wide determinations" respecting 1983 limitations, and it argued that Congress could not have intended the "impossible burden" of "individual consideration to the circumstances of each . . . discharger."[27] It also quoted from the Senate Report that the Administrator was "to set a base level for all plants in a given category"; from the Conference Report that "the determination of the economic impact of an effluent limitation" was to be made "on the basis of classes and categories . . ."; and from Senator Muskie that the Conferees had agreed upon a class-wide cost-benefit analysis for 1977 "in order to maintain uniformity within a class . . . and to avoid imposing . . . any requirement to consider the location of sources within a category or to ascertain water quality impact of effluent controls, or to determine the economic impact of controls on any individual plant."[28] It ended by declaring: "[W]e hold that EPA has the authority to issue regulations setting forth uniform effluent limitations for categories of plants."[29]

Appearances, however, can be deceiving. The Court's reference to "uniform" limitations is seriously undercut by its earlier conclusion that 1977 limitations, for which § 301 makes no reference to "categories," may be set by regulation "so long as some allowance is made for variations in individual plants, as EPA has done by including a variance clause in its 1977 limitations."[30] This passage not only demonstrates, as I have argued above, that the question of flexibility is independent of the question of the power to act by regulation; it also shows that the Court did not decide the 1977

[27] 430 U.S. at 127, 132.

[28] *Id.* at 129–30. Leg. Hist. at 1468, 304, 170.

[29] 430 U.S. at 136.

[30] *Id.* at 128.

limitations must or may be uniform. And a footnote leaves no doubt that the Court meant to leave the uniformity issue altogether open with regard to 1977: "We agree with the Court of Appeals . . . that consideration of whether EPA's variance provision has the proper scope would be premature."[31]

Thus the battle through the courts of appeals and the Supreme Court over the crucial question of uniformity of the 1977 standards has produced no answer. The troops have marched up the hill, and they have marched back down. They might as well not have bothered.[32]

IV

Standing alone, § 301 appears to contemplate greater uniformity in the 1983 than in 1977 limitations, for only the former are said to apply to "categories and classes" of sources.[33] Of course the unmodified reference to "sources" with regard to 1977 need not exclude uniformity as a matter of language, and the discrepancy may be accidental.[34] Though the Supreme Court seems to have thought it significant, the parties did not, and § 304 confirms the hypothesis that no sharp distinction was intended. Both for 1977 and 1983, the guideline regulations to be adopted under § 304 are to do two things: (1) to "identify . . . the degree of effluent reduction attainable through the application" of the respective (best practicable and best available) technology "for classes and catego-

---

[31] *Id.* at 128 n. 19. Just when the issue can be determined is not clear. Industry was challenging the validity of what the Court viewed as an effluent limitation under § 301. § 509(b) forbids making such challenges more than 90 days after adoption. 33 U.S.C. § 1369(b). See Currie, note 15 *supra*, at 1254–60, for analysis and criticism of this provision.

[32] The Supreme Court is not to blame for this. Industry's petitions for certiorari raised only two questions (labeled as three): which court had review jurisdiction, and whether EPA regulations were to be based upon § 301 or § 304. See Petitions for Certiorari, No. 75-978, at p. 2; No. 75-1473, at pp. 2–3. The EPA's cross-petition raised only the issue of variances under § 306. Cross-petition for Certiorari, No. 75-1705, at p. 2. Since uniformity was not relevant to either of these questions, the Court said more rather than less about uniformity than the case demanded.

The failure of industry to raise the uniformity question explicitly may be attributable to its partial victory on that matter below. The court of appeals had held the limitation regulations only "presumptively applicable."

[33] See text *supra*, at notes 3–4.

[34] See American Iron & Steel Inst. v. EPA, 526 F.2d 1027, 1042 n.32 (3d Cir. 1975), calling the difference "inadvertent" and "a result of imprecise legislative drafting." Accord, Comment, note 19 *supra*, at 152.

ries of point sources"; and (2) to "specify factors to be taken into account in determining . . . measures and practices . . . to be applicable to point sources [or "to any point source"] . . . within such categories or classes."[35]

Thus, for both years there are to be guidelines formulated by category, specifying, for example, that suspended solids from pickling mills may be reduced to *x* or *y* milligrams per liter. And while the EPA will have to exercise judgment in deciding whether to make separate categories for mills pickling with different acids, the very idea of categorical guidelines suggests that where appropriate it may prescribe a single "degree of effluent reduction" within each category.[36]

At the same time, the requirement that the guidelines "specify factors to be taken into account in determining . . . practices . . . applicable to point sources . . . within such categories"—not discussed by the Supreme Court—unmistakably allows the EPA to permit variation according to the circumstances of each plant.[37] This is not to say that the EPA necessarily must be more lenient with older plants, for example, for theoretically there may be industries in which there are no factors justifying a departure from what has been generally determined to be the best practicable or

[35] 33 U.S.C. § 1314(b)(1),(2). The 1983 provision contains a few additional words that seem to add nothing of substance. The regulations are to "specify factors to be taken into account in determining the best measures and practices available *to comply with subsection (b)(2) of section 301 of this Act* to be applicable to any point source . . . within such categories or classes." (Emphasis added.) Since a similar reference to § 301(b)(1) appears in another sentence of the 1977 provision, the difference appears to be no more than an alteration of word order.

[36] The Senate Report, Leg. Hist. at 1468, stated that the Administrator would be "expect[ed]" to identify a "range" of permissible values above a "base" level to which everyone would have to comply. To the Third Circuit this was gospel. The expectations of a committee were equated with the command of the Congress. American Iron & Steel Inst. v. EPA, 526 F.2d 1027, 1045 (1975). While the statute certainly allows the guidelines to establish "ranges" where the Administrator deems them appropriate, it says nothing to require them, least of all when there is no justification for them. Nor did the Committee, however authoritative its interpretation, say it did.

[37] Several commentators have viewed the quoted language as a direction to the Administrator to divide "categories" into "subcategories" where warranted by relevant factors. See Zener, *The Federal Law of Water Pollution Control*, in Env. Law Inst., Federal Environmental Law 682, 703 (Dolgin & Guilbert, eds. 1974); Arnold, *Effluent Limitations and NPDES: Federal and State Implementation of the FWPCA Amendments of 1972*, 15 B.C. Indus. & Comm. L. Rev. 767, 770 (1974); Parenteau & Tauman, note 20 *supra*, at 36–37. This argument fails to explain the direction to list those factors in the guidelines themselves. If the EPA planned to create subcategories by later regulation, why would it not create them in the guidelines to begin with?

best available technology. Congress could hardly have ordered age to make a difference when it is irrelevant. But § 304 does seem to mean that, both for 1977 and for 1983, the guidelines are to make such allowances wherever they are justified and must state what factors are relevant.

Section 301's cryptic references to "categories" and to technology "economically achievable for such category or class," added without explanation in conference, leans in the other direction for 1983. But this ambiguous repetition of a phrase already found in § 304 cannot be given significant weight without ignoring the plain and specific provisions of § 304.[38]

The earlier legislative history supports the natural reading of § 304. The Senate Report is clear enough. Not only is the Administrator to consider the various factors listed in that section when defining "best practicable" or "best available" for any "category," but "[i]n applying effluent limitations to any individual plant, the factors cited above should be applied to that specific plant."[39] When asked point-blank whether § 301 contemplated that best-available limitations would be set "almost on an individual point source by point source basis," Senator Muskie, the sponsor of the bill, either agreed or evaded the question. For both years § 301 "anticipate[d] individual application of controls on point sources through the procedures under the permit program established under section 402."[40] The House Report essentially repeated the language of § 304: "In specifying the factors to be taken into account in determining the control measures and practices to be applicable

[38] § 301(c), 33 U.S.C. § 1311(c), also added in Conference, authorizes the Administrator to modify the 1983 requirements upon a showing "that such modified requirements (1) will represent the maximum use of technology within the economic capability of the owner or operator; and (2) will result in reasonable further progress toward the elimination of the discharge of pollutants." At first glance the presence of an authorization for individual variances suggests that except for its provisions the determination of best available technology is to be made on an industry-wide basis, and the Supreme Court so suggested, 430 U.S. at 127 n.17. But closer examination reveals that the determinations to be made may be substantively different. § 301(b) requires use of the best technology economically achievable, which implies a balance of costs and benefits. § 301(c) appears to allow a variance for a discharger even when the benefits of control outweigh the costs, if to comply would be beyond his "economic capability," *e.g.*, would put him out of business. See Zener, note 37 *supra*, at 702, arguing that § 301(c) provides the sole avenue of relief when a discharger's difficulty results from his "weak financial picture." Thus, § 301(c) does not demonstrate that the economic achievability of technology must be determined on an industry-wide basis under § 301(b).

[39] Leg. Hist. at 1468.

[40] *Id.* at 1391.

to any point source within a category and class, the Administrator is expected to give specific and detailed consideration to the age of the equipment . . . , cost and the economic, social, and environmental impacts of achieving such effluent reduction."[41] Representative Clausen, a committee member supporting the bill, spoke of the "best practicable" requirement as "a standard that would be applied to all plants of a similar nature, regardless of location, if the applicable factors that I just enumerated were the same in each plant."[42] Up to this point the explanations of both House and Senate bills were consistent with the language of § 304.

With the Conference Report things began to get murky. In a passage quoted by the Supreme Court, that report flatly contradicted § 304: "The conferees intend that the Administrator or the State . . . will make the determination of the economic impact of an effluent limitation on the basis of classes and categories of point sources, as distinguished from a plant by plant determination."[43]

The report went on, however, to contradict itself, explicitly explaining, as both committees had previously, that the Administrator under § 304 was to "specify factors to be taken into account in determining the control measures and practices to be applicable to point sources . . . within categories or classes."[44] It summarized, with an expectation of uniformity that fell short of the absolute, limitations within a class should be "as uniform as possible"; the guidelines should "assure that similar point sources with similar characteristics, regardless of their location or the nature of the water into which the discharge is made, will meet similar effluent limitations."[45]

Then came Senator Muskie, explaining the Conference action to the Senate. He chose the half of the Conference Report he preferred, insisting that the modified bill provided for "nationally uniform effluent limitations based on 'best practicable' technology."[46] He then added to the record a written statement in which this theme was further expanded:[47]

> The Conferees agreed upon this limited cost-benefit analysis in order to maintain uniformity within a class and category of point sources subject to effluent limitations, and to avoid im-

[41] *Id.* at 794.

[42] *Id.* at 378.

[43] *Id.* at 304.

[44] *Id.* at 308.

[45] *Id.* at 309.

[46] *Id.* at 162.

[47] *Id.* at 170, 172.

> posing on the Administrator any requirement to consider the location of sources within a category or to ascertain water quality impact of effluent controls, or to determine the economic impact of controls on any individual plant in a single community. . . .
>
> The Conferees intend that the factors described in section 304(b) be considered only within classes or categories of point sources and that such factors not be considered at the time of the application of an effluent limitation to an individual point source within such a category or class.

Neither Senator Muskie nor anyone else called attention to the difference in phrasing between the 1977 and 1983 provisions or suggested that the later limitations were to be more uniform.

Thus the legislative history suggests, though rather inconclusively, that the Conference Committee may have wished to modify § 304's requirement of plant-by-plant consideration. Yet it left that section intact, while adding a few ambiguous words to § 301.

It was in a water-pollution case decided only two years before *duPont* that the Supreme Court reminded us that "legislative intention, without more, is not legislation."[48] If legislative history shows that the language of a statute reflects a drafting error, it may be permissible to ignore the language.[49] But the draftsman can scarcely have written inadvertently of "factors to be taken into account in determining . . . practices . . . applicable to point sources . . . within such categories." The statute, not explanatory statements made by individual members of Congress or written by their anonymous employees, is the law.[50]

---

[48] Train v. City of New York, 420 U.S. 35, 45 (1975). See also Piper v. Chris-Craft Industries, Inc., 430 U.S. 1, 26 (1977), decided the same day as *duPont:* "Reliance on legislative history in divining the intent of Congress is, as has often been observed, a step to be taken cautiously."

[49] See, *e.g.*, Arizona v. California, 373 U.S. 546, 567–75 (1963).

[50] The Petitioners' Brief in No. 75-978, pp. 61–62, quotes Senator Jackson's criticism of another portion of the Muskie statement as "a back-door attempt at legislation through last minute speeches on the floor of the Senate," Leg. Hist. at 204; Rep. Dingell's objection to the same passages as " 'bootstrap' legislative history," Leg. Hist. at 107; and an article by then-EPA counsel Robert Zener speaking of Muskie's remarks about uniformity: "[S]tatements of individual conferees that go farther than the Conference Report are dubious indications of congressional intent, since frequently such statements were made on the floor only because the individual conferee failed to get conference agreement to put the statement in the Report." Zener, note 37 *supra*, at 703 n.98. Senator Muskie was the one who explained that in applying the statutory phrase "best available technology *economically achievable*" the Administrator "should reflect an evaluation of what needs to be done to move toward the elimination of the discharge of pollutants

Much has been made by the courts and commentators of the Supreme Court's recent statement that it would defer to the EPA in the construction of a complex statute it administers[51] because the EPA's construction was "sufficiently reasonable to preclude the Court of Appeals from substituting its judgment for that of the Agency."[52] As one of these commentators concedes, however, "the Court's pronouncements on when a reviewing court may substitute its judgment for that of an administrative agency have been somewhat irregular."[53] I find compelling the conclusion of Professor Jaffe:[54]

> [W]here the *judges* are themselves *convinced* that certain reading, or application, of the statute is the *correct*—or the only *faithful*—reading or application, they should intervene and so declare. Where the result of their study leaves them without a definite preference, they can and often should abstain if the agency's preference is "reasonable."

What is "practicable" or "best available" technology, in sum, may vary from plant to plant under the clear dictates of § 304.

V

At stake in *duPont* were the EPA's "effluent limitations guidelines" for the inorganic chemicals industry. Illustrative are the regulations respecting the "Chlorine and Sodium or Potassium Hy-

---

and what is achievable through the application of available technology—without regard to cost." Leg. Hist. at 170. (Emphasis added.)

Note, note 19 *supra*, at 1021 complains that the courts in the effluent-limitation cases have shown "an undue concern with the language of the Act [sic] and its legislative history." See also Parenteau & Tauman, note 20 *supra*, at 35, observing of a decision the authors dislike that the court had "based . . . [its] conclusion on the language of § 304(b) itself, finding the legislative history too confusing to be dispositive." The Fourth Circuit, concluding that "read literally the 1977 requirement is for determination on the basis of individual discharges," refused to hold accordingly because "practical considerations may not be ignored." *duPont II*, 541 F.2d at 1029. No comment is necessary.

[51] See, *e.g.*, American Meat Inst. v. EPA, 526 F.2d 442, 449–50 (7th Cir. 1975); American Frozen Food Inst. v. Train, 539 F.2d 107, 131 (D.C. Cir. 1976); Parenteau & Tauman, note 20 *supra*, at 20 n.92; Comment, note 19 *supra*, at 138; Note, note 19 *supra*, at 1002–03.

[52] Train v. Natural Resources Defense Council, Inc., 421 U.S. 60, 87 (1975), quoted by the Court in support of its decision in *duPont*. 430 U.S. at 135.

[53] Comment, note 19 *supra*, at 138 n.104.

[54] Jaffe, Judicial Control of Administrative Action 572 (1965).

droxide Production Subcategory."[55] This subcategory is further divided between plants using the mercury-cell and those using the diaphragm-cell process. For each type of plant one 1977 figure is prescribed for a thirty-day average and another for a single day. Thus for mercury-cell plants total suspended solids discharged are not to exceed 0.32 kilograms for each 1,000 kilograms of chlorine manufactured over any thirty consecutive days, nor 0.64 on any day.[56] In recognition, however, of the possibility that data not yet known to the EPA may require that these limitations "be adjusted for certain plants in this industry," the regulation allows a "discharger or other interested person" to submit evidence to the permitting authority "that factors relating to the equipment or facilities involved, the process applied, or other such factors related to such discharger are fundamentally different from the factors considered in the establishment of the guidelines." Upon adequate proof the permit issuer is to establish limitations "either more or less stringent than the limitations established herein, to the extent dictated by such fundamentally different factors."[57]

A comparison of this regulation with § 304 suggests that the EPA is merely paying lip service to the statutory requirement. While the statute demands a specification of factors relevant to an individual determination, the regulation prescribes a single standard to be adhered to absent proof of "fundamentally different" circumstances, leaving the relevant factors essentially undefined. As for specifying factors, the regulation is less specific than the statute,[58] although Congress apparently thought EPA's study of an industry would enable it to go into detail: "In specifying the factors to be taken into account . . . the Administrator is expected to give specific and detailed consideration to the age of the equipment . . . , the cost."[59] Of course, if the EPA's information indicated that the figures prescribed were practicable for the whole industry, it would not be required to pretend otherwise.[60] But in leaving the door open

---

[55] 40 C.F.R. §§ 415.60–.66 (1976).

[56] 40 C.F.R. § 415.62(a) (1976).

[57] 40 C.F.R. § 415.62 (1976).

[58] See note 10 *supra*.

[59] Leg. Hist. at 794, which supports the natural meaning of § 304.

[60] Having subdivided certain inorganic-chemical categories "to reflect different manufacturing processes used to produce the same chemical," the EPA found that "factors such as plant age, plant size and geographical location did not justify further

for unforeseen exceptions it should be as specific and as broad as the statute itself.[61] Yet the EPA construed its own variance regulations to allow only technical and engineering factors, not cost or adverse environmental impact, to be considered at the permit stage.[62] This is an unnatural reading, for cost at least may be a factor "relating to the equipment or facilities involved," or an "other such factor related to such discharger." Moreover, as the Fourth Circuit held in *Appalachian Power Co. v. Train*,[63] a variance clause that does not allow cost or environmental impact to be considered does not satisfy § 304, which requires a case-by-case determination of what is "practicable" and expressly lists costs and environmental impact as factors relevant to that determination.

Not only do the regulations as construed lack specificity and improperly exclude certain relevant factors from consideration at the permit stage. In requiring that the discharger show that his case is "fundamentally" different, the EPA has created a strong presumption of uniformity that the statute does not appear to demand. The regulation transforms a statutory directive for case-by-case determination into a single rule applicable except in extraordinary circumstances. Section 304 seems to contemplate that dischargers are to meet different limitations whenever their differences are significant, not just when they are "fundamental." As the Third Circuit held in *American Iron & Steel Inst. v. EPA*, "the variance procedure provides for less flexibility than . . . Congress contemplated."[64]

---

segmentation of the industry." Development Document for Effluent Limitations Guidelines and New Source Performance Standards for the Major Inorganic Chemicals Manufacturing Point Source Category (1974), p. 1, in Appendix Exhibit Vol., No. 75-978, at 5586. See also *id.* at 61–63 (App. Ex. at 5644–46) for greater specificity respecting this conclusion.

[61] An example of the anticipated specific enumeration of factors is found in 40 C.F.R. § 420.12(b) (1976), respecting discharges from coke ovens: "The limitations specified may be exceeded up to 15 percent by those facilities equipped with gas desulfurization units to the extent that such measured discharge is necessary by reason of the increased effluent volume generated by these facilities."

[62] See 39 Fed. Reg. 28926–27, 30073 (1974), cited in Appalachian Power Co. v. Train, 545 F.2d 1351, 1360 n.22 (4th Cir. 1976).

[63] 545 F.2d 1351, 1359 (1976).

[64] 526 F.2d 1027, 1046 (1975). The variance provisions were held sufficiently broad in Natural Resources Defense Council, Inc. v. EPA, 537 F.2d 642, 645 (2d Cir. 1976), and in American Petroleum Inst. v. EPA, 540 F.2d 1023, 1033 (10th Cir. 1976). The former based its decision on the conclusion that uniformity was the basic goal; the latter gave no discernible reason.

The 1983 regulations typically contain no variance clause at all. The chlorine guideline, for example, flatly provides for "no discharge of process waste water pollutants" from diaphragm-cell plants by 1983.[65] The sodium-carbonate regulation prescribes flat daily and monthly maxima.[66] The latter is quite inconsistent with § 304, which contemplates plant-to-plant variation when dictated by relevant factors. The legality of the former may appear more debatable, since the paragraph of § 304 relating specifically to measures for complete elimination of discharges does not itself speak of factors relevant to the individual plant. But the elimination of all discharge is a possible and congressionally hoped-for means of complying with § 301(b)(2)'s requirement of the best available technology economically achievable. And § 304 is explicit that the guidelines specify factors to be considered in applying that concept to individual sources.

VI

In the Third Circuit *Iron and Steel* case, industry offered examples to show the significance of its argument that the statute required plant-by-plant determinations of practicability:[67]

> Youngstown claims that its plants in the Mahoning Valley provide one third of the direct employment in that area . . . , that its plants are very old . . . , that many will be forced to close if the limitations promulgated by the Administrator are enforced, and that because of the heavy concentration of steel plants along the shores, the river is unavailable for recreational uses anyway. . . . CF & I . . . contends that the installation of antipollution devices in its Colorado plants would cause a significant net loss of water through evaporation, which would have serious consequences in a state where water is a scarce and valuable resource.

That compliance with an effluent limitation found "practicable" for the steel industry generally would disemploy a third of the workers in the Mahoning Valley is undeniably a "cost" of imposing that requirement.[68] That it would aggravate water scarcity in

[65] 40 C.F.R. § 415.63 (1976).

[66] 40 C.F.R. § 415.153 (1976).

[67] American Iron & Steel Inst. v. EPA, 526 F.2d 1027, 1036 (1975).

[68] The ordinary sense of the term is supported by the statement of Rep. Jones, Leg. Hist. at 231: "The term 'total cost of application of technology' as used in section 304(b)(1)(B) is meant to include those internal, or plant, costs sustained by the owner

Colorado is an unmistakable "non-water quality environmental impact." Under § 304 both are to be considered. Whether those circumstances justify a relaxation of what the guideline finds generally practicable will depend upon all the facts. The "effluent reduction benefits," to quote § 304, may be worth the suggested hardships. That the Mahoning may be unusable even if clean, however, is deemed irrelevant. The whole thrust of the movement that led to the 1972 amendments requiring "best practicable" and "best available" technology was a desire to shift away from the earlier focus on water quality and to base effluent requirements on the ability of the discharger.[69] Against this background, "effluent reduction benefits" does not mean the ultimate water-quality benefits to be achieved from reducing effluents. It means a comparison of contaminants in effluent with and without the best practicable treatment.[70]

VII

What is to be said for this statutory scheme? First of all, one may agree with the Fourth Circuit as to draftsmanship: "The conflict among the circuits emphasizes the confusion caused by this poorly drafted and astonishingly imprecise statute."[71]

---

or operator and those external costs such as potential unemployment, dislocation, and rural area economic development sustained by the community, area, or region."

[69] See, *e.g.*, Leg. Hist. at 1461: "The application of Phase I technology to industrial point sources is based upon the control technologies for those sources. . . . It is not based upon ambient water quality considerations." See also *id.* at 1426, 1459; *id.* at 1304 (Senator Cooper); *id.* at 787: "Subsection (b) of section 301 establishes a technological basis for the determination of effluent limitations." The bills as reported said only that "costs" should be considered, without relating them to "effluent reduction benefits." See *id.* at 980, 1615. Senator Muskie explained that the Conference's new phrase was meant to express a "limited cost-benefit analysis." *Id.* at 170. But neither he nor anyone else suggested it was meant to reverse the whole legislative direction by making water quality relevant. Muskie paraphrased the statutory "effluent reduction benefits" as "degree of effluent reduction." *Ibid.* "Under this interpretation," says Zener, "EPA apparently could limit its cost-benefit analysis to a determination of whether its standard was set at the point of the cost curve where the marginal cost of an additional degree of effluent reduction rises steeply." Zener, note 37 *supra*, at 697–98. Both Zener and Davis & Glasser, *The Discharge Permit Program under the FWPCA of 1972*, 2 Ford. Urb. L. J. 179, 210 (1974), note the ambiguity of the statutory language; neither resolves it.

[70] The EPA wrote several of the regulations to exempt steel plants in the Mahoning Valley from otherwise applicable limitations altogether. 40 C.F.R. § 420.132 (1976). The Third Circuit, over EPA's argument that the regulation left it to the state to define "best practicable" for these plants on an individual basis, held the exemptions invalid: "§ 301 (e) requires the EPA to establish specific effluent limitations for all point sources." That other means might be found for "accommodating diversity," the court did not dispute. American Iron & Steel Inst. v. EPA, 10 E.R.C. 1689, 1706–07 (1977).

[71] *duPont II*, 541 F.2d at 1026.

Second, we may lament the insistence of Congress on prescribing the contents of agency regulations in such great detail. Congress is no expert on pollution control; that is why it delegates responsibility to the EPA. The more specific Congress gets the more it risks making mistakes and the more likely it becomes that additional legislation will be necessary. Perhaps the extreme example is the requirement in the Clean Air Act that EPA regulations require by 1977 "a reduction of at least 90 per centum from emissions of carbon monoxide and hydrocarbons allowable . . . in model year 1970."[72] Congress is in no position to determine whether a 90 percent reduction is either necessary or practicable. The upshot, predictably, has been continued lobbying for minor adjustments best made at the agency level in light of general congressional policy. In the water statute, too, a sensible Congress would have left it to the agency to decide how to administer a requirement of best practicable technology. In attempting to specify the details, Congress got into an unnecessary tangle.

Third, as the Supreme Court in *duPont* recognized,[73] administrative costs may make truly independent plant-by-plant comparisons of costs and benefits undesirable. Moreover, the absence of generally applicable standards is conducive to uncertainty, to consequent delays in compliance, and to discrepant treament by various permit granters of persons similarly situated. The EPA's program of uniform standards with an allowance for cases "fundamentally different"—I would have said for "unreasonable hardship"[74]—seems a lesser evil than that envisioned by the present statute.

Fourth, though the statute goes too far in requiring de novo consideration of practicability for each plant, it holds everyone in the country to rigid time deadlines with no escape clause whatever.[75] In my thirty months as a state pollution officer,[76] I encountered several hundred petitions for variances from generally appli-

---

[72] Clean Air Act, § 202(b)(1)(A), 42 U.S.C. § 1857 f-1(b)(1)(A).

[73] 430 U.S. at 132.

[74] *Cf.* Ill. Rev. Stat., Ch. 111 1/2, § 1035.

[75] See Bethlehem Steel Corp. v. Train, 544 F.2d 657, 659 (3d Cir. 1976), where the EPA "agreed that compliance by July 1, 1977 was not feasible." A provision in the House bill allowing up to two-year extensions of the Phase I (now 1977) date upon a finding that it was "not possible either physically or legally to complete the necessary construction within the statutory time limit" or when more time was allowed in a plan for implementing water-quality standards, LEG. HIST. at 964–65, was deleted.

[76] I was chairman of the Illinois Pollution Control Board, 1970–72.

cable standards. By far the bulk of them dealt with time problems.[77] Many things beyond the polluter's control can upset the most carefully calculated compliance schedule. A strike may preclude timely manufacture of control equipment. A storm, an explosion, or other misadventure may delay timely installation. Unanticipated fuel shortages may necessitate a tardy change of plans. The EPA itself may miss its statutory deadlines for promulgating guidelines,[78] so that there is insufficient time for industry to plan and build by the date prescribed. In a few such cases the discharge may be so intolerable that society benefits by closing the plant down, but my experience leads me to believe they are rare. Nor does it seem to me desirable to inflict punitive money sanctions on the victim of such a misfortune, or to brand him, as the present law demands, a wrongdoer. Prosecutorial or equitable discretion may of course be exercised to prevent serious injustice,[79] but discretion is uncertain. It would be better to recognize explicitly that schedules cannot always be met by allowing variances respecting time as well as technology on proof of unreasonable hardship.

Fifth, the individual circumstances to be considered in applying or modifying effluent limitations ought to include water quality and the value of improving it. It makes no sense to spend millions of dollars to render a river clean enough to swim in if, as argued in the case of the Mahoning steel mills, physical conditions make it unswimmable anyway.[80]

Sixth, I doubt the wisdom of requiring by statute, even subject to suitable variance provision, that a given level of technology be applied everywhere without regard to the nature of the receiving

---

[77] See, *e.g.*, Ozark-Mahoning Co. v. EPA, 1 Ill. P.C.B. 121 (1970); Wagner Castings Co. v. EPA, 1 Ill. P.C.B. 155 (1971); Marblehead Lime Co. v. EPA, 1 Ill. P.C.B. 335 (1971).

[78] See Natural Resources Defense Council, Inc. v. Train, 510 F.2d 692 (D.C. Cir. 1975). The Sixth Circuit has just held that EPA's delay is an excuse, since § 301 requires use of the best practicable technology "as defined by the Administrator pursuant to § 304(b)." Republic Steel Corp. v. Train, 557 F.2d 91 (1977). Nothing in this opinion suggests that any other excuse can justify delay.

[79] See Bethlehem Steel Corp. v. Train, 544 F.2d 657, 660 (3d Cir. 1976), in which the EPA indicated that it did not contemplate enforcement. As the court noted, the EPA's position would not preclude citizen suits under § 505, 33 U.S.C. § 1365. See also Reserve Mining Co. v. EPA, 514 F.2d 492 (8th Cir. 1975) (Refuse Act); Friends of the Earth v. Potomac Elec. Power Co., 419 F. Supp. 528, 535 (D.D.C. 1976) (Clean Air Act); but see United States v. United States Steel Corp., 9 E.R.C. 1002, 1005 (N.D. Ala. 1976), *aff'd* 548 F.2d 1232 (5th Cir. 1977) (same statute).

[80] See text *supra*, at notes 68–70.

water. The reason we legislate against water pollution is to prevent harm: to make water safe for drinking, pleasant for swimming, hospitable to fish. A small discharge to a large river may have no significant adverse effect, and to require it to be extensively treated would be a waste of money. Yet the same discharge to a small stream might destroy a valuable sport fishery and wipe out a town's public water supply.

It is this variability of the harm caused by similar discharges that led to the focus on the quality of the receiving water in federal law before the 1972 amendments. What one might discharge was determined by its effect on the receiving stream. The important thing was that the water in that stream was safe for its designated uses.[81]

Dissatisfaction with this approach led to the 1972 amendments.[82] There was some reason for dissatisfaction. One problem with an absolute water-quality approach is the difficulty of predicting accurately the effect of a given discharge on a particular body of water. The variables are numerous and the calculations subject to substantial margins of error.[83] Another is the cost and time required to make such determinations as compared with a single decision as to available technology. Added to these is the incompleteness of knowledge as to the levels of various pollutants that may be harmful. That limited tests to date have not shown the ingestion of a poison to be deleterious below *x* milligrams per day does not prove that level to be safe.[84] Moreover, unless the wastewater itself is clean enough to be harmless, in even the largest body of water there will be mixing zones in which contaminant values are high enough to cause harm.[85] Further, if the pollutant is not quick to degrade, it will accumulate

---

[81] See the Administration testimony by CEQ Chairman Train and EPA Administrator Ruckelshaus in favor of continuing this basic approach. Leg. Hist. at 1114–18, 1179–84.

[82] See, *e.g.*, *id.* at 1426.

[83] See Ackerman & Sawyer, *The Uncertain Search for Environmental Policy: Scientific Factfinding and Rational Decisionmaking along the Delaware River*, 120 U. Pa. L. Rev. 419, 479–80 (1972).

[84] See NAPCA, Guidelines for the Development of Air Quality Standards and Implementation Plans 16 (1969): "The exposure levels which have thus far been associated with identifiable effects, particularly effects on man and on the ecological system of which man is part, are not necessarily the lowest levels of exposure that will produce such effects. Nor are those effects necessarily the only ones produced by such exposures."

[85] See, *e.g.*, Ill. P.C.B. Regs., Ch. 3, Rule 201(a).

downstream in the ocean, as salt has done, and may eventually become harmful. Beyond this, if we allow present dischargers to load the water with as much of a contaminant as it can take without causing harm, we leave no room for future development. If we are not to forgo new industry, we will have to revise our standards whenever a newcomer comes along.[86] Finally, in an aesthetic sense it may be that no discharge can be viewed as totally harmless. Just as some folks bathe every week "whether they need it or not," there can be satisfaction in knowing that a stream is undefiled by man.[87]

For all these reasons, there are instances in which it makes sense to require certain controls to be installed everywhere, although immediate discernible harm could be avoided in some places without them. Thus when I was there the Illinois Pollution Control Board required a minimum of secondary treatment of all sewage,[88] as does the federal statute,[89] and the statewide use of relatively inexpensive lime precipitation to reduce heavy metals to levels not likely to cause serious harm in substantial streams.[90] Yet to carry this philosophy too far can lead to enormous overexpenditures in pollution control, or worse. Mindful of this danger, the Illinois Board required control of phosphorus effluents to Lake Michigan, where there was a proven danger of eutrophication,[91] but not to flowing streams in which high phosphorus had proved no problem.[92] It prescribed expensive tertiary treatment of sewage only for discharges to streams whose low dilution ratio indicated it was necessary to maintain enough oxygen for fish.[93] And in a dramatic air-pollution example, it refused to extend statewide a stringent sulfur-

[86] See In the Matter of Emission Standards, 4 ILL. P.C.B. 298, 309 (1972).

[87] See Hines, *A Decade of Nondegradation Policy in Congress and the Courts*, 62 IOWA L. REV. 643, 646–49 (1977), urging that this policy, underlying the wilderness movement, also supports a policy against degradation of air and water of current quality better than necessary to meet ambient standards based on perceptible harm.

[88] Ill. P.C.B. Regs., Ch. 3, Rule 404(a).

[89] § 301(b)(1)(B), 33 U.S.C. § 1311(b)(1)(B).

[90] Ill. P.C.B. Regs., Ch. 3, Rule 408; see In the Matter of Effluent Criteria, 3 ILL. P.C.B. 401, 407–20 (1972).

[91] In re Phosphorus Water Standards, 1 ILL. P.C.B. 515 (1971).

[92] In the Matter of Effluent Criteria, 3 ILL. P.C.B. 401, 407 (1972).

[93] Ill. P.C.B. Regs., Ch. 3, Rule 404(c), (f); see In the Matter of Effluent Criteria, 3 ILL. P.C.B. 755, 766–71 (1972).

oxide emission standard which would divert scarce clean fuel from highly polluted areas in which it was most needed.[94]

The federal water-pollution statute does not allow this needed flexibility. While it commendably requires measures beyond the uniform effluent limitations where necessary to assure satisfactory water quality,[95] it requires all dischargers to install not one but two levels of control equipment without regard to varying effects on water quality. It could scarcely be doubted that 90 percent reduction of phosphorus discharges, for example, is "practicable" in the sense of producing enormous benefits in some situations at acceptable cost.[96] Evidently the EPA must require it throughout the country. And while I would be inclined to agree that the liming of heavy metals is "practicable" everywhere,[97] the federal law requires a second step "which will result in reasonable further progress" toward eliminating discharge.[98] When the receiving stream needs protection beyond lime treatment, filtration may be called for, or even the recirculation of the effluent with sewer discharge of a little blowdown. But to require these across the board may be to spend considerable sums with little to show for them.

In short, the EPA needs more latitude than the statute gives it to determine when uniform effluent limitations are appropriate and when they are not. A variance procedure, though desirable, is not enough. To avoid the burden of multiple adjudications, the agency should have power to tailor the regulations themselves to the need.

VIII

In sum, *duPont* leaves largely unresolved the question that prompted the filing of suit. The hints the Court threw out on that question contradict the statute. And the statute itself is misguided in several critical respects. The war against pollution is important enough to deserve better treatment.

---

[94] See In the Matter of Emission Standards, 4 Ill. P.C.B. 298, 334–35 (1972).

[95] § 301(b)(1)(C), 33 U.S.C. § 1311(b)(1)(C).

[96] See notes 91 and 92 *supra.*

[97] See note 90 *supra.*

[98] § 301(b)(2)(A), 33 U.S.C. § 1311(b)(2)(A).

ELEANOR P. WOLF

NORTHERN SCHOOL DESEGREGATION AND RESIDENTIAL CHOICE

In the Northern school cases, both the findings of discrimination and the effectiveness and feasibility of the remedy involve the acceptance of a sociological generalization: that there is a "corresponding" or reciprocal effect between racial composition of schools and racial composition of neighborhoods. The first part of this paper is concerned with the assertions made in court decisions about the causal relationship between racial concentration ("segregation") in schools and residential racial concentration.

The desegregation remedy, unless it is to be a permanent system of racial quotas in school assignments, requires the assumption that altering the racial composition of schools will inhibit the processes that produce residential segregation. In the second part of this paper, I evaluate some of the evidence in support of this hypothesis.

I. Racial Reciprocity between School and Neighborhood

In the absence of legislatively mandated dual school systems, the conclusion that racially concentrated schools are to a substantial degree the outcome of government action, and therefore reveal *de jure* segregation, is not self-evident and requires elaborate reasoning

---

Eleanor P. Wolf is Professor of Sociology at Wayne State University.

0-226-46429-6/78/1977-4000$01.86

to justify. This has not proved easy. Sociologists have generally described Northern school segregation as *de facto*, in the sense that it was an obvious outcome of racial separation in residence. Given the nearly universal practice of assigning children to the school closest to where they live, it seemed clear that a very high degree of racial segregation would be inevitable, especially since children who attend public schools are even more concentrated spatially, by race, than the two adult populations. "Busing" was, therefore, necessary to eliminate segregation only because most children who live within walking distance of each other are of the same race.

How, then, in the effort to maintain continuity with legal precedent established in the Southern cases, can the courts find Northern schools segregated *de jure?* One way would be to seek evidence that government actions were so decisive an influence in the development of racial segregation in housing that the school segregation that flows from it amounts to *de jure* segregation, once removed. This was the main burden of the district court opinion by the late Judge Roth in the Detroit case, *Bradley v. Milliken.*[1] Perhaps because of some uncertainty as to how this new and bold approach would be viewed by higher courts, Roth also included findings of a series of constitutional violations by school authorities. These, and only these, became the basis for the affirmance by the Court of Appeals of the findings of *de jure* segregation in Detroit. The Sixth Circuit specifically rejected reliance on housing segregation, and the future of the "housing approach" remains in some doubt.[2] Thus, in Northern cities where a very high degree of racial separation in residence exists and the geographical method of student assignment is used, findings of *de jure* segregation have been based on actions of school authorities, such as drawing of boundaries, selection of sites, establishment of feeder patterns from primary to secondary schools, etc., to justify classifying the overall result as constitutionally invalid. It is this doctrine that is epitomized by Mr. Justice White in *Detroit:* ". . . had the Detroit school system not followed an official policy of segregation throughout the 1950's and 1960's Negroes and whites would have been going to school together."[3]

---

[1] Bradley v. Milliken, 338 F. Supp. 582 (E.D. Mich. 1971).

[2] Bradley v. Milliken, 484 F.2d 215, 242 (6th Cir. 1973); see Taylor, *The Supreme Court and Urban Reality: A Tactical Analysis of Milliken v. Bradley*, 21 WAYNE L. REV. 751 (1975); Pettigrew, *A Sociological View of the Post-Bradley Era*, 21 WAYNE L. REV. 813 (1975).

[3] Milliken v. Bradley, 418 U.S. 717, 779 (1974).

White's is not a statement of law, it is an empirical generalization about the cause of racial separation in Detroit schools. Given a city with a residential segregation index that has been over 80 for at least thirty-five years and given the lawfulness of assigning children on a neighborhood basis, this statement is unsupportable. I do not contend that certain constitutional violations never took place in Detroit, but that it was not these acts that caused the schools to become racially concentrated.[4] The questionable validity of the proposition that such school violations caused Northern school segregation has been recognized by constitutional scholars who appear to favor the outcome, although criticizing the doctrine as "contrived" and even harmful to judicial credibility.[5]

Among sociologists expert in the field of residential choice, most are either unaware of the federal judiciary's causal anlysis of school segregation or disinclined, for other reasons, to challenge it. Because of its patent weakness there is an effort to shore up this dubious theory by describing the relationship between school and neighborhood composition as "interactive" or "reciprocal"; they have, it is said, a "corresponding effect" upon each other. I have found no reference by the Supreme Court to this doctrine before the *Swann* decision in 1971,[6] although the phrase was used by Professor Fiss in a 1965 article.[7] In an apparent effort to explain how school segregation can be attributed to anything other than residential segregation—although a system of neighborhood school assignment is permissible—a sociological generalization was enunciated

[4] I have found that much of the factual material on the alleged constitutional violations by Detroit school authorities is plainly inaccurate. Even if true, however, they could not possibly be the cause of school segregation. Detroit's black population has been highly segregated since at least 1880: ". . . increasingly during the late nineteenth century, blacks clustered within a narrow area on Detroit's near east side. The third ward, a two-block-wide strip . . . became synonymous with black Detroit." KATZMAN, BEFORE THE GHETTO 67, 79 (1973). Long ago "[t]he vigorous exclusion of Negroes from white residential neighborhoods made escape from the ghetto virtually impossible. . . . By 1847 the residents of South Boston could boast that 'not a single colored family' lived among them." LITWACK, NORTH OF SLAVERY: THE NEGRO IN THE FREE STATES, 1790–1860 169–70 (1961).

[5] See Fiss, *The Charlotte-Mecklenburg Case—Its Significance for Northern School Desegregation*, 38 U. CHI. L. REV. 697, 705 (1971); Fiss, *Groups and the Equal Protection Clause*, 5 PHIL. & PUB. AFFAIRS 107, 145 (1976).

[6] Swann v. Charlotte-Mecklenburg Board of Education, 402 U.S. 1, 20–21 (1971).

[7] Fiss, *Racial Imbalance in the Public Schools: The Constitutional Concepts*, 78 HARV. L. REV. 564, 587 (1965); see also United States v. Jefferson County Bd. of Ed., 372 F.2d 836, 888–89 (5th Cir. 1966). It would seem reasonable, however, that when black children were legally restricted to all-black schools, the location of those schools would have some influence on residential choices.

by the district court in *Bradley v. Milliken* that has been repeated in other school cases: "[J]ust as there is an interaction between residential patterns and the racial composition of the schools, so there is a corresponding effect on the residential pattern by the racial composition of the schools."[8]

Upon reflection there is very much less here than meets the eye. In fact, there is virtually nothing at all. If a school system uses a strict and innocent method of establishing an attendance area for an elementary school, proceeding outward from the school building in all directions (as physical barriers permit), it is clear that the school population must reflect the racial composition of the public school children who live on the blocks surrounding it. But the only way in which the racial composition of a school could exert a corresponding effect upon the racial composition of a neighborhood would be through an indirect causal relationship. The number of black and white children in the school—*i.e.*, the area's children, gathered under one roof—is asserted to exercise a decisive influence upon the residence decisions of those black and white households able to translate their housing desires into actuality. Only thus could the effect of school racial composition upon neighborhood racial composition be fairly characterized as corresponding.

The evidence cited to show how constitutional violations, such as gerrymandering and other departures from the neighborhood school policy, worsened the effects of an assignment policy which, if scrupulously followed, would produce school segregation more intense than that of households segregation is flimsy and unconvincing. Although the Court in *Swann*[9] (and later, in *Keyes*)[10] suggested that school-site selection has both a short- and long-term effect on residential patterns, no evidence was offered in support of these statements. It is a curious fact that some of the same experts who declare that rather small shifts in pupil assignment (school violations) are a substantial cause of segregated schools simultaneously deny that massive reassignment via busing contributes to white attrition. During the Detroit trial the chief expert witness for the plaintiffs, Dr. Gordon Foster, comparing the 1950 and 1960 census, concluded that the existence of an optional area between two schools

[8] 338 F. Supp. at 587.

[9] 402 U.S. at 20–21.

[10] Keyes v. School District No. 1, 413 U.S. 189, 201–02 (1973).

made a racially mixed residential area unstable because "they [the residents] generally feel this is an ad hoc temporary interim situation and it increases white flight."[11] Why an opportunity to select the less black of two schools would stimulate white families to "flee" the city was not explained. (If anything, families who have such an option are likely to stay a bit longer in mixed areas.)[12]

Foster also contended that altering the boundary of a school attendance area or changing feeder patterns of elementary to secondary schools would have "stabilized the racial situation"—or "held the integration status"[13]—of various schools. But no data to support these claims were forthcoming. As far back as 1967 the United States Commission on Civil Rights (unwaveringly prointegration) concluded, after a study of such efforts, that in cities with a majority black student body any "solution" of this type was not possible.[14] Sheldon and Glazier,[15] Farley,[16] Pettigrew,[17] and others have come to similar conclusions, which simply means that altering the racial composition of a school in changing neighborhoods within such a city does not have a corresponding effect upon residential patterns. Indeed, this is the empirical basis used to justify the imposition of a district-wide solution: desegregation is, after all, to be imposed, not as a penalty, but as a remedy.

The fact is that there are numerous natural experiments that clearly reveal that a mixed school does not create a mixed residential area. In some large cities there are a few instances where poor whites live in neighborhoods close enough to those occupied by blacks so that some secondary schools are mixed. Professor Suttles

---

[11] Transcript, Bradley v. Milliken, p. 1420 (hereafter cited as Transcript).

[12] See Hanley, *Keyes v. School District No. 1: Unlocking the Northern Schoolhouse Doors*, 9 Harv. Civ. Rts.—Civ. Lib. L. Rev. 124, 130–31, and n. 38 (1974); and see Wolf & Lebeaux, Change and Renewal in an Urban Community 76–80, 155–65 (1969); Molotch, Managed Integration 61 (1972).

[13] Transcript, pp. 1433, 1511, 1523, 1526.

[14] U.S. Commission on Civil Rights, Racial Isolation in the Public Schools 154 (1967). Detroit's public schools, for example, had become majority black almost ten years before the start of the trial.

[15] Sheldon & Glazier, Pupils and Schools in New York City 75–76, 105–19 (1965).

[16] Farley, *Residential Segregation and Its Implications for School Integration*, 39 Law & Contemp. Prob. 164, 169, 193 (1975).

[17] Pettigrew, *The Negro and Education*, in Katz & Gurin, eds., Race and the Social Sciences 49, 95 (1969). Pettigrew stated that if the black school population was substantial and growing, efforts short of overall reassignment were "mere band-aid[s]."

has made an intensive study of such an area.[18] A recent survey done for the Illinois State Board of Education under Anthony Down's supervision reveals the existence of others, again often associated with the presence of low-income whites with limited residential mobility.[19] Detroit has had instances where a relatively small residential enclave contributed to the enrollment of a high school, making it—for several years—about 20 percent black.[20] In the past, when the black school population in Detroit was very small, no secondary school and only a few elementary schools were predominantly black. None of these mixed school situations in Detroit had a corresponding effect upon the neighborhoods from which they drew. What the effect on residential patterns might have been had the Detroit school system in 1910 rejected the geographical assignment system and built an educational park or embarked upon a program of student racial dispersion by trolley car—or horse and buggy—I cannot say.

Small towns with small black populations typically have but one secondary school, but its biracial character has not created racial dispersion. A study of a number of Philadelphia suburbs with busing programs that include even the elementary schools found residential segregation to be unchanged as a consequence.[21] Nor is there any evidence—or even claims—that the system-wide school dispersion programs in Berkeley, Pasadena, Princeton, Evanston, and elsewhere have had a corresponding effect on housing patterns, although these programs have been in existence for several years.

Summarizing their findings on the ubiquity of racial separation in housing, Taeuber and Taeuber said, "It occurs regardless of the character of local laws and policies, and regardless of the extent of other forms of segregation or discrimination . . . whether there are hundreds of thousands of Negro residents, or only a few thousand."[22] Elsewhere Karl Taeuber concluded that:

---

[18] SUTTLES, THE SOCIAL ORDER OF THE SLUM (1968).

[19] REAL ESTATE RESEARCH CORP., STABILITY OF RACIAL MIX IN ILLINOIS SCHOOLS (1976).

[20] Mumford High School in northwest Detroit was such an example until rapid increase in the proportion of black high school students made it an all-black school.

[21] Blumberg & Lalli, *Little Ghettoes: A Study of Negroes in the Suburbs*, 27 PHYLON 117 (1966).

[22] TAEUBER & TAEUBER, NEGROES IN CITIES 35–36 (1965); see also Farley & Taeuber, *Population Trends and Residential Segregation since 1960*, 159 SCIENCE 953, 955 (1968);

> The racial composition of city schools is becoming more homogeneously Negro. *This occurs whether or not the pattern of segregated public schools changes*, simply because the relative number of Negroes increases. As black children replace white children in a public school system, administrators, even if they attempt to utilize the available repertoire of desegregation techniques, are likely to find the number of blacks in predominantly black schools increasing . . . even if the all-white schools are integrated, the other schools will simultaneously become more predominantly Negro.[23]

Although there are thousands of examples of mixed areas temporarily creating mixed schools and many instances where a reasonably biracial area with few white children in it has coexisted with a predominantly black school, there is no noted instance where a mixed school produced a mixed neighborhood. A city-wide school with an admission requirement (such as Detroit's Cass Technical) does hold some middle-class families—black and white—within the city but only at the expense of other geographically based schools from which it skims the cream, thus making those schools less attractive to those families who have residential alternatives.

It is well known that in the Old South, when racially separate schools were legally required, there was somewhat more residential mixture than exists today.[24] A similar situation exists in those few central-city areas where high-income households of both races share urban space, but nothing else, with the poor black families surrounding them. The Gold Coast uses private schools, not those attended by children from the nearby slums.

There can be no doubt that changes in the race/class composition of schools in transition neighborhoods often crystallize or precipitate a decision, by those families able to execute such an inclination, to move. The population mix of an area influences the

---

but see Taeuber, *Demographic Perspectives on Housing and School Segregation*, 21 WAYNE L. REV. 833, 843 (1975).

[23] Statement of Karl Taeuber, Hearings before the Select Committee on Equal Educational Opportunity, United States Senate, 91st Cong., 2d Sess. pt. V, 2731, (1970). (Emphasis added.) In his oral testimony, however, Taeuber altered this statement by stating that the "reverse process is just as much in force." *Id.* at 2747. See also WOLF & LEBEAUX, note 12 *supra*, at 19–20.

[24] PALEN, THE URBAN WORLD 216, 218 (1975); see also TAEUBER & TAEUBER, note 22 *supra*, at 3; Clotfelter, *Spatial Rearrangement and the Tiebout Hypothesis: The Case of School Desegregation*, 42 SO. ECON. J. 263, 268 (1975). Clotfelter shows that ending Jim Crow schools decreased neighborhood integration.

residential decisions of those who are most directly affected by that composition more rapidly than those not so much affected. A child is in the fifth grade only once in his life, and this creates a sense of urgency not found during other stages of the life cycle. Thus, those more insulated from the population mix by the use of nonpublic schools, or no schools at all (childless families), are, other factors being equal, likely to stay a bit longer in mixed areas or are more likely to enter them, especially if they can rent rather than buy. But this should not be exaggerated. Areas with small proportions of public school users, *e.g.*, 15 percent of all households in the South Shore area of Chicago and about 30 percent in the Bagley area in Detroit, did not look much different ten years after black in-movement began than similar areas with much larger proportions of households with children.[25] There are very few instances, usually associated with some extraordinary attraction, where such households enter in sufficient numbers to maintain biracial stability. But there are a great many instances of retirement communities without schools—or children—just as separated by race as other areas.

The corresponding effect may be a useful legal rationalization, but sociologically the statement is a tautology. Residential patterns are conjunctural phenomena, the outcome of a myriad of residential decisions that, in the aggregate, create the population composition of an area. The present and anticipated class-ethnic mix of an area influences the future mix to the extent that residents (or prospective residents) are able to actualize their preferences. If they rarely encounter the mix, it will, of course, have less impact or a slower impact upon their residential behavior than on those whose children do. But to say that the racial composition of an area-based school has a corresponding effect on the area's racial composition is to say that the children playing on the neighborhood's streets have a corresponding effect on the neighborhood composition. They do not affect the makeup of the population; they are that population, or a portion of it, gathered together for several hours of the day.

II. Effects of a Metropolitan Remedy on Residential Decisions

When a court, finding *de jure* segregation, orders a desegregation remedy, pupil placement is divorced from place of residence

---

[25] Molotch, note 12 *supra*, at 91; Wolf & Lebeaux, note 12 *supra*, at 5.

to varying degrees. This alone is proof, if any is needed, that it is not violations of the neighborhood school assignment system but adherence to it that "causes" the schools to be segregated. A placement method based on racial proportions must be used so that school composition will not reflect the residential composition of the area that surrounds a school. To what extent, if at all, will this method of assignment, if it could be imposed on a metropolitan area, begin to generate a diminution of residential segregation? Or will this new system, because it imposes contact and interaction on many who were previously quite insulated from it, generate an opposite tendency: increased spatial segregation through departure from or avoidance of the area by those families able to do so?

The aggregate studies of the rate of racial change before and after a judicial desegregation decree, with and without busing, are difficult to interpret. They certainly reveal, however, that the effects of programs of involuntary student dispersion cannot be understood without considering the size of the area, the racial and class proportions, the amount of change created by a busing program, the time span, and events before a busing program began. For example, a Northern city with a large black population will have had a history of racial transition in many neighborhoods, and much of that segment of the white population most able to relocate will have already done so gradually over a period of many years. One would expect that the larger the proportion of whites who previously were insulated from black residential movement, the greater the effect on their movement a drastic busing remedy would have. A similar effect might be imagined if prosperous white families who had been using private schools were suddenly precluded from doing so. It was reported several years ago that many metropolitan areas were losing population, but it was also found that "the rate of out-migration does not vary with local hardship. Migrants leave at a steady rate regardless of local conditions, although such local conditions do affect the rate of *in*-migration."[26] This may be due to the fact that a decision to leave is more disruptive and difficult than a decision to avoid an area—or that a decision to leave at certain late stages of metropolitan growth is a decision affecting a disproportionately poor white population. The steady rate of out-migration may also reflect the operation of regulator market mecha-

---

[26] Alonso, *The Mirage of New Towns*, 19 PUB. INT. 3, 9 (1970).

nisms. Many whose homes represent all of their savings cannot afford to sell at the depressed prices that result from increased supply and lessened demand.

To explore fully the probable impact of metropolitan busing on housing patterns would require a review of the substantial literature on residential behavior, especially that which is concerned with the influence of class-ethnic factors. This is impossible here. I will, instead, indicate a number of faulty or questionable assumptions about residential decision making that have been widespread in the current controversy over the expected effects of metropolitan busing on residential segregation. We lack a firm empirical foundation for assessing these effects because the instances are so few and the time lapse has been too short. No metropolitan busing plan has yet been implemented in the North. The absence of such data is a disadvantage but should not be a disabling handicap because, whether the area is a neighborhood, a city, or a metropolis, the same underlying sociological principles should apply.

In all residential behavior, regardless of scale, the variables involved may be classified as those related to inclinations or preferences and those related to the ability or capacity to execute them. Complex calculations in which ability factors are weighed against preference factors are undertaken in rather deliberate fashion. Most families with children are homeowners, and house sale and purchase is not impulse buying. For this reason, if a busing program does alter residential trends and patterns, one would not expect the full effect to be apparent for some time. Residential decisions take time to incubate and more time to execute, and the behavior of those who act first greatly affects the behavior of those who have not yet acted. For example, there is a depressing effect on house prices if many are placed on the market at the same time, and this tends to slow down the decisions of others to sell. They must buy elsewhere, usually at normal prices, *i.e.*, higher than their present house would fetch if sold on a glutted market. Obviously, a prosperous white family can and does leave (or avoid) a situation which is only moderately unsatisfactory while a poor family may be intensely unhappy but unable, for varying time periods, to do anything about it. Thus we find that, on the whole, white households remaining in predominantly black areas are those less able to leave, rather than those who have stronger preferences for such neighborhoods.[27] Residential inclinations are rarely altered by ability factors, but their implementation is often long delayed.

Metropolitan school desegregation is viewed by many as preventing more intense residential segregation than a program confined to the city. ("It would tend to halt white flight.") For others it offers good prospects for generating residential integration. ("It might lure people back to the city.")[28] These outcomes are predicted (with various degrees of certainty, depending on who is offering them) because a metropolitan remedy appears to promise a strong effect on both inclination to move and ability to do so. It is seen as reducing inclinations to withdraw from area schools primarily because metropolitanism dilutes the proportion of black and poor—thus altering the schools' class-ethnic mix—while factors of time and distance would seem to make it more difficult to escape even if there is some degree of dissatisfaction. This dissatisfaction is often predicted to be temporary because it is thought to be based on nonrational fears and false beliefs, *i.e.*, prejudice, that will be dispelled by experience.

A. CONSTRAINTS ON MOBILITY IN METROPOLITAN BUSING PLANS

Residential behavior of both whites and blacks is involved in the formation of housing patterns. There is much disagreement as to the relative strength of the factors that produce black concentration. Whatever economic factors constrain black residential mobility would not, of course, be affected by student reassignment. Estimates of the importance of these constraints vary from Anthony Pascal's, that between 40 and 50 percent of housing segregation is thus accounted for, to Karl Taeuber's estimate of from 20 to 25 percent.[29] Approximately 250,000 people in Detroit, for example,

---

[27] Aldrich, *Ecological Succession in Racially Changing Neighborhoods, A Review of the Literature*, 10 URB. AFF. Q. 327 (1975); see also note 25 *supra*.

[28] See, *e.g.*, Orfield, *White Flight Research: Its Importance, Perplexities, and Possible Policy Implications*, N.I.E., SYMPOSIUM ON SCHOOL DESEGREGATION AND WHITE FLIGHT 43, 60–61 (1975); Rossell, *School Desegregation and White Flight*, 90 POL. SCI. Q. 675, 688–89 (1976), for suggestions that metropolitan desegregation might encourage a return to the city. Confidence that metropolitan plans would tend to deter white flight is expressed in Pettigrew & Green, *School Desegregation in Large Cities: A Critique of the Coleman "White Flight" Thesis*, 46 HARV. ED. REV. 1, 49–50 (1976).

[29] PASCAL, ECONOMICS OF HOUSING SEGREGATION 177–78 (Rand Corp. research memo #5510, 1967); TAEUBER, PATTERNS OF NEGRO-WHITE RESIDENTIAL SEGREGATION 18 (Rand Corp. paper #4288, 1970).

now receive public assistance; approximately 80 percent are black.[30] Busing will not add to their economic ability. Nor can it be expected to alter the disinclination of others for a residential location near many of these households. These preference factors will be considered later. Nor will school dispersion reduce the various forms of covert discrimination still practiced in the sale or rental of housing to black families.

The ability to withdraw to private schools, for those who can afford them, would also be unaffected except perhaps to increase their use by those who cannot quite so conveniently avoid busing by choosing a suburban location. According to reports this has become a substantial and ongoing development in some Southern areas under far-reaching desegregation orders.[31] On the basis of the larger proportion of prosperous families in Northern metropolitan areas, one could predict a greater use of the private school option under Northern metropolitan-wide busing programs. The loss to the public schools of this more affluent and influential segment of the population, should this occur, has a number of consequences that some consider quite serious.

There seems to be general agreement, however, that the capacity to withdraw by changing residence is sharply diminished by a metropolitan, as compared with a city-only, remedy. During the remedy hearings in *Bradley v. Milliken* in 1972, expert witnesses repeatedly told Judge Roth that he should order a metropolitan plan because: "White flight will be minimized to the point that . . . it will become insignificant . . . there comes a time when one can no longer commute to one's work from massive distances . . . It becomes economically over-burdening to continue to move further and further away."[32]

Some of the assumptions here are dubious. First, "further and further away" from what? Rapid and continuing economic decentralization has already meant that over 70 percent of suburbanites in some large metropolitan areas work in suburban areas, not in the

[30] This estimate was provided by Professor Lebeaux, School of Social Work, Wayne State University, on the basis of data for summer 1976.

[31] The use of private schools in some Southern districts is described as "a mass movement" that "has drastically altered racial balances in the public schools," in Giles, Cataldo, & Gatlin, *Desegregation and the Private School Alternative*, in N.I.E., note 28 *supra*, at 21, 22.

[32] Remedy Hearings, Transcript, pp. 72–73.

city.[33] In large metropolitan areas, such as Detroit, suburban families spend less time, on the average, traveling to services and facilities they want to reach than do city households.[34] Second, substantial research data confirm that the length of the journey to work is one of the lowest priority and most readily compromised aspects of residential behavior.[35] Adults might well decide on a longer trip to work for themselves to avoid a long trip to school for their children when the latter appears to have no offsetting advantages. "Economic over-burden," like other costs, turns out, within limits that are not at all clear, to be a matter of choices between values. Third, wherever the perimeter of the desegregation area is drawn, those who already live in its vicinity will not have to go very far to avoid inclusion. It was for this reason that the NAACP, during the metropolitan remedy hearings in the Detroit case, spoke of an intention, if such a remedy were imposed, to seek a court order restricting school construction in the area outside the perimeter.[36] It is not at all certain, however, that this interference with residential mobility would or could be granted, or that it would be possible to distinguish between the legitimate school needs of an exurban community and those generated by refugees from a busing program and therefore defined as illegitimate.

It is unfortunate that the controversy about the effects of busing on residential decisions has been framed in terms of accelerated exodus, out-movement, or "white flight." Racial transition is often, perhaps usually, unaccompanied by an increase in the rate of residential mobility.[37] With normal residential turnover somewhere

---

[33] PALEN, note 24 *supra*, at 152.

[34] Stegman, *Accessibility Models and Residential Location*, 35 J. AM. INST. PLANNERS 22, 28 (Jan. 1969).

[35] Michelson, *Most People Don't Want What Architects Want*, 5 TRANSACTION 37 (July–Aug. 1968); see also Stegman, note 34 *supra*, at 25.

[36] Remedy Hearings, Transcript, pp. 840, 1023, 1197, 1436, 1454. An alternative solution offered for this problem was continuous boundary adjustment operating "much like a rubber band in connection with white flight. As parents move out the borough extends and snaps the students back into the district from which they fled." *Id.* at 99. This, of course, is another form of a permanent system of racial quotas.

[37] *Molotch*, note 12 *supra*, at 123, 157; Aldrich & Reiss, *Continuities in the Study of Ecological Succession*, 81 AM. J. SOC. 846, 864 (1976); Guest & Zuiches, *Another Look at Residential Turnover in Urban Neighborhoods*, 77 AM. J. SOC. 457 (1971); WOLF & LEBEAUX, note 12 *supra*, at 37–43, 48, 86, 93; SUTKER & SUTKER, RACIAL TRANSITION IN THE INNER SUBURB 32, 48 (1974) (reporting that one transition area had increased mobility and one had not).

between 10 and 20 percent annually, there need be no accelerated mobility for an area to change from all white to predominantly black in a few years simply through white avoidance.[38] This has happened frequently to neighborhoods, and it has been happening, more gradually, to entire cities. If the political boundary becomes no barrier to racial dispersion in schools, the metropolitan area should be considered as if it were a large city with, of course, a different class-ethnic mix. Since 1965 the chief source of growth of the primarily white suburbs of many of our metropolitan areas has not been movement or flight from the city but movement from one suburb to another or from elsewhere in the nation.[39] There need be no "flight," *i.e.*, accelerated out-movement, for metropolitan areas to continue to lose whites, and prosperous blacks as well, from their central cities.

If the source of suburban growth is increasingly not that area's central city, can it not be anticipated that the area to be avoided will simply be widened? Findings on population movement since 1970 suggest the possibility that some older metropolitan regions are being avoided by middle-class white families in favor of rural and semirural areas or the suburbs of newer metropolitan areas in the Southwest and elsewhere.[40] Thus, decreasing the ease with which whites can flee by increasing the size of the area involved in a metropolitan busing program may not, because of the factors that have been enumerated, constitute much of a barrier, assuming of course that inclinations remain constant. But the other basis for hopefulness about the metropolitan desegregation strategy is that the altered class-ethnic mix in the schools will make a substantial difference in residential preferences.

B. RESIDENTIAL INCLINATIONS AND THE SCHOOL POPULATION MIX

The sociological relevance of the city-suburban boundary is that outlying residential areas, taken as a whole, generally have higher-

---

[38] A commonly used figure is 20 percent per year, but this includes renters as well as owners. See REPORT OF THE NATIONAL ADVISORY COMMISSION ON CIVIL DISORDERS 244–45 (1968); MOLOTCH, note 12 *supra*, at 151, 172.

[39] See PALEN, note 24 *supra*, at 420. For data and analysis to support the existence of this trend, see Zikmund, *Sources of the Suburban Population: 1955–1960 and 1965–1970*, 5 PUBLIUS 27 (Winter 1975).

[40] Mobility of the Population of the U.S. (March 1970–March 1975), Series P.-20, No. 285. Survey data suggest that these movements are the actualization of long-standing inclinations to be "well away from the center of things." See Michelson, note 35 *supra*, at 39.

income households than their central cities. For example, in Detroit, in 1972, the fifty-three–district metropolitan busing plan selected by the district court, rejected two years later by the Supreme Court, would have produced overall a student population about 25 percent black, in contrast to the then almost 70 percent proportion in the city of Detroit, with associated differences in social-class proportions.

During those remedy hearings expert witnesses repeatedly testified that a metropolitan-based student mix would offer the inestimable benefit of a "middle-class majority" in the classroom. This, they assured the Court, would enhance educational achievement and remove inclinations to flee. Suburban counsel made some attempts to challenge the educational benefits of this mix,[41] but its existence was not refuted. The explanation offered for its positive impact, however, was that college-educated parents are helpful to "aspirations" and "values" and in the development of academic skills. Of course, there would not be a middle-class majority, defined as public school children of college-educated parents, in Detroit or most other metropolitan areas.[42]

Overall birthrate differences between the races,[43] a factor which also partially accounts for the population loss in some close-in white suburbs,[44] has, four years later, increased the proportion of black and poor in Detroit. Extension of the geographic area increases travel time for some children beyond the daily two-hour round-trip maximum the courts have generally regarded as acceptable. Implementation of a metropolitan busing plan is generally seen as disadvantageous by high-income whites, since the average social-class level of their childrens' classrooms is instantly lowered, and a certain proportion of these children could be expected to be withdrawn to private schools. These changes, the net effect of which is

---

[41] The courts generally have not permitted testimony to challenge the alleged educational benefits of integration after a finding of *de jure* segregation has been made, or even at earlier stages of litigation; see Yudof, *Equal Educational Opportunity and the Courts*, 51 Tex. L. Rev. 411, 439 (1973).

[42] The proportion of college-educated adults in the Detroit SMSA is estimated to be 9.5 percent; 19 percent have had some college education. Six percent of Detroit adults are college graduates.

[43] Orfield, *Federal Policy, Local Power and Metropolitan Segregation*, 89 Pol. Sci. Q. 777, 781–82 (1975).

[44] Southeast Michigan Council of Governments recently released estimates showing a population decrease in some all-white Detroit suburbs as well as in Wayne County as a whole. Detroit News, 6 June 1976, p. 11, col. 1; see also note 40 *supra*.

not now estimable, all suggest that white attrition is likely to occur even under metropolitan busing even without any initial acceleration of white residential movement.

The probable impact of metropolitan school dispersion on black residential preferences must also be considered, for if an area proves more attractive to blacks than to whites, racial transition will occur. If the school situation is an important attraction for upwardly mobile black families, the uniform composition of schools under metropolitan desegregation would be expected to reduce somewhat the inclination for residential dispersion among blacks. These inclinations have not been very pronounced. Opinion data on black residential preferences, like similar material from white respondents, have an uncertain relationship to overt acts. But these data are often derived from poor questions using ambiguous terms such as "integrated neighborhoods." More carefully worded questions reveal that the right to enter any area is considered essential, but a desire for mixture is qualified. Little preference is shown for predominantly white neighborhoods.[45] When the question specifies a similar social-class level regardless of integration in the neighborhood, black preferences for mixture, like white objections to it, are sharply reduced.[46] Hermalin and Farley have noted that the proportion of blacks desired by Negroes is probably not the proportion whites have in mind when they indicate approval of residential integration.[47] There is no research to suggest that, even in the absence of

---

[45] Poll data show fewer than 10 percent preferring "mostly white" neighborhoods. Marx, Protest and Prejudice 175–76 (1967); see also Bradburn, Sudman, & Gockel, Side by Side 134 (1971); Campbell & Schuman, *Racial Attitudes in Fifteen American Cities*, in Supplemental Studies for the National Advisory Commission 1, 15 (1968); Watts et al., The Middle-Income Negro Family Faces Urban Renewal (1964). Even a moderate tendency toward black clustering is enhanced by the fact that high-quality homes in transition or black areas are usually less expensive than similar homes farther from large concentrations of poor blacks. Thus, a black household would need both more money and a strong wish to avoid clustering to reject this path of least resistance.

[46] Marx, note 45 *supra*, at 175; Hermalin & Farley, *The Potential for Residential Integration in Cities and Suburbs: Implications for the Busing Controversy*, 38 Am. Soc. Rev. 595, 597 (1973).

[47] Hermalin & Farley, note 46 *supra*, at 609. See also Morrill, *The Negro Ghetto: Problems and Alternatives*, 55 Geog. Rev. 339, 360 (1965), which notes that "a fundamental dilemma arises" because blacks usually prefer a larger proportion of their own group than is readily acceptable to whites. For a discussion of own-group residential preferences among blacks, see, *e.g.*, Perry & Feagin, *Stereotyping in Black and White*, in Hahn, ed., People and Politics in Urban Society 433, 438–41 (1972); Berger, *Suburbia and the American Dream*, 2 Pub. Int. 80 (1960).

discrimination, blacks would distribute themselves randomly. All that we know about the social construction of black ethnicity would argue against such an outcome. If an approximately random distribution continues to be the core meaning attached by the NAACP to school desegregation, a continued system of racial quotas would be required. There is little reason to anticipate that metropolitan-wide racial dispersion in schools would affect black residential preferences, except to remove one of the motives sometimes reported by blacks for seeking homes in white neighborhoods.

What about own-group preferences within that mosaic of groups to which we attach the deceptive label "white"? "White" does not, as does "black," refer to an ethnic group, but is a composite or residual category: nonblack. The Joint Center for Urban Studies recently found that 75 percent of all Boston adults were living in the same sector of the city in which they had lived as teenagers. A similar pattern was found in Houston, where "nearly three-fourths of those interviewed were living in the same sector as their neighborhood of previous residence. The next neighborhood to which they were thinking of moving was again in the same sector."[48] Such residential movement which, when it involves blacks, is labeled "the extension of the ghetto" is common among groups with a network of social relations. These social ties are the mechanism underlying locational decisions.[49] "In Kansas City . . . as members of each [ethnic group] . . . have prospered and deserted the city center, movements of individual group members . . . have been predictable according to where the lead-edge of the group's members have moved."[50] These moves by whites have the consequence of further isolating blacks, whether or not participants so intend.

Ethnic ties are of course not the only basis for own-group preferences. It is not easy to disentangle ethnic from social-class differences. What would the response to metropolitan busing be if social-class diversity were as great but all the children were white,

---

[48] HARVARD & M.I.T. JOINT CENTER FOR URBAN STUDIES, RESEARCH PROJECT ON NEIGHBORHOOD EVOLUTION AND DECLINE, INTERIM REPORT 35–36 (1975). For persistence of white ethnic residential segregation, see KANTROWITZ, ETHNIC AND RACIAL SEGREGATION IN THE NEW YORK METROPOLIS (1973); Guest & Weed, *Ethnic Residential Segregation: Patterns of Change*, 81 AM. J. SOC. 1088 (1976).

[49] The process is similar to that reported in finding a job (Granovetter, *The Strength of Weak Ties*, 78 AM. J. SOC. 1360 [1973]).

[50] HARVARD & M.I.T. JOINT CENTER FOR URBAN STUDIES, note 48 *supra*, at 35.

or if black social-class distribution, including its school-related manifestations, were the same as that in the category we call white? The preference for association with those whose behavior and general style of life resembles that which we share or want to emulate is at least as strong among people in general as it is among college professors.[51] It is hard to exaggerate its importance, especially for parents who are convinced of the importance of social climate and the power of peer-group influence in and out of school. A metropolitan busing plan produces considerably more social-class diversity in the classroom than that which usually occurs in unplanned neighborhood racial transition because the cost of housing acts as a screen—although not nearly as fine a one as is generally contended in the fair-housing literature. But compared with a city-only remedy, metropolitan busing is believed to affect not only the ability but also the wish to escape by decreasing the proportion of poor and black in the classroom. In cities where this proportion is small, the difference may be inconsequential. In situations like that in Detroit, where the difference is great,[52] the question will be, Is the difference great enough? Unfortunately, discussions of this matter usually involve the use of the "tipping-point" concept. Numbers make a difference, but the factors involved in the difference they make are not reducible to a tipping point or "band," and this spongy and deceptive concept should be discarded.[53] It fails to distinguish between residential preferences, residential decisions, and overt residential behavior. It treats blacks, and responses to blacks, as if proportions alone, without reference to social class and associated behavior, were decisive. It fails to take account of the fact that decisions about buying or selling a house are based on the best estimates people can make of the future as well as the present. Thus, renters reveal somewhat different evaluations and inclinations than

---

[51] GANS, PEOPLE AND PLANS 154–58, 168–71, 176–78 (1968); see also MOLOTCH, note 12 *supra*, at 174–203; WOLF & LEBEAUX, note 12 *supra*, at 125.

[52] Approximately 80 percent of Detroit's public-school children are black, and approximately one-third of these are from households on public assistance.

[53] Wolf, *The Tipping-Point in Racially Changing Neighborhoods*, in FRIEDEN & MORRIS, eds., URBAN PLANNING AND SOCIAL POLICY 148 (1968); Stinchcombe, McDill, & Walker, *Is There a Racial Tipping Point in Changing Schools?* 25 J. SOC. ISSUES 127 (Jan. 1969); KANTROWITZ, note 48 *supra*, at 59; Pryor, *An Empirical Note on the Tipping Point*, 47 LAND. EC. 413 (1971); Aldrich, note 27 *supra*, at 343; MOLOTCH, note 12 *supra*, at 163; REAL ESTATE RESEARCH CORP., note 19 *supra*, at 10; SUTKER & SUTKER, note 37 *supra*, at 28.

those who buy. What would the preference point (with respect to proportion of blacks) be in a school that had very high admission standards? It clearly would bear little similarity to that in a school situation where a smaller proportion of black students included many who did poorly in school and some who were known to engage in delinquency associated with violence. With regard to academic achievement, the sad fact at present is that adding black students to white classrooms generally lowers average levels of achievement.[54] If numbers are small, this difference is negligible. But some behavior is so feared that, even if statistically rare, those who can will avoid placing their children in such situations. Ordinary citizens, like sociologists, observe the association between class, ethnicity, and behavioral differences and make crude estimates of the probability of encountering such actions. The degree of risk considered acceptable, however, is a factor that those whose children are involved evaluate quite differently from those who are not involved, and the extent to which these risk calculations are rational or not—in which case they are defined as "prejudice"—is a tricky business.

The use of the term "prejudice" to mean both irrational racist beliefs and the wish to avoid situations where one's children are in contact with a greater volume of dangerous, unpleasant, or educationally disadvantageous behavior can only becloud analysis. If social-class and ethnic differences in behavior are real, how can responses to them, admittedly based on self-interest, be defined as nonrational prejudgment? It is true that social scientists have superior understanding of the sources of these differences, but this greater knowledge of causality is irrelevant to the parent who must decide on a course of action on the basis of present and predicted behavior, not its origin and development. And if there is an empirical basis for some of these negative assessments, how can we expect involuntary association to erase rather than confirm them? As a strategy for improving the attitudes and thus altering the residential preferences of the more advantaged group, contact with black children of a lower social class than that usually found in transition neighborhoods is not at all promising.

---

[54] U.S. Commission on Civil Rights, note 14 *supra*, at 80; Campbell, *Defining and Attaining Equal Educational Opportunity in a Pluralistic Society*, 26 Vand. L. Rev. 461, 463–65 (1973).

III. Conclusion

Unless metropolitan desegregation remedies are accepted as an ongoing system of student-quota reassignment by race, this remedy must offer some promise of altering the residential behavior of blacks and whites in sufficient numbers to overcome (1) the unbalancing effect of existing age and birthrate differences between the races; (2) the constraints on black residential mobility exerted by both economic limitations and covert forms of discrimination; (3) varying degrees of own-group clustering of whites with ethnic ties; (4) tendencies to residential own-group clustering of blacks; (5) avoidance by those households able to do so of areas with or near large numbers of poor families, in response to class-ethnic behavioral differences as well as prejudice; (6) an apparently growing national trend of middle-class white migration away from Northeast and Midwest metropolitan areas to smaller, less central locations; and (7) increased use of nonpublic schools by prosperous members of both races.

There is no hard evidence to suggest that metropolitan busing would entice whites "back to the city," where an increasing proportion of suburbanites have never lived. The chief advantage to most of them would be that their children could avoid a long bus ride. But this hardly seems sufficient. Even with some degree of reversal of the various enumerated factors, it is clear that to disestablish the enormous existing concentrations of blacks and whites would require massive residential interchange in metropolitan areas like Detroit, Chicago, Cleveland, New York, Los Angeles, and Philadelphia. The conclusion in recent articles that grim social and economic conditions (violent crime, unemployment, abandoned housing, deteriorated city services), rather than in-school contact (busing), account for white movement offers a more, rather than less, pessimistic outlook.[55] These conditions are quite unaffected by alterations in pupil assignment unless one subscribes to some naive version of the "hostage theory," *i.e.*, if the children can't escape contact with the city, their parents will "do something" to cure its ills. Problems of this order are not ameliorated within a time span relevant to a pupil's school experience, and those who can will, when they can, withdraw from or avoid such encounters for their children.

---

[55] *E.g.*, Rossell, note 28 *supra*, at 688; Orfield, note 28 *supra*, at 49–51.

The judiciary has hesitated to move toward institutionalization of racial quotas in school assignment. But if desegregation is to be measured against the standard of a random racial distribution, there is no basis for expecting this outcome save by permanent and universal compulsion. Perhaps judges do not realize that these means will be required to maintain desegregation as they have come to define it. Perhaps they have been persuaded that there is a corresponding effect between school and neighborhood composition, or that residential racial concentrations are largely the product of prejudice that will be dispelled by the contact of children in the classroom.

The reasoning of the courts on the entire issue of the relationship between school and residential segregation is illogical and confused. To this is added, at the remedy stage, a cloud of uncertainty as to what desegregation means. Is it to be defined in NAACP terms as the elimination of "racially identifiable schools," requiring schools of approximately similar racial percentages within the school district, whether the proportion black is 8 or 80 percent? Or does desegregation require some substantial presence—a majority, or what—of whites? If so, they must be sought and retained. The courts have generally held that anticipated objections and nonacceptance by whites may not be considered in fashioning a remedy, but their position is unclear and inconsistent.[56] The late Judge Roth, from the very start of the Detroit trial, spoke openly in court about the danger that a Detroit-only plan would drive remaining whites from the city. The Sixth Circuit Court of Appeals and four dissenters on the Supreme Court based their objection to a Detroit-only plan on the grounds that owing to the city's racial composition such a plan "did not desegregate." This can mean only that including and retaining whites is at the heart of a desegregation remedy and that white reaction is indeed a factor to be reckoned with. District Judge Robert DeMascio freely stated his concern about further loss of white children from Detroit's schools, now about 80 percent black; and because the Supreme Court had rejected a metropolitan remedy on grounds that the suburbs had not been found guilty of *de jure* segregation, he ordered a minimum of racial reassignment. The NAACP has attacked the DeMascio plan and

---

[56] Levin & Moise, *School Desegregation Litigation in the Seventies and the Use of Social Science Evidence: An Annotated Guide*, 39 LAW & CONT. PROB. 50, 93–106 (1975).

the rationale offered for it in the strongest language.[57] The outcome of these proceedings may clarify the issue whether concern about white attrition is a legally permissible consideration for both the courts and for school authorities. The latter, it has been held, are not to take white hostility or attrition into account when contemplating various forms of reassignment to overcome racial concentration. If such concern is not permissible, then the NAACP position should prevail: The right to a "desegregated education"—operationally defined as assignment to a school which roughly approximates the racial composition of the district—cannot depend on whether the white community or anyone else considers the proportion of blacks too high for their taste.

The root of this uncertainty and confusion as to the meaning of the desegregation remedy is that the courts have not yet crystallized their task in the Northern school cases. They seek, with great difficulty, by strained logic and inadequate evidence, to move beyond their original purpose of eliminating mandatory segregation, while trying to maintain continuity with the 1954 *Brown* decision. They attempt to graft mechanisms for achieving stable integration onto constitutional principles intended to strike down state-mandated separation. A judicial command to cease racial discrimination entails no concern for the achievement of certain racial proportions and need give no thought to the problem of how long racial mixture will continue to exist. Antidiscrimination orders thus logically and properly take no heed of adverse white reaction. But an enduring racial mixture cannot be secured by issuing judicial commands.

Finally, from a social-policy perspective, do we pose the proper question when we ask: To what extent will involuntary student reassignment make the loss of whites occur more rapidly than would otherwise have been the case? If we see no evidence thus far of any corresponding effect from student dispersion and little support from existing research to predict such an outcome, then the

[57] Judge DeMascio's order was described by NAACP officials as "a judicial calamity"; "a travesty of justice"; "takes us back to the days of Dred Scott"; "racist, evil, and a rape of the constitutional rights of black children" because it did not sufficiently redistribute the then 75 percent black/25 percent white pupil population. Detroit Free Press, 17 Aug. 1975, p. 1, col. 6. The NAACP has filed a new complaint for an interdistrict remedy, citing acts of *de jure* segregation by suburban districts and "allegations relating to metropolitan housing." See Beer, *The Nature of the Violation and the Scope of the Remedy*, 21 WAYNE L. REV. 903, 914 (1975).

best that can be said is that the attrition of middle-class families, both white and black, will simply continue. What, then, is the social-policy justification for a costly program that is widely disliked, divisive in its effects on the labor-liberal political coalition, uncertain in its effects on academic achievement and racial attitudes, and leaves demographic sorting-out processes much as before.[58] We usually consider a finding of no difference an indication that a given strategy should not be undertaken, rather than the reverse. At this point, proponents of busing remedies usually remind us that the courts are required to remedy a condition that has been judged to have been created in substantial degree by constitutionally violative acts. But if the condition was not caused by these violations and the desegregation remedy is not likely to correct it, what then?

[58] For a comprehensive review and evaluation of research on both attitudes and achievement, see St. John, School Desegregation: Outcomes for Children (1975).

GERHARD CASPER and

RICHARD A. POSNER

THE CASELOAD OF THE SUPREME COURT: 1975 AND 1976 TERMS

I. Introduction

In 1976 the American Bar Foundation published our study of the workload of the United States Supreme Court.[1] In it we traced the evolution in the Court's jurisdiction since 1790, ascertained the growth in the Court's workload by a variety of statistical measures, attempted statistical appraisal of the impact of caseload growth on the Court's workload, and evaluated a variety of current proposals for relieving the Court of some of its burdens. We concluded that the Court's workload had not yet reached the point at which radical corrective measures could be justified. It is important to note that we did not deny that the Court has a heavy load to carry.[2] But we did take strong issue with the analysis underlying

---

Gerhard Casper is Max Pam Professor of Law and Professor of Political Science, The University of Chicago. Richard A. Posner is Professor of Law, The University of Chicago. The authors are grateful for the research assistance of Frederick and Priscilla Sperling, The University of Chicago Law School class of 1979, which was funded by The Law School.

[1] Casper & Posner, The Workload of the Supreme Court (1976).

[2] Some Justices continue to express their concern about the impact of the Court's workload on the quality of its performance. See, *e.g.*, Mr. Justice Stewart's dissent in United States v. Jacobs, 429 U.S. 909, 910 (1976), and the Chief Justice in dissent in Moore v. City of East Cleveland, Ohio, 97 S. Ct. 1932, 1948 (1977).

0-226-46429-6/78/1977-3000$01.09

the proposals in particular of the Freund Study Group and the Hruska Commission.[3] We also questioned the efficacy of, and the need for, most of the reforms then advocated, particularly the creation of a National Court of Appeals.

The latest Term for which we had complete data in our 1976 study was that of 1973, though we had scattered information for the 1974 Term. Data for two more Terms—1975 and 1976—have since become available. Given the importance of the question of whether to alter the structure, methods, or jurisdiction of the Supreme Court in order to relieve its workload, we have decided to bring our 1976 study up to date, at least to the extent necessary for purposes of reexamining the crucial policy question addressed in that study. In addition, the paucity of regularly published statistics concerning the nation's most important court prompts us to try to keep up to date, to the extent possible within our limited resources and without regard to immediate policy questions, the principal statistics compiled in our 1976 study.

What follows, therefore, is a continuation of some of the principal statistical series contained in the 1976 study. (We hope to present a regular updating of these statistics until such time as the Clerk's Office of the Supreme Court or the Administrative Office of the United States Courts expands their statistical reporting program, a matter touched on in the conclusion of this article.)

II. The Statistics

A. Overall Caseload

Table 1 presents the total number of cases filed in the Supreme Court in the 1975 and 1976 Terms. Figures for the 1973 and 1974 Terms, which appeared in our 1976 study, are included for purposes of comparison.

The 1973 Term was not only the busiest in the Court's history,[4] but it was the seventh consecutive Term in which the annual filings had increased. Since 1973, the annual filings in the Court have actually declined. It would be premature to draw any long-term con-

[3] See Federal Judicial Center Report of the Study Group on the Case Load of the Supreme Court (Paul A. Freund, chairman, 1972); Commission on Revision of the Federal Court Appellate System, Structure and Internal Procedures: Recommendations for Change (1975).

[4] The figures we used for 1973 and 1974 were adjusted by the Clerk of the Supreme Court to offset the distortions created by the fact that the 1973 Term was an unusually long one.

TABLE 1

CASES FILED IN SUPREME COURT, 1973–76

Term	Number
1973	3,943
1974	3,661
1975	3,934
1976	3,872

SOURCE.—Office of the Clerk, U.S. Supreme Court (original cases not included).

clusions from the experience of three Terms, given the lack of information about the causality of the Supreme Court caseload change. (Anyone writing at the end of the Court's 1964 Term would have noted that the Court's annual filings had declined for two consecutive Terms, but had he predicted a continuation of this trend he would have been grievously mistaken.) It would be equally unfounded, however, to dismiss the experience of the last three Terms as necessarily aberrant. As we emphasized in our 1976 study, theory does not teach—contrary to the conclusions of some earlier writings on this question—that a court's docket is bound to grow over time as a function of an increasing level of the underlying activities—accidents, commercial transactions, personal income, divorce, or whatever—out of which litigation arises. Furthermore, it is not the experience of the last three Terms alone that suggests the possibility that the Court's docket may be leveling off, perhaps for a significant period (long enough, at any rate, to avoid having to rush into radical cures for the workload problem that may be worse than the disease). For, as shown in table 2, while it is only recently that the annual rise in the caseload has actually stopped, the rate of caseload growth has been slowing since 1968.

TABLE 2

GROWTH IN APPLICATIONS CASELOAD, THREE-YEAR PERIODS, 1965–76

Period	Percentage Increase over Previous Three-Year Period
1965–67	24
1968–70	17
1971–73	12
1974–76	1

SOURCES.—Table 1, *supra;* CASPER & POSNER, note 1 *supra*, at 58 (table 3.15).

Again, no firm conclusions can be drawn from such data. The causes of the trend are not clear; its continuation cannot be predicted with any confidence. At the same time, it would seem unjustified to disregard the evidence in tables 1 and 2 and press ahead with drastic proposals for change in the Supreme Court's jurisdiction or structure premised on the assumed inevitability of a further substantial growth in the Court's caseload in the immediate future.

For those who think the Court's caseload has long since reached unmanageable proportions, nothing short of our assurance—which, for the reasons just stated, we cannot give—that the caseload will decline significantly will suffice to deflect the proposals for radical change. But as we tried to show in our 1976 study, there is no evidence that the caseload has yet reached such crisis proportions that the modest meliorative steps we suggested should not be attempted before moving directly to more radical solutions.[5]

B. TRENDS IN SPECIFIED AREAS

The caseload trend of the last three Terms seems fairly evenly distributed, affecting "indigent" as well as "paid" cases, as shown in table 3.

TABLE 3

PAID AND INDIGENT CASES FILED, SUPREME COURT, 1973–76

Term	Paid	Indigent
1973	2,068	2,118
1974	1,768	1,891
1975	1,921	2,013
1976	1,872	2,000

SOURCE.—Office of the Clerk, U.S. Supreme Court. The figures for 1973 are unadjusted for the unusual length of term. See note 4 *supra*.

This impression of even distribution persists if we examine broad subject-matter categories within the civil appellate (*i.e.*, paid) docket, as shown in table 4. A major exception is the rise in federal question litigation, balanced by a decline in diversity cases—perhaps reflecting a dawning awareness on the part of the bar of the futility of seeking review in diversity cases given the very small probability that review will be granted.

[5] CASPER & POSNER, note 1 *supra*, at 108–18.

TABLE 4

CIVIL CASES FILED ON APPELLATE DOCKET, 1973–76

	Cases from Lower Federal Courts									Cases from State Courts			
	Federal Government Litigation					Private Litigation							
Term	Review of Administrative Action	Taxation	Other	Total Federal Government Litigation	State and Local Government Litigation	Federal Question	Diversity	Total Private Litigation	Total Federal Court Cases	Government Litigation	Private Litigation	Total State Court Cases	Total Civil Case Filed
1973. . . .	198 (14)*	87 (15)	150 (26)	435 (18)	193 (58)	305 (19)	137 (31)	442 (23)	1,070 (27)	218 (91)	103 (79)	321 (87)	1,391 (41)
1974. . . .	134 (13)	52 (15)	127 (26)	313 (19)	158 (70)	290 (12)	75 (19)	365 (13)	836 (26)	147 (87)	122 (89)	269 (88)	1,105 (41)
1975. . . .	209 (22)	61 (10)	84 (19)	354 (19)	166 (66)	379 (13)	59 (15)	438 (13)	958 (24)	182 (85)	143 (87)	325 (86)	1,283 (40)
1976. . . .	220 (13)	66 (17)	102 (28)	388 (18)	187 (75)	372 (10)	62 (23)	434 (12)	1,009 (26)	184 (89)	107 (81)	291 (86)	1,300 (39)

* Percent of constitutional cases shown in parentheses.

One of the points emphasized in our 1976 study was the growth in the percentage of constitutional cases on the Supreme Court's docket. We were therefore surprised to find that the percentage of constitutional cases on the appellate docket in the 1974–76 Terms, for which the relevant data were not available in time for the 1976 study, was lower–below 50 percent–than in the immediately preceding years, when it had ranged as high as 60 percent. We were sufficiently perplexed to redo our original analysis of the percentage of constitutional cases in the Terms studied in our 1976 monograph, and we found that the percentage of federal constitutional cases among the federal criminal cases on the Court's docket had been somewhat overstated and the percentage of constitutional cases on the Court's state criminal docket slightly understated. The result of these corrections, shown for selected years in table 5, is a reduction in our estimate of the growth of the percentage of constitutional cases on the appellate (and hence on the total) docket of the Court. The qualitative conclusion of our original study, however–that the percentage of constitutional cases on the Court's docket has increased substantially since 1956–continues to hold, as does the finding that the Court has become primarily a constitutional court.

Unfortunately, because we have not classified the indigent cases filed in the last three Terms by subject matter (a task that would have required actual inspection of a sample of indigent petitions, as in our 1976 study), we do not know the exact percentage of indigent petitions that raise constitutional issues. We used the 1973

TABLE 5

PERCENTAGE OF CONSTITUTIONAL CASES ON SUPREME COURT'S DOCKET, SELECTED TERMS, 1956–76

	Appellate Docket						
		Criminal					
Term	Civil	State	Federal	Total	Total Civil and Criminal	Miscellaneous Docket	Total of All Cases
1956...	24	100	37	60	31	77	52
1961...	29	100	47	70	39	83	65
1967...	35	100	49	73	46	80	66
1973...	41	100	52	72	51	76	64
1974...	41	100	55	70	51	76	62
1975...	40	100	51	64	47	76	62
1976...	39	100	52	64	47	76	62

SOURCE.—See CASPER & POSNER, note 1 *supra*, at 51 (Method II).

figure for the subsequent Terms. As a result, the last column in table 5 must be used with caution. It should be noted, however, that the most striking implication of that column—that the entire growth in the percentage of constitutional cases on the Court's caseload occurred before 1961 and there has been no growth since then—is in fact broadly consistent with the results in our original study, though we did not then state that interesting fact.

TABLE 6

CRIMINAL CASES ON APPELLATE DOCKET, 1956–76

Type of Case	Average No. Cases per Term		
	1956–58	1971–73	1974–76
Federal cases	112	372	418
State cases	61	264	163
Total federal and state cases	173	636	581

As shown in table 6, the rather startling growth in the number of paid federal cases on which we commented in our 1976 study[6] has continued, while state criminal cases on the appellate docket have dropped substantially. Although state cases have always constituted a minority of criminal cases on the appellate docket (in 1973 they provided 59 percent of all indigent criminal cases),[7] their share of the appellate criminal cases has dropped to 28 percent for the 1974–76 Terms, which is less than what it was during the 1956–58 base period. This, combined with continued growth in the number of federal cases, lends support to our 1976 findings which forced us to abandon the attribution of the overall growth in the Court's criminal docket to the Warren Court's criminal jurisprudence as such,[8] which would have affected state cases more than federal cases.

On the civil docket, as shown in table 7, categories that had declined or remained roughly the same over the period covered in the 1976 study show the same pattern in the more recent Terms, the principal exception being a fairly sharp increase in the number of maritime cases. However, as shown in table 8, several of the major growth areas in the original study have shown a decline in the most recent period, military cases, racial cases, election cases,

[6] *Id.* at 42.

[7] *Id.* at 36 (table 3.3).

[8] *Id.* at 42.

TABLE 7

AREAS IN WHICH THE CIVIL APPELLATE DOCKET CASELOAD DID NOT INCREASE SUBSTANTIALLY OR DECLINED

Area	Average No. Cases per Term		
	1956–58	1971–73	1974–76
Civil action from lower federal courts:			
Taxation	62	85	60
FPC	13	15	11
FTC	12	7	6
ICC	17	15	19
Immigration and Naturalization Service	8	8	8
Antitrust (Department of Justice)	8	11	3
Eminent domain	8	3	0
Federal tort claims	7	5	11
Priority of government liens	5	3	0
Federal government personnel	11	10	15
Public (federal) contracts	12	5	7
FELA	10	6	3
Interstate Commerce Act (private)	7	5	0
Jones Act and other maritime	13	16	29
Patents, copyrights, trademarks	32	39	35
Railway Labor Act	6	6	6
Diversity cases	100	116	65
Total federal	331	355	278
Civil action from state courts:			
FELA	9	3	3
Labor relations	3	3	4
Total state	12	6	7
Total cases	343	361	285

TABLE 8

AREAS IN WHICH THE CIVIL APPELLATE DOCKET CASELOAD INCREASED SUBSTANTIALLY

Area	Average No. Cases per Term		
	1956–58	1971–73	1974–76
Military	14	30	10
NLRB	19	49	43
Civil rights acts and racial discrimination	19	83	60
Education	1	28	44
Reapportionment and elections	1	44	28
Health/welfare	3	32	42
Private antitrust	9	37	40
Private SEC	2	22	24
Government personnel (state)	15	45	15
State liquor control	2	6	0
Domestic relations	7	18	21
Zoning	4	10	13
Property	3	12	47
Torts	5	19	26
Total	104	435	413

and cases involving state government personnel being the most important examples. Some of the slack has been taken up by continued growth in education, health/welfare, property, and torts cases.

A comparison of tables 7 and 8 indicates that areas that were declining or at least not growing rapidly in 1971–73 remained stable in the next three-Term period, while the growth areas tended (as shown in the last row of table 8) to level off. This suggests that trends within specific subject-matter areas which contribute to overall caseload change may hold the key to explaining the overall moderation in caseload growth evident in the last three Terms.

A similar stability in the workload of the Court is revealed by an examination of the merits docket, *i.e.*, the cases that are decided on the merits, ordinarily after full briefing and oral argument. Tables 9 and 10 show no growth pattern in signed majority opinions,

TABLE 9

SIGNED MAJORITY AND PER CURIAM OPINIONS, SUPREME COURT, 1970–76

Term	No. Signed Majority Opinions	No. per Curiams
1970	109	22
1971	129	24
1972	140	18
1973	140	8
1974	123	20
1975	138	16
1976	126	22

SOURCE.—Office of the Clerk, U.S. Supreme Court. (Per curiams include only those rendered after oral argument.)

NOTE.—We went back to 1970 in this table to correct certain errors appearing in our original study.

per curiam opinions, or numbers of words produced by the Court in its opinions.

III. CONCLUSIONS

The study of the three most recent Terms has revealed several interesting facts. First, there has been no growth in the annual number of filings. We are reluctant to draw conclusions from so brief a trend but would note that the leveling off is con-

TABLE 10

WORD OUTPUT OF SUPREME COURT, 1974–76

	Majority Opinions*			Dissenting Opinions			Concurring Opinions			Concurring-Dissenting Opinions			
Term	No.	Average Words per Opinion	Total Words (Thousands)	No.	Average Words per Opinion	Total Words (Thousands)	No.	Average Words per Opinion	Total Words (Thousands)	No.	Average Words per Opinion	Total Words (Thousands)	Total Output of Words (Thousands)
1974..	155	4,200	645	125	2,100	264	54	900	46	13	3,100	40	995
1975..	177	4,300	753	100	2,700	268	74	1,300	97	16	3,400	54	1,172
1976..	152	4,700	712	98	2,700	269	69	1,100	77	15	1,700	26	1,084

SOURCES.—U.S. Reports; for 1976 also Supreme Court Reporter and U.S. Law Week.

* Includes both per curiam and signed majority opinions. The number of such opinions is somewhat larger than those given in table 9 due to the fact that the Clerk's data include only per curiams rendered after oral argument.

sistent with an argument that we first detailed in June 1974.[9] Second, the leveling off was fairly generally distributed across major categories of cases; it was not the result of a dramatic fall in the number of filings in any particular area. We were able to identify specific areas where the annual filings had continued, or begun, to decline significantly. We speculate that the overall drop in filings might reflect simply the balancing out of trends, affected by a multitude of unrelated phenomena such as the completion of litigation growing out of the Vietnam War and the creation of a considerable amount of precedent in such areas as elections. The decline in the annual filings in diversity cases may reflect a growing awareness of the extremely low probability of the Court's granting review in such cases, and hence the low value of seeking such review. We noted a continued growth in federal criminal cases on the appellate docket balanced by a decline in paid state cases.

This follow-up study reinforces the major policy conclusion of the earlier study. Congress should defer the adoption of radical proposals for Supreme Court reform, such as creating an additional judicial layer between the lower courts and the Supreme Court or depriving the Court of some of its major heads of jurisdiction. We said then that there was still time—and we repeat the statement with greater confidence today—to explore the possibilities for solving the workload problem, or at least keeping it within manageable proportions, through the modest reforms discussed in our original study. There is no evidence of a worsening crisis requiring precipitate measures. We think this conclusion, itself somewhat radical when first stated by us, is gaining acceptance. The proposals for far-reaching changes in the Court's structure and jurisdiction to alleviate its workload pressures have receded in recent months.[10]

We continue to believe that the key to understanding the workload problem lies in the collection and analysis of detailed statistics, kept and reported regularly and consistently. Our own resources to act as a statistical arm of the Supreme Court are limited, and we

---

[9] Casper & Posner, *A Study of the Supreme Court's Caseload*, 3 J. LEG. STUDIES 339, 346–49 (1974).

[10] The Subcommittee on Improvements in Judicial Machinery of the Senate Judiciary Committee held hearings on the National Court of Appeals proposal during the course of 1976. See Hearings on S. 2762 and S. 3423—the National Court of Appeals Act—before the Subcommittee on Improvements in Judicial Machinery of the Committee on the Judiciary, United States Senate, 94th Cong., 2d Sess., pt. 1 (1977).

have assumed this informal office only because of the failure of the Office of the Clerk of the Court or the Administrative Office to maintain and publish an adequate set of annual statistics. We hope we will not seem ungracious in urging the Clerk, whose office has been so helpful to us in our own studies, to assume a greater role in providing the students of the Court's work, and the legislators who must appraise proposals for changes designed to reduce the Court's workload, with statistical series even more detailed than those presented in our studies.

GEOFFREY R. STONE

THE MIRANDA DOCTRINE IN THE BURGER COURT

The task of a court confronted with a precedent that a majority of its members believe to be seriously misguided or worse is never an easy one. And the difficulty is exacerbated when that precedent is recent, highly controversial, and deeply embedded in the public consciousness. In such a context, the expedient of direct overruling may seem unattractive, for such action would inescapably raise strong doubts about the integrity and the stability of the judicial process.[1] Faced with this problem, a court may attempt to avoid or to postpone a direct overruling of the disfavored precedent. The very existence of the conflict, however, is likely to exert considerable strain on the court in its efforts to deal forthrightly with issues posed by the precedent. This seems to be the current plight of the Burger Court[2] with respect to *Miranda v. Arizona*.[3]

Geoffrey R. Stone is Associate Professor of Law, The University of Chicago.

AUTHOR'S NOTE: I should like to thank Walter Blum, Richard Epstein, Walter Hellerstein, Edmund Kitch, Bernard Meltzer, and Franklin Zimring for their helpful comments on an earlier draft of this article.

[1] See Israel, *Gideon v. Wainwright: The "Art" of Overruling*, 1963 SUPREME COURT REVIEW 211, 218–19.

[2] There is a danger in the use of such labels, for they may convey a false impression that the Court is essentially monolithic in nature. In fact, changes within the Court are ordinarily gradual, and the Court usually operates though shifting majorities. See Linde, *Judges, Critics, and The Realist Tradition*, 82 YALE L. J. 227, 244–47 (1972). Nevertheless, such labels do serve a useful shorthand function so long as they are not taken too literally. Warren Burger became Chief Justice on June 23, 1969. The other members of the Court at that time were Black, Douglas, Brennan, Marshall, Harlan, Stewart, and White, the last three of whom dissented in *Miranda*. 384 U.S. at 504–45. It does not seem to me un-

0-226-46429-6/78/1977-5000$05.29

That *Miranda* has fallen into disfavor with the present majority of the Court is reflected both in its substantive decisions and in the manner in which it has exercised its power to decide which cases on its docket to review. In the past four years, the Court has granted certiorari in only one of the thirty-five cases on its appellate docket in which a defendant sought review of a lower court decision holding evidence admissible over a claimed violation of *Miranda*.[4] During this same period, the Court has granted certiorari in thirteen of the twenty-five cases in which the government sought review of a lower court decision excluding evidence on the authority of *Miranda*.[5] In terms of its decisions on the merits, the Court, in the years since Warren Burger assumed the role of Chief Justice, has handed down eleven decisions concerning the scope and application of *Miranda*. In ten of these cases, the Court interpreted *Miranda* so as not to exclude the challenged evidence.[6] In the remaining case, the Court avoided a direct ruling on the *Miranda* issue, holding the evidence inadmissible on other grounds.[7] In effect, then, the Court

duly rash to assume, based upon their prior writings and the views they have expressed concerning *Miranda* since appointment to the Court, that at least a majority of the Justices appointed by Presidents Nixon and Ford would not have joined *Miranda*. As to the prior writing, see Frazier v. United States, 419 F.2d 1161, 1171–72 (D.C. Cir. 1969) (separate opinion by Judge Burger); Burger, *Who Will Watch the Watchman?*, 14 AM. U. L. REV. 1 (1964); Powell, *The President's Page*, 50 A.B.A.J. 891 (1964).

[3] 384 U.S. 436 (1966).

[4] Beckwith v. United States, 425 U.S. 341 (1976). These figures were drawn from an analysis of volumes 42–45 of *United States Law Week—Supreme Court*, covering the 1973–76 Terms. The only other *Miranda* decision in these years in which the Court granted review to a defendant was Doyle v. Ohio, 426 U.S. 610 (1976) and its companion case, Wood v. Ohio, both of which were on the miscellaneous docket.

[5] Michigan v. Tucker, 417 U.S. 433 (1974); Pennsylvania v. Romberger, 417 U.S. 964 (1974); Oregon v. Hass, 420 U.S. 714 (1975); United States v. Hale, 422 U.S. 171 (1975); Michigan v. Mosley, 423 U.S. 96 (1975); Ohio v. Gallagher, 425 U.S. 257 (1976); Baxter v. Palmigiano, 425 U.S. 308 (1976); Enomoto v. Clutchette (a companion case to *Baxter*); United States v. Mandujano, 425 U.S. 564 (1976); Oregon v. Mathiason, 429 U.S. 492 (1977); Brewer v. Williams, 97 S.Ct. 1232 (1977); United States v. Washington, 97 S.Ct. 1814 (1977); United States v. Wong, 97 S.Ct. 1823 (1977).

[6] Those decisions, in the order in which they will be discussed in this article, are as follows: Harris v. New York, 401 U.S. 222 (1971); Michigan v. Tucker, 417 U.S. 433 (1974); Oregon v. Hass, 420 U.S. 714 (1975); Michigan v. Mosley, 423 U.S. 96 (1975); Baxter v. Palmigiano, 425 U.S. 308 (1976); Beckwith v. United States, 425 U.S. 341 (1976); Oregon v. Mathiason, 429 U.S. 492 (1977); United States v. Mandujano, 425 U.S. 564 (1976); United States v. Wong, 97 S.Ct. 1823 (1977); United States v. Washington, 97 S.Ct. 1814 (1977).

[7] Doyle v. Ohio, 426 U.S. 610 (1976). In several other cases, the Court has not ruled directly on the *Miranda* issue. Brewer v. Williams, 97 S. Ct. 1232 (1977); Ohio v. Gallagher, 425 U.S. 257 (1976); United States v. Hale, 422 U.S. 171 (1975); Pennsyl-

has not held a single item of evidence inadmissible on the authority of *Miranda*. Moreover, despite the relative frequency and complexity of these decisions, neither Justices White or Stewart, both of whom dissented in *Miranda*, nor any of the four Justices appointed by Richard Nixon, has found it necessary to cast even a single vote to exclude evidence because of a violation of *Miranda*.

This article will examine these eleven decisions with essentially three questions in mind. First, how has the Court reacted to the pressures inherent in this situation? That is, to what extent, if any, has the Court sacrificed the judicial ideals of candor, logic, craftsmanship, and reasoned elaboration in the cases that came before it? Second, what, in fact, is the status of *Miranda* today? That is, to what extent, if any, are charges that the Court is actively engaged in dismantling *Miranda* warranted?[8] And third, to what extent, if any, are these decisions premised upon a coherent, principled interpretation of *Miranda* or of the privilege against compelled self-incrimination?

I. MIRANDA: THE PRECEDENT

The use of improper police interrogation for the purpose of eliciting confessions from persons suspected of crime has been a subject of special concern in this country at least since the Wickersham Commission report on police abuses in 1931.[9] Five years later, the Supreme Court addressed the problem in *Brown v. Mississippi*,[10] which involved a state homicide conviction based upon a confession obtained through physical torture. Although there was no patent

---

vania v. Romberger, 417 U.S. 964 (1974). In a few instances, the Court has dealt with *Miranda* only indirectly. Garner v. United States, 424 U.S. 648 (1976); Brown v. Illinois, 422 U.S. 590 (1975); Schneckloth v. Bustamonte, 412 U.S. 218 (1973).

[8] Michigan v. Mosley, 423 U.S. 96, 112 (1975) (Brennan, J., dissenting); Bartram v. State, 33 Md. App. 115 (1976); see Ritchie, *Compulsion That Violates the Fifth Amendment: The Burger Court's Definition*, 61 MINN. L. REV. 383, 430–31 (1977); Note, 17 ARIZ. L. REV. 188, 213 (1975).

[9] 4 NATIONAL COMMISSION ON LAW OBSERVANCE AND ENFORCEMENT, REPORT ON LAWLESSNESS IN LAW ENFORCEMENT (1931).

[10] 297 U.S. 278 (1936). Prior to *Brown*, the Court had considered a smattering of coerced confession cases arising out of federal prosecutions. These cases were decided on the basis either of the constitutional privilege against compelled self-incrimination, Bram v. United States, 168 U.S. 532 (1897), or of common law principles, Pierce v. United States, 160 U.S. 355 (1896); Hopt v. Utah, 110 U.S. 574 (1884).

ground for reversing the conviction,[11] the Court found the whole procedure "revolting to the sense of justice,"[12] and therefore violative of the Due Process Clause of the Fourteenth Amendment.

In the next thirty years, the Court handed down more than thirty opinions concerning the use of allegedly coerced confessions.[13] It was during this period that the "voluntariness" doctrine matured. At first, the Court's primary concern was with the use of confessions coerced by physical brutality,[14] but it soon brought psychological coercion within the doctrine as well.[15] Moreover, although the due process rationale was directed initially at the potential unreliability of the evidence,[16] the doctrine gradually expanded, focusing also on the fairness of the police practices[17] and on the individual's state of mind and capacity for effective choice.[18] Thus, despite the apparent simplicity of the "voluntariness" concept on its face, it proved to be highly subtle and elusive, involving a delicate balancing of a whole complex of variables concerning the behavior of the police and the subjective attributes of the suspect.[19]

Given the Court's inability to articulate a clear and predictable definition of "voluntariness," the apparent persistence of state courts in utilizing the ambiguity of the concept to validate confessions of doubtful constitutionality, and the resultant burden on its own

---

[11] The Fifth Amendment privilege against compelled self-incrimination had not yet been held applicable to the states, and in 1936 it was far from evident that the Due Process Clause required anything more than a fair trial. See Amsterdam, *The Supreme Court and the Rights of Suspects in Criminal Cases*, 45 N.Y.U.L. Rev. 785, 805–06 (1970).

[12] 297 U.S. at 286.

[13] Kamisar, *A Dissent from the Miranda Dissents: Some Comments on the "New" Fifth Amendment and the Old "Voluntariness" Test*, 65 Mich. L. Rev. 59, 102 n.184 (1966); Comment, *The Coerced Confession Cases in Search of a Rationale*, 31 U. Chi. L. Rev. 313 & n.1 (1964).

[14] White v. Texas, 310 U.S. 530 (1940); Brown v. Mississippi, 297 U.S. 278 (1936).

[15] Leyra v. Denno, 347 U.S. 556 (1954); Watts v. Indiana, 338 U.S. 49 (1949); Chambers v. Florida, 309 U.S. 227 (1940).

[16] Ward v. Texas, 316 U.S. 547 (1942).

[17] Rogers v. Richmond, 365 U.S. 534 (1961); Ashcraft v. Tennessee, 322 U.S. 143 (1944).

[18] Lynum v. Illinois, 372 U.S. 528 (1963); Gallegos v. Colorado, 370 U.S. 49 (1962); Blackburn v. Alabama, 361 U.S. 199 (1960).

[19] McCormick, Evidence §§ 149–50 (2d ed. 1972); Note, 79 Harv. L. Rev. 935, 961–84 (1966); Kamisar, *What Is an "Involuntary" Confession?*, 17 Rutgers L. Rev. 728 (1963).

workload,[20] it seemed inevitable that the Court would seek "some automatic device by which the potential evils of incommunicado interrogation [could] be controlled."[21] Its first major step in this direction rested on the Sixth Amendment guarantee of the right to counsel in criminal cases. Prior to 1964, the refusal of police to permit the subject of interrogation to consult with counsel was regarded as only one of the "totality of circumstances" relevant to the voluntariness of the confession.[22] In *Massiah v. United States*,[23] however, the Court held that a postindictment interrogation was a "critical stage" of the prosecution to which the right to counsel attaches, and that the Sixth Amendment therefore required the exclusion of incriminating statements elicited from the accused after he had been indicted and in the absence of counsel.[24] *Massiah*, however, was limited to postindictment confessions, and thus did not affect the vast majority of police interrogations. A month later, in *Escobedo v. Illinois*,[25] the Court extended its Sixth Amendment approach to preindictment interrogation. The precise reach of this decision was clouded, however, by a combination of sweeping language with an express limitation of the holding to the specific facts at issue. This ambiguity generated considerable debate and confusion.[26] Two years later, the Court shifted its emphasis from the Sixth Amendment to the Fifth, and granted certiorari in *Miranda* "to explore some facets of the problems . . . of applying the privilege against

---

[20] See Amsterdam, note 11 *supra*, at 806–07; Note, note 19 *supra*, at 1021.

[21] SCHAEFER, THE SUSPECT AND SOCIETY 10 (1967). In federal prosecutions, the Court attempted to establish such a device through the exercise of its supervisory powers. See McNabb v. United States, 318 U.S. 332 (1943); Mallory v. United States, 354 U.S. 449 (1957).

[22] Crooker v. California, 357 U.S. 433 (1958); Cicenia v. Lagay, 357 U.S. 504 (1958).

[23] 377 U.S. 201 (1964).

[24] Within a year the Court made clear that this rule was equally binding on the states. McLeod v. Ohio, 381 U.S. 356 (1965). The Sixth Amendment had been held applicable to the states a year before *Massiah*. Gideon v. Wainwright, 372 U.S. 335, 342 (1963).

[25] 378 U.S. 478 (1964).

[26] Enker & Elsen, *Counsel for the Suspect: Massiah v. United States and Escobedo v. Illinois*, 49 MINN. L. REV. 47 (1964); Kamisar, *Equal Justice in the Gatehouses and Mansions of American Criminal Procedure*, in KAMISAR, INBAU & ARNOLD, CRIMINAL JUSTICE IN OUR TIME 1, 53–81 (1965); Comment, *The Curious Confusion Surrounding Escobedo v. Illinois*, 32 U. CHI. L. REV. 560 (1965); Note, note 19 *supra*, at 1001–20; Herman, *The Supreme Court and Restrictions on Police Interrogation*, 25 OHIO ST. L. J. 449 (1964). See also United States v. Childress, 347 F.2d 448 (7th Cir. 1965); Collins v. Beto, 348 F. 2d 823 (5th Cir. 1965); People v. Dorado, 62 Cal. 2d 338 (1965); People v. Hartgraves, 31 Ill. 2d 375 (1964).

self-incrimination to in-custody interrogation, and to give concrete constitutional guidelines for law enforcement agencies and courts to follow."[27]

In each of the four companion cases involved in *Miranda*, the defendant had been arrested, taken to a police station, and interrogated without full warnings of his constitutional rights. In each case, the police secured a confession that was used at trial to obtain a conviction. In each case the Court held that use of the confession violated the privilege against compelled self-incrimination. The first hurdle confronting the Court concerned the applicability of the privilege in the extrajudicial context of police interrogation. Although the Court had so applied the privilege some seventy years earlier in *Bram v. United States*,[28] that decision had been vigorously criticized as founded upon a confusion between the constitutional privilege and the common law rule governing coerced confessions.[29] The Court in *Miranda* reaffirmed *Bram*.[30]

The Court next turned its attention to the nature of custodial interrogation. At the outset, the Court noted that, in part because of the traditionally incommunicado setting of police interrogation, the use of physical brutality to secure confessions—although the exception in 1966—could not effectively be eradicated without additional limitations on the interrogation process.[31] The Court then observed that the modern practice of in-custody interrogation is primarily psychologically rather than physically oriented and, after describing various psychological ploys and tactics advocated in police manuals as effective means of obtaining confessions, the Court stressed that it had long recognized that coercion can exist even in the absence of physical brutality.[32] Having cleared away the underbrush, the Court then turned to the heart of the problem. Thus, the Court maintained that "[e]ven without employing brutality, the

---

[27] 384 U.S. at 441–42. The self-incrimination clause had been held applicable to the states in Malloy v. Hogan, 378 U.S. 1 (1964).

[28] 168 U.S. 532 (1897).

[29] See McCormick, note 19 *supra*, at § 125, and sources cited, at 266 n. 62; 8 Wigmore, Evidence § 2252, at 329 & n. 27 (McNaughton rev. ed. 1961).

[30] 384 U.S. at 460–65. It should be noted that between *Bram* and *Miranda*, several cases suggested that the privilege applied in the coerced confession context. See Shotwell Mfg. Co. v. United States, 371 U.S. 341 (1963); Wan v. United States, 266 U.S. 1 (1924); Hardy v. United States, 186 U.S. 224 (1902). For a defense of *Miranda* on this point, see Kamisar, note 13 *supra*.

[31] 384 U.S. at 445–47.

[32] *Id.* at 448–55.

'third degree' or the specific stratagems described above, the very fact of custodial interrogation exacts a heavy toll on individual liberty and trades on the weakness of individuals."[33] The very atmosphere of custodial interrogation, the Court reasoned, "carries its own badge of intimidation" and involves "inherently compelling pressures which work to undermine the individual's will to resist and to compel him to speak where he would not otherwise do so freely."[34] Although conceding that the confessions of the four defendants involved in *Miranda* might not "have been involuntary in traditional terms," the Court concluded that to offset the coercive pressures inherent in custodial interrogation, safeguards must be employed to assure that the suspect has a "full opportunity to exercise the privilege against self-incrimination."[35]

Accordingly, the Court held that the prosecution in a criminal case may not use statements, whether exculpatory or inculpatory, stemming from custodial interrogation of the defendant unless it demonstrates the use of procedures effective to protect the privilege. Custodial interrogation was ambiguously defined as questioning initiated by law enforcement officers "after a person has been taken into custody or otherwise deprived of his freedom of action in any significant way."[36] Recognizing that the Constitution does not require any particular solution to the problem, the Court declared that unless "other procedures which are at least as effective in apprising accused persons of their right of silence and in assuring a continuous opportunity to exercise it" are employed,[37] prior to any questioning, the person must be warned that he has a right to remain silent, that any statement that he makes may be used as evidence against him, and that he has a right to the assistance of counsel, either retained or appointed. Finally, the Court stated that the defendant may waive these rights, provided that the waiver is made voluntarily, knowingly, and intelligently, but that if the defendant indicates in any manner at any stage of the process that he wishes to consult with an attorney or not to be questioned, the interrogation must cease.[38]

---

[33] *Id.* at 455.

[34] *Id.* at 457, 467.

[35] *Ibid.*

[36] *Id.* at 444.

[37] *Id.* at 467.

[38] *Id.* at 444–45. The Warren Court handed down four other decisions concerning *Miranda*. Johnson v. New Jersey, 384 U.S. 719 (1966) (holding *Miranda* inapplicable to cases in which trial began before the *Miranda* decision); Jenkins v. Delaware, 395 U.S. 213 (1969) (holding *Miranda* inapplicable to cases in which retrials began after the date

Miranda was perhaps the most controversial of the Warren Court's criminal procedure decisions, and it has been the subject of spirited debate for more than a decade.[39] The decision raised complex questions concerning history, policy, and the proper role of the Supreme Court in our system of government. It is not my intent here, however, to enter the debate on those issues. Rather, for my purposes, *Miranda* is simply—although at times ambiguously—a given. My concern here is not with the merits of *Miranda* itself, but with what the Burger Court has done to it in its "*Miranda* decisions" and with what those decisions have done to the Burger Court. As noted earlier, through the end of the 1976 Term, the Burger Court has handed down eleven decisions concerning the scope and application of *Miranda*. It is to these eleven decisions that we now turn.

II. Harris v. New York: Impeaching Miranda

Harris v. New York,[40] the Burger Court's first confrontation with *Miranda*, presented the question whether statements elicited from a defendant without full compliance with the *Miranda* safeguards could be used to impeach the defendant's credibility when he testified at trial. Harris was arrested on January 7, 1966, and taken to police headquarters, where he was interrogated about drug transactions allegedly consummated on January 4 and 6. This interrogation was not preceded by a warning of his right to appointed counsel.[41] At his interrogation, Harris made several incriminating statements.[42] At his trial on two counts of drug sale, Harris testified

of that decision); Mathis v. United States, 391 U.S. 1 (1968) (holding *Miranda* applicable to interrogation of a state prisoner in jail for an offense unrelated to the federal tax offense under investigation); Orozco v. Texas, 394 U.S. 324 (1969) (holding *Miranda* applicable to a custodial interrogation in the suspect's home).

[39] See George, Constitutional Limitations on Evidence in Criminal Cases 273–96 (1973); Graham, *What Is "Custodial Interrogation?": California's Anticipatory Application of Miranda v. Arizona*, 14 U.C.L.A. L. Rev. 59 (1966); Kamisar, note 13 *supra*; see also *Interrogation of Criminal Defendants—Some Views on Miranda v. Arizona*, 35 Fordham L. Rev. 169 (1966). It is also noteworthy that in Title II of the Omnibus Crime Control and Safe Streets Act of 1968, 18 U.S.C. § 3501, Congress attempted to override *Miranda* through legislation. See Note, 82 Harv. L. Rev. 1392 (1969).

[40] 401 U.S. 222 (1971).

[41] Although the interrogation occurred prior to the decision in *Miranda*, the trial was held after it. Thus, under Johnson v. New Jersey, 384 U.S. 719 (1966), *Miranda* was applicable.

[42] Harris was accused of selling narcotics to an undercover police officer. At the interrogation, Harris admitted that he had purchased narcotics for the officer.

in his own behalf and denied committing the alleged crimes. On cross-examination, over Harris's objection, the prosecution was permitted to bring the prior incriminating statements to the jury's attention. The trial judge instructed the jury that it could consider those statements solely for the purpose of evaluating Harris's credibility. Harris was convicted on the second count, but the jury deadlocked on the first. The New York appellate courts affirmed the conviction.[43] In a brief, almost cryptic opinion, the Supreme Court, speaking through Chief Justice Burger, held the evidence properly admitted.[44]

In *Miranda,* the Court had unambiguously indicated that statements obtained in violation of its dictates could not be used to impeach[45] and, prior to *Harris,* most state and lower federal courts had therefore held such evidence inadmissible for that purpose.[46] In *Harris,* however, the Chief Justice maintained that *Miranda's* discussion of the impeachment issue "was not at all necessary to the Court's holding and cannot be regarded as controlling."[47] Reliance upon that fact rejects the fundamental nature of the *Miranda* decision as seen by the Court that formulated it. Rightly or wrongly, *Miranda* was deliberately structured to canvass a wide range of problems, many of which were not directly raised by the cases before the Court. This approach was thought necessary in order to "give concrete constitutional guidelines for law enforcement agencies and courts to follow."[48] Thus, a technical reading of *Miranda,* such as that employed in *Harris,* would enable the Court to label many critical aspects of the decision mere dictum and therefore not

---

[43] People v. Harris, 31 App. Div. 2d 828, *aff'd* 25 N.Y. 2d 175, (1969) (per curiam).

[44] Chief Justice Burger was joined by Justices Harlan, Stewart, White, and Blackmun. Justices Black, Douglas, Brennan, and Marshall dissented.

[45] For example, in explaining why exculpatory as well as inculpatory statements obtained without the proper safeguards must be inadmissible, the *Miranda* Court noted that "statements merely intended to be exculpatory by the defendant are often used to impeach his testimony at trial. . . . These statements are incriminating in any meaningful sense of the word and may not be used without the full warnings and effective waiver required for any other statement." 384 U.S. at 477. See also Dershowitz & Ely, *Harris v. New York: Some Anxious Observations on the Candor and Logic of the Emerging Nixon Majority,* 80 YALE L. J. 1198, 1208–10 (1971).

[46] Prior to *Harris,* six federal Courts of Appeals and appellate courts of fourteen states had held statements obtained in violation of *Miranda* inadmissible for the purpose of impeachment; three state appellate courts had reached the contrary result. See 401 U.S. at 231 n. 4 (Brennan, J., dissenting).

[47] 401 U.S. at 224.

[48] 384 U.S. at 441–42.

"controlling." Interestingly, although it has had several opportunities to do so, the Court has not employed the "dictum" approach to *Miranda* since *Harris*. It may be that, in light of the critical response of commentators to this aspect of *Harris*,[49] the Court has concluded that this is not an appropriate way to analyze opinions like *Miranda*. Alternatively, the Court may have come to appreciate the value of such "legislative" opinions, and may not wish to undermine its own ability to use this technique.[50]

In any event, having concluded that *Miranda* was not dispositive, the Court turned its attention to resolution of the question at issue. To bolster its conclusion that evidence obtained in violation of *Miranda* could be used to impeach, the Court placed primary reliance upon *Walder v. United States*.[51] To appreciate the Court's use of *Walder* in *Harris*, it is necessary first to take note of the Court's 1925 decision in *Agnello v. United States*.[52] In *Agnello*, the prosecution sought to use evidence seized in an unlawful search by asking Agnello on cross-examination whether he had ever seen it before. When Agnello answered in the negative, the trial judge permitted the prosecution to introduce the evidence for the purpose of impeaching his credibility. The Supreme Court reversed, noting that Agnello had not mentioned the evidence in his direct examination and that he had done nothing to waive his right to have the evidence excluded. Some thirty years later, in *Walder*, the Court carved a narrow exception out of the *Agnello* principle. The government unlawfully seized heroin from Walder, and the evidence was thereafter suppressed and the indictment dismissed. Two years later, Walder was indicted for an entirely separate narcotics offense. At his trial for this latter offense, Walder took the stand and, after denying the specific acts with which he was charged, voluntarily and gratuitously went on to claim that he had never possessed narcotics. In these circumstances, the trial judge permitted the government to introduce evidence of the prior possession to impeach his credibility. The Supreme Court affirmed, emphasizing however that "the Constitution guarantees a defendant the fullest opportunity to meet the accusation against him," and that the defendant "must be

[49] See Dershowitz & Ely, note 45 *supra*, at 1210.

[50] See Roe v. Wade, 410 U.S. 113 (1973).

[51] 347 U.S. 62 (1954).

[52] 269 U.S. 20 (1925).

free to deny all the elements of the case against him without thereby giving leave to the Government to introduce by way of rebuttal evidence illegally secured by it, and therefore not available for its case in chief."[53] But Walder "went beyond a mere denial of complicity in the crimes of which he was charged and made the sweeping claim that he had never dealt in or possessed any narcotics," and in that situation "there is hardly justification for letting the defendant affirmatively resort to perjurious testimony in reliance on the Government's disability to challenge his credibility."[54]

Whatever the merits of the *Walder* exception,[55] it did not control *Harris*. Harris, unlike Agnello, made his statement that was the basis of impeachment on direct examination, but he did not go beyond a mere denial of guilt of the crimes charged. Nevertheless, the Chief Justice in *Harris*, quoting selectively from *Walder*, presented that decision as supporting—indeed, controlling—precedent for his position.[56] In effect, he construed *Walder* as holding that unconstitutionally obtained evidence may always be used to impeach. No mention is made of *Agnello*. Although the Chief Justice conceded that "Walder was impeached as to collateral matters," whereas Harris "was impeached as to testimony bearing more directly on the crimes charged," he baldly concluded that this is not "a difference in principle that warrants a result different from that reached by the Court in *Walder*."[57] Thus, not only did *Harris* disregard a clear command of *Miranda*, it also swept aside a carefully crafted limitation on the *Walder* doctrine.

There are in fact several significant differences "in principle" between *Walder* and *Harris*. Most obviously, unlike Harris, Walder was impeached, not as to his denial of the elements of the crime charged but, rather, as to a wholly gratuitous statement on a collateral matter. The *Walder* Court, sensitive to the defendant's constitutional right to testify in his own behalf and to the potential impact on the ability to exercise that right of the threat of impeachment by unconstitutionally obtained evidence, thought this to be a

---

[53] 347 U.S. at 65.

[54] *Ibid.*

[55] *Walder* has been much criticized. Wright, Federal Practice and Procedure § 408, at 107 (1969); Comment, *The Impeachment Exception to the Exclusionary Rules*, 34 U. Chi. L. Rev. 939 (1967); Note, 42 N.Y.U.L. Rev. 772 (1967).

[56] *Compare* 401 U.S. at 224, *with* 347 U.S. at 65.

[57] 401 U.S. at 225.

critical distinction. The *Harris* Court, in a blink, found it an unprincipled one. The "collateral matter/element of the crime" distinction is relevant in another sense. When a defendant is impeached by illegally obtained evidence that bears directly on the crime charged, there is a substantial risk, not present when the impeachment concerns only collateral matters, that the evidence will be considered by the jury as direct substantive proof of the defendant's guilt.[58] Thus, in *Walder*, the defendant's prior possession of narcotics, although not unharmful to his cause, did not itself establish any elements of the crime charged, whereas in *Harris* the incriminating statement, if used by the jury for substantive purposes, could itself virtually clinch the case for the prosecution. In practical effect, then, evidence which the Burger Court conceded cannot, under *Miranda*, constitutionally be used as evidence of guilt may, under *Harris*, in fact be so used through indirection. And aware of these realities, the defendant may for this reason alone decline to testify even as to the elements of the crime charged, thus underscoring the Court's concern in *Walder*.[59] It is true, of course, that the jury in *Harris* was instructed to use the incriminating statement solely for purposes of evaluating Harris's credibility. But it has long been recognized that such instructions are more often than not an exercise in futility,[60] and the Court, cognizant of this fact, has viewed such instructions with considerable skepticism when constitutional rights are implicated.[61] Such skepticism was sorely lacking in *Harris*. Finally, the Court in *Harris* simply overlooked the fact that, unlike Walder, Harris was impeached with evidence obtained in violation of the Fifth Amendment, rather than the Fourth. The Fourth Amendment exclusionary rule is not mandated by the language of the Amendment itself but, rather, is a court-created device designed

---

[58] See Kent, *Harris v. New York: The Death Knell of Miranda and Walder?*, 38 Brooklyn L. Rev. 357, 360–61 (1971); Dershowitz & Ely, note 45 *supra*, at 1215–17; Comment, 73 Colum. L. Rev. 1476 (1973); Note, 85 Harv. L. Rev. 3, 47–49 (1971).

[59] See Note, note 58 *supra*, at 51–52; see also United States v. Steele, 419 F. Supp. 1387 (W.D. Pa. 1976); United States v. Steele, 419 F. Supp. 1389 (W.D. Pa. 1976); People v. Bacino, 41 Ill. App. 3d 738 (1976).

[60] See Kalven & Zeisel, The American Jury 127–28, 177–80 (1966); Hoffman & Brodley, *Jurors on Trial*, 17 Mo. L. Rev. 235, 243–45 (1952); Kalven, *A Report on the Jury Project of the University of Chicago Law School*, 24 Ins. Counsel J. 368, 371 (1957); see also Krulewitch v. United States, 336 U.S. 440, 453 (1949) (Jackson, J., concurring).

[61] Loper v. Beto, 405 U.S. 473, 482–83 n.11 (1972); Bruton v. United States, 391 U.S. 123 (1968); Jackson v. Denno, 378 U.S. 368 (1964).

primarily to discourage unreasonable searches and seizures.[62] The Self-Incrimination Clause of the Fifth Amendment, however, by its own terms seems to dictate the exclusion of evidence obtained in violation of its commands.[63] As the Burger Court has itself observed, "In contrast to the Fifth Amendment's direct command against the admission of compelled testimony, the issue of admissibility of evidence obtained in violation of the Fourth Amendment is determined after, and apart from, the violation."[64] Thus, although balancing of the sort engaged in in *Walder* might be appropriate in the Fourth Amendment context, it was out of place in *Harris.*[65]

Not content to rest exclusively upon the precedential force of *Walder*, the Chief Justice proceeded to offer policy justifications for the result in *Harris:* first, that use of Harris's prior incriminating statement "undoubtedly provided valuable aid to the jury in assessing [his] credibility"; and second, that it is unnecessary to exclude the evidence for deterrent purposes since "sufficient deterrence flows when the evidence in question is made unavailable to the prosecution in its case in chief."[66] The Court was surely correct in recognizing that this evidence is valuable to the jury when used to impeach. But it would also be valuable to the jury if used as substantive evidence of guilt. Simply to identify a legitimate government interest ought not in itself dispose of the issue. Although the need to prevent perjury is important, both *Agnello* and *Walder* concluded

---

[62] Stone v. Powell, 428 U.S. 465, 486 (1976); United States v. Janis, 428 U.S. 433, 446 (1976); United States v. Peltier, 422 U.S. 531, 536–39 (1975); United States v. Calandra, 414 U.S. 338, 347–48, 364 (1974); but see, *e.g.*, *Peltier*, *supra*, at 550–62 (Brennan, J., dissenting); *Calandra*, *supra*, at 355–67 (Brennan, J., dissenting).

[63] See Ritchie, note 8 *supra*, at 389 n.37, 417 n.168; Dershowitz & Ely, note 45 *supra*, at 1214–15; Note, 41 Brooklyn L. Rev. 325, 337–39, 348 (1974); Comment, 82 Yale L.J. 171, 178 (1972); Note, note 58 *supra*, at 49–51.

[64] United States v. Janis, 428 U.S. 433, 443 (1976).

[65] It should not make any difference under the Fifth Amendment that the evidence is used to impeach rather than in the prosecution's case-in-chief, for in both cases the individual is compelled "to be a witness against himself." See *Miranda*, 384 U.S. at 476–77; Note, note 19 *supra*, at 1030. It might be argued, of course, that by voluntarily electing to testify, the accused has "waived" the privilege. See 8 Wigmore, note 29 *supra*, at § 2276. The traditional concept of "waiver," however, should not be viewed as extending to earlier violations of the privilege. See Note, note 19 *supra*, at 1030; *cf.* Leary v. United States, 395 U.S. 6 (1969). Indeed, prior to *Harris*, the general rule among state and lower federal courts was that evidence obtained in violation of the Fifth Amendment could never be used to impeach. See Annot., 89 A.L.R. 2d 478 (1963) and cases cited therein.

[66] 401 U.S. at 225. The Court also apparently took solace from the seemingly irrelevant observation that prior inconsistent statements "made by the accused to some third person" would be admissible. *Id.* at 226. See Dershowitz & Ely, note 45 *supra*, at 1224–26.

that it does not override all countervailing concerns.[67] Thus, if the result in *Harris* were supportable as a matter of policy, it would have to rest on the Court's analysis of the deterrence issue. Regrettably, there was no such analysis; the Court offered only its conclusion. That conclusion, however, seems questionable, at best.

The underlying rationale of the constitutional rules of exclusion is that by forbidding the use of evidence obtained in an unlawful manner, the incentive for the police to employ unconstitutional tactics is removed, or at least reduced. To what extent, then, does the result in *Harris* provide an incentive to police not to warn a suspect of his rights, in violation of *Miranda?* The incentive would seem substantial. If the officer informs the suspect of his rights, the suspect might nevertheless confess, and that confession would then be admissible as substantive evidence of guilt. But the officer runs the risk that, having been alerted to his rights, the suspect will refuse to speak or ask to consult an attorney. Although it is impossible to prove the point conclusively,[68] it seems only reasonable to assume that this risk would be reduced, and the likelihood of a confession increased, if the suspect is kept ignorant of his rights. And if the suspect does confess without warnings, the police, after *Harris*, have much to gain. If the suspect chooses to testify at trial, the confession can be used to impeach and, because of the ineffectiveness of limiting instructions,[69] is likely to be used as substantive evidence of guilt as well. On the other hand, if the suspect attempts to avoid this dilemma by exercising his right not to testify at trial, the jury is likely, despite cautionary instructions, to regard his silence as evidence of guilt.[70] Thus, for the police, it is virtually a no-lose situation, and

[67] Similarly, the Court's observation that the defendant's privilege to testify in his own behalf "cannot be construed to include the right to commit perjury" is correct, but unhelpful. 401 U.S. at 225. See Dershowitz & Ely, note 45 *supra*, at 1221–22.

[68] For studies of the actual impact of *Miranda*, see Seeburger & Wettick, *Miranda in Pittsburgh—A Statistical Study*, 29 U. Pitt. L. Rev. 1 (1967); Medalie, Zeitz & Alexander, *Custodial Police Interrogation in Our Nation's Capital: The Attempt to Implement Miranda*, 66 Mich. L. Rev. 1347 (1968); Leiken, *Police Interrogation in Colorado: The Implementation of Miranda*, 47 Denver L.J. 1 (1970); Comment, 76 Yale L.J. 1519 (1967).

[69] See authorities cited in note 60, *supra*.

[70] See Williams, *The Trial of a Criminal Case*, 29 N.Y.B.A. Bull. 36, 41–42 (1957); Meltzer, *Required Records, the McCarran Act, and the Privilege against Self-Incrimination*, 18 U. Chi. L. Rev. 687, 690 (1951); Bruce, *The Right to Comment on the Failure of the Defendant to Testify*, 31 Mich. L. Rev. 226, 230 (1932); Note, 4 Colum. J.L. & Soc. Prob. 215, 221–22 (1968).

Harris therefore seems to carry at least the potential seriously to undercut the incentive of the police to comply with the dictates of *Miranda*.[71]

Finally, it should be noted that the Court in *Harris* stated that evidence obtained in an unconstitutional manner may not be admissible even for impeachment purposes if "the trustworthiness of the evidence" does not satisfy "legal standards."[72] The Court did not explain, however, whether this refers to some general due process requirement of reliability, or to some other unexplored, unidentified notion of "trustworthiness" independent of the Due Process Clause.[73] *Miranda* itself was intended in part to guard against the possibility that the inherently coercive atmosphere of custodial interrogation would elicit untrue and hence unreliable statements.[74] The result in *Harris* was necessarily premised on the implicit judgment that the risk of unreliability arising out of the failure to comply with *Miranda* does not itself violate these "legal standards" of "trustworthiness." What, then, of confessions that are "involuntary" under traditional standards? Despite the involuntariness, such confessions are not invariably unreliable.[75] Must a court called upon after *Harris* to rule on the admissibility of a confession for purposes of impeachment determine not only whether the confession was "involuntary" but also whether it is untrustworthy? The Court in

---

[71] See Dershowitz & Ely, note 45 *supra*, at 1218–21; Kent, note 58 *supra*; Note, note 58 *supra*, at 51–52. There is considerable skepticism today as to whether the Fourth Amendment exclusionary rule has any appreciable deterrent effect. United States v. Janis, 428 U.S. 433, 449–53 (1976), and authorities cited therein. That skepticism should not be extended too readily to *Miranda*, however, for unlike the Fourth Amendment exclusionary rule, *Miranda* is likely to have a significant deterrent impact because "the predominant incentive for interrogation is to obtain evidence for use in court. Consequently, police conduct in this area is likely to be responsive to judicial rules governing the admissibility of that evidence." Oaks, *Studying the Exclusionary Rule in Search and Seizure*, 37 U. Chi. L. Rev. 665, 722 (1970).

[72] 401 U.S. at 224.

[73] This issue was clouded still further by the Court's later decision in Loper v. Beto, 405 U.S. 473 (1972), in which the Court held that a prior conviction obtained in violation of defendant's Sixth Amendment right to counsel could not be used to impeach his veracity as a witness when he testified in his own behalf in a separate and unrelated criminal trial. Although the "trustworthiness" of such a conviction is surely suspect, the Court did not seem to rest its result on that ground.

[74] 384 U.S. at 470. See Michigan v. Payne, 412 U.S. 47, 53 (1973); Johnson v. New Jersey, 384 U.S. 719, 730 (1966).

[75] It should be noted that even when the confession itself is unreliable, the fruits of that confession might nevertheless be reliable and therefore, under *Harris*, perhaps admissible to impeach.

Harris found it unnecessary to address this question since, according to the Chief Justice, Harris did not "claim that the statements made to the police were coerced or involuntary."[76] This statement, however, is flatly untrue. At his trial, throughout the state appellate proceedings, and in his brief and oral argument before the Supreme Court, Harris consistently maintained that his statements to the police were involuntary.[77] The Court's assertion to the contrary is simply inexplicable.

Whatever one's views of the result in *Harris*, the opinion from beginning to end, from the Court's treatment of the record, to its use of precedent, to its analysis of policy, lacks candor, meticulousness, and reasoned elaboration. In short, *Harris* was an exercise of raw judicial power, with little or no effort made to explain or to justify its premises or conclusions.[78] The opinion raises many more questions than it answers. What are the implications of the Court's balancing approach in *Harris* for other issues that arise under *Miranda*, such as whether the "fruits" of a statement obtained in violation of *Miranda* are admissible? Does *Harris* reject *Agnello*, as well as the "collateral matter" limitation of *Walder*, with respect to evidence obtained in violation of *Miranda*?[79] Does *Harris* extend, not only to evidence obtained through the particular type of *Miranda* violation at issue in *Harris* (failure to give complete warnings), but to evidence obtained through other sorts of violations of *Miranda* as well? Does *Harris* extend, not only to evidence obtained through violations of *Miranda*, but also to evidence obtained through more traditional violations of the privilege against self-incrimination[80] and through violations of other constitutional rights?[81] Does

---

[76] 401 U.S. at 224.

[77] See Dershowitz & Ely, note 45 *supra*, at 1201–04. In support of this contention, Harris alleged, among other things, that at the time he made the statements he was suffering from withdrawal symptoms and may have been suffering the aftereffects of a recent automobile accident which caused a concussion. See *id.* at 1204.

[78] Several state courts have rejected *Harris* in interpreting their own constitutions. People v. Disbrow, 16 Cal. 3d 101 (1976); Commonwealth v. Triplett, 462 Pa. 244 (1975); State v. Santiago, 53 Haw. 254 (1971).

[79] *Compare* United States v. Mariani, 539 F. 2d 915 (2d Cir. 1976), *with* United States v. Carrasquillo, 412 F. Supp. 289 (E.D. Pa. 1976).

[80] Several courts seem to have concluded that *Harris* does not extend to the use for impeachment purposes of confessions found to be "involuntary" under traditional standards, without regard to trustworthiness. LaFrance v. Bohlinger, 499 F. 2d 29 (1st Cir. 1974); Booker v. State, 326 So. 2d 791 (Miss. 1976); State v. Langley, 25 N.C. App. 298 (1975). If *Harris* does govern the use of all statements obtained in violation of the privilege, the

Harris extend, not only to the use of unconstitutionally obtained evidence to contradict specific testimony of the accused, but to the use of such evidence to impeach his character generally in terms of veracity as well?[82] Does *Harris* extend, not only to the use of unlawfully obtained evidence to impeach the accused, but also to the use of such evidence to contradict the testimony of a defense witness when the accused does not take the stand?[83] At least a few of these questions have been answered in the Court's subsequent decisions.

III. Michigan v. Tucker: Miranda Rewritten

Michigan v. Tucker[84] posed but did not resolve the question whether "fruits" of a statement elicited in violation of *Miranda* are admissible against the defendant in a subsequent criminal trial. Tucker was arrested for rape and assault and taken to the police station for questioning. He was not warned of his right to appointed counsel prior to interrogation. Tucker told the police that at the time of the crime he had been with one Robert Henderson. The police contacted Henderson, whose story served to discredit rather than to support Tucker's alibi. Henderson also told the police that on the day after the crime Tucker had made several statements that implicated him in the crime. At trial, Tucker objected to Henderson's testimony as to these incriminating statements on the ground that the police would never have learned of Henderson's existence but for Tucker's unlawful interrogation. The trial court permitted Henderson to testify, although Tucker's own statements to the police were excluded. Tucker was convicted, and the Michigan appel-

---

scope of immunity offered in return for otherwise incriminatory revelations could be narrowed accordingly. See Ritchie, note 8 *supra*, at 415 n. 163.

[81] Several courts have simply assumed that *Harris's* emasculation of *Walder* governs the use of evidence obtained in violation of the Fourth Amendment. United States v. Mariani, 539 F. 2d 915 (2d Cir. 1976); United States v. Bermudez, 526 F. 2d 89 (2d Cir. 1975); United States v. Penta, 475 F. 2d 92 (1st Cir. 1973). In Loper v. Beto, 405 U.S. 473, 482 n. 11 (1972), the Court indicated, without holding, that *Harris* might be relevant to the use for impeachment purposes of evidence obtained in violation of the Sixth Amendment. See also Walker v. Follette, 443 F. 2d 167 (2d Cir. 1971) (applying *Harris* in Sixth Amendment context).

[82] Loper v. Beto, 405 U.S. 473, 482 n. 11 (1972), suggests, without clearly holding, that *Harris* does not extend to this situation. But see United States v. Penta, 475 F. 2d 92 (1st Cir. 1973); see generally Comment, note 58 *supra*, at 1492–1500.

[83] At least one court has concluded that *Harris* does not go this far. State v. Davis, 67 N. J. 222 (1975).

[84] 417 U.S. 433 (1974).

late courts affirmed the conviction.[85] Tucker then sought habeas corpus in federal district court. That court held the use of Henderson's testimony violative of *Miranda* and granted the relief sought.[86] The Court of Appeals affirmed.[87] The Supreme Court reversed.[88]

At the outset, it might be useful simply to mention various approaches a court intent on upholding the use of the evidence in *Tucker* might conceivably have embraced. First, there is the analysis suggested by Mr. Justice Brennan in his concurring opinion.[89] Shortly after *Miranda*, the Court held in *Johnson v. New Jersey*[90] that *Miranda* was not to be applied retroactively, and declared that it could be invoked only in trials begun after the date of the *Miranda* decision. Although the interrogation in *Tucker* preceded *Miranda*, the trial began thereafter. Mr. Justice Brennan argued in *Tucker* that there are good reasons to modify *Johnson* so as not to apply the fruits rule to any confession elicited prior to *Miranda*.[91] Although this analysis disposes of *Tucker*, it has no significant impact on *Miranda* generally. The Court in *Tucker* specifically rejected this analysis.[92] Second, one might modify *Johnson* directly, so that *Miranda* itself is held applicable only to confessions elicited after the date of the *Miranda* decision. The statement in *Johnson* that, regardless of the date of the interrogation, *Miranda* is applicable in all post-*Miranda* trials was dictum. Moreover, such a rule makes considerable sense and, indeed, has been employed by the Court in virtually all of its post-*Johnson* nonretroactivity decisions.[93] This approach, too, would dispose of *Tucker* with little effect on *Miranda* generally. Although the State of Michigan urged this approach in

[85] 19 Mich. App. 320 (1969), *aff'd* 385 Mich. 594 (1971).

[86] 352 F. Supp. 266 (E.D. Mich. 1972).

[87] 480 F. 2d 927 (6th Cir. 1973).

[88] Mr. Justice Rehnquist's majority opinion was joined by Chief Justice Burger and Justices Stewart, Blackmun, and Powell. Mr. Justice Brennan, joined by Mr. Justice Marshall, filed a separate concurring opinion, as did Mr. Justice White. Mr. Justice Douglas dissented.

[89] 417 U.S. at 453–60.

[90] 384 U.S. 719 (1966).

[91] This theory is not without its flaws. See 417 U.S. at 452–53 n. 26.

[92] *Ibid.*

[93] United States v. Peltier, 422 U.S. 531 (1975); Williams v. United States, 401 U.S. 646 (1971); Desist v. United States, 394 U.S. 244 (1969); Stovall v. Denno, 388 U.S. 293 (1967); see also Gagnon v. Scarpelli, 411 U.S. 778 (1973); Morrissey v. Brewer, 408 U.S. 471 (1972).

its brief,[94] the Court did not mention it. Finally, one might, like Mr. Justice White in his *Tucker* concurrence,[95] conclude that the fruits doctrine is simply inapplicable in the *Miranda* context. The Court has long recognized that the fruits of statements obtained in violation of the Self-Incrimination Clause are inadmissible,[96] and most state and lower federal courts have applied the doctrine to violations of *Miranda*.[97] But the Court, as we have already seen, has not hesitated to reject precedents. And this time, of course, the Court could draw upon *Harris* for support. Nevertheless, the Court in *Tucker* found it unnecessary to decide this question, resting its holding instead on what it termed "narrower ground."[98]

Mr. Justice Rehnquist, writing for the majority, began by asking "whether the police conduct complained of directly infringed upon [Tucker's] right against compulsory self-incrimination or whether it instead violated only the prophylactic rules developed to protect that right."[99] After noting that the privilege has been given broad scope "[w]here there has been genuine compulsion of testimony,"[100] he turned his attention to *Miranda*. The Court in that decision, he

---

[94] Brief of Petitioner, at pp. 6–10. It should be noted that although the relevant portion of *Johnson* was dictum, that dictum was at least implicitly relied on in several cases which, like *Tucker*, involved pre-*Miranda* confessions and post-*Miranda* trials. See Mathis v. United States, 391 U.S. 1 (1968); Orozco v. Texas, 394 U.S. 324 (1969); Harris v. New York, 401 U.S. 222 (1971).

[95] 417 U.S. at 460–61. It is unclear from his opinion whether Mr. Justice White rejected the application of the fruits rule to *Miranda* in its entirety, or whether he rejected its application only when, as in *Tucker*, the "fruit" consists of the testimony of a third person.

[96] United States v. Mandujano, 425 U.S. 564, 576 (1976); Lefkowitz v. Turley, 414 U.S. 70, 78, 84 (1973); Kastigar v. United States, 406 U.S. 441, 444–45 (1972); Murphy v. Waterfront Comm'n, 378 U.S. 52, 79 (1964); Counselman v. Hitchcock, 142 U.S. 547, 584–86 (1892).

[97] United States v. Pellegrini, 309 F. Supp. 250 (S.D.N.Y. 1970); United States v. Harrison, 265 F. Supp. 660 (S.D.N.Y. 1967); People v. Algien, 180 Colo. 1 (1972); People v. Schader, 71 Cal. 2d 761 (1969); People v. Peacock, 29 App. Div. 2d 762 (1st Dept. 1968); but see Keister v. Cox, 307 F. Supp. 1173 (W.D. Va. 1969). Interestingly, the dissenters in *Miranda* themselves thought the fruits doctrine is triggered by violations of *Miranda*. See 384 U.S. at 500 (Clark, J., concurring & dissenting); *id.* at 545 (White, J., joined by Harlan & Stewart, J J., dissenting). There is language in *Miranda* which supports this interpretation. See 384 U.S. at 479.

[98] 417 U.S. at 447.

[99] *Id.* at 439.

[100] *Id.* at 440. Thus, the right has been held applicable to proceedings before a grand jury, Counselman v. Hitchcock, 142 U.S. 547 (1892); to civil proceedings, McCarthy v. Arndstein, 266 U.S. 34 (1924); to congressional investigations, Watkins v. United States, 354 U.S. 178 (1957); and so on.

observed, held for the first time "that a defendant's statements might be excluded at trial despite their voluntary character under traditional principles."[101] "To supplement this new doctrine," *Miranda* established a series of "recommended" procedural safeguards designed "to provide practical reinforcement for the right against compulsory self-incrimination."[102] Then, pointing to the statement in *Miranda* that the Constitution does not necessarily require "adherence to any particular solution" to the problems posed by the " 'inherent compulsions of the interrogation process,' "[103] Mr. Justice Rehnquist maintained that the Court in *Miranda* itself "recognized that these procedural safeguards were not themselves rights protected by the Constitution."[104] He then compared "the facts in this case with the historical circumstances underlying the privilege," and concluded that there had been no violation of Tucker's rights under the Fifth Amendment since his statement "could hardly be termed involuntary as that term has been defined in the decisions of this Court."[105] Accordingly, only the "recommended procedural safeguards" of *Miranda* had been violated.[106]

Mr. Justice Rehnquist's conclusion that there is a violation of the Self-Incrimination Clause only if a confession is involuntary under traditional standards is an outright rejection of the core premises of *Miranda*. As even he conceded, the Court in *Miranda* thought that the privilege against self-incrimination offered "a more comprehensive and less subjective protection"[107] than the Due Process Clause which had been the basis of the traditional voluntariness test. Thus, recognizing that "the process of in-custody interrogation . . . contains inherently compelling pressures which work to undermine the individual's will to resist and to compel him to speak where he would not otherwise do so freely,"[108] the Court in *Miranda* had

---

[101] 417 U.S. at 443.

[102] *Id.* at 443–44.

[103] *Id.* at 444, quoting 384 U.S. at 467.

[104] *Id.* at 444.

[105] *Id.* at 444–45.

[106] For a general analysis of Justice Rehnquist's overall performance since his appointment to the Court, see Shapiro, *Mr. Justice Rehnquist: A Preliminary View*, 90 HARV. L. REV. 293 (1976).

[107] 417 U.S. at 442–43.

[108] 384 U.S. at 469. See also *id.* at 467, 474; and text *supra* at notes 33–35.

held that, in the absence of appropriate safeguards, a statement obtained in such circumstances is elicited in violation of the privilege despite its voluntary character under traditional standards. Mr. Justice Rehnquist's analysis in *Tucker*—viewing the privilege solely in terms of the voluntariness test—simply rejects this aspect of *Miranda;* the conclusion that a violation of *Miranda* is not a violation of the privilege is flatly inconsistent with the Court's declaration in *Miranda* that "[t]he requirement of warnings and waiver of rights is a fundamental with respect to the Fifth Amendment privilege."[109] And in *Orozco v. Texas*,[110] decided shortly after *Miranda*, the Court, in ruling a statement inadmissible because obtained in violation of *Miranda*, specifically stated that "the use of these admissions obtained in the absence of the required warnings was a flat violation of the Self-Incrimination Clause of the Fifth Amendment." The only evidence Mr. Justice Rehnquist offered to support his conclusion was the Court's statement in *Miranda* that the Constitution does not necessarily require "adherence to any particular solution" to the problem of custodial interrogation. He neglected to mention, however, that the *Miranda* Court added that, "unless we are shown other procedures which are at least as effective in apprising accused persons of their right of silence and in assuring a continuous opportunity to exercise it," the procedures established in *Miranda* must be obeyed.[111] Thus, although the Fifth Amendment does not require use of the precise safeguards set out in *Miranda*, it does require use of some safeguards of at least equal effectiveness. Finally, it might be noted that the conclusion that the *Miranda* safeguards are not constitutionally based poses an interesting puzzle. If these safeguards are not derived from the Constitution, whence do they spring? As Justice Douglas observed in dissent, "The Court is not free to prescribe preferred modes of interrogation absent a constitutional basis."[112] Since the Court has no supervisory power over the states, the Rehnquist analysis, if taken seriously, would

[109] *Id.* at 476. See also *id.* at 474, 491.

[110] 394 U.S. 324, 326 (1969). Just a year before *Tucker*, Mr. Justice Rehnquist observed that a violation of *Miranda* involves the violation of a "constitutional right." See United States v. Russell, 411 U.S. 423, 430 (1973).

[111] 384 U.S. at 467.

[112] 417 U.S. at 462. See also McNabb v. United States, 318 U.S. 332, 340 (1943).

seem in practical effect to overrule *Miranda*.[113] Mr. Justice Rehnquist, however, apparently did not see his analysis as having that effect, for he did not end the opinion at this point.

Having concluded that the conduct of the police did not violate Tucker's rights under the Fifth Amendment, Mr. Justice Rehnquist turned next to the question whether Henderson's testimony should have been excluded because it was the fruit of a statement elicited in violation of the *Miranda* safeguards. In *Wong Sun v. United States*,[114] the Court held that the fruits of an unconstitutional search and seizure must be suppressed. Mr. Justice Rehnquist distinguished *Wong Sun*, however, for unlike the situation in *Wong Sun*, the police conduct in *Tucker* did not violate the Constitution.[115] The implications of the earlier analysis now come to light. Although *Miranda* was not overruled, it now stands a notch beneath even the disfavored Fourth Amendment exclusionary rule in importance. Stripped of its constitutional basis, *Miranda* exists in an analytical vacuum. Thus, with *Wong Sun* out of the way, Mr. Justice Rehnquist declared that "there is no controlling precedent of this Court to guide us," and "[w]e must therefore examine the matter as a question of principle."[116]

---

[113] It is often said that the Fourth Amendment exclusionary rule is a "judicially created remedy designed to safeguard Fourth Amendment rights" even though it is not necessarily mandated by the amendment itself. United States v. Calandra, 414 U.S. 338, 348 (1974); accord Stone v. Powell, 428 U.S. 465, 486 (1976); United States v. Janis, 428 U.S. 433, 446 (1976). It might be argued that the majority's analysis in *Tucker* should be construed as suggesting that the *Miranda* safeguards are similarly "judicially created" even though not mandated by the Fifth Amendment. The difficulty with the analogy, however, is that, as Mr. Justice Rehnquist himself noted in *Tucker*, the Fourth Amendment exclusionary rule is triggered only by an actual constitutional violation, whereas the *Miranda* safeguards, according to *Tucker*, exist independently of any constitutional violation. See 417 U.S. at 445–46. Alternatively, one might interpret *Tucker* as suggesting that although the safeguards themselves are derived from the Fifth Amendment in order to prevent "real" violations of the amendment, they do not constitute personal constitutional rights belonging to any particular individual. *Cf.* United States v. Calandra, 414 U.S. at 348; Stone v. Powell, 428 U.S. at 486; United States v. Janis, 428 U.S. at 446. Such an interpretation seems foreclosed, however, by *Tucker* itself, for the majority opinion seems to have rejected the idea that the *Miranda* safeguards are even derived from the Constitution. See 417 U.S. at 444. See generally, Monaghan, *Constitutional Common Law*, 89 HARV. L. REV. 1 (1975).

[114] 371 U.S. 471 (1963).

[115] 417 U.S. at 445–46.

[116] *Id.* at 446. Interestingly, the Justice made no reference to the Court's decisions applying the fruits doctrine to violations of the Fifth Amendment. See note 96 *supra*. Presumably, these decisions would in any event be distinguished in the same manner as *Wong Sun*. Even more interestingly, he made no reference to Harrison v. United States, 392 U.S. 219 (1968), in which the Court held the fruits doctrine applicable to violations of the *McNabb-Mallory* rule. Since that rule is not derived from the Constitution, it would seem to be at least a relevant, if not controlling, precedent.

Mr. Justice Rehnquist then proceeded to resolve this "question of principle" by balancing the government's interest in using the evidence against the competing interests that might arguably be served by exclusion. One conceivable justification for the exclusion of unlawfully obtained evidence is, of course, "protection of the courts from reliance on untrustworthy evidence."[117] This might be the case, for example, when a confession is actually coerced. There is no problem of unreliability here, however, for Henderson, like any other witness, was present in court and available for cross-examination to test the veracity of his assertions. That the police learned of Henderson's existence through a violation of Tucker's "rights" does not in itself cast doubt upon the trustworthiness of Henderson's testimony. The opinion turned next to what the Court in recent years has termed the "prime purpose" of the exclusionary rule–deterrence of future unlawful police conduct.[118] The analysis is brief and to the point. Since this purpose "necessarily assumes that the police have engaged in willful, or at the very least negligent, conduct," the "deterrence rationale loses much of its force" when the police acted in "good faith."[119] In *Tucker*, the interrogation took place prior to the decision in *Miranda*. Accordingly, although the police failed to provide full warnings, they clearly acted in good faith under then-prevailing law, and exclusion of Henderson's testimony would therefore serve no significant deterrent function. Thus, in a rather nifty sleight of hand, Mr. Justice Rehnquist reaffirmed the seemingly anomalous retroactivity rule of *Johnson v. New Jersey* but then turned it to his own advantage so as to render the rule itself virtually meaningless by engrafting a new "good faith" limitation onto *Miranda*.[120]

Finally, Mr. Justice Rehnquist addressed Tucker's contention that Henderson's testimony should be held inadmissible in recognition

---

[117] 417 U.S. at 448.

[118] *Id.* at 446; see also Stone v. Powell, 428 U.S. 465, 486 (1976); United States v. Janis, 428 U.S. 433, 446 (1976); United States v. Calandra, 414 U.S. 338, 347 (1974).

[119] 417 U.S. at 447.

[120] Mr. Justice Rehnquist did note that Tucker's own statement to the police was excluded at trial under the authority of *Johnson*. 417 U.S. at 447–48, 451. Thus, he may see *Johnson* as retaining its validity at least with respect to statements of the defendant himself. It is difficult to see why exclusion of those statements is proper, however, given the Court's analysis of the deterrence issue and its creation of a "good faith" limitation. *Cf.* United States v. Peltier, 422 U.S. 531 (1975). But see text *infra* at notes 138–40.

of "the imperative of judicial integrity."[121] The "judicial integrity" rationale of the exclusionary rule can be traced to the Court's 1914 decision in *Weeks v. United States*.[122] It is founded on the notion that a judge who does not exercise his authority to exclude unlawfully obtained evidence becomes a "partner in wrongdoing" with the police officer who obtained the evidence.[123] Although this concept played a major, albeit ambiguous, role in the development of the exclusionary rule for some sixty years,[124] the Burger Court has relegated it to subordinate status.[125] In effect, the Court has interpreted, or reinterpreted, the doctrine to mean only that courts must not themselves commit or actually encourage unlawful conduct.[126] So viewed, the "judicial integrity" concept appears to merge with the deterrence rationale and, consonant with this view, the majority in *Tucker* dismissed the concept in a footnote, noting simply that it does not "provide an independent basis for excluding challenged evidence."[127] To complete his analysis of this "question of principle," Mr. Justice Rehnquist balanced the "strong interest" in "making available to the trier of fact all concededly relevant and trustworthy evidence" against the not "very persuasive" arguments supporting its exclusion.[128] Not surprisingly, he concluded that, in the circumstances of this case, use of the evidence, although derived from a violation of *Miranda*, was nevertheless proper.

---

[121] Elkins v. United States, 364 U.S. 206, 222 (1960).

[122] 232 U.S. 383 (1914).

[123] See Monaghan, note 113 *supra*, at 5.

[124] Harrison v. United States, 392 U.S. 219, 224 n.10 (1968); Terry v. Ohio, 392 U.S. 1, 12–13 (1968); Elkins v. United States, 364 U.S. 206, 222 (1960); Weeks v. United States, 232 U.S. 383, 391–92, 394 (1914). See also Olmstead v. United States, 277 U.S. 438, 470 (Holmes, J., dissenting), 484 (Brandeis, J., dissenting) (1928). The theory underlying the "judicial integrity" concept has never been extended in application to the logical extreme. Brown v. United States, 411 U.S. 223 (1973); Alderman v. United States, 394 U.S. 165 (1969); Jones v. United States, 362 U.S. 257 (1960); Walder v. United States, 347 U.S. 62 (1954). For analyses of the "judicial integrity" doctrine, see Monaghan, note 113 *supra*, at 5–6; Kaplan, *The Limits of the Exclusionary Rule*, 26 Stan. L. Rev. 1027 (1974); Schrock & Welsh, *Up from Calandra: The Exclusionary Rule as a Constitutional Requirement*, 59 Minn. L. Rev. 251, 263–71 (1974); Note, 20 U.C.L.A. L. Rev. 1129 (1973).

[125] Stone v. Powell, 428 U.S. 465, 485 (1976); United States v. Janis, 428 U.S. 433, 458 n.35 (1976); United States v. Peltier, 422 U.S. 531, 537 (1975).

[126] See authorities cited in note 125 *supra*.

[127] 417 U.S. at 450 n.25. Mr. Justice Rehnquist also dismissed Tucker's contention that the evidence should be excluded in order to preserve the adversary system. *Id.* at 449–50.

[128] *Id.* at 450. *Cf.* United States v. Nixon, 418 U.S. 683 (1974).

The implications of both aspects of the *Tucker* opinion are potentially devastating for *Miranda*. The Court deprived *Miranda* of a constitutional basis but did not explain what other basis for it there might be. Thus, *Tucker* seems certainly to have laid the groundwork to overrule *Miranda*.[129] Moreover, even if *Tucker* did not entirely dismantle *Miranda*, it clearly severed it from the privilege against compelled self-incrimination. As a result, the Court in future *Miranda* cases need not face the inherent command of the privilege that evidence obtained in violation of its dictates is *per se* inadmissible.[130] The Court is now free to balance at will. And, as the Court's treatment of *Wong Sun* illustrates, *Tucker* leaves the Court with a convenient dearth of "controlling precedents" for the future. For precedential purposes, *Miranda* now stands in isolation.[131] The advantage of this state of affairs is apparent. For example, although the Court in *Tucker* did not decide whether the "fruits" doctrine is applicable to *Miranda*, a holding of inapplicability would now seem to be within easy reach. Such a result could be premised upon the sort of balancing "analysis" employed in *Harris*, and could be achieved without unsettling the use of the doctrine when Fifth, Sixth, or even Fourth Amendment rights are involved.[132] There is, or at least might be, one final feature of this aspect of *Tucker* worth noting. In short, *Tucker* might arguably be viewed as implicitly explaining and thereby limiting *Harris*. One question left unanswered in *Harris* was the extent to which it governs, not only the use of evidence obtained in violation of *Miranda*, but evidence obtained in violation of other rights as well. If one reads *Tucker* back into *Harris*, some of the analytical gaps in that

[129] One court has suggested that *Tucker* did in fact overrule *Miranda* and reinstate the traditional voluntariness test. See United States v. Crocker, 510 F.2d 1129 (10th Cir. 1975).

[130] See authorities cited in note 63 *supra*.

[131] To be more precise, *Tucker* has paved a one-way precedential street. Although decisions in related areas which may be viewed as "protective" of individual rights are, like *Wong Sun*, distinguishable, decisions "restricting" the scope or application of such rights may be deemed "controlling" in light of *Miranda*'s lesser stature.

[132] Several courts, relying heavily upon *Tucker*, have already held the "fruits" doctrine inapplicable to *Miranda*. United States ex rel. Hudson v. Cannon, 529 F.2d 890 (7th Cir. 1976); Rhodes v. State, 91 Nev. 17 (1975); Bartram v. State, 33 Md. App. 115 (1976). Another court, relying upon *Tucker*, has held that violations of *Miranda* cannot be raised in federal habeas corpus proceedings. Richardson v. Stone, 421 F. Supp. 577 (N.D. Cal. 1976). As a final example, a court has suggested that state action decisions concerning the Fourth Amendment are, in light of *Tucker*, inapposite to the state action issue in the *Miranda* context. See Commonwealth v. Mahnke, 335 N.E.2d 660 (1975).

opinion are filled,[133] and *Harris* might then be construed exclusively as a *Miranda* decision, without any ripple effect.[134]

The second aspect of *Tucker* is equally problematic. If one assumes that the "prime purpose" of the exclusionary rule is to deter and accepts the Court's crabbed view of the "judicial integrity" concept, adoption of a good faith exception has considerable surface appeal. After all, if the officer genuinely acts in good faith, he is not culpable and, as Mr. Justice Rehnquist argued, little deterrence would seem to be gained by excluding the evidence. On closer examination, however, the issue grows more complex. Although the immediate impact of an application of the exclusionary rule is to penalize past police error, its longer-range impact should be to induce individual police officers to learn the law governing their activities and to provide an incentive to police departments to train their employees as fully and completely as possible. Use of a good faith defense undercuts this potential, for it places a premium on ignorance.[135] Moreover, a good faith defense would add an additional, and exceptionally difficult, fact-finding operation to the already overburdened criminal process. Except in the most unusual circumstances, determination of whether a mistake of law was "reasonable" is hardly an easy task.[136] The existence of such a defense could generate uncertainty and invite calculated risks on the part of the police, thereby defeating a primary goal of *Miranda*. Despite these considerations, it is at least conceivable that adoption of a good faith defense in the *Miranda* context is warranted. But surely such a radical modification of *Miranda* merits more careful attention than it received in the few conclusory sentences in *Tucker*.[137]

---

[133] For example, the unexplained conflict between *Harris* and the inherent requirement of exclusion of the privilege against self-incrimination is explained, however unsatisfactorily, in *Tucker*.

[134] See Kidd v. State, 33 Md. App. 445 (1977).

[135] See Kaplan, note 124 *supra*, at 1044.

[136] *Id.* at 1045. In *Tucker* the issue was more clouded than the Court admitted. Although the interrogation occurred prior to *Miranda*, it was post-*Escobedo*. There was no violation of *Escobedo* in *Tucker*, because "*Escobedo* is not to be broadly extended beyond the facts of that particular case." 417 U.S. at 438. But at the time of the interrogation, the meaning of *Escobedo* was unclear. See note 26 *supra*. Thus, whether the police were acting reasonably at the time under then-prevailing law is not an easy question. For other fact patterns posing difficult "good faith" issues, see Tanner v. Vincent, 541 F.2d 932 (2d Cir. 1976); Bracco v. Reed, 540 F.2d 1019 (9th Cir. 1976); Cranford v. Rodriguez, 512 F.2d 860 (10th Cir. 1975).

[137] Several Justices have suggested use of a good faith defense in the Fourth Amendment context as well. See Stone v. Powell, 428 U.S. 465, 496 (Burger, J., concurring), *id.* at 536 (White, J., dissenting) (1976); Brown v. Illinois, 422 U.S. 590, 606 (1975) (Powell, J., concurring).

Wholly apart from the merits or substantive content of the good faith defense, *Tucker* left unresolved the scope of its application. Although the good faith defense is now clearly applicable in the fruits context, Mr. Justice Rehnquist emphasized several times in *Tucker* that Tucker's own statements to the police had been excluded, thus implying that the defense might not govern use of the suspect's statements themselves.[138] Such a distinction might arguably be defensible on the theory that *per se* inadmissibility of at least the evidence derived directly from the unlawful conduct is necessary to further the general educative goals of the exclusionary rule. Nevertheless, one week after *Tucker*, the Court vacated the judgment in *Pennsylvania v. Romberger* and remanded for reconsideration in light of *Tucker*.[139] In *Romberger*, the Pennsylvania Supreme Court had held inadmissible the defendant's own statement, obtained in violation of *Miranda* in a pre-*Miranda* interrogation. The order in *Romberger* would seem to suggest that the good faith defense may not, after all, be limited to the fruits situation.[140]

IV. Oregon v. Hass: Harris Revisited

Unlike its predecessors, the Court's decision in *Oregon v. Hass*[141] answered more questions than it raised. In August 1972, bicycles were stolen from two residential garages near Klamath Falls, Oregon. On the day of the thefts, Officer Osterholme of the Oregon State Police, investigating one of the crimes, arrested Hass at his home. At Hass's trial,[142] Osterholme testified *in camera* that after being given the *Miranda* warnings, Hass admitted that he had taken two bicycles, but stated that he was not sure which one Osterholme was talking about. He said that he had returned one of the bicycles and that the other was where he had left it. Osterholme and Hass then departed in a patrol car for the site. On the way,

---

[138] 417 U.S. at 447–48, 451.

[139] 417 U.S. 964 (1974), vacating Commonwealth v. Romberger, 454 Pa. 279 (1973).

[140] On remand, the Pennsylvania Supreme Court reaffirmed its earlier result, this time relying upon its own as well as the federal Constitution, thereby preventing further review by the Supreme Court. 464 Pa. 488 (1975). Since *Tucker*, many state and lower federal courts have simply assumed that the good faith defense is applicable in all *Miranda* situations. United States v. Kinsman, 540 F.2d 1017 (9th Cir. 1976); Cranford v. Rodriguez, 512 F.2d 860 (10th Cir. 1975); Statewright v. Florida, 394 F. Supp. 849 (S.D. Fla. 1975); State v. Harbaugh, 132 Vt. 569 (1974).

[141] 420 U.S. 714 (1975).

[142] Hass was charged with only one of the thefts.

however, Hass had some misgivings and said he wished to telephone his attorney. Osterholme responded that Hass could contact his attorney when they returned to the office but, instead of returning immediately, he continued the investigation.[143] Thereafter, Hass located the stolen bicycle and, according to Osterholme, identified the houses from which the bicycles had been stolen. The trial judge, finding a clear violation of *Miranda's* command that when "the individual states that he wants an attorney, the interrogation must cease until an attorney is present,"[144] held that statements made by Hass after his request to contact his lawyer were inadmissible in the prosecution's case-in-chief. At the trial, Hass conceded that he had helped to conceal the bicycles after learning that they had been stolen but denied any involvement in the thefts themselves. To impeach this testimony, Osterholme was permitted to testify in rebuttal that Hass had identified the houses from which the bicycles had been stolen. Hass denied that he had done so, but was nevertheless convicted. The Oregon appellate courts overturned the conviction, holding the evidence inadmissible even for purposes of impeachment.[145] The Supreme Court reversed.[146]

Three facets of *Hass* merit attention. First, Mr. Justice Marshall argued in dissent that, rather than disposing of this case on the merits, the Court should properly have remanded to the Oregon Supreme Court so that it might clarify the basis of its decision. The Court has long held that when a state court rests its judgment upon independent state grounds as well as on federal law, the Court will not review the case.[147] This rule is founded on the notion that "if the same judgment would be rendered by the state court after we corrected its views of federal laws, our review could amount to

---

[143] The Court does not describe this event with complete accuracy. Although Osterholme clearly postponed their return to the office in order to continue the investigation, the Court's opinion leaves this ambiguous, thus implying that the statements might have been made on the way back to the office. See 420 U.S. at 715–16. This is irrelevant, however, to the Court's ultimate disposition of the case.

[144] 384 U.S. at 474. The Court added that "[i]f authorities conclude that they will not provide counsel during a reasonable period of time in which investigation in the field is carried out, they may refrain from doing so without violating the person's Fifth Amendment privilege so long as they do not question him during that time." *Ibid.*

[145] 13 Ore. App. 368, *aff'd* 267 Ore. 489 (1973).

[146] Justices Brennan and Marshall dissented. Justice Douglas did not participate.

[147] Jankovich v. Indiana Toll Road Comm'n, 379 U.S. 487 (1965); Herb v. Pitcairn, 324 U.S. 117 (1945); Minnesota v. National Tea Co., 309 U.S. 551 (1940); Fox Film Corp. v. Muller, 296 U.S. 207 (1935).

nothing more than an [impermissible] advisory opinion."[148] Moreover, in those cases in which it is unclear whether the state court relied upon state law, the Court has generally sought clarification.[149] The question posed by Mr. Justice Marshall was whether *Hass* was such a case. Several years before *Harris*, the Oregon Supreme Court had held that unlawfully obtained evidence could not be used to impeach.[150] The Oregon Supreme Court noted in *Hass* that it initially agreed to review the case in order to decide whether it "wished" to overrule that earlier decision in light of *Harris*. Although the court found it unnecessary to decide that question, it might have viewed *Harris* as persuasive rather than controlling authority, thus implying a state-law basis for its decision. On the other hand, in neither *Hass* nor the prior decision did the Oregon Supreme Court make any express reference to its own constitution, and this is certainly evidence that its decisions were premised solely on federal law. Nevertheless, a Court sensitive to "the respect due the highest courts of states" and seeking "scrupulously to observe" its own long-standing jurisdictional rules might properly have sought clarification in these circumstances.[151] The Court in *Hass*, however, simply declared that the decision of the Oregon Supreme Court was based exclusively upon federal law, and that review was therefore appropriate.

Second, *Hass* at least implicitly raised a question of the possible impact of *Tucker* on *Harris*. In *Harris*, the Court held that the exclusion of unlawfully obtained evidence for impeachment purposes would not sufficiently further the goal of deterring illegal police conduct to warrant such a ban. Whatever the merits of *Harris* itself, as a general matter such *per se* rules, based on speculative judgments as to deterrent effect, may arguably be justifiable so long as the Court chooses to avoid case-by-case determination as to whether the officers acted in good or bad faith. Once such determinations must in any event be made, however, the administrative advantages of a *per se* approach are substantially reduced, and once

---

[148] Herb v. Pitcairn, 324 U.S. 117, 126 (1945).

[149] California v. Krivda, 409 U.S. 33 (1972); Mental Hygiene Dept. v. Kirchner, 380 U.S. 194 (1965); Adams v. Russell, 229 U.S. 353 (1913); DeSaussure v. Gaillard, 127 U.S. 216 (1888).

[150] State v. Brewton, 247 Ore. 241 (1967).

[151] Herb v. Pitcairn, 324 U.S. 117, 128 (1945).

it is established that the violation was committed in bad faith, there would seem to be significant deterrent potential. In *Hass*, unlike *Tucker* and *Harris*,[152] the officer's conduct was flagrantly violative of a clear command of *Miranda*, and he can hardly be said to have acted in good faith. Thus, *Hass* would seem to pose the question whether evidence obtained in a bad faith violation of *Miranda* may nevertheless be used to impeach. Although the Court in *Hass* held the evidence admissible for this purpose, this argument was not presented by the parties, and *Hass* therefore should not be read as undertaking to resolve the issue.

Finally, there is the question whether the holding of *Harris* should govern *Hass*. *Harris* was premised on the assumption that a suspect is almost as likely to reveal incriminating information after the receipt of *Miranda* warnings as when no warnings are given. Accordingly, permitting the use for impeachment purposes of incriminating statements elicited without proper warnings is not likely to induce the police to violate *Miranda*. That is, the only marginally increased probability of obtaining a confession if no warnings are given would not provide sufficient incentive for the police to refuse to give warnings, for such a refusal would surrender the right to use such statements in their case-in-chief without yielding any substantial benefit in return. Whatever the force of this reasoning in *Harris*, it would be wholly unconvincing in *Hass*. In *Hass*, Officer Osterholme read Hass his rights, but when Hass asked permission to contact his attorney, Osterholme disregarded the request and continued the "interrogation." This continued interrogation resulted in the revelation of the incriminating information at issue. Had Hass been permitted to consult with his attorney, it is all but certain that the attorney would have advised him at the very least not to make any potentially incriminating statements.[153] Thus, if evidence obtained in these circumstances may be used to impeach, the officer has virtually nothing to lose and everything to gain by ignoring the request for counsel, in clear violation of *Miranda*. Although conceding that extension of *Harris* to this situation might have this effect, Mr. Justice Blackmun, speaking for the Court, simply declared that "the balance was struck in *Harris*, and we are not disposed to change it

---

[152] As in *Tucker*, the interrogation in *Harris* was pre-*Miranda*.

[153] See Enker & Elsen, note 26 *supra*, at 66; Dershowitz & Ely, note 45 *supra*, at 1220; see also Watts v. Indiana, 338 U.S. 49, 59 (1949) (Jackson, J., concurring).

now."[154] *Hass* thus made clear the true nature of the "balance" struck in *Harris. Harris* was interpreted to be based, not on a balancing of the impeachment value of the evidence against the degree of actual deterrent value of exclusion, but rather on a judgment that the state's interest in using the evidence for this purpose must always prevail, without regard to the effect this might have on the willingness of the police to comply with the dictates of *Miranda.* In practical effect, *Hass* constituted an open invitation to the police to disregard the suspect's right to the assistance of counsel.[155] And given the reasoning of *Hass*, one can only assume that, when the issue arises, the Court will similarly approve the use for impeachment purposes of statements elicited from a suspect through continued interrogation in disregard of his assertion of his right to terminate questioning, thereby undermining that aspect of *Miranda* as well.[156]

V. Michigan v. Mosley: If at First You Don't Succeed . . .

In *Michigan v. Mosley*,[157] the Court was called upon to interpret the requirement of *Miranda* that once "the individual indicates in any manner, at any time prior to or during questioning, that he wishes to remain silent, the interrogation must cease."[158] This requirement was based in part on a presumption that, in the inherently coercive atmosphere of custodial interrogation, "any statement taken after the person invokes his privilege cannot be other than the product of compulsion, subtle or otherwise."[159] The problem confronting the Court in *Mosley* was that, although *Miranda* made clear that "the interrogation must cease" when the suspect indicates that "he wishes to remain silent," it did not state the circumstances, if any, in which interrogation may be resumed.

---

[154] 420 U.S. at 723.

[155] An examination of post-*Hass* cases indicates that police have eagerly accepted the invitation. United States v. Smith, 538 F.2d 1359 (9th Cir. 1976); Murphy v. State, 336 So.2d 213 (Miss. 1976); Stevens v. State, 354 N.E.2d 727 (Ind. 1976); State v. Boone, 220 Kan. 758 (1976); Wilson v. State, 56 Ala. App. 13 (1975); Commonwealth v. Mahnke, 335 N.E.2d 660 (Mass. 1975).

[156] 384 U.S. at 445, 473–74.

[157] 423 U.S. 96 (1975).

[158] 384 U.S. at 473–74.

[159] *Id.* at 474. The procedures to be followed when the individual requests advice of counsel are set out *ibid.*

Prior to *Mosley*, the case law on this issue was in a state of disarray. Almost all courts agreed that, once the suspect asserted his right of silence, any immediate attempt to continue interrogation or to persuade him to change his mind was prohibited.[160] Faced with even a brief lapse of time before the second effort to interrogate, however, the courts were sharply divided. Under one approach, any attempt to interrogate a suspect who had previously refused to speak was deemed *per se* unlawful unless the suspect was accompanied by counsel.[161] A second approach focused on the presence or absence of changed circumstances, apparently barring any subsequent attempt to question in the absence of some intervening event which might justify renewed interrogation.[162] Most pre-*Mosley* courts, however, seem to have adopted an *ad hoc* approach to the problem, implicitly undertaking a two-pronged inquiry.[163] First, was the subsequent attempt to question merely an impermissible continuation of the prior attempt, or was it a genuinely independent event? In effect, these courts seem to have interpreted *Miranda's* requirement that "the interrogation must cease" as referring only to the initial attempt to question. Under this view, renewed efforts to interrogate were not absolutely forbidden. Second, if the subsequent attempt to interrogate was in fact an independent event, was the suspect's eventual waiver of his rights knowing, intelligent, and voluntary within the meaning of *Miranda?*[164] In making both of these determinations, these courts considered such factors as the number of prior unsuccessful attempts to interrogate;[165] the length of time

---

[160] United States v. Crisp, 435 F.2d 354 (7th Cir. 1970); United States v. Barnes, 432 F.2d 89 (9th Cir. 1970); *cf.* Combs v. Wingo, 465 F.2d 96 (6th Cir. 1972); United States v. Priest, 409 F.2d 491 (5th Cir. 1969).

[161] People v. Fioritto, 68 Cal.2d 714 (1968).

[162] Commonwealth v. Grandison, 449 Pa. 231 (1972); Commonwealth v. Jefferson, 445 Pa. 1 (1971).

[163] Hill v. Whealon, 490 F.2d 629 (6th Cir. 1974); United States v. Clark, 499 F.2d 802 (4th Cir. 1974); United States v. Collins, 462 F.2d 792 (2d Cir. 1972); Jennings v. United States, 391 F.2d 512 (5th Cir. 1968); People v. Pittman, 55 Ill. 2d 39 (1973); State v. Bishop, 272 N.C. 283 (1968).

[164] 384 U.S. at 444.

[165] United States ex rel. Doss v. Bensinger, 463 F.2d 576 (7th Cir. 1972) (two prior attempts); United States v. Collins, 462 F.2d 792 (2d Cir. 1972) (three prior attempts); People v. Naranjo, 181 Colo. 273 (1973) (two prior attempts).

between the attempts;[166] whether the attempts to interrogate concerned the same or different crimes;[167] whether new warnings were given;[168] whether the location had changed;[169] whether the same or different officers were present;[170] whether the officers present at the subsequent interrogation knew of the suspect's prior assertion of his rights;[171] whether new evidence had been obtained and revealed to the suspect prior to the subsequent interrogation;[172] and so on. As might be expected, because of the absence of any clear standards, the results under this approach were unpredictable and often inconsistent. Finally, some courts modified this approach by employing an especially high standard of knowing, intelligent, and voluntary waiver in the face of renewed attempts to question.[173] It was this confusion that the Court was asked to resolve in *Mosley*.

After receiving an anonymous tip implicating Mosley in robberies that had recently occurred at the Blue Goose Bar, the White Tower Restaurant, and the 101 Ranch Bar, the last of which resulted in a murder, Detective Cowie of the Armed Robbery Section of the Detroit Police Department arrested Mosley. Cowie brought Mosley to the Robbery, Breaking, and Entering Bureau of the Police Department, located on the fourth floor of the departmental headquarters building. He then advised Mosley of his rights and, ac-

[166] United States v. Clark, 499 F.2d 802 (4th Cir. 1974) (four hours); United States v. Jackson, 436 F.2d 39 (9th Cir. 1970) (four days); Jennings v. United States, 391 F.2d 512 (5th Cir. 1968) (one hour); State v. Robinson, 87 S.D. 375 (1973) (fifteen minutes).

[167] Hill v. Whealon, 490 F.2d 629 (6th Cir. 1974) (same crime); United States v. Vasquez, 476 F.2d 730 (5th Cir. 1973) (different crime); United States v. Collins, 462 F.2d 792 (2d Cir. 1972) (same crime); McIntyre v. New York, 329 F.Supp. 9 (E.D.N.Y. 1971) (different crime).

[168] United States v. Grady, 423 F.2d 1091 (5th Cir. 1970) (new warnings); Jennings v. United States, 391 F.2d 512 (5th Cir. 1968) (new warnings); State v. McClelland, 164 N.W. 2d 189 (Iowa 1969) (no new warnings).

[169] United States v. Choice, 392 F.Supp. 460 (E.D. Pa. 1975) (different location); People v. Pittman, 55 Ill. 2d 39 (1973) (different location); State v. Godfrey, 182 Neb. 451 (1968) (same location).

[170] United States v. Jackson, 436 F.2d 39 (9th Cir. 1970) (same officers); McIntyre v. New York, 329 F.Supp. 9 (E.D.N.Y. 1971) (different officers); People v. Pittman, 55 Ill. 2d 39 (1973) (same officers); People v. Gary, 31 N.Y. 2d 68 (1972) (different officers).

[171] Hill v. Whealon, 490 F.2d 629 (6th Cir. 1974) (knew); Jennings v. United States, 391 F.2d 512 (5th Cir. 1968) (did not know).

[172] United States ex rel. Doss v. Bensinger, 463 F. 2d 576 (7th Cir. 1972) (new evidence presented); United States v. Barnes, 432 F.2d 89 (9th Cir. 1970) (new evidence presented); People v. Naranjo, 181 Colo. 273 (1973) (new evidence presented).

[173] McIntyre v. New York, 329 F.Supp. 9 (E.D.N.Y. 1971); United States v. Bird, 293 F.Supp. 1265 (D. Mont. 1968).

cording to Cowie, attempted to question him about the robbery of the White Tower Restaurant. When Mosley said he did not want to answer any questions "about the robberies," Cowie ceased the interrogation and Mosley was taken to a ninth-floor cell block. Thereafter, Cowie informed Detective Hill of the Homicide Bureau that Mosley had been arrested.[174] About two hours after Cowie's attempt to interrogate Mosley, Hill brought him to the fifth-floor Homicide Bureau for questioning about the robbery-murder. Hill warned Mosley of his rights and, after Mosley denied any involvement in the crime, Hill informed him that another person had confessed and had named him as the "shooter."[175] Mosley then made a statement implicating himself in the homicide. At his subsequent trial for murder, Mosley objected to the use of this statement in the prosecution's case-in-chief on the grounds that it had been elicited in violation of *Miranda*.[176] The trial judge permitted the statement to be used, however, and Mosley was convicted. The Michigan Court of Appeals overturned the conviction, holding that "*Miranda* cannot be circumvented by the simple expedient of shuttling a person from one police officer to another for purposes of questioning . . . thus justifying subsequent interrogations after an election to remain silent."[177] The Supreme Court reversed.[178]

Mr. Justice Stewart, speaking for the Court, began his analysis by noting that in order to resolve this issue, one must look beyond the precise language of the key passage in *Miranda*, for any strictly literal interpretation of the phrase "the interrogation must cease" would necessarily "lead to absurd and unintended results."[179] He

---

[174] It is unclear whether Cowie informed Hill that Mosley had asserted his right to remain silent. See Michigan v. Mosley, Appendix at pp. 16, 23.

[175] During cross-examination by Mosley's attorney at the suppression hearing, Hill admitted that he had lied to Mosley and that the other person had not in fact confessed but had "denied a physical participation in the robbery." *Id.* at pp. 37, 40–41.

[176] Mosley also contended that the statement was the product of an illegal arrest, that it was inadmissible because he had not been taken before a judicial officer without unreasonable delay, and that it had been obtained through trickery and promises of leniency. The Michigan appellate courts found it unnecessary to rule on these claims, as did the Supreme Court.

[177] 51 Mich. App. 105, 108 (1974). The Michigan Supreme Court denied review. 392 Mich. 764 (1974).

[178] Mr. Justice White filed a separate concurring opinion. Justices Brennan and Marshall dissented.

[179] 423 U.S. at 102. The Justice rejected three specific literal interpretations: (1) "that a person who has invoked his 'right to silence' can never again be subjected to custodial

then observed that the Court in *Miranda* had stated that its intent was "to adopt 'fully effective means . . . to notify the person of his right of silence and to assure that the exercise of the right will be scrupulously honored.' "[180] He therefore concluded that "a reasonable and faithful interpretation" of *Miranda* requires that any statement elicited after the suspect has elected to remain silent must be held inadmissible unless his assertion of the right was " 'scrupulously honored.' "[181] Turning to the specific facts of *Mosley*, Mr. Justice Stewart held that the police conduct clearly satisfied that standard. In reaching this result, he considered it relevant that Detective Cowie had ceased the interrogation immediately when Mosley invoked his right of silence, that questioning was resumed by another officer at "another location" only after the passage of "a significant period of time," that a new set of warnings preceded the second interrogation, and that the second interrogation concerned a different and "unrelated" crime.[182]

At the outset, it should be noted that the Court in *Mosley* did not adopt the most restrictive possible interpretation of *Miranda*. In a concurring opinion,[183] Mr. Justice White maintained that when an individual makes a statement after he is properly advised of his rights, the sole question should be whether the waiver of those rights was knowing, intelligent, and voluntary. The fact of repeated attempts to interrogate, he argued, should be relevant only insofar as it bears on the ultimate issue of voluntariness. The Court recognized that this approach is flatly inconsistent with the language, spirit, and underlying assumptions of *Miranda* and rejected it as "absurd."[184] In so doing, the Court made clear that the requirement that the police "scrupulously honor" the suspect's assertion of his right to remain silent is independent of the requirement that any waiver be knowing, intelligent, and voluntary. Although the Court's refusal to embrace White's analysis is welcome, *Mosley* is not without its faults.

In holding that Mosley's rights had been "scrupulously hon-

---

interrogation by any police officer at any time or place on any subject"; (2) that even "volunteered" statements made while in custody and after an assertion of the right to remain silent must be excluded; and (3) that only an "immediate cessation of questioning" is required. *Id.* at 101–02.

[180] *Id.* at 103, quoting 384 U.S. at 479.

[181] *Id.* at 103, 104.

[182] *Id.* at 104–06.

[183] *Id.* at 107–11 (White, J., concurring).

[184] *Id.* at 102.

ored," Mr. Justice Stewart seemed to give considerable weight to the fact that the second interrogation concerned a separate and "unrelated" offense. Indeed, if the Court's standard is to be taken seriously, this fact seems critical, for in its absence one is left only with a renewed effort to question by a different member of the same police force, in a different room in the same building, only two hours after Mosley's assertion of his right not to be questioned. The Michigan courts, however, never found as a matter of fact that the initial attempt to interrogate did not concern the robbery-murder at the 101 Ranch Bar.[185] Moreover, the Michigan Court of Appeals expressed skepticism with respect to the State's contention that the robbery-murder was not raised at the Cowie interrogation.[186] The anonymous tip that triggered Mosley's arrest implicated him in three crimes. It seems unlikely that Cowie would not have mentioned the 101 Ranch Bar incident to Mosley simply because it involved a murder as well as a robbery. At the suppression hearing, Detective Cowie initially testified that he discussed "several robberies" with Mosley.[187] He then changed his testimony, and insisted that he questioned Mosley only about the White Tower Restaurant robbery.[188] According to Cowie, however, Mosley declined to say anything "about the robberies."[189] Thus, although Cowie claimed that he never asked Mosley about the robbery-murder,[190] the matter seems open to doubt, and one does not expect this sort of question to be decided in the first instance in the Supreme Court.[191]

Turning to the *Mosley* standard itself, the requirement that an individual's rights be "scrupulously honored" surely has a nice ring to it but, as formulated and applied in *Mosley*, is devoid of any clear substantive content. The Court made no effort to explain how the test is to be interpreted. It did not indicate which, if any, of the factors present in *Mosley* are essential to satisfy the standard. At

[185] The trial court made no finding of fact on this issue. See Appendix at 45.

[186] 51 Mich. App. at 108.

[187] Appendix at 9.

[188] *Id.* at 19.

[189] *Id.* at 13.

[190] *Id.* at 9.

[191] Even if Cowie did not actually mention the 101 Ranch Bar incident to Mosley, the question remains whether his refusal to talk "about the robberies" should be construed to cover that event. The Court concluded that the officers could reasonably interpret this statement as not including the robbery-murder. See 423 U.S. at 105. This conclusion seems questionable. See *id.* at 119–20 (Brennan, J., dissenting). In addition, it assumes without explanation that the critical factor is the reasonableness of the officers' interpretation rather than the actual intent of the suspect.

one level, *Mosley* might mean that in the absence of different crimes, or some similarly extraordinary factor, it is unlawful to attempt to question an individual who has previously asserted his right to remain silent. Several courts have interpreted *Mosley* in this manner.[192] At the other extreme, the Court noted at one point that *Mosley* was not a case in which "the police failed to honor a decision of a person in custody to cut off questioning, either by refusing to discontinue the interrogation upon request or by persisting in repeated efforts to wear down his resistance and make him change his mind."[193] If this passage indicates the true meaning of the "scrupulously honored" test, it would seem to differ only marginally from the approach endorsed by Mr. Justice White. Almost no courts have embraced this interpretation of *Mosley*.[194] Finally, *Mosley* might be construed as adopting a balancing approach, under which a whole set of variables must be considered in each case to determine whether the individual's rights have been "scrupulously honored." If this is what *Mosley* means, it would not seem to be a "reasonable and faithful interpretation" of *Miranda*, if for no other reason than that it could hardly be labeled a "concrete" constitutional guideline. *Miranda* sought to add clarity to the law; *Mosley*, under this view, can add only confusion. Nevertheless, most courts, probably correctly, have adopted this construction of *Mosley*. As a consequence, the post-*Mosley* case law is as unpredictable and inconsistent as it was before.[195]

Ultimately there is the question whether the *Mosley* standard is, as a substantive matter, compatible with *Miranda*. The primary concern of *Miranda* in this context was that, in the already inherently coercive atmosphere of custodial interrogation, repeated efforts to question an individual who has previously decided to remain silent can effectively wear down his will to resist and lead him to speak where he would not otherwise do so freely. Moreover, any attempt to determine in each case whether these pressures in fact produced

---

[192] United States v. Maddox, 413 F. Supp. 60 (W.D. Okla. 1976); Commonwealth v. Walker, 368 A.2d 1284 (1977); Matter of T.T.T., 365 A.2d 366 (D.C. Ct. App. 1976).

[193] 423 U.S. at 105–06.

[194] But *cf.* People v. Almond, 67 Mich. App. 713 (1976).

[195] Williams v. Ohio, 547 F.2d 40 (6th Cir. 1976); United States v. Clayton, 407 F. Supp. 204 (E.D. Wis. 1976); United States v. Jakakas, 423 F. Supp. 564 (E.D. N.Y. 1976); State v. Clemons, 27 Ariz. App. 193 (1976); State v. Lee, 114 Ariz. 101 (1976); Hearne v. State, 534 S.W.2d 703 (Tex. Ct. Crim. App. 1976).

a "coerced" statement would prove hopelessly difficult. Due to the very complexity of the task, many confessions which were not truly "voluntary" might simply slip by. Thus, *Miranda* erected a presumption that any statement elicited through interrogation after the person has invoked his privilege is "the product of compulsion."[196] The problem in *Mosley*, then, is to determine the circumstances in which the potentially coercive impact of renewed attempts to question may be held to be so low as to justify a waiver of this presumption. *Mosley* concluded that this is the case when the individual's assertion of his rights was "scrupulously honored," apparently on the theory that if the individual knows that his rights have been respected in the past, he will not be afraid to assert them again and will not feel that it is a mere exercise in futility.[197] However sound the theory, it is impossible to determine from *Mosley* itself whether the Court will apply the doctrine in strict conformity with that theory.[198] In any event, the inherent ambiguity of the concept would seem to make its utility as a practical matter questionable at best.

Is there a realistic alternative? In his dissenting opinion in *Mosley*, Mr. Justice Brennan argued that the police should not be permitted to attempt to question an individual who has previously invoked his privilege unless the individual is accompanied by counsel.[199] This approach has the obvious advantage of clarity, is sensitive to *Miranda's* concern with the coercive impact of renewed efforts to interrogate, and is consistent with *Miranda's* recognition that presence of counsel is in itself an important safeguard in offsetting the inherent coercion of custodial interrogation.[200] The majority's only response to this suggested alternative was to refer to a passage in *Miranda*. In its discussion of the proper procedures to be followed when a suspect requests counsel, the Court observed in *Miranda*

---

[196] 384 U.S. at 474.

[197] 423 U.S. at 104.

[198] That the two attempts to question Mosley at least arguably concern different crimes would seem to be an important consideration under this theory. For in that situation, the second effort to interrogate does not indicate a lack of respect for the prior assertion of silence, and the potential coercive impact would therefore seem to be relatively slight. Given this fact, the actual decision in *Mosley* is not necessarily inconsistent with the theory underlying its standard.

[199] See 423 U.S. at 116 (Brennan, J., dissenting). The dissent also suggested that a renewed effort to question might be permissible at arraignment. *Ibid.*

[200] See 384 U.S. at 466, 474 n.44. This approach would not, of course, prohibit the suspect himself from changing his mind and speaking on his own initiative.

that "[i]f the individual states that he wants an attorney, the interrogation must cease until an attorney is present."[201] As sole support for its rejection of Brennan's approach, the Court in *Mosley* declared that *Miranda* "directed that 'the interrogation must cease until an attorney is present' only '[i]f the individual states that he wants an attorney.' "[202] If, as some commentators have suggested,[203] this statement was intended to assert that *Miranda* itself rejected the Brennan position, it is patently false. On the other hand, if it was intended to mean only that *Miranda* did not specifically adopt the Brennan approach, it is accurate, but not an adequate response, for Mr. Justice Brennan agreed that *Miranda* did not expressly resolve the issue presented in *Mosley*. Although the Brennan view seems to have considerable merit,[204] the Court in *Mosley* simply refused to address it. Instead, it chose to chart a middle course which offers only ambiguous protection to the accused and virtually no guidance to the police or the courts who must live with the rule.

VI. Baxter v. Palmigiano: Miranda and the Prison Disciplinary Hearing

In *Wolff v. McDonnell*,[205] the Court held that an inmate has no right under the Due Process Clause to the assistance of counsel, either retained or appointed, at a prison disciplinary hearing.[206] Shortly thereafter, the Courts of Appeals for the First and Ninth Circuits, in separate suits for injunctive relief, held that, despite

---

[201] *Id.* at 474.

[202] 423 U.S. at 104 n.10, quoting 384 U.S. at 474.

[203] See, *e.g.*, Comment, 13 San Diego L. Rev. 861 (1976).

[204] Even if one accepts the basic premises of the position, it might nevertheless be reasonable to permit the police to attempt to question the suspect about a wholly different crime in the absence of counsel. See note 198 *supra*. Mr. Justice Brennan apparently rejected such an "exception." In his concurring opinion, Mr. Justice White criticized the dissent's approach, as well as that of the Court, on the ground that it prevents the police from keeping the suspect informed of the evidence against him, thereby depriving the suspect himself of relevant information. See 423 U.S. at 109 n.1 (White, J., concurring). This criticism is unpersuasive, for if the suspect wants to know the nature of the evidence against him at any point in time, he can simply ask. Moreover, the practice of continually notifying the accused of the evidence against him would seem to have a potentially substantial coercive impact.

[205] 418 U.S. 539 (1974).

[206] The Court did suggest, however, that there might be some special circumstances, as when the inmate is illiterate, in which assistance of a counsel-substitute is required. *Id.* at 570.

Wolff, the inmate does have a right to counsel under *Miranda* when the conduct which is the subject of the hearing might constitute a crime as well as a violation of prison regulations.[207] In reaching this result, these courts relied heavily upon the Court's 1968 decision in *Mathis v. United States*.[208] In *Mathis*, a federal tax investigator questioned an individual who was already in prison on other charges about certain tax returns in a routine tax investigation. The Court, noting that the individual was formally in "custody" and that such investigations frequently result in criminal prosecutions, held that statements elicited in these circumstances without full compliance with *Miranda* are inadmissible in a subsequent criminal trial. In the prison disciplinary hearing cases, the Courts of Appeals reasoned that *Mathis* must logically govern the situations before them as well. The Supreme Court granted certiorari in both cases,[209] consolidated them for argument and decision, and reversed.[210]

The Court disposed of the issue in a single, brief paragraph:[211]

> Neither *Miranda*, *supra*, nor *Mathis*, *supra*, has any substantial bearing on the question whether counsel must be provided at '[p]rison disciplinary hearings [which] are not part of a criminal prosecution.' *Wolff* v. *McDonnell*, *supra*, at 556. The Court has never held, and we decline to do so now, that the requirements of those cases must be met to render pretrial statements admissible in other than criminal cases.

The underlying assumption of this paragraph seems to be that *Miranda* is violated only when a statement elicited without full compliance with its demands is used in a criminal prosecution. The mere fact of interrogation without compliance with *Miranda* is not in itself unlawful, and the use of statements obtained in such cir-

---

[207] Clutchette v. Procunier, 510 F.2d 613 (9th Cir. 1975); Palmigiano v. Baxter, 510 F.2d 534 (1st Cir. 1974). Both suits were filed under 42 U.S.C. § 1983. *Clutchette* was a class action, in which the plaintiffs sought declarative as well as injunctive relief. *Palmigiano* was an individual action, in which the plaintiff sought damages as well as an injunction.

[208] 391 U.S. 1 (1968).

[209] See 421 U.S. 1010 (1975).

[210] Baxter v. Palmigiano, 425 U.S. 308 (1976). Justices Brennan and Marshall dissented on this point but relied upon the Due Process Clause without addressing the *Miranda* issue. *Id.* at 325 (Brennan, J., concurring in part and dissenting in part). Mr. Justice Stevens did not participate. The Court reversed the Courts of Appeals on several other issues outside the scope of this article.

[211] 425 U.S. at 315.

cumstances in anything other than a criminal prosecution is not prohibited. Since neither of these cases specifically raised the issue, the Court did not decide whether *Mathis* forbids the use in a criminal case of statements elicited in this sort of situation without compliance with *Miranda*. *Baxter* did hold, however, that statements obtained without use of the *Miranda* safeguards may be used in any proceeding other than a criminal prosecution. This would presumably include not only prison disciplinary hearings, but also parole and probation revocation hearings, civil actions brought by the government, and so on.[212] The Court has had considerable difficulty with such issues in the Fourth Amendment context.[213] In *Baxter*, however, the Court attempted to settle the problem in the *Miranda* context in two sentences.

The Court's holding in *Baxter* rested upon two key assumptions about the nature of *Miranda* and, inferentially, about the nature of the privilege against self-incrimination. First, the Court's conclusion that the fact of interrogation without compliance with *Miranda* is not in itself unlawful seems to assume that the privilege is violated only when compelled evidence is actually used against the defendant in a criminal case. The mere act of compelling the statement is not unconstitutional. Although the precise wording of the Clause might lend itself to such an interpretation, the Court had never before limited it in this manner. In a long line of decisions, the Court has consistently held that an individual may assert the privilege "in any proceeding, civil or criminal, administrative or judicial, investigatory or adjudicatory."[214] These decisions are founded on the notion that the privilege "has two primary interrelated facets."[215] The privilege guards not only against the use of statements elicited by

---

[212] The Court has held that parole and probation revocation hearings are not phases of the "criminal prosecution." Gagnon v. Scarpelli, 411 U.S. 778 (1973); Morrissey v. Brewer, 408 U.S. 471 (1972).

[213] See United States v. Janis, 428 U.S. 433 (1976).

[214] Kastigar v. United States, 406 U.S. 441, 444 (1972); see Counselman v. Hitchcock, 142 U.S. 547 (1892) (grand jury); McCarthy v. Arndstein, 266 U.S. 34 (1924) (civil action); Watkins v. United States, 354 U.S. 178 (1957) (congressional investigation); In re Groban, 352 U.S. 330 (1957) (administrative investigation); In re Gault, 387 U.S. 1 (1967) (juvenile proceedings). It should be noted that if the sole concern of these cases was with the use of evidence, it would be sufficient simply to allow the defendant to move to suppress if and when that problem arises. These cases clearly go beyond that. See Lefkowitz v. Cunningham, 97 S. Ct. 2132 (1977); Maness v. Meyers, 419 U.S. 449 (1975).

[215] Murphy v. Waterfront Comm'n, 378 U.S. 52, 57 n.6 (1964).

compulsion, but also against the very act of compelling such statements whether or not they are ever actually used in a criminal case. Indeed, only two weeks before *Baxter*, the Court declared that "the privilege protects against the use of compelled statements as well as guarantees the right to remain silent absent immunity."[216] The Court's assumption in *Baxter* that the failure to comply with *Miranda* is not in itself unlawful either flies in the face of this precedent or is premised upon a disassociation of *Miranda* from the privilege. The Court, of course, provided the groundwork for the latter in *Tucker*. But even if *Tucker* explains *Baxter*, one might reasonably have expected some discussion of the issue or, at the very least, some reference to *Tucker*. The Court, however, offered only a bald, unsupported conclusion.[217]

The second fundamental assumption of the Court in *Baxter* is that statements elicited without the *Miranda* safeguards may be used in any proceeding other than a criminal prosecution. Once again, the language of the Clause—including, as it does, the phrase "in any criminal case"—may seem to support this assumption. But once it is established that the privilege may be violated by the very act of compelling self-incriminating statements, it may arguably be necessary to create an exclusionary rule similar to that employed in the Fourth Amendment context to deter such violations. And the need for such a rule may be particularly great when, as in the prison disciplinary hearing situation, use of the evidence in a criminal case "falls outside the offending officer's zone of primary interest."[218] Although the Court has never squarely addressed this issue with respect to the privilege,[219] it simply assumed it out of existence with

[216] Garner v. United States, 424 U.S. 648, 653 (1976). See also Maness v. Meyers, 419 U.S. 449 (1975).

[217] It should be noted that the Court's assumption in *Baxter* that the act of obtaining a confession without *Miranda* warnings is not in itself unlawful seems inconsistent with the assumption of all the Justices participating in *Harris*, *Tucker*, and *Hass*. In each of those cases, the Justices proceeded on the assumption that a relevant issue was whether use of the evidence would undercut the deterrent force of *Miranda*. But if the failure to give warnings is not in itself unlawful, the deterrent concern seems irrelevant. If the only illegality consists of use of the evidence, that can be handled simply by excluding the evidence when the situation arises; it is unnecessary to consider whether allowing the evidence to be used will encourage the police not to give warnings.

[218] United States v. Janis, 428 U.S. 433, 458 (1976).

[219] The Court's assumption in its immunity decisions that a guarantee that compelled testimony and its fruits will not be used in a criminal prosecution is coextensive with the privilege, Kastigar v. United States, 406 U.S. 441 (1972), does not settle the issue. For

respect to *Miranda*. In sum, whether or not one agrees with the result in *Baxter*, the Court's opinion falls short of the ideal. In its rush to judgment, the Court simply refused to come to grips with the complex and intriguing questions presented.

VII. Doyle v. Ohio: Miranda and Impeachment by Silence

In *Doyle v. Ohio*,[220] decided in 1976, the Court faced the question whether a prosecutor may constitutionally impeach a defendant's exculpatory story by bringing out on cross-examination the defendant's failure to relate the story to the police after receiving *Miranda* warnings at the time of his arrest.[221] William Bonnell, a well-known "street person" with a long criminal record, arranged to assist local narcotics investigators in setting up drug dealers in return for prosecutorial help in his latest legal problems. Shortly thereafter he informed the agents that he had arranged to buy ten pounds of marijuana from defendants Doyle and Wood. The agents provided Bonnell with funds and, after the transaction allegedly occurred, Doyle and Wood were arrested and charged with selling marijuana. At their separate trials, the defendants testified that Bonnell had framed them and that in fact he had attempted to sell the marijuana to them. Unfortunately for the state, this explanation of the event was "not entirely implausible," and there was little if any direct evidence to contradict it.[222] In order to undercut the defendants' explanation and to impeach their credibility, the prosecutor was permitted in each case to reveal to the jury through cross-examination that neither Doyle nor Wood, after being advised of his rights under *Miranda*, had offered this explanation to the police

---

once immunity is granted, there is no longer any unlawful compulsion to self-incriminate and therefore no unlawful conduct to deter. For a discussion of the possibility of establishing a Fourth Amendment–type exclusionary rule for Fifth Amendment violations, see Comment, 73 Colum. L. Rev. 1288 (1973).

[220] 426 U.S. 610 (1976). *Doyle* was consolidated for purposes of argument and decision with *Wood v. Ohio*, a companion case arising out of the same event.

[221] The evidentiary theory underlying the use of silence as proof is that an individual confronted with false accusations of guilt will ordinarily deny the accusations. Thus, silence in this context may be viewed as an admission of the truth of the accusations. See McCormick, note 19 *supra*, at §§ 161, 270. When, as in *Doyle*, the silence is used only to impeach, the inference is that the individual's failure to tell the exculpatory story in the face of an accusation indicates that the story is false.

[222] 426 U.S. at 613. Although several narcotics agents observed the transaction, only one claimed actually to have seen the defendants pass the marijuana to Bonnell.

at the time of his arrest.[223] The defendants were convicted and the Ohio appellate courts affirmed. The Supreme Court reversed.[224]

The leading decision on the use of a defendant's silence for evidentiary purposes is *Griffin v. California*,[225] in which the Court held that an instruction to the jury permitting it to construe the defendant's failure to testify as evidence of guilt constituted an unconstitutional "penalty" on the exercise of the privilege against self-incrimination.[226] A year later, the Court in *Miranda* extended *Griffin* to silence in the context of custodial interrogation, declaring that "it is impermissible to penalize an individual for exercising his Fifth Amendment privilege," and that the prosecution therefore may not "use at trial the fact that he stood mute or claimed his privilege in the face of accusation."[227] The problem confronting the Court in *Doyle* was that *Griffin* itself dealt specifically only with the use of a defendant's silence as substantive evidence of guilt. It did not address the question whether such evidence may be used to impeach. Moreover, some forty years before *Griffin*, the Court, in *Raffel v.*

---

[223] In addition, the defendants were cross-examined as to their failure to tell this version of the event at their preliminary hearings or at any other time prior to the trials. Finally, each defendant was cross-examined about this matter when he testified as a defense witness at the other's trial. The Court found it unnecessary in *Doyle*, however, to rule on the constitutionality of these tactics. See 426 U.S. at 616 n.6.

[224] Mr. Justice Stevens, joined by Justices Blackmun and Rehnquist, dissented.

[225] 380 U.S. 609 (1965).

[226] *Id.* at 614. The precise analytical support of *Griffin* is obscure. Since the defendant did not actually testify, it cannot be said that he was "compelled" to incriminate himself. Thus, the "penalty" concept added a new dimension to analysis of the privilege. In a series of subsequent decisions, the Court has extended the penalty doctrine to situations in which assertion of the privilege results in some state-imposed economic loss. Lefkowitz v. Turley, 414 U.S. 70 (1973); Uniformed Sanitation Men Ass'n v. Comm'r of Sanitation, 392 U.S. 280 (1968); Gardner v. Broderick, 392 U.S. 273 (1968); Garrity v. New Jersey, 385 U.S. 493 (1967). For analyses of the application of this doctrine in other contexts, see Chaffin v. Stynchcombe, 412 U.S. 17 (1973); Brooks v. Tennessee, 406 U.S. 605 (1972); McGautha v. California, 402 U.S. 183 (1971); Simmons v. United States, 390 U.S. 377 (1968). For an excellent discussion of the doctrine, see Comment, 123 U. Pa. L. Rev. 940, 954–61 (1975).

[227] 384 U.S. at 468 n.37. Once it is established that the privilege is available in the context of custodial interrogation, see text *supra* at notes 28–57, this extension of *Griffin* seems eminently reasonable, for the nature and extent of the "penalty" seem virtually identical in the two situations. Accordingly, courts have agreed that the defendant's silence during custodial interrogation may not be used as substantive evidence of guilt. United States v. Faulkenbery, 472 F.2d 879 (9th Cir. 1973); United States v. Nolan, 416 F.2d 588 (10th Cir. 1969); United States v. Nielsen, 392 F.2d 849 (7th Cir. 1968); United States v. Mullings, 364 F.2d 173 (2d Cir. 1966). Indeed, several courts reached this conclusion even before *Griffin* and *Miranda*. Helton v. United States, 221 F.2d 338 (5th Cir. 1955); United States v. LoBiondo, 135 F.2d 130 (2d Cir. 1943).

United States,[228] upheld the constitutionality of this tactic. At his first trial, Raffel did not take the stand. That trial ended in a hung jury, and upon retrial Raffel elected to testify in order to deny the truth of some of the evidence against him. On cross-examination, the prosecutor was permitted to bring to the jury's attention his failure to testify earlier, on the theory that this tended to undercut the credibility of his testimony. The Court affirmed the conviction, noting that Raffel had completely waived his privilege by deciding to testify, and that use of the evidence in these circumstances would not deter defendants from remaining silent at their first trial, because the possibility of a second trial would then seem remote. In a series of subsequent decisions, the Court limited the evidentiary impact of *Raffel*, holding in each instance that use of the defendant's silence to impeach was impermissible because the probative value of the evidence was outweighed by the risk of undue prejudice to the defendant.[229] Although these decisions were premised on the Court's supervisory powers over the federal courts and did not expressly consider the constitutional issue, their reasoning seemed substantially to undercut the force of *Raffel* at the constitutional level as well.[230] To complicate matters still further, the Court's decisions in *Harris* and *Hass* placed considerable emphasis on the distinction between the use of evidence for impeachment rather than substantive purposes and stressed the importance of the state's interest in challenging the veracity of the defendant. Accordingly, those decisions might be seen as at least implicitly revitalizing *Raffel*. Given this background, it seems obvious that the issue presented in *Doyle* could not be resolved by straightforward resort to precedent alone.[231]

---

[228] 271 U.S. 494 (1926).

[229] United States v. Hale, 422 U.S. 171 (1975); Stewart v. United States, 366 U.S. 1 (1961); Grunewald v. United States, 353 U.S. 391 (1957). See also Johnson v. United States, 318 U.S. 189 (1943).

[230] *Compare* United States v. Hale, 422 U.S. 171, 180 and n.7 (1975), and Grunewald v. United States, 353 U.S. 391, 423–24 (1957), *with* Raffel v. United States, 271 U.S. 494, 499 (1926). See also Johnson v. United States, 318 U.S. 189, 196–97 (1943). The Court did attempt, however, to reconcile these decisions with *Raffel*.

[231] Prior to *Doyle*, most state and lower federal courts held that the defendant's silence during custodial interrogation could not constitutionally be used to impeach. Minor v. Black, 527 F.2d 1 (6th Cir. 1975); United States v. Anderson, 498 F.2d 1038 (D.C. Cir. 1974), *aff'd sub nom.* United States v. Hale, 422 U.S. 171 (1975); Johnson v. Patterson, 475 F.2d 1066 (10th Cir. 1973); Fowle v. United States, 410 F.2d 48 (9th Cir. 1969); People v. Bobo, 390 Mich. 355 (1973); State v. Anderson, 110 Ariz. 238 (1973). But

Perhaps not surprisingly, then, the Court in *Doyle* chose simply to sidestep the question whether use of the defendant's silence to impeach violated the privilege against self-incrimination, holding instead that, in the circumstances of this case, the practice constituted a deprivation of due process. Mr. Justice Powell, speaking for the Court, began by observing that, in accordance with *Miranda*, the defendants were advised at the time of their arrest that they had a right to remain silent. He then reasoned that, although "the *Miranda* warnings contain no express assurance that silence will carry no penalty, such assurance is implicit to any person who receives the warnings."[232] Thus, although recognizing that prosecutors must ordinarily be granted "wide leeway in the scope of impeachment cross-examination" in order to detect and prevent perjury, the Court nevertheless concluded that, given the implicit assurance of the warnings, it is "fundamentally unfair" to allow the arrestee's silence to be used to impeach an explanation subsequently offered at trial.[233] In short, it violates due process for the government to inform an individual that he may do something free of any adverse consequences and then later penalize him for doing that very thing. Exclusion of the evidence in *Doyle*, it should be noted, seems inconsistent with one interpretation of *Harris*, where the Court suggested that unlawfully obtained evidence may be used to impeach the defendant so long as it satisfies legal standards of trustworthiness. One might argue, I suppose, that *Harris* is distinguishable because the evidence in *Doyle* was not obtained unlawfully—the illegality arose solely out of its use at trial. That distinction does not seem useful, however, in light of the fact that the Court in *Baxter* viewed *Miranda* itself in precisely that manner. Thus, although the Court did not appear to recognize the inconsistency, *Doyle* seems clearly to limit *Harris*. At the same time, however, the Court's analysis in *Doyle* did not in any sense constitute a reaffirmation of *Miranda*. Rather, the fact that the defendants in this case were informed of their rights under *Miranda* was simply an unalterable given. The result in *Doyle* would have been no different had the arresting officers been under no legal obligation to provide the warnings. Interestingly, the sole authority cited by Mr. Justice Powell for his approach in *Doyle* was a case in which the Court employed similar

---

see United States ex rel. Burt v. New Jersey, 475 F.2d 234 (3rd Cir. 1973); United States v. Ramirez, 441 F.2d 950 (5th Cir. 1971); Thomas v. State, 285 So.2d 148 (Miss. 1973).

[232] 426 U.S. at 618.

[233] *Id.* at 617 n. 7, 618.

reasoning where the defendant erroneously had been permitted to invoke the privilege.[234]

In any event, the remaining issue in *Doyle* was whether these defendants could themselves properly take advantage of the estoppel theory. In his dissenting opinion, Mr. Justice Stevens maintained that, since the defendants did not specifically testify that their failure to tell their version of the event to the police was an exercise of the right to remain silent, the Court's theory had no application in this case. In his view, the proper approach would be to permit the defendant to explain his motivations to the jury and then to allow the jurors to evaluate the probative value of the evidence accordingly. As Mr. Justice Powell recognized, however, "every post-arrest silence is insolubly ambiguous because of what the State is required to advise the person arrested."[235] The motivations for silence are so inherently subtle and complex that it is simply unrealistic to expect a juror to disentangle them with any degree of certainty. Moreover, once the cat is out of the bag, there is a substantial danger that the jury will draw an impermissible inference of guilt from the very fact that the defendant chose to remain silent.[236] Thus, as Mr. Justice Powell concluded, "the unfairness occurs when the prosecution, in the presence of the jury, is allowed to undertake impeachment on the basis of what may be the exercise of that right."[237] In practical effect, then, the Court embraced a prophylactic rule at least vaguely reminiscent of the sort of analysis prevalent in *Miranda.*

Doyle, however, left several important questions unanswered. First, suppose the arresting officer, in clear violation of *Miranda*, did not advise the defendant of his rights. May the defendant's silence be used to impeach his testimony at trial? *Doyle* does not govern because the defendant was not misled as to the nature of his rights. It seems anomalous to permit use of the defendant's silence to impeach when *Miranda* is violated, but not when it is obeyed. Such a distinction, however, is consistent with *Doyle.* To avoid this dilemma, one might argue that the very existence of this anomaly would provide an incentive to the police to refuse to advise suspects

---

[234] See Johnson v. United States, 318 U.S. 189 (1943), discussed at 426 U.S. at 618–19 n.9.

[235] 426 U.S. at 617.

[236] See United States v. Hale, 422 U.S. 171, 180 (1975).

[237] 426 U.S. at 619 n.10.

of their rights, and that use of the evidence should therefore be prohibited even if the police fail to provide warnings. Given the Court's treatment of the deterrence issue in *Harris* and *Hass*, however, such an argument seems likely to fail. Second, suppose the arresting officer informed the defendant not only of his rights under *Miranda*, but also that if he elects to exercise his right to remain silent, and later testifies in his own defense at trial, his silence at this point might then be used to impeach his credibility as a witness. The use of such an additional warning would seem to eliminate the Court's concerns in *Doyle* but would create new problems, for it would almost certainly confuse the suspect and intensify the already coercive atmosphere of custodial interrogation.[238] Nevertheless, the Court in *Doyle* at least hinted that such an additional warning might well be permissible.[239] Finally, *Doyle* left unresolved the question whether a defendant's silence during custodial interrogation may be used to impeach if *Miranda* itself is ever overruled.

All of these problems would of course be eliminated were the Court to hold, under the *Griffin* principle, that this use of the defendant's silence constitutes an impermissible penalty on the exercise of the privilege against self-incrimination.[240] Although a defendant in Doyle's position would seem to have a strong claim to the protection of *Griffin*,[241] the Court in recent years has taken an in-

[238] Indeed, the Court in *Miranda* specifically condemned police suggestions to the accused that "silence in the face of accusation is itself damning and will bode ill when presented to a jury." 384 U.S. at 468.

[239] The Court noted that the defendant " 'was not informed here that his silence, as well as his words, could be used against him at trial.' " 426 U.S. at 619, quoting United States v. Hale, 422 U.S. 171, 183 (1975) (White, J., concurring).

[240] Alternatively, the Court, building upon its own nonconstitutional decisions, see cases cited in note 229 *supra*, might examine the use of silence to impeach on a case-by-case basis in terms of a due process standard of trustworthiness. *Cf.* Minor v. Black, 527 F.2d 1 (6th Cir. 1975). Such an approach would limit, although not eliminate, the problems noted in the text.

[241] The "penalty" that troubled the Court in *Griffin* arose out of the instruction to the jury that it might properly view the defendant's failure to testify at trial as evidence of guilt. The penalty in *Doyle* seems at least equally severe. Although technically the silence in the *Doyle* situation is used for impeachment purposes, such limiting instructions are woefully ineffective and, as a practical matter, once the jury learns of the evidence it is likely to use it for substantive purposes as well. United States v. Hale, 422 U.S. 171, 180 (1975), and authorities cited in note 60 *supra*. It might be argued, however, that the defendant in *Doyle* can avoid this problem simply by declining to testify at trial. That in itself would seem to be a substantial penalty and, in any event, such a tactic would only exacerbate the situation, for now the defendant is remaining silent before the jury itself. It might also be argued that, at the time of arrest, the defendant is so far removed from

creasingly dim view of the penalty doctrine.[242] Indeed, only two months before *Doyle*, the Court held in *Baxter* that officials at a prison disciplinary hearing may constitutionally draw adverse inferences against the inmate from his refusal to testify, even though the hearing concerns conduct which could constitute a crime under state law. The Court distinguished *Griffin* on essentially two grounds. First, unlike the situation in *Griffin*, prison disciplinary proceedings involve "important state interests other than conviction for crime."[243] And second, since the stakes at such hearings are not as high as at criminal trials, evidentiary use of the silence does not constitute as serious a penalty. If such considerations are sufficient to distinguish *Baxter* from *Griffin*, they might arguably be sufficient to distinguish *Doyle* as well. As *Harris* emphasized, the state's need to impeach a defendant's credibility is founded not only upon its interest in "conviction for crime," but also upon its independent interest in preventing and detecting perjury. Moreover, if the penalty in *Baxter* is not of sufficient magnitude to trigger *Griffin*, use of the defendant's silence at a criminal trial for impeachment rather than substantive purposes might likewise be insufficient.[244]

VIII. Beckwith v. United States and Oregon v. Mathiason: Miranda without Custody?

In *Beckwith v. United States*,[245] two special agents of the Intelligence Division of the Internal Revenue Service met with

trial that a concern that his silence might eventually be used to impeach him simply will not affect his decision whether to remain silent at this early stage in the proceedings. As noted earlier, the Court made precisely this sort of argument in *Raffel*. Whatever the merits of this concern in the circumstances of *Raffel*, it does not seem particularly persuasive here. Once the defendant is taken into custody, he knows that a trial may follow, and although the "chilling effect" may not be as great in *Doyle* as in *Griffin*, it cannot be dismissed entirely. Finally, it should be noted that the jury will always be aware of defendant's silence at trial, even if no instruction is given. Thus, the penalty in *Griffin* consists only of the additional impact of the prohibited instruction. In the *Doyle* situation, however, the jury will know nothing of the defendant's prior decision to remain silent unless it is expressly brought to its attention. In this sense, then, the actual penalty is greater in *Doyle* than in *Griffin*. Thus, given all these considerations, although the question is always one of degree, *Griffin* should govern the situation presented in *Doyle*.

[242] Chaffin v. Stynchcombe, 412 U.S. 17 (1973); McGautha v. California, 402 U.S. 183 (1971); but see Brooks v. Tennessee, 406 U.S. 605 (1972). See also Comment, note 226 *supra*, at 954–61.

[243] 425 U.S. at 319.

[244] But see note 242 *supra*.

[245] 425 U.S. 341 (1976).

Beckwith in a private home where he occasionally stayed. The agents informed Beckwith that one of their functions was to investigate the possibility of criminal tax fraud, and that they were then investigating his federal income tax liability for the years 1966 through 1971. Beckwith answered their questions and turned over several relevant documents. When the interview ended, the agents left.[246] Thereafter, Beckwith was formally charged with evasion of income taxes. Prior to trial, Beckwith, although conceding that at the time of the interview he was not "in custody or otherwise deprived of his freedom of action in any significant way" within the meaning of *Miranda*, nevertheless moved to suppress all statements he made to the agents on the ground that he had not been given the warnings mandated by *Miranda*.[247] The district court denied the motion, holding that, in the absence of custodial interrogation, no warnings were necessary. The United States Court of Appeals for the District of Columbia Circuit agreed with this conclusion,[248] and the Supreme Court affirmed.[249]

The Court's holding that *Miranda* does not govern this situation seems reasonable. Although at the time of the interview the investigation had "focused" on Beckwith in the sense that he was already suspected of criminal activity, *Miranda* was not premised upon that factor alone. Rather, the primary concern of *Miranda*, as the Court recognized in *Beckwith*, was that the inherently coercive atmos-

---

[246] During the interview, Beckwith stated that the relevant records were at his place of employment. The agents met Beckwith there later and picked up the records.

[247] In fact, the agents did provide partial warnings. Thus, they informed him that he could not be compelled to provide self-incriminating information, that any information he provided could be used against him, and that he could seek the assistance of an attorney. They did not warn him, however, of his absolute right to remain silent, or that counsel would be appointed if necessary.

[248] 510 F.2d 741 (D.C.Cir. 1975). Almost all courts that had previously addressed this question had reached the same result. United States v. Robson, 477 F.2d 13 (9th Cir. 1973); United States v. Stribling, 437 F. 2d 765 (6th Cir. 1971); United States v. MacLeod, 436 F.2d 947 (8th Cir. 1971); United States v. Prudden, 424 F.2d 1021 (5th Cir. 1970); United States v. Mackiewicz, 401 F.2d 219 (2d Cir. 1968); but see United States v. Oliver, 505 F.2d 301 (7th Cir. 1974); United States v. Lockyer, 448 F.2d 417 (10th Cir. 1971); United States v. Dickerson, 413 F.2d 1111 (7th Cir. 1969). Several commentators agree with the minority view. See Note, 20 Syracuse L. Rev. 725 (1969); Lay, *Right to Counsel in Criminal Tax Investigations*, 43 Ind.L.J. 69 (1967); Duke, *Prosecution for Attempts to Evade Income Tax: A Discordant View of a Procedural Hybrid*, 76 Yale L.J. 1 (1966).

[249] Mr. Justice Marshall filed a separate concurring opinion. Mr. Justice Brennan dissented. Mr. Justice Stevens did not participate.

phere of in-custody interrogation could operate to overbear the individual's will to resist and make it difficult, if not impossible, for the individual freely and effectively to assert his rights in the absence of special safeguards. Thus, although the "focus" concept may play an important role with respect to other aspects of Fifth Amendment analysis,[250] it is not in itself sufficient to trigger *Miranda*.[251] The critical issue in *Beckwith*, then, would seem to be whether, at the time of the interview, Beckwith was confronted with a situation in which he was similarly unable freely to invoke the privilege. Any questioning of an individual by governmental officials in the course of a criminal investigation will, of course, generate some pressures and anxieties, but those pressures do not in themselves amount to the sort of "inherent coercion" at issue in *Miranda*.[252] Beckwith argued further, however, that there is a special form of compulsion present in this situation, for the United States employs a self-reporting tax system, and the average taxpayer will therefore assume that "he must cooperate when actually visited by revenue agents."[253] Standing alone, the compulsive impact of that assumption would seem to be similar to that present when the individual is compelled to file a return, and *Miranda* surely does not apply in that context.[254] The real question, however, is whether the combination of these pressures creates an "inherently coercive" atmosphere similar to that confronting the Court in *Miranda*. The Court's negative answer to this question seems reasonable, and the decision in *Beckwith* therefore stands on a strict but not improper

---

[250] See Garner v. United States, 424 U.S. 648, 655–58 (1976).

[251] In Escobedo v. Illinois, 378 U.S. 478, 490 (1964), the Court suggested that certain rights attach when the "investigation is no longer a general inquiry into an unsolved crime but has begun to focus on a particular suspect." In *Miranda*, however, the Court declared that the phrase "focus" as employed in *Escobedo* really meant "custody" as defined in *Miranda*. See 384 U.S., at 444 n.4. Thus, although there was some debate after *Miranda* concerning the continued vitality of the "focus" concept, most commentators agreed that it was not the critical factor in *Miranda*. See generally Kamisar, *"Custodial Interrogation" within the Meaning of Miranda*, in Inst. Cont. Leg. Ed., Criminal Law and the Constitution 335, 338–51 (1968); Smith, *The Threshold Question in Applying Miranda: What Constitutes Custodial Interrogation?* 25 S.Car.L.Rev. 699, 707–10 (1974).

[252] Kamisar, note 251 *supra*, at 342–43. Indeed, in *Miranda* itself the Court observed that general questioning of citizens "not under restraint" does not necessarily involve "the compelling atmosphere inherent in the process of in-custody interrogation." 384 U.S. at 477, 478.

[253] Brief for Petitioner, at p. 19.

[254] Garner v. United States, 424 U.S. 648, 657–58 (1976).

interpretation of *Miranda*.[255] There is, however, at least one potentially troubling aspect of the opinion. Throughout his analysis, Chief Justice Burger, speaking for the Court, repeatedly emphasized *Miranda's* specific concern with the problem of custodial interrogation rather than its somewhat broader concern with inherently coercive settings. *Beckwith* therefore seems to imply that the underlying principles of *Miranda* will be limited in application exclusively to custodial interrogation of the sort involved in *Miranda* itself and will not be extended to other, similarly coercive, settings.[256] It is at least plausible, as the Court observed, that to apply *Miranda* in *Beckwith* "would cut this Court's holding in that case completely loose from its own explicitly stated rationale."[257] But it is even more clearly true that to limit *Miranda* to its facts would in effect strip it of any principled basis and destroy its vitality by obviating the need carefully to consider the values implicit in its rationale.

In *Oregon v. Mathiason*,[258] decided some nine months later, the implication of *Beckwith* became a reality. After being informed that Mathiason might possibly have committed a burglary, an officer of the State Police attempted to contact him for questioning.

---

[255] The truly compelling aspect of Beckwith's claim, I think, is not so much that a person in his position is unable freely to assert his rights, but rather that in the absence of warnings and an understanding of the nature of the investigation, he cannot fairly be said knowingly and intelligently to have waived the privilege. This theory would seem to involve considerations somewhat different from those underlying *Miranda*. In Garner v. United States, 424 U.S. 648 (1976), the Court made clear that, "in the ordinary case," if an individual "makes disclosures instead of claiming the privilege, the Government has not 'compelled' him to incriminate himself." *Id*. at 654. And if there is no compulsion to incriminate, there is no need to inquire as to whether there was a knowing and intelligent waiver of the privilege. On the other hand, the Court specifically distinguished those situations in which the "government deliberately seeks to avoid the burdens of independent investigation" by knowingly and intentionally attempting to compel self-incriminating disclosures. *Id*. at 655–56. In other words, it is one thing for the government to attempt to compel an individual to reveal information without intending it to be self-incriminating, and quite another for it to attempt to compel what it knows to be incriminating information. Although the Court did not make clear what safeguards, if any, must be employed in the latter situation, a warning of the right to exercise the privilege might arguably be required. The Court did not address this question in *Beckwith*, however, either because it did not find sufficient "compulsion" to trigger this doctrine, or because Beckwith relied solely upon *Miranda*. For further discussion of this issue, see text *infra* at notes 278–98.

[256] Indeed, the Court noted that although there may be some situations of even noncustodial interrogation involving coercion, the proper analysis in such instances would focus on the traditional "voluntariness" standard. 425 U.S. at 347–48.

[257] *Id*. at 345.

[258] 429 U.S. 492 (1977).

The officer tried to reach Mathiason on several occasions without success. He then decided simply to leave his card at Mathiason's apartment with a note asking him to call because "I'd like to discuss something with you." Mathiason, who was on parole at the time, called the officer the next day, and they agreed to meet later that afternoon at the State Patrol Office. The officer met Mathiason in the hallway, took him into an office, and closed the door. He advised Mathiason that the police believed that he was involved in the burglary, and falsely stated that his fingerprints had been found at the scene. The officer also advised Mathiason that his truthfulness in discussing this matter might possibly be considered by the district attorney or the judge. Mathiason confessed. The officer then informed Mathiason of his rights under *Miranda* and took a taped confession. Mathiason was then permitted to leave. Thereafter, he was charged with first-degree burglary, and at his trial the prosecution was permitted, over his objection, to use the confession as evidence of guilt. Mathiason was convicted, but the Oregon Supreme Court reversed, holding that the "interrogation took place in a 'coercive environment,' " and that *Miranda* therefore governed.[259] The Supreme Court, without the benefit of briefs, oral argument, or an opportunity to examine the record, summarily reversed in a *per curiam* opinion.[260]

The first question presented in *Mathiason* is whether, at the time he first confessed, Mathiason was "in custody or otherwise deprived of his freedom of action in any significant way" within the meaning of *Miranda*. Although the Court in *Miranda* made no effort to clarify this standard, it clearly intended that *Miranda* not be limited in application to police-station interrogations[261] or to situations in which the suspect is technically or formally under "arrest."[262] It is also clear from *Miranda* that once this standard is satisfied, the *Miranda* safeguards must be observed. No further inquiry into the degree of "inherent coercion" in the particular situation at issue is necessary.[263] How, then, is a court to determine in any given case

---

[259] 275 Ore. 1 (1976), *rev'g* 22 Ore. App. 494 (1975).

[260] Justices Brennan and Stevens dissented from the Court's summary disposition; Mr. Justice Marshall dissented on the merits.

[261] Orozco v. Texas, 394 U.S. 324 (1969); Mathis v. United States, 391 U.S. 1 (1968).

[262] The Court in *Miranda* studiously avoided reliance upon this concept. See Kamisar, *supra* note 251, at 336.

[263] *Cf.* Mathis v. United States, 391 U.S. 1 (1968); see Graham, note 39 *supra*.

whether the standard is satisfied? One approach might be for a court to attempt to ascertain whether the individual was in fact "in custody or otherwise deprived of his freedom of action in any significant way."[264] Such an approach would necessitate an inquiry into the actual subjective intent of the officer. As Judge Friendly has observed, however, *Miranda* "could scarcely have intended" this to be the critical inquiry, for it would lead to "swearing contests in which officers would regularly maintain their lack of intention to assert power over a suspect" and, moreover, "would fail to recognize *Miranda's* concern with the coercive effect of the 'atmosphere' from the point of view of the person being questioned."[265] Alternatively, a court might hold the crucial consideration to be whether the individual himself subjectively believed that he had been significantly deprived of his liberty.[266] This approach is founded on the view that the individual who thinks his liberty has been restrained is subjected to precisely the sorts of custodial pressures of concern to the Court in *Miranda*, whether or not this belief is correct or even reasonable.[267] Although this approach has a certain analytical appeal, it would enable defendants regularly to assert that they believed themselves to have been under restraint and, in practice, "would require a prescience neither the police nor anyone else possesses."[268] Finally, a court might conclude that the critical issue should be whether, applying an objective standard, a reasonable person in the individual's position could believe that he was not free to leave. In making this determination, a court would presumably consider such factors as the behavior of the police, the nature of the setting, the extent to which the investigation had already focused on the individual, the extent to which the individual was aware of the evidence against him, and so on. This approach seems generally consistent with the underlying concerns of *Miranda*, and at the same time it avoids reliance upon self-serving state-

[264] State v. Evans, 439 S.W.2d 170 (Mo. 1969); Myers v. State, 3 Md. App. 534 (1968); Seagroves v. State, 282 Ala. 354 (1968).

[265] United States v. Hall, 421 F.2d 540, 544 (2d Cir. 1969).

[266] Hicks v. United States, 382 F.2d 158 (D.C. Cir. 1967); United States v. Harrison, 265 F. Supp. 660 (S.D. N.Y. 1967); State v. Lay, 427 S.W.2d 394 (Mo. 1968).

[267] LaFave, "*Street Encounters*" *and the Constitution: Terry, Sibron, Peters, and Beyond*, 67 MICH. L. REV. 40, 99 (1968).

[268] United States v. Hall, 421 F.2d 540, 544 (2d Cir. 1969).

ments of the police or the defendant, eliminates the difficulties of determining states of mind, and does not hold the police responsible for the idiosyncrasies of particular defendants. Accordingly, this approach seems the most sensible of the three, and it has been widely endorsed by courts and commentators alike.[269]

The Court in *Mathiason* held that at the time of his confession, Mathiason was not "in custody or otherwise deprived of his freedom of action in any significant way." In reaching this result, the Court stressed that Mathiason "came voluntarily to the police station," that "he was immediately informed that he was not under arrest," and that after confessing he "did in fact leave the police station without hindrance."[270] The Court apparently thought it irrelevant or at least unimportant that Mathiason was on parole at the time, that the officer indicated that the police had substantial evidence of his guilt, that the officer implied that a prosecution was likely, and that the questioning took place behind closed doors at a police station. Thus, although the Court did not expressly address the question, the particular set of factors which the Court deemed controlling would seem to suggest that *Mathiason* is premised upon the "subjective intent of the officer" approach. Indeed, under either of the other approaches, the factors ignored by the Court would seem critical, whereas at least one of the factors considered significant—that Mathiason was ultimately permitted to leave—would seem almost irrelevant under those other approaches. Assuming that the Court did in fact adopt the "subjective intent of the officer" standard in *Mathiason*, its conclusion that Mathiason was not under restraint might be defensible. But, as indicated earlier, that standard is seriously flawed, most importantly in that it is plainly unresponsive to the underlying concerns of *Miranda*. It is possible, of course, that the Court in *Mathiason* thought it was applying the "objective" standard. If so, its conclusion seems dubious. Whatever Mathiason's original reasons for agreeing to the meeting, it seems to me that, once he reached the threshold of actually confessing, a person in his position would not reasonably have believed himself free simply to

---

[269] United States v. Bekowies, 432 F.2d 8 (9th Cir. 1970); United States v. Hall, 421 F.2d 540 (2d Cir. 1969); Lowe v. United States, 407 F.2d 1391 (9th Cir. 1969); Freije v. United States, 408 F.2d 100 (1st Cir. 1969); People v. Arnold, 66 Cal.2d 438 (1967); People v. P., 21 N.Y.2d 1 (1967); Smith, note 251 *supra*, at 713–14; Kamisar, note 251 *supra*, at 362; see also Annot., 31 A.L.R.3d 565 (1970) and (1977 Supp.).

[270] 429 U.S. at 495.

get up and leave the building.[271] Thus, however one reads *Mathiason*, it seems clearly to embrace a rather crabbed interpretation of *Miranda.*

The remaining question in *Mathiason* was whether, even if Mathiason was not "in custody or otherwise deprived of his freedom of action in any significant way" at the time he confessed, *Miranda* should nevertheless govern this situation. Unlike Beckwith, Mathiason was questioned in a police station behind closed doors, he was on parole, and he was informed, not just that he was being investigated, but that the police already believed him to be guilty. It would therefore seem that, whether or not he was free to leave, Mathiason was questioned in an "inherently coercive" environment at least arguably similar, if not identical, to that involved in *Miranda* itself. The Court, however, declined even to undertake such an inquiry. Rather, after observing that *Miranda* was concerned with custodial interrogation, the Court declared that "[i]t was *that* sort of coercive environment to which *Miranda* by its terms was made applicable, and to which it is limited."[272] Thus, not only does *Mathiason* restrict the meaning of "custodial interrogation," it also holds that the principles underlying *Miranda* are henceforth to be applied only in that limited context. And all of this was accomplished without briefs, oral argument, or a record.

IX. United States v. Mandujano, United States v. Wong, and United States v. Washington: Miranda and the Grand Jury

In March 1973, Roy Mandujano agreed to obtain heroin for an undercover narcotics agent. Although the deal fell through, the agent reported the incident to federal prosecutors who were then

---

[271] At least two commentators have suggested that *Miranda* should apply whenever an individual suspected of criminal activity is "asked" to come to the station house for questioning. Smith, note 251 *supra*, at 732; Graham, note 39 *supra*, at 79–80. Mathiason was in an even worse position than most. He was expressly informed that the police believed him to be guilty, and knowledge of this fact could well lead a person reasonably to believe that he is not free to leave. Moreover, Mathiason was on parole. As Mr. Justice Stevens recognized in *Mathiason*, "a parolee is technically in legal custody continuously until his sentence has been served." 429 U.S. at 500 (Stevens, J., dissenting). Perhaps more importantly, a parolee is in a particularly vulnerable position and is likely to feel substantial pressure to cooperate with the authorities. And the pressure might be especially severe when he is "asked" to submit to questioning about a crime of which he is suspected.

[272] 429 U.S. at 495.

seeking information on local drug traffic to present to a special grand jury. Several weeks later, Mandujano was subpoenaed to testify before the grand jury. Upon entering the grand jury room, he was informed that he was required to answer all questions except where the answer would incriminate him and that, if he wished the assistance of counsel, the lawyer could not enter the room. Although Mandujano stated that he could not afford to hire an attorney, he was not advised that he had a right to appointed counsel.[273] The prosecutor then proceeded to question Mandujano about his familiarity with the local narcotics trade. During the course of this questioning, Mandujano specifically denied having offered to procure heroin for the undercover agent. He was subsequently charged in a two-count indictment with attempting to distribute heroin and with willfully and knowingly making a false material declaration to the grand jury.[274] Prior to trial on the perjury charge, Mandujano moved to suppress his testimony before the grand jury on the ground that it had been elicited in violation of *Miranda*. The district court held that, since Mandujano was a "putative" defendant at the time of his grand jury appearance, he was entitled to full *Miranda* warnings, and therefore granted the motion. The United States Court of Appeals for the Fifth Circuit affirmed.[275] The Supreme Court reversed.[276] The Court held, without dissent, that whether or not *Miranda* is applicable in this context, the privilege against compelled self-incrimination does not sanction perjury. In a plurality opinion authored by the Chief Justice, four members of the Court went further, however, and maintained that *Miranda* does not govern this situation at all.[277] Before turning to those issues, it

[273] Thus, the warnings actually given to Mandujano differ from those mandated by *Miranda* in several respects: (1) he was warned of his right not to incriminate himself, rather than of a right to remain silent; (2) he was not warned that anything he said might be used against him; (3) he was informed that his counsel, if he retained one, could not enter the room with him; and (4) he was not warned of his right to appointed counsel.

[274] Mandujano was convicted for attempting to distribute heroin. The grand jury testimony was not utilized by the prosecution at that trial.

[275] 496 F.2d 1050 (5th Cir. 1974), *aff'g* 365 F.Supp. 155 (W.D. Tex. 1973).

[276] United States v. Mandujano, 425 U.S. 564 (1976).

[277] Justices White, Powell, and Rehnquist joined Chief Justice Burger. Justice Brennan, joined by Mr. Justice Marshall, filed a separate concurring opinion in which he argued that Mandujano had a right to be warned of the privilege, and that he had a right to the aid of counsel. This argument was premised upon general principles arising out of the privilege, rather than upon *Miranda* itself. Mr. Justice Stewart, joined by Mr. Justice Blackmun, concurred without reaching any of the questions debated in dictum by Justices Burger and Brennan. Mr. Justice Stevens did not participate.

might first be worthwhile to examine whether, wholly apart from *Miranda*, there is any other basis in the privilege for holding that an individual in Mandujano's position is entitled to be warned of his right to assert the privilege and is entitled to the assistance of counsel.

The Court has often stated that, as a general rule, an individual who desires the protection of the privilege "must claim it or he will not be considered to have been 'compelled' within the meaning of the Amendment."[278] In *Garner v. United States*,[279] decided only two months before *Mandujano*, the Court explained that this rule derives from the essential nature of the privilege itself. Since "the fundamental purpose of the Fifth Amendment [is] the preservation of an adversary system of criminal justice,"[280] the privilege is not implicated unless the government's questioning subverts that system and becomes inquisitorial. In an inquisitorial process, the purpose of questioning is to elicit evidence to be used against the individual at his own criminal prosecution, and "the inquiring government is acutely aware of the potentially incriminatory nature of the disclosures sought."[281] When the government questions an individual for other purposes, however, the integrity of the adversary system may not be threatened. Thus, in those instances in which "[o]nly the witness knows whether the apparently innocent disclosure sought may incriminate him," the "government ordinarily may assume that its compulsory processes are not eliciting testimony that he deems to be incriminating."[282] In such circumstances, the government is not seeking deliberately "to avoid the burdens of independent investigation by compelling self-incriminating disclosures."[283] Accordingly, "the burden appropriately lies" with the individual "to make a timely assertion of the privilege," and if he elects instead to disclose "the information sought, any incriminations properly are viewed as not compelled."[284] Under this view of the

[278] United States v. Monia, 317 U.S. 424, 427 (1943). See Garner v. United States, 424 U.S. 648, 654–55 (1976); United States v. Kordel, 397 U.S. 1, 7–10 (1970); Rogers v. United States, 340 U.S. 367, 370–71 (1951); Vajtauer v. Commissioner of Immigration, 273 U.S. 103, 112–13 (1927).

[279] 424 U.S. 648 (1976). The Court held in *Garner* that an individual who disclosed incriminating information on his tax return rather than claiming the privilege was not unconstitutionally compelled to incriminate himself.

[280] *Id.* at 655.

[281] *Id.* at 657.

[282] *Id.* at 655.

[283] *Id.* at 655–56.

[284] *Id.* at 655.

privilege, it seems clear that a witness subpoenaed to testify before a grand jury ordinarily must assert the privilege on his own initiative. Since the government is not attempting to compel self-incriminating answers, no warning of the right not to answer is required, and the concept of a "knowing and intelligent" waiver is inapplicable.[285] What, though, of the situation in which the government embarks upon an inquisitorial enterprise and attempts deliberately to compel the witness to disclose information for use against him at a later criminal prosecution? Although *Garner* is founded upon the distinction between these two situations, it does not state expressly what procedures, if any, are to be employed when the government seeks to undermine the adversary system in this manner. It would seem reasonable to conclude, however, that in this context there must be a "knowing and intelligent" waiver of the privilege and, presumably, a warning to the witness that he need not answer any question if the answer would tend to incriminate him.[286] It should be noted that even the Chief Justice, in his plurality opinion in *Mandujano*, left open the possibility that such a warning might constitutionally be required.[287] Assuming that such a warning is indeed required, the remaining issue is whether it must be given to every "putative" defendant,[288] or rather only to those "putative" defendants whom the prosecutor subjectively intends to charge by indictment. As an analytical matter, this distinction is not without importance, for it poses the question whether *Garner*'s linkage of the privilege and subversion of the adversary process is limited to

---

[285] This assumes, of course, that *Miranda* does not govern this situation. It should also be noted that, as *Garner* makes clear, even in this situation the privilege may be violated if the individual is not free to assert the privilege. *Id.* at 657.

[286] *Cf. id.* at 657. See Ritchie, note 8 *supra*, at 428. But see note 330 *infra*. The state and lower federal courts have long wrestled with these issues. Under the traditional view, a witness called to testify before a grand jury need not be warned of his right to assert the privilege even if he was the "focus" of the investigation. In recent years, however, there has been a trend toward requiring such a warning. See McCormick, note 19 *supra*, at § 137. *Compare* United States v. Luxenberg, 374 F.2d 241 (6th Cir. 1967); Powell v. United States, 226 F.2d 269 (D.C. Cir. 1955); United States v. Bernard, 411 F. Supp. 304 (E.D. Mich. 1976); United States v. Pepe, 367 F. Supp. 1365 (D. Conn. 1973); United States v. Lawn, 115 F. Supp. 674 (S.D.N.Y. 1953); *with* United States v. Levinson, 405 F.2d 971 (6th Cir. 1968); United States v. Cleary, 265 F.2d 459 (2d Cir. 1959); United States v. Scully, 225 F.2d 113 (2d Cir. 1955); United States v. Gilboy, 160 F. Supp. 442 (M.D. Pa. 1958); United States v. Klein, 124 F. Supp. 476 (S.D.N.Y. 1954).

[287] 425 U.S. at 582 n.7.

[288] The phrase "putative" defendant has generally been defined as a witness whom the prosecutor has probable cause to suspect of having committed a crime bearing some relation to the investigation. 425 U.S. at 598–99 and n.16 (Brennan, J., concurring).

those instances in which the government deliberately seeks to compel self-incriminating disclosures in order to use them against the individual at a later prosecution, or rather whether it extends to any effort to compel such disclosures, without regard to any present intention to use them against the individual. As a practical matter, however, any inquiry into the actual subjective intent of the prosecutor is likely to be so burdensome from an administrative standpoint as not to be worth the effort.[289]

The second issue raised, but not decided, in *Mandujano* is whether, wholly apart from *Miranda*, the privilege guarantees a "putative" defendant subpoenaed to testify before a grand jury the right to the advice of counsel.[290] In *Miranda*, of course, the Court held that the privilege may of its own force require that an individual be permitted to consult with an attorney. Until recently, that doctrine had not been extended beyond the "inherently coercive" atmosphere concept of *Miranda*. In *Maness v. Meyers*,[291] however, the Court added a new wrinkle. *Maness* held that a lawyer may not constitutionally be held in contempt for advising his client, during trial of a civil case, to refuse to produce material demanded by a subpoena *duces tecum* when the lawyer believed in good faith that the material might tend to incriminate his client. This holding was premised specifically upon the privilege against self-incrimination. The Court began by observing that "assertion of a testimonial privilege, as of many other rights, often depends upon legal advice from someone who is trained and skilled in the subject matter, and who may offer a more objective opinion."[292] Indeed, a layman often "may not be aware of the precise scope, the nuances, and boundaries of his Fifth Amendment privilege."[293] As the Court recognized, the privilege "is not a self-executing mechanism; it can be affirmatively waived, or lost by not asserting it in a timely fashion."[294] Moreover, if a lawyer can be held in contempt for erroneously, but in good

[289] Indeed, the difficulties involved in such an inquiry are well illustrated in *Mandujano* itself. The agents involved and the prosecuting attorney testified that they had no intention to seek an indictment against Mandujano when he was first subpoenaed to testify. The district court, after an extensive hearing, rejected this assertion, concluding that "it strains credulity to suggest that the special attorney did not have one eye on a possible prosecution." 365 F.Supp. at 158.

[290] Under existing law, the Sixth Amendment right to counsel is inapplicable, since the witness has not as yet been indicted. See Kirby v. Illinois, 406 U.S. 682 (1972).

[291] 419 U.S. 449 (1975).

[292] *Id.* at 466.

[293] *Ibid.*

[294] *Ibid.*

faith, advising his client to assert the privilege, "some advocates may lose their zeal for forthrightness and independence."[295] As a consequence, some clients will not be advised of their rights, and this "would deny the constitutional privilege against self-incrimination the means of its own implementation."[296] The possible implications of this decision are substantial. To be sure, the Court in *Maness* attempted valiantly to limit the scope of its holding. I doubt, however, that it can be so easily cabined. Under *Maness*, if a state permits a witness before a grand jury to consult with counsel, it may not, consonant with the privilege, punish the attorney for giving the witness erroneous, but good faith, advice as to his assertion of the privilege, because such punishment would deter other attorneys from advising their clients without fear. Does it not logically follow that the privilege guarantees any such witness—or at least any putative defendant—the right to consult with counsel? On what principled basis can these situations be distinguished?[297] And if a witness may consult with retained counsel, does not the poor witness have a right to consult with appointed counsel? And if a witness may consult his attorney outside the grand jury room, why not inside as well?[298] My point is not that all these results necessarily flow from *Maness*, nor is it to demonstrate, by parading what some might see as a list of horribles, that *Maness* was wrongly decided. Rather, I believe that *Maness* was founded upon an important insight about the nature of the privilege, and although it undoubtedly raises a whole set of new and difficult problems, the Court should not be too quick to retreat from that insight. Unfortunately, in his plurality opinion in *Mandujano*, the Chief Justice maintained that a putative defendant has no right to consult with counsel about his asser-

[295] *Ibid.*

[296] *Id.* at 468.

[297] It might be argued, I suppose, that such a requirement would disrupt and delay the grand jury process. The argument, however, seems unpersuasive. See 425 U.S. at 606–07 (Brennan, J., concurring).

[298] Counsel's presence in the grand jury room would surely enhance his ability effectively to advise his client, for he would be able to hear the questions personally and in context. Moreover, this would not seriously threaten the need for secrecy in the grand jury, for a client is permitted to reveal his own testimony to his attorney in any event. Finally, this would be less disruptive of the proceedings than for the witness repeatedly to leave the room in order to speak with his attorney. See generally Newman, *The Suspect and the Grand Jury: A Need for Constitutional Protection*, 11 U. RICHMOND L. REV. 1 (1976); Dash, *The Indicting Grand Jury: A Critical Stage?*, 10 AM.CRIM.L.REV. 807 (1972); Steele, *Right to Counsel at the Grand Jury Stage of Criminal Proceedings*, 36 MO.L. REV. 193 (1971); Meshbesher, *Right to Counsel Before Grand Jury*, 41 F.R.D. 189 (1967).

tion of the privilege. In so doing, Chief Justice Burger made no mention of *Maness*, an opinion he authored.

Although the Chief Justice concluded in *Mandujano* that application of the principles underlying *Miranda* in this context would be "an extravagant expansion never remotely contemplated by this Court,"[299] the Court as a whole did not decide this question. The considerations involved when a putative defendant is subpoenaed to testify before a grand jury are somewhat different from those involved in the custodial interrogation situation at issue in *Miranda*. Accordingly, *Mathiason*, which was decided several months after *Mandujano*, might be seen as implicitly settling this issue. Since the grand jury situation involves at least some element of "custody," however, *Mathiason* may not be controlling. In any event, analysis of the *Miranda* issue should properly involve a dual inquiry. First, is the putative defendant called to testify before a grand jury confronted with an "inherently coercive" atmosphere sufficiently similar to that involved in *Miranda* to trigger its concerns? Second, if so, do the special circumstances of testimony before a grand jury justify the use of safeguards different from those employed in *Miranda?*

In a literal sense, an individual subpoenaed to testify before a grand jury has been "deprived of his freedom of action in [a] significant way." He is required by law to be at a certain place, at a certain time, whether or not he wishes to comply. He is not free simply to leave or to terminate the questioning at will. The compulsion exerted by a subpoena, however, differs substantially from that exerted by the sort of "custody" involved in *Miranda*, where the restriction on the individual's liberty is ordinarily effected with the use or threat of force in what often may be demeaning circumstances.[300] Thus, although the fact that the grand jury witness is compelled to appear may be relevant, it does not in itself establish the existence of a situation in which the individual is unable freely to assert the privilege. The critical factor, then, would seem to be the atmosphere of the grand jury room itself. In his plurality opinion in *Mandujano*, Chief Justice Burger noted that, unlike the type of custodial interrogation at issue in *Miranda*, interrogation before a grand jury is not likely to involve the use of physical brutality or psychologically oriented techniques designed to coerce the indi-

---

[299] 425 U.S. at 580.

[300] See United States v. Dionisio, 410 U.S. 1, 10 (1973).

vidual to incriminate himself. Indeed, it was primarily on this basis that the Chief Justice rested his conclusion that *Miranda* is inapplicable in this context.[301] Although this observation may be correct, it cannot be deemed dispositive. The Court in *Miranda* was, of course, concerned with the use of such tactics by the police. Its primary concern, however, and the one upon which the decision was ultimately premised, was that the very atmosphere of custodial interrogation "carries its own badge of intimidation" and involves "inherently compelling pressures which work to undermine the individual's will to resist and to compel him to speak where he would not otherwise do so freely."[302] Thus, the Burger treatment of *Miranda* in *Mandujano* missed the mark entirely. In fact, the argument that the grand jury room constitutes an "inherently coercive" atmosphere within the meaning of *Miranda* would seem to have considerable merit. A witness subpoenaed to testify before a grand jury may find himself alone in an unfamiliar and intimidating setting. He must take an oath in which he swears to testify fully and truthfully. He knows that that oath is backed by the force of law. Even if he knows of his right to invoke the privilege, he must still decide whether to respond to questions, and risk having his answers used against him at a later criminal trial, or to attempt to claim the privilege, creating suspicion in the eyes of the grand jurors and risking a possible citation for contempt. And all the while, he may be subjected to constant interrogation, directed by a skilled prosecutor, that may gradually wear down his willingness to continue to assert the privilege. These coercive pressures would seem to be particularly acute for the putative defendant, who may know or at least suspect that he is a target of the investigation and who is likely to be subjected to the most intense and vigorous questioning. As one commentator has observed, the grand jury interrogation of a putative defendant would seem to recreate "the very setting in which the privilege historically developed."[303] There is, however, another side of the coin. As the Court recognized in *Miranda*, the "compulsion to speak in the isolated setting of the police station may well be greater than in courts or other official investigations, where there are often impartial observers to guard against intimidation or trick-

---

[301] 425 U.S. at 579–80.

[302] 384 U.S. at 457, 467. See also text *supra*, at notes 30–35.

[303] McCormick, note 19 *supra*, at § 137, at 290. See also Newman, note 298 *supra;* Dash, note 298 *supra;* Meshbesher, note 298 *supra*.

ery."[304] Moreover, unlike the individual interrogated in the ordinary *Miranda*-like setting, the witness subpoenaed to testify before a grand jury has an opportunity in advance to prepare himself legally and psychologically for the ordeal. In sum, the question is, I think, a close one that could reasonably be decided either way. It should be emphasized, however, that even if *Miranda* is held to govern, this does not necessarily mean that all of the rights mandated by *Miranda* must automatically be extended to the grand jury situation without variation. Although the putative defendant compelled to testify before a grand jury, like the individual subjected to the more common form of custodial interrogation, may be confronted with an "inherently coercive" atmosphere, there are differences between these situations which might justify differences in treatment. For example, under *Miranda*, the individual is afforded an absolute right to remain silent. In the grand jury context, however, there may be a legitimate and substantial need to obtain information from the witness that would not tend to incriminate him. The grand jury is a special and important institution in our system of government. Unnecessary obstacles should not be imposed lest they render it powerless to serve its essential functions. It therefore may be reasonable to warn the witness only of his right to invoke the privilege, rather than of an absolute right not to answer any questions. On the other hand, if *Miranda* governs this situation, the witness before the grand jury should be guaranteed the right to consult with counsel, both to obtain his advice concerning assertion of the privilege and as a means to offset the coercive pressures of the setting. It may be, however, that since there are impartial observers present in the room, the attorney need not be permitted to enter.[305] The basic point is that *Miranda* establishes certain fundamental principles that need not be applied mechanistically. Rather, they should be applied with sensitivity to the special and distinguishing characteristics of the problem at hand.[306]

The final question presented in *Mandujano* was whether, even if

[304] 384 U.S. at 461.

[305] But see note 298 *supra*.

[306] Thus it would seem reasonable to conclude that these rights and warnings must be accorded not to all witnesses but rather only to putative defendants. As *Garner* recognized, the interrogation process is inquisitional in nature only when the government is attempting to elicit self-incriminating information. Moreover, the nature of the questioning itself is likely to be most intense and hence coercive in this context.

Mandujano was not properly advised of his rights under *Miranda*, *Garner*, or *Maness*, his testimony at the grand jury should nevertheless be admissible against him in the prosecution for perjury. The Court held, without dissent, that such evidence is indeed admissible. Moreover, a year later, in *United States v. Wong*, the Court unanimously reaffirmed this holding even though Wong, unlike Mandujano, had as a practical matter been given no warnings at all.[307] In reaching this result, the Court relied upon the general rule that "[o]ur legal system provides methods for challenging the Government's right to ask questions–lying is not one of them. A citizen may decline to answer the question, or answer it honestly, but he cannot with impunity knowingly and willfully answer with a falsehood."[308] The right not to be compelled to incriminate oneself, in other words, does not guarantee a right to commit perjury. This rule seems sensible if the individual has a fair opportunity to assert the privilege but elects instead to lie. Suppose, however, as in *Miranda*, that the individual is interrogated in circumstances in which he is unable freely and effectively to assert the privilege. In that situation, the individual desiring not to incriminate himself may have no recourse but to lie. Or, to take an even more dramatic example, suppose the individual is compelled by government officials specifically to incriminate himself falsely. Although these variations may seem somewhat more problematic, the Court has long recognized that the immunity afforded by the privilege "relates to the past and does not endow the person who testifies with a license to commit perjury."[309] That is, when an individual is compelled to make false statements, his real complaint is not that he has been compelled to incriminate himself within the meaning of the privilege but rather that he has been compelled to commit an independent

[307] 97 S.Ct. 1823 (1977). At the time of her grand jury appearance, the government had received reports that Wong had bribed two undercover police officers. When questioned about these events, she falsely denied the bribes. Prior to testifying, she was given relatively complete warnings, *id.* at 1824 n.2., but the district court found that, because of a language problem, she had not understood the warnings. The court, adopting reasoning similar to that employed by the Fifth Circuit in *Mandujano*, held her testimony inadmissible in the prosecution for perjury. The Court of Appeals for the Ninth Circuit affirmed. 553 F.2d 576 (9th Cir. 1974).

[308] Bryson v. United States, 396 U.S. 64, 72 (1969); see United States v. Knox, 396 U.S. 77 (1969); Dennis v. United States, 384 U.S. 855 (1966); Kay v. United States, 303 U.S. 1 (1938); United States v. Kapp, 302 U.S. 214 (1937); Glickstein v. United States, 222 U.S. 139 (1911).

[309] Glickstein v. United States, 222 U.S. 139, 142 (1911).

criminal act.[310] In light of these principles, it seems clear that neither *Mandujano* nor *Wong* involved any violation of the privilege.[311]

In an effort to circumvent these principles, the Courts of Appeals in these cases held the evidence inadmissible, not on the authority of the privilege but rather on the theory that the defendants had been deprived of due process of law. These courts maintained that it is fundamentally unfair for the government to compel a putative defendant to appear before a grand jury and then to question him about his activities, without adequately advising him of his rights, in the hope of eliciting self-incriminating or perjurious responses. Such a practice, the courts concluded, "smacks of entrapment" and is therefore violative of due process. Whatever the merits of this theory in the abstract, it seems unpersuasive in the context of *Mandujano*, for he was at least warned of his right to invoke the privilege. Wong was in a somewhat more sympathetic position, for the district court found that she did not know that she need not incriminate herself and, to the contrary, thought that she was required to answer all questions. From her standpoint, then, Wong was subjected "to the cruel trilemma of self-accusation, perjury or contempt."[312] The Court, however, rejected this theory, reasoning that it "in reality relates to the protection of values served by the Fifth Amendment privilege, a privilege which does not protect perjury."[313] Thus, although the Court did indicate that there might conceivably be circumstances in which prosecutorial conduct leading to the commission of perjury might violate due process,[314] it apparently will define those circumstances quite narrowly.

On the same day that the Court decided *Wong*, it also handed down its decision in *United States v. Washington*.[315] In December 1972, an officer of the Washington, D.C., police department, after

---

[310] United States v. Knox, 396 U.S. 77, 82–83 (1969).

[311] It might be argued, however, that the evidence should be held inadmissible in order to remove any incentive the prosecutor might have not to provide the required warnings in the hope of eliciting perjurious testimony. *Harris* and *Baxter* would seem implicitly to have disposed of any such theory.

[312] Murphy v. Waterfront Commission, 378 U.S. 52, 55 (1964).

[313] 97 S.Ct. at 1827.

[314] Each of the opinions in *Mandujano* left open such a possibility, referring specifically to Brown v. United States, 245 F.2d 549 (8th Cir. 1957), in which it was established that the sole purpose for calling the witness before the grand jury was to induce him to commit perjury. 425 U.S. at 583 (plurality opinion); *id.* at 585 (Brennan, J., concurring); *id.* at 609 (Stewart, J., concurring).

[315] 97 S.Ct. 1814 (1977).

stopping a van for a traffic offense, spotted a motorcycle in the back of the van. The motorcycle was listed as having recently been stolen, and the officer arrested the two persons in the van. Upon learning that Washington owned the van, the police notified him that it was in their possession. When Washington attempted to reclaim the van, he told a rather bizarre story to explain the presence of the motorcycle.[316] The officer to whom Washington related this tale expressed skepticism and declined to release the van. Washington then went to the United States Attorney's office where he met with a prosecutor in an effort to arrange for release of the van. The prosecutor, although dubious of his story, nevertheless permitted Washington to take the van. At the same time, however, he served him with a subpoena to testify before the grand jury investigating the motorcycle theft. After entering the grand jury room, Washington was fully advised of his rights under *Miranda*.[317] On the other hand, although Washington "was a potential defendant whose indictment was considered likely by the prosecution,"[318] he was told only that "he was needed as a witness in prosecuting the two who were occupants of the van at the time of its impoundment."[319] Washington repeated his explanation of the event to the grand jury, and he was thereafter indicted for grand larceny and receiving stolen property. Prior to trial, the Superior Court for the District of Columbia granted Washington's motion to suppress the testimony, holding that since he had not been informed that he was a potential defendant, he could not be said to have "knowingly and intelligently" waived the privilege. The District of Columbia Court of Appeals affirmed.[320] The Supreme Court reversed.[321]

---

[316] Washington explained that while driving the van himself he had stopped to help an unknown motorcyclist. He allowed the motorcycle to be placed in his van to take it for repairs. Soon after this, however, the van stalled and he walked to a nearby gasoline station to telephone the persons eventually found driving the van for help. He waited a while for them to arrive, and when they did not appear he returned to the spot where he had left the van. When he arrived, the van was gone, and he assumed his friends had repaired the van and driven it away.

[317] 97 S.Ct. at 1817.

[318] *Id.* at 1818 n.4.

[319] 328 A.2d 98, 100 (D.C. 1974).

[320] *Ibid.* The Superior Court also quashed the indictment. The Court of Appeals held this to be an improper remedy, however, and the Supreme Court declined to rule on this issue. See 97 S.Ct. at 1818 n.3. The Court of Appeals also held that the warnings given to Washington were improper because they were given "in the cloister of the grand jury." 328 A.2d at 100. The Supreme Court rejected this argument. See 97 S.Ct. at 1820–21.

[321] Mr. Justice Brennan, joined by Mr. Justice Marshall, dissented.

At the outset, Chief Justice Burger, speaking for the Court, noted that it was unnecessary to decide in *Washington* whether *Miranda* governs this situation, since the warnings Washington received "plainly satisfied any possible claim to warnings."[322] The Court in *Miranda* did not address the question whether an individual interrogated in "inherently coercive" surroundings must be warned that he is a potential defendant, for in each of the cases before the Court in *Miranda* the defendant was under arrest at the time of the interrogation and was therefore fully aware of his status. The Court did declare in *Miranda*, however, that "[i]f the interrogation continues without the presence of an attorney and a statement is taken, a heavy burden rests on the government to demonstrate that the defendant knowingly and intelligently waived his privilege against self-incrimination and his right to retained or appointed counsel."[323] Regrettably, *Miranda* did not clarify the precise meaning of "knowing and intelligent" waiver in this context. One approach might be to interpret this concept as requiring only that the individual be aware of and capable of understanding his rights at the time of the confession. Under this view, proof that the individual was advised of his rights and that he in fact "waived" them would, in most instances, end the matter.[324] Alternatively, the concept might be interpreted as requiring that the individual be aware of and understand not only his rights but also the surrounding circumstances and the practical and legal consequences of a waiver.[325] If this is the proper inquiry, it would seem reasonable to conclude that, whether or not an express warning to this effect is required, the prosecution should at the very least be required to prove that an individual in Washington's position knew that, at the time of his testimony, he was in fact a suspect rather than a mere witness. Knowledge of this fact would seem essential for the individual attempting "knowingly and intelligently" to decide whether to as-

---

[322] 97 S.Ct. at 1818. The Court observed, however, that even if *Miranda* does govern this situation, the witness need not be warned that he has a right to remain silent. At most, he need be warned only that he need not answer questions if the answers would incriminate him. See *id.* at 1817 n.2.

[323] 384 U.S. at 475.

[324] For an excellent defense of this approach, see State v. McKnight, 52 N.J. 35 (1968).

[325] The Court has adopted this interpretation of "knowing and intelligent" in its guilty plea cases. Brady v. United States, 397 U.S. 742, 748 (1970); see also Von Moltke v. Gillies, 332 U.S. 708, 724 (1948) (plurality opinion); United States v. Frazier, 476 F.2d 891 (D.C. Cir. 1973).

sert his rights and would seem likely to have a substantial impact upon his willingness to cooperate with the investigation. Moreover, if the individual is in fact innocent and does not know that he is a potential defendant, he is in no position to decide whether his answers might incriminate him.[326] Rather than address the meaning of the "knowing and intelligent" waiver concept, the Court in *Washington* approached the problem from a somewhat different perspective. Chief Justice Burger emphasized that the guarantee of the privilege "is only that the witness be not *compelled* to give self-incriminating testimony."[327] Even if it is assumed that Washington was questioned in an "inherently coercive" environment, however, the warnings he was given were sufficient to offset those coercive pressures. In any event, even if Washington did not know that he was a potential defendant rather than a mere witness, his ignorance on that score has no bearing on the question of compulsion. Accordingly, the Chief Justice concluded that given the absence of compulsion, Washington's incriminating testimony before the grand jury "cannot conflict with any constitutional guarantees of the privilege."[328] In effect, then, the Court in *Washington* seems simply to have ignored *Miranda's* requirement of a "knowing and intelligent" waiver. Once the individual is advised of his rights, the sole remaining question under *Washington* "is whether, considering the totality of the circumstances, the free will of the witness was overborne."[329] In reaching this conclusion, the Court expressed not even the slightest hint that it was in reality disregarding a major feature of *Miranda's* protections.[330]

---

[326] A third possible approach, not adopted in *Miranda*, might be to hold that there can never be a "knowing and intelligent" waiver unless the individual is in fact advised to speak by counsel. *Cf.* A.L.I. Model Code of Pre-Arraignment Procedure 39–40 (Study Draft No. 1 1968); Kuh, *Some Views on Miranda v. Arizona*, 35 Fordham L. Rev. 233, 234–35 (1966).

[327] 97 S. Ct. at 1819. [328] *Ibid.* [329] *Ibid.*

[330] To complete its task, the Court held further that use of Washington's testimony would not conflict with any of the principles enunciated in *Garner*. Although the government was deliberately attempting to elicit self-incriminating disclosures from Washington, he was not, the Chief Justice concluded, "compelled" to make such disclosures, since any inherent coercion present in the grand jury setting was offset by the warnings he received. The Court relied upon *Beckwith* to support this conclusion. In effect, it confused two concepts which the Court in *Garner* took pains to distinguish. The Court in *Garner* observed that "voluntariness" refers to those situations, like *Miranda*, in which "some factor prevents a [person] desiring to claim the privilege from doing so." 424 U.S. at 654 n.9. Thus, although Washington's testimony, like Beckwith's statements, might have been voluntary, unlike Beckwith Washington was under legal compulsion to testify. By

X. Conclusion

What, then, is the present status of *Miranda?* It would be an understatement, I suppose, to say that the Burger Court has taken a dim view of *Miranda*. The Court has stated that the principles underlying *Miranda* are not to be extended beyond the sort of custodial interrogation involved in *Miranda* itself, and it has narrowly defined the concept of "custodial interrogation." It has declared that evidence obtained without compliance with the *Miranda* safeguards is admissible in any proceeding other than a criminal prosecution, and it has held that such evidence is admissible even in a criminal prosecution if used for the purpose of impeachment. It has embraced an uncertain standard for determining when the police may renew efforts to interrogate an individual who has previously asserted his right to remain silent, and it has impliedly undercut *Miranda's* requirement of a "knowing and intelligent" waiver. It has hinted that evidence obtained in violation of *Miranda* will be excluded only if the police did not act in good faith, and it has announced that the *Miranda* safeguards are not derived from the privilege against compelled self-incrimination. Although the results in these cases are consistent, in that the Court has steadfastly declined to exclude even a single item of evidence on the authority of *Miranda*, the decisions do not appear to rest upon any unifying, coherent principle other than a fundamental rejection of the premises of *Miranda* and an apparent desire to return, ultimately, to the "voluntariness" standard.[331] This is not to say, however, that all of the Court's holdings, implications, suggestions, and declarations are necessarily "wrong," even given *Miranda*. To the contrary, in at least some instances, the weaknesses in the Court's opinions are primarily stylistic and analytical rather than substantive. And given the heightened social concern with the maintenance of "law and order" and the essentially "legislative" nature of the *Miranda* opin-

obliterating this distinction, *Washington* seems to imply that *Garner* is applicable only to "involuntariness" situations. Wholly apart from this, *Washington* implies that, whether or not Washington had a right under *Garner* to be warned of the privilege, *Garner* does not also require a "knowing and intelligent" waiver.

[331] This is reflected most clearly in *Tucker* and *Washington*. See also Brewer v. Williams, 97 S. Ct. 1232, 1252–54 (Burger, C.J., dissenting), 1260–61 (Blackmun, J., dissenting) (1977). The Burger Court seems to have taken a relatively restrictive view of the privilege in other respects as well. Andresen v. Maryland, 427 U.S. 463 (1976); Fisher v. United States, 425 U.S. 391 (1976); Kastigar v. United States, 406 U.S. 441 (1972); McGautha v. California, 402 U.S. 183 (1971). See Ritchie, note 8 *supra*.

ion, it is at least conceivable that one or more of the Justices who formed the *Miranda* majority would have joined the result, if not the opinion, in some of these cases. Moreover, it should be noted that, on the whole, the Burger Court's decisions have focused primarily on fringe issues. As a practical matter, the core of *Miranda*—the prohibition of the use in the prosecution's case in chief of evidence elicited from an individual through custodial interrogation without proper warnings—remains largely intact.[332] From the standpoint of candor and craftsmanship, however, the opinions, taken as a whole, are highly unsatisfactory. In its unyielding determination to reach the desired result, the Court has too often resorted to distortion of the record, disregard of the precedents, and an unwillingness honestly to explain or to justify its conclusions.

In *Brewer v. Williams*, decided last Term, more than twenty briefs were filed urging the Court to overrule *Miranda*. The Court, however, found it unnecessary to address that question.[333] My prediction is that the Court will not overrule *Miranda*. *Miranda* was a highly controversial decision, and it is closely identified with the Warren era. Those Justices who were appointed for the express purpose of "strengthening the peace forces" are almost surely sensitive to what would be the inescapably political overtones of a direct reversal. Such a decision would raise grave doubts, even among those who might disagree with *Miranda* as a matter of policy, "as to the Court's impersonality and as to the principled foundations of its decisions."[334] Moreover, as the foregoing analysis demonstrates, the Court could, with little or no fanfare, gradually dismantle *Miranda* piecemeal. That, I think, is the course of the future.

---

[332] It is unclear to what extent, if any, the Court's decisions have affected the willingness of law enforcement personnel to comply with the core requirements of *Miranda*. The most important empirical studies of the impact of *Miranda* on police behavior were conducted prior to these decisions. See authorities cited in note 68 *supra*.

[333] 97 S. Ct. 1232, 1239 (1977). The Court held the evidence in *Brewer* inadmissible because of a violation of the Sixth Amendment right to counsel.

[334] Israel, note 1 *supra*, at 218.

ROBERT H. BORK

VERTICAL RESTRAINTS: SCHWINN OVERRULED

The Supreme Court's decision in *Continental T.V., Inc. v. GTE Sylvania Inc.*[1] is either the most important and promising antitrust decision of the past two or three decades or merely the latest inconclusive episode in the Court's continuing travail in the wilderness of the law of vertical restraints. Lest hope stir prematurely, it must be said that the evidence supporting the latter view is strong. Though the Court overruled the *Schwinn*[2] *per se* rule and upheld Sylvania's practice of requiring its dealers to sell only from specified locations, a practice that amounts to vertical market division, the opinion also took care to distinguish indistinguishable business practices and to suggest that vertical market divisions might be unlawful under some (unspecified) circumstances. The field of vertical restraints was by no means swept clear of legal inhibition, as it deserves to be.

Caution is appropriate. We have, after all, been this way before. The 1963 *White Motor* decision,[3] by refusing to apply a *per se* rule

Robert H. Bork is Chancellor Kent Professor of Law, Yale University.

[1] 97 S. Ct. 2549.

[2] United States v. Arnold, Schwinn & Co., 388 U.S. 365 (1967).

[3] White Motor Co. v. United States, 372 U.S. 253 (1963).

0-226-46429-6/78/1977-7000$01.79

despite the logic of prior cases, seemed to presage the beginning of useful, economically intelligible law in this area. But *White Motor* was followed in four years by the *per se* rule of *Schwinn*. *Schwinn's* result was not only wrong, but its rationale verged on mere wittiness. It is entirely possible that *Sylvania's* promising start will be ended in a few years by another *Schwinn*. This law has bumped in the dark from one inconsistency to another since *Dr. Miles* in 1911,[4] and so far it has always proved premature to announce the dawn.

There is, however, an argument to be made the other way—that *Sylvania* holds the promise of fundamental reform, not only in the law of vertical restraints but in antitrust generally. The present misshapen look of antitrust doctrine is due in large measure to the Supreme Court's habit of regarding business efficiency as either irrelevant or harmful. Whether this view arose from simple misunderstanding of the requirements of consumer welfare or from a belief that the antitrust laws were most appropriately interpreted as protective tariffs for small business need not concern us here. The point is that insufficient regard for efficient methods of production and distribution meant that hardly any business practice challenged could survive. The sole benefit the practice might confer was ruled out of court, and only possible dangers were considered. It was for this reason that the government had for some years an almost unbroken succession of victories in the Supreme Court.

The Court's *Sylvania* opinion not only counted efficiencies in favor of a challenged business practice but did so in a sophisticated way, perceiving that the elimination or mitigation of competition among a manufacturer's dealers was essential to the achievement of certain distributional efficiencies. Moreover, in resting its decision on those grounds, the Court necessarily accepted the premise that the antitrust laws are, primarily if not solely, concerned with consumer welfare. A great deal of doctrinal baggage about the social purposes of these laws, much of which was served up to them again in petitioners' brief, was silently jettisoned. This approach—concern for consumer welfare and an intelligent inquiry into the efficiency potential of challenged business practices—is capable of altering the entire corpus of antitrust jurisprudence, which now stands in considerable need of repair.

---

[4] Dr. Miles Medical Co. v. John D. Park & Sons Co., 220 U.S. 373 (1911).

The litigation over Sylvania's dealer market division was fascinating as well because of the tactical dilemmas it posed for the parties and for the courts. The difficulty from everybody's point of view was that vertical restraints are, in economic terms, all of a piece. There are no distinctions to be made among them. They should be either all illegal *per se* or all unqualifiedly lawful. But legal doctrine is not in line with economic reality; it draws lines and makes distinctions that do not exist in the world it purports to describe and control. To uphold one vertical restraint is, if an economic rationale is followed, necessarily to adopt a principle that sustains all. Similarly, to condemn one is, in strict logic, to condemn all. A law which equivocates—upholds some and condemns some—is constrained to deny the unitary character of vertical restraints. But the difficulty is that business reality keeps threatening to break through the law's words, and that poses a very touchy tactical problem. Each side in the *Sylvania* litigation attempted to deny the full implications of what it sought; for either petitioners or respondent to admit the full sweep of the principle immanent in its position would have been to risk losing the case. Either way, too much solidly established doctrine would have had to have been leveled. Either course would also have received a very bad press. Antitrust is of serious, even passionate, interest to far more people than those who understand it. That may be the greatest obstacle to reform. The microeconomic theory relevant to consumer welfare, however rigorous and inescapable it may be, does not persuade most of the constituencies the Court addresses, and any institution, even the Supreme Court, must pay attention to its constituencies.

The relevant facts in *Sylvania* were few, simple, and not greatly in dispute.[5] Sylvania entered television manufacturing in the days of black-and-white sets after World War II along with many other manufacturers. Though it survived into the days of color television, Sylvania was never a major factor in the industry. Like most other manufacturers, Sylvania sold to wholesalers and exercised no selection of or control over the retailers to whom the sets were resold. Whatever the reason, Sylvania's market position deteriorated, until by 1960 it had a share of the national market between 1 and 2 per-

[5] The facts referred to here are taken from the opinions of the Supreme Court and the Court of Appeals for the Ninth Circuit and from the Joint Appendix filed in the Supreme Court.

cent. This volume was considered inadequate to long-term profitable operation.

A new management group reassessed the corporation's marketing strategy and decided to sell directly to retailers, to select the retailers and have fewer of them, and to adopt a dealer "elbow room" policy. "Elbow room" was, in fact, a variety of dealer market division which, according to the currently reigning precedent,[6] was *per se* illegal under Section 1 of the Sherman Act.[7] Sylvania signed franchise agreements with selected dealers and explained the elbow room policy. The idea was to limit competition between resellers of Sylvania products by spacing the franchisees. In a large marketing area, such as San Francisco, there might be more than one Sylvania franchisee; in smaller areas there would probably be only one. The franchised retailers remained free to sell competing makes of television, and Sylvania remained free to cancel the franchise or to appoint additional franchisees in the area if, in its view, the area was not developed properly. The crux of the policy was that Sylvania would not add dealers if the dealer already in the area performed well. To prevent dealers from invading each other's territories, Sylvania representatives made it clear orally—it was not in the written agreement—that the franchise was for a specified location only. The dealer could change locations or open new locations but would not receive Sylvania products for sale at the new address unless Sylvania agreed.

In formal terms, this was not quite the same as a strict division of territories. Larger communities had, as mentioned, more than one franchise and any franchisee could sell outside his area. But the purpose and effect of elbow room was the same as a formal division of territories. The location clause divides dealer territories because of the cost and inconvenience of selling at a distance. A law concerned with substance would view the two practices as the same, and *Schwinn* a few years later held that vertical market division, where the manufacturer sells rather than consigns goods, was illegal *per se*.

Probably few manufacturers dropped their location clauses after *Schwinn*, and that fact reflects the recognized instability of much

---

[6] Timken Roller Bearing Co. v. United States, 341 U.S. 593 (1951) (horizontal market division).

[7] 26 Stat. 209 (1890), 15 U.S.C. § 1.

antitrust doctrine. Counseling on antitrust matters is peculiarly difficult precisely because the courts do not treat as the same things that are the same. The lawyer is not professionally obliged to advise his client to obey all the logical ramifications of *Schwinn* when he has very good reason to believe that the courts will not enforce those ramifications. Given the inconsistencies of antitrust doctrine, any competent antitrust lawyer must frequently proceed by "feel" rather than dry logic. He must often advise clients that the rule as stated is broad enough to apply to their proposed conduct, but it is most unlikely that the rule will remain as broad when the courts see what it means in their situation. In such circumstances, it is legitimate, though risky, for the lawyer to approve business practices that test the rule.

Sylvania adopted the elbow room policy and the location clause in 1962, before *Schwinn*. Whether because of that policy or for other reasons, Sylvania's national market share grew by 1965 to about 5 percent, and it stood eighth among the nation's television manufacturers. Also in 1965, however, Sylvania got into a complicated dispute with Continental T.V., one of its most successful dealers. Continental and its associated corporations, all referred to as Continental here, had franchises in several California communities, including San Francisco. The complications of the dispute are of little interest, but the upshot was that Continental opened a store in Sacramento, where it was not franchised, and moved Sylvania sets from franchised locations to the Sacramento premises.

Sylvania's franchisee in Sacramento, Handy Andy, had performed exceptionally well, getting over 15 percent of that market, or better than three times Sylvania's national average share. Sylvania was not prepared to franchise a new dealer in an area where the existing dealer was performing so well, and Handy Andy was not pleased with the prospect either. Continental would not withdraw its Sylvania sets, apparently on advice of counsel, and the result was the cancellation of Continental as a Sylvania franchisee everywhere.

Part of the dispute between Sylvania and Continental was about credit, and the finance company involved brought suit for money owed and merchandise held. Continental cross-claimed against Sylvania and the finance company on the theory that the location clauses violated Section 1 of the Sherman Act.

Once the location clause was identified as vertical market division, a highly unsatisfactory and internally inconsistent body of precedent came into play. Moreover, that body of legal doctrine interacts unpredictably with a more coherent body of economic theory. The interaction of law and economics, generally considered an unmixed good in academic circles, here takes on a different aspect and creates great tactical difficulties, though of very different orders, for counsel and the courts. It may be useful to sketch both the legal and the economic terrain over which the *Sylvania* litigation was fought out.

Restraints may involve price fixing or market division, and they may be horizontal or vertical.[8] The argument from the case law that vertical market division must be illegal *per se* is simple and inexorable. It also produces an obviously incorrect result. The argument runs this way. At least since *Addyston Pipe & Steel*,[9] courts have recognized that for the purposes of the Sherman Act there is no difference between horizontal price fixing and horizontal market division: they are identical and illegal *per se*. At least since *Dr. Miles*,[10] the courts have said that there is no difference between horizontal and vertical price fixing: they are identical and illegal *per se*. Since things which are equal to the same thing are equal to each other, it follows that vertical market division is *per se* illegal. The perfect symmetry, the logical impeccability, of that argument is not to be faulted merely because the conclusion turns out not to be true. Courts insist upon perceiving that vertical market division is not clearly bad, that it may be a useful and efficient means of doing business, and that enormous commercial disruption would follow if all forms of vertical market division were really outlawed. They are quite right. Yet, if vertical market division may often be good for consumers, and if the logic is impeccable by which the opposed conclusion is deduced, the trouble must lie in the premises from which the argument proceeds. The law has either been mistaken in its treatment of vertical price fixing or it has been mistaken in treating price fixing and market division as equivalents. There appears to be no other possibility. I shall subsequently inquire which

---

[8] See Levi, *The Parke, Davis–Colgate Doctrine: The Ban on Resale Price Maintenance*, 1960 SUPREME COURT REVIEW 258.

[9] United States v. Addyston Pipe & Steel Co., 85 Fed. 271 (6th Cir. 1898); *modified and aff'd*, 175 U.S. 211 (1899).

[10] Note 4 *supra*.

premise, that of *Addyston Pipe & Steel* or that of *Dr. Miles*, must be judged flawed. Once the nature of the error in the law of vertical restraints is seen, it becomes easier to see as well that the rules of *per se* illegality for horizontal price fixing and market division are overbroad.

Sylvania is not the first occasion on which the Supreme Court has balked at taking the logic of the related *per se* rules to its conclusion. The syllogistic argument set out above is essentially that used by the government to obtain summary judgment in *White Motor*.[11] The district court found the argument irresistible, as it is if the premises are left intact. White, a truck manufacturer, employed written dealer agreements that limited dealer resales to specified geographic areas and reserved sales to governmental units to White. White appealed to the Supreme Court, arguing that the territorial clause encouraged its dealers to compete against sellers of rival makes rather than each other, and that the customer clause ensured that the highly complex business with government would be properly handled.

The Supreme Court reversed the summary judgment for the government and remanded for trial.[12] Justice Douglas, writing for the majority, said: "This is the first case involving a territorial restriction in a *vertical* arrangement; and we know too little of the actual impact of both that restriction and the one respecting customers to reach a conclusion on the bare bones of the documentary evidence before us."[13] He was unsure whether the elimination of rivalry restricted output, as a cartel would, or created efficiency, which he thought might be permissible in special cases:[14]

> We do not know enough of the economic and business stuff out of which these arrangements emerge to be certain [of their purpose or effect]. They may be too dangerous to sanction or they may be allowable protections against aggressive competitors or the only practicable means a small company has for breaking into or staying in business. . . .

A dissent by Justice Clark, joined by Chief Justice Warren and Justice Black, said that White's arrangements were not susceptible

---

[11] United States v. White Motor Co., 194 F. Supp. 562 (N.D. Ohio 1961).

[12] Note 3 *supra*.

[13] 372 U.S. at 261.

[14] *Id*. at 263.

of justification because they eliminated competition,[15] a principle so sweeping that it would outlaw all forms of economic integration.

The majority's wish for a trial to develop the purpose and effects of the restraints imposed by White was frustrated when the parties worked out a settlement. A remand for trial was, in any event, a dubious idea. The other *per se* rules were formed on the basis of economic reasoning—some of it valid, some of it erroneous—not on the basis of trials to determine real economic tendencies. There is little a factual investigation can contribute to the judgment the law must make. Horizontal price fixing, for example, was held illegal *per se* because economic reasoning showed its inevitable tendency, not because that tendency was demonstrated by a factual record.[16] So it is, and must be, in the formulation of many antitrust rules.

Whatever its shortcomings, *White Motor* seemed a highly promising decision. The Court had recognized the possibility that one form of vertical restraint and one form of market division could create efficiencies, and therefore that a *per se* rule might be inappropriate. If that possibility were explored, it seemed possible the Court would ultimately realize that something was very wrong with each of the other *per se* doctrines that had led the district court, quite logically, to a wrong conclusion. It was not to be.

Four years later, in 1967, the Court dealt again with the problem of vertical market division.[17] Arnold, Schwinn & Co. sold bicycles it manufactured in a variety of ways but always insisted that its wholesalers sell only within assigned territories and only to retailers franchised by Schwinn, and that its retailers sell only to ultimate consumers. The Supreme Court was in no better position to answer the questions about the purpose and effect of vertical restrictions than it had been in *White Motor*. Indeed, it now avoided the need for one answer by suggesting that efficiency was not, after all, of particular concern: "The antitrust outcome does not turn merely on the presence of sound business reason or motive," but upon the question whether "the effect upon competition in the marketplace is substantially adverse."[18] One might have thought the two ques-

---

15 *Id.* at 275, 281.

16 United States v. Trans-Missouri Freight Ass'n, 166 U.S. 290 (1897); United States v. Addyston Pipe & Steel Co., note 9 *supra*; United States v. Trenton Potteries Co., 273 U.S. 392 (1927).

17 Note 2 *supra*.

18 388 U.S. at 375.

tions closely related, if not identical. In any case, the opinion did not answer either the question of efficiency (beyond denigrating it by saying that cartels increase profits, too) or the question of restriction of output. Instead, it offered a rule that turned upon no conventional antitrust or economic criteria but, of all things, upon the passage of title:[19]

> We conclude that the proper application of § 1 of the Sherman Act to this problem requires differentiation between the situation where the manufacturer parts with title, dominion, or risk with respect to the article, and where he completely retains ownership and risk of loss. . . . [W]e are not prepared to introduce the inflexibility which a *per se* rule might bring if it were applied to prohibit all vertical restrictions of territory and all franchising. . . . But to allow this freedom where the manufacturer has parted with dominion over the goods—the usual marketing situation—would violate the ancient rule against restraints on alienation and open the door to exclusivity of outlets and limitation of territory further than prudence permits.

This unfortunate passage seemed so far from concerns relevant to antitrust that it inspired criticism bordering on ribaldry. It was said that the fusion of law and economics had at last produced a synthesis: equitable servitudes do not run with chattels personal. It was suggested that the antitrust bar at last had a guide to the permissible length of requirements contracts: a life or lives in being, plus twenty-one years—anything longer would violate the ancient rule against perpetuities. The parodies were symptoms of exasperation and, perhaps, of sensed insult. Nobody ever thought of a satisfactory explanation of the asserted competitive significance of who had title to the bicycles. The law seemed further from a satisfactory solution, further even from satisfactory questions or terms of discourse, than it had been after *White Motor*.

The proximate cause of the Court's difficulty seemed obvious. It was struggling, as it continues to struggle, with the logical but patently unrealistic results of a wrong premise laid down by Justice Hughes in the 1911 *Dr. Miles* decision, a premise rigidly adhered to ever since. In holding a resale price maintenance program illegal *per se*, Justice Hughes reasoned from the *per se* illegality of horizontal agreements among competitors. He said there was no more

[19] *Id.* at 378–80.

valid reason to permit a manufacturer to eliminate competition among his retailers than to permit the retailers to do it themselves. The Court has been unwilling to reexamine that proposition, though it is obviously incorrect. It also adheres to the obviously correct position that price fixing and market division are alike and should be treated so. The trouble is that it is apparent that vertical market division is capable of creating distributive efficiencies that the Court does not wish to destroy. The consequence is that the Court adheres to the premises that require *per se* illegality for market division and refuses to reach that result. That intellectual posture is bound to produce opinions that walk a little funny.

The economic analysis of vertical restraints, and hence the fallacy of Justice Hughes's argument in *Dr. Miles*, is by now fairly well known.[20] The analysis begins, and very nearly ends, with the postulate that businessmen prefer to make money and find little satisfaction in giving it away needlessly to their customers. If that rather stodgy proposition is accepted, the conclusion follows that all vertical restraints should be lawful. It is easy to see why. No manufacturer wants to allow his retailers a profit above normal. That is more than he has to pay for retailing services; it is money out of his own pocket for no particular purpose. The last thing he wants to do, therefore, is assist his retailers in forming a cartel. They would restrict output and make more money, while he would make less. When we observe a manufacturer setting a minimum resale price or dividing his dealers' territories, the one thing we know for certain is that he is not limiting their rivalry in order to help them mulct the public and, incidentally, himself. That would be the same as if the manufacturer acquired a valuable patent and donated it to his retailers so that they could charge him a fee to practice his own invention. We do not observe behavior of that sort, and a legal doctrine which supposes it to be common is plainly mistaken.

The manufacturer who employs a vertical restraint does so because he believes he thereby induces dealer behavior that makes distribution more efficient. There are a variety of ways in which

---

[20] See Bowman, *The Prerequisites and Effects of Resale Price Maintenance*, 22 U. Chi. L. Rev. 825 (1955); Telser, *Why Should Manufacturers Want Fair Trade?*, 3 J. Law & Econ. 86 (1960); Bork, *The Rule of Reason and the Per Se Concept: Price Fixing and Market Division, II*, 75 Yale L. J. 373 (1966); Posner, *Antitrust Policy and the Supreme Court: An Analysis of the Restricted Distribution, Horizontal Merger and Potential Competition Decisions*, 75 Column L. Rev. 282 (1975). The majority opinion in *Sylvania* relies upon portions of this literature.

restraints may enhance efficiency. The one most commonly discussed in the literature is the optimization of dealer sales effort, including the provision of information to consumers, through the elimination of "free riding." All selling involves the provision of information and persuasion. The more detailed the information, the more efficient it will be to provide it at the point of sale to persons who have identified themselves as potential buyers and who, in addition, may have questions not easily anticipated and addressed in mass market advertising. The manufacturer, therefore, will often want his dealers to invest money and time in carrying a full line of his models for display, instructing sales personnel in the product's features and comparative advantages, explaining the product and its use to potential customers, and performing similar functions. The dealer will do these things only if he can recapture their cost in the price at which he sells. But some dealers will perceive that they can let others incur the costs of persuasion and capture the customer by offering a lower price. Such dealers take a free ride. If free riding becomes common, no dealer will find it worthwhile to provide the sales effort that would otherwise be optimal.

The manufacturer can ensure optimal dealer sales effort by dividing territories or by fixing minimum resale prices. Where the product is effectively sold through one or a few outlets in an area, the manufacturer may use market division (or some variant of the species, such as exclusive dealing or location clauses). Where many outlets in an area are preferable, the manufacturer may choose resale price maintenance.

These practices are pro-consumer in the only sense that a free enterprise law such as antitrust can define that term. The manufacturer will employ vertical restraints only if consumers respond more to the information provided than they would to lower prices without the information. It is true that some consumers would prefer the lower prices without the information, but the technology of distribution may not allow the preferences of both groups of consumers to be met, and the manufacturer will choose to satisfy the larger number. That is not an uncommon problem. Manufacturing economies may dictate a single model of a product, even though a minority of consumers would prefer a lower-priced model. If antitrust sees no problem in that, it should see no problem in a manufacturer's decision to sell a model with dealer-provided information rather than without. This analysis demonstrates (it is not too strong a word) that antitrust should have no concern with vertical restraints; all should be lawful.

After trial on Continental T.V.'s Sherman Act claim, Justice Tom C. Clark, sitting by designation as a district judge, ruled that *Schwinn* was the controlling precedent and instructed the jury that it was *per se* illegal for a manufacturer to agree on their locations with dealers. The jury found for Continental T.V. and fixed damages at $591,505. The court automatically tripled that to $1,774,515 and also awarded plaintiff $275,000 in attorneys' fees.[21] Sylvania appealed, and a panel of the Court of Appeals for the Ninth Circuit affirmed the district court, two to one. Rehearing en banc was granted, however, and the panel opinion was withdrawn.

The en banc court of appeals, dividing seven to four, reversed the judgment of the district court and remanded for further proceedings, holding that the location clause was not *per se* unreasonable.[22] Both the majority and the minority opinions had difficulty in arriving at their conclusions because a decision either way undercut established law, and each side was correct in accusing the other of doing just that.

Judge Ely's opinion for the majority had, as might be expected, its greatest difficulty with *Schwinn*. Sylvania had achieved vertical market division by a location clause; Schwinn had achieved it by a territorial clause and a customer clause. This difference in form tempted the majority to argue that "Sylvania imposed neither of the restrictions that *Schwinn* appropriately condemned."[23] The argument continued: "Thus a critical and very obvious distinction between the restrictions in *Schwinn* and those of Sylvania is that *Schwinn* involved a restriction on the locations and types of permissible *vendees*, while Sylvania only imposed restrictions on the permissible locations of *vendors*."[24]

It never became clear why that difference in form made a difference in competitive substance. But the judges in the majority quite correctly perceived that Sylvania's system created valuable efficiencies, and they appear to have engaged in somewhat tortuous reasoning in an effort to save those efficiencies from the stultifying force of *Schwinn*.

---

21 GTE Sylvania, Inc. v. Continental T.V., Inc., 537 F.2d 980, 986 (9th Cir. 1976).

22 *Id*. at 989, 990.

23 *Id*. at 989.

24 *Id*. at 990.

The main dissenting opinion, written by Judge Kilkenny,[25] relied upon *Schwinn* and had its difficulties with what the majority called the "veritable avalanche of precedent" upholding the legality of exclusive dealership contracts.[26] Exclusive dealerships divide territories:[27]

> The majority conveniently confuses and integrates location clauses and exclusive dealerships, claiming them to be so interdependent as to make exclusive dealerships useless without resale-type location clauses as an enforcement option. The two are clearly distinguishable. In an exclusive dealership, the distributor, dealer, or franchisee obtains a manufacturer's *self-imposed promise not to contract with another distributor in the general area*. . . . It is one thing for a manufacturer to restrict its own behavior. It is quite another to try to restrict that of an independent business entity.

Of course, if the dealer asked for the exclusive dealing promise then it, too, would be restricting the behavior of an independent business entity, and the distinction would collapse. Not that it is much of a distinction, in any event. All commercial contracts restrict the behavior of independent business entities; that is their function.

The dissent, moreover, did not face up to the majority's point that, formalities of who made the promise aside, exclusive dealing agreements are worthless to both manufacturer and dealer without a location clause. As the majority said, under *Schwinn's* "rule of *per se* illegality, *if a dealer is franchised anywhere he is franchised everywhere*."[28] The manufacturer may promise dealer A that he will franchise nobody else in his area, but he cannot keep the promise if dealer B, franchised anywhere else, is free because of *Schwinn* to open next door to dealer A.

The distinctions offered by the two sides were inevitably inadequate. The majority opinion failed to persuade that location clauses are not within the *Schwinn* rule of *per se* illegality, and the dissent failed to persuade that outlawing location clauses does not destroy exclusive dealing and franchising. Neither the majority nor the dis-

---

[25] *Id.* at 1004.

[26] *Id.* at 997.

[27] *Id.* at 1013–14.

[28] *Id.* at 998.

sent is to be faulted for this. They were trapped by doctrine they lacked the authority to revise. It might have been a contribution, however, if each side had said as much.

The Supreme Court granted certiorari, and, since the parties faced the same dilemma as did the two wings of the Ninth Circuit, a delicate problem of appellate advocacy arose. Sylvania's attorneys felt unable to admit flatly that a decision their way would undercut *Schwinn* and, for that matter, *Dr. Miles.*[29] Continental's attorneys felt constrained to deny that a decision their way meant that to franchise anywhere is to franchise everywhere.[30] They are not to be faulted either. The advocate's duty to his client is to try to gain a majority of the Court, and it is impossible to say that a rigorously logical presentation will do that in a field where the Court has created inconsistencies. Better, the advocate may well reason, not to ask too much, but to suggest that a decision your way is safe because it would have few ramifications, while a decision for your opponent would have vast, unsettling, and not fully known implications. In *Sylvania* each side was correct, at least about the implications of its adversary's position.

The Supreme Court affirmed the judgment of the court of appeals. Mr. Justice Powell wrote the opinion for five members of the majority; Mr. Justice White concurred on different reasoning; Mr. Justice Brennan, joined by Mr. Justice Marshall, dissented; and Mr. Justice Rehnquist took no part in the case.

Mr. Justice Powell's opinion is noteworthy both because of its argument and because it commanded a majority of the Court while making a sharp philosophical break with the antitrust approach with which we have become familiar if not content. The opinion began, as candor required it should, by stating an inability to distinguish *Schwinn*:[31]

> In intent and competitive impact, the retail customer restriction in *Schwinn* is indistinguishable from the location restriction in the present case. In both cases the restrictions limited the freedom of the retailer to dispose of the purchased products as he desired. The fact that one restriction was addressed

[29] Brief for Respondent, pp. 29–44.

[30] Brief for Petitioners, pp. 42–49.

[31] 97 S.Ct. at 2556.

> to territory and the other to customers is irrelevant to functional antitrust analysis, and indeed, to the language and broad thrust of the opinion in *Schwinn.*

Mr. Justice Powell then undertook a reconsideration of *Schwinn* and began with the basic issue of the justification necessary for a *per se* rule: "*Per se* rules of illegality are appropriate only when they relate to conduct that is manifestly anti-competitive"[32] or, as the language he quoted from the *Northern Pacific* opinion put it, when a practice or agreement displays a "pernicious effect on competition and lack of any redeeming virtue."[33] But the "market impact of vertical restrictions is complex because of their potential for a simultaneous reduction of intrabrand competition and stimulation of interbrand competition."[34] Mr. Justice Powell cited examples of distributive efficiencies that must be considered "redeeming virtues." Manufacturers may use them, for example, to "induce retailers to engage in promotional activities or to provide service and repair facilities necessary to the efficient marketing of their products."[35] He referred to the "free rider" effect discussed earlier.

Since the distinction in Schwinn between sale and nonsale transactions did not correspond to any real difference in competitive impacts, the question arose whether to extend the *Schwinn per se* rule to nonsale transactions or return sale transactions to a reasonableness test. Here Mr. Justice Powell adverted to the test stated in *Northern Pacific* and noted that vertical restrictions of a nonprice variety did not meet the standard for *per se* illegality:[36]

> Such restrictions, in varying forms, are widely used in our free market economy. . . . [T]here is substantial scholarly and judicial authority supporting their economic utility. There is relatively little authority to the contrary. Certainly, there has been no showing in this case, either generally or with respect to Sylvania's agreements, that vertical restrictions have or are likely to have a "pernicious effect on competition" or that they "lack . . . any redeeming virtue." . . . Accordingly, we conclude that the *per se* rule stated in *Schwinn* must be overruled.

---

[32] *Id.* at 2558.

[33] Northern Pacific Ry. Co. v. United States, 356 U.S. 1, 5 (1958).

[34] 97 S.Ct. at 2558–59.

[35] *Id.* at 2561.

[36] *Id.* at 2562.

The opinion was a straightforward performance that rid the law of a bad rule and a hapless precedent. The economic argument, only part of which has been summarized here, was crisp, on point, and far better than the antitrust standard. These virtues alone should win the opinion high marks, but the news is even better than that. First, though he did not argue the point, Mr. Justice Powell proceeded on the asumption, which runs contrary to much Supreme Court reasoning in the past,[37] that the creation of business efficiency helps justify a practice under the antitrust laws. Had that same, indisputably proper, assumption been made earlier by the Supreme Court, much of antitrust, including all law about vertical relationships and all law about mergers, would be different and consumers better served. If that assumption continues in the law of the future, antitrust may yet be made a policy that clearly does more good than harm rather than remaining a policy whose net effects are in doubt. Concern for efficiencies also implies that a major, if not the sole, end of antitrust is consumer welfare, a point disputed in Mr. Justice White's concurring opinion.

Having said this much about the greatly encouraging aspects of Mr. Justice Powell's opinion and the adherence of a majority to its principles, I must also say that the decision is not quite an occasion for euphoria. It, too, draws distinctions and expresses reservations that, if taken seriously in the future, are capable of continuing the confusion that has so long characterized both the law of vertical restraints and the law of horizontal price fixing and market division. These matters are best taken up in connection with Mr. Justice White's concurrence.

Mr. Justice White argued that *Schwinn* could be distinguished and need not be overruled in order to uphold Sylvania's dealer location clause.[38] The distinction he suggested would, however, plunge the courts into complicated analyses of the differences between types of vertical restraint. The problem is less that the analysis is complex than that it relies upon differences that do not exist.

Mr. Justice White thought Sylvania's case "distinguishable from *Schwinn* because there is less potential for restraint of intrabrand competition and more potential for stimulating interbrand competition."[39] The majority opinion left itself open for this counter by

---

[37] See, *e.g.*, Brown Shoe Co. v. United States, 370 U.S. 294, 344 (1962); F.T.C. v. Procter & Gamble Co., 386 U.S. 568, 580 (1967).

[38] 97 S.Ct. at 2563.

[39] *Ibid.*

suggesting that the market impact of vertical restrictions was complex, thus inviting inquiry whether it might not vary from case to case. Mr. Justice White noted that *Schwinn* involved, among other things, a restriction "prohibiting franchised retailers from selling Schwinn products to nonfranchised retailers."[40] This was worse for intrabrand competition than Sylvania's location clause, he thought, because it might prevent reselling to discounters. That is quite true, of course, but it does not militate against Schwinn's restraint any more than against Sylvania's. The efficiency sought depends precisely upon preventing a discounter from taking a free ride.

The two cases were also said to differ, in Sylvania's favor, with respect to interbrand competition. Sylvania had no economic power in the product market, whereas Mr. Justice White believed that Schwinn had. When Sylvania introduced the location clause as part of the elbow room policy, it had between 1 and 2 percent of the market, and that share had since risen to 5 percent. When Schwinn adopted its policy, it was the leading bicycle producer in the country with 22.5 percent of the market, and that share fell over the next ten years to 12.8 percent as another manufacturer replaced Schwinn as the leader. This observation led up to Mr. Justice White's distinction of *Schwinn*. Two considerations permitted that to be done:[41]

> The first is that, as the majority puts it, "when interbrand competition exists, as it does among television manufacturers, it provides a significant check on the exploitation of intrabrand market power because of the ability of consumers to substitute a different brand of the same product." . . . Second is the view, argued forcefully in the economic literature cited by the majority, that the potential benefits of vertical restraints in promoting interbrand competition are particularly strong where the manufacturer imposing the restraints is seeking to enter a new market or to expand a small market share.

Neither of these distinctions would be useful in the law, because neither corresponds to any difference in economic effect that courts need concern themselves with. Each consideration leads, and led Mr. Justice White, to the conclusion that the ability to employ vertical restraints should be limited to firms of very small market share. Market share analysis properly affects the application of some

---

[40] *Ibid.*

[41] *Id.* at 2566.

rules in antitrust, but this is not one of them. Whatever the manufacturer's market share, 1 percent or 100 percent, our basic postulate holds that he will not adopt marketing strategies that transfer money from his pocket to the pockets of his retailers. Competitor or monopolist, if the manufacturer imposes a vertical restraint, he thinks he is getting more efficient distribution. Greater efficiency is valuable to consumers without regard to the market share of the firm that achieves it. Courts should not examine a manufacturer's decision about comparative distributive efficiencies any more than they would use an antitrust suit as the occasion to inquire whether the manufacturer has the machinery in his plant lined up in the most effective sequence and, if in the judge's estimation he does not, to enjoin a new floor plan.

Mr. Justice White also produced a noneconomic argument to bolster his conclusion. He saw the distinction in *Schwinn* between sale and nonsale transactions as resting on "the notion in many of our cases involving vertical restraints that independent businessmen should have the freedom to dispose of the goods they own as they see fit."[42] That notion is indeed to be found in some cases, but that is not the same as saying that the notion has merit and should be retained. The manufacturer and the retailer are in a continuing relationship that is made more effective in serving consumers by the restraints. Moreover, the retailer is free to dispose of the goods he owns as he sees fit; it is just that a retailer who destroys efficiency by doing so will not be sold additional goods.

But this is sparring. The real objection to the noneconomic theme Mr. Justice White correctly identifies in the cases is that it is so undefined as to be virtually useless as an analytical concept. No businessman who has signed a contract is independent in the sense that he may, without penalty, do with his business, goods, resources, etc., as he sees fit. The antitrust theme, as stated, is commercially anarchic; it would deny the utility of contractual control in increasing efficiency. There seems no way the concept can be refined and narrowed that is particularly intelligible. Why do we worry only about the independence of the retailer from any contractual obligations to the manufacturer? What of the manufacturer who owns goods, would like to ship them to Canada for higher profits, but is under contract to deliver them to a retailer in Chicago? That manufacturer is an independent businessman whose freedom to dispose of

---

[42] *Id.* at 2567.

goods he owns as he sees fit is curtailed. If, in both cases, it is true that compelling the performance of obligations voluntarily undertaken creates efficiency, how can the law distinguish between them? There appears to be no way except for uncritical sentimentality about the "small" man, though it is not clear why the retailer is any "smaller" than the consumer who loses due to the retailer's refusal to accept the restraint on the location of his franchise. It is true that the dealer freedom principle is embedded in the cases, some of them at least, but if it is an idea that serves no purpose and harms consumers, perhaps it ought to be pried loose from antitrust jurisprudence and discarded.

The majority opinion was vulnerable on another point, however, and Mr. Justice White pointed that out. Objecting to reliance on "relevant economic impact" as the test, he noted:[43]

> It is common ground among the leading advocates of a purely economic approach to the question of distribution restraints that the economic arguments in favor of allowing vertical nonprice restraints generally apply to vertical price restraints as well. . . . The effect, if not the intention, of the Court's opinion is necessarily to call into question the firmly established *per se* rule against price restraints.

This economic perception constantly troubled those, attorneys and judges, who wished to undercut *Schwinn* and was used as a rhetorical weapon by those who wished to preserve the precedent. The rule against vertical price fixing seems sacrosanct. Thus Continental T.V. argued that those writers who urged the legalization of vertical market division were wrong about its beneficent effects but quite right in seeing it as equivalent to vertical price fixing. ("For this Court to accept that view would be to reject *Dr. Miles* and every vertical case after *Dr. Miles*.")[44] Sylvania, meanwhile, engaged in an awkward attempt to suggest differences between the two forms of restraint, such as that vertical market division does not prevent a dealer from lowering prices as resale price maintenance does.[45] That is no more than a description of the different forms of restraint that have the same tendencies.

Mr. Justice Powell's opinion for the majority attempted to dispose of the awkward similarities between the two forms of restraint

---

[43] *Id.* at 2568.

[44] Brief for Petitioners, p. 51.

[45] Brief for Respondent, pp. 62–64.

in a footnote, suggesting that there are "significant differences that could easily justify different treatment":[46]

> In his concurring opinion in *White Motor Co.*, Mr. Justice Brennan noted that, unlike nonprice restrictions, "[r]esale price maintenance is not designed to, but almost invariably does in fact, reduce price competition not only *among* sellers of the affected product, but quite as much *between* that product and competing brands.". . . Professor Posner also recognized that "industry-wide resale price maintenance might facilitate cartelizing." . . . Furthermore, Congress recently has expressed its approval of a *per se* analysis of vertical price restrictions by repealing those provisions of the Miller-Tydings and McGuire Acts allowing fair trade pricing at the option of the individual States. . . . No similar expression of congressional intent exists for nonprice restrictions.

That is, I agree, the best case that can be made for treating price and nonprice vertical restraints differently—two economic statements and a statement of congressional attitude. The economic statements are easily shown not to be significant, and we are then left with a congressional misunderstanding of the problem, but a misunderstanding that has not been written into law. Perhaps different treatment can be justified, as the majority states, but not really "easily."

Mr. Justice Brennan's observation is an accurate description of resale price maintenance but does not distinguish that restraint from vertical market division. The purpose of both vertical price and nonprice restraints is to allow a higher price to induce additional activity and to compensate for its costs. Both, therefore, have an effect in the same direction on price competition with other brands. Nor is there reason to doubt that the net effect of each restraint is, despite formal differences, beneficial.

Industry-wide use of resale price maintenance might facilitate cartelization, but it is not likely and it is easily detected if it should occur. Industry-wide use of telephones may also facilitate cartelization, but if the general effect of such use is to make industry more efficient, as is the case with both resale price maintenance and telephones, there is little utility in a *per se* rule against either.

Professor Posner, who is cited in the footnote, did no more than

[46] 97 S.Ct. at 2558–59 n. 18.

recognize, as others have done, the theoretical possibility that resale price maintenance may be used as an implement either of a dealers' or of a manufacturers' cartel.[47] Dealers, the argument usually runs, may organize and force manufacturers to use resale price maintenance that does not purchase efficiency but simply gives the cartel extra profits. The manufacturers must be coerced to do this, and it is not apparent why the dealers would not in most cases find it simpler and less expensive simply to agree on prices without involving unwilling manfacturers. The dealers would have to coerce all or almost all manufacturers to make the cartel effective. The likelihood of detection seems enormous. Some manufacturers would complain, the amount of organizational and maintenance activity would be large and visible, and the antitrust authorities could pay special attention to cases of the industry-wide use of resale price maintenance. The idea that manufacturers often employ resale price maintenance to assist their cartelization is implausible. It assumes the manufacturers have no other means of detecting price cuts and agree to fix resale prices so that manufacturer cuts can be seen in retailer cuts. But manufacturer price cutting will be made known by retailers who bargain for prices with other manufacturers; the theory could apply only where each manufacturer has exclusive outlets. That means the products are probably highly differentiated, so that a cartel agreement would be difficult to run and competition would break out through dealer sales effort. Again, all or almost all the industry would have to be involved and detection would be relatively simple.

The final point made by Mr. Justice Powell to distinguish vertical price and nonprice restraints was that Congress had recently repealed its exemption of resale price maintenance carried on under state statutes from the interdiction of the Sherman Act.[48] The weight to be given that action is not free from doubt. Congress originally passed the authorizing statutes because it then disagreed with the Supreme Court's rule that resale price maintenance should be illegal *per se*. The later repeal indicates that it has changed its view. But Congress has not legislated *per se* illegality, either through this repeal or in the original Sherman Act. It has said, at most, that

---

[47] I have argued elsewhere, at a length not to be tolerated here, that the theoretical possibility is not an adequate basis for a rule against resale price maintenance. Bork, note 20 *supra*, at 405–15.

[48] 89 Stat. 801 (1975).

it thinks the Court's *per se* rule was correct, but said it in a form that does not have the binding force of a statute, almost as if it had passed a nonbinding resolution. The Court, presumably, still has its original obligation to develop the law of the Sherman Act according to its best economic understanding. Should the Court become persuaded that vertical price restraints are means of creating distributive efficiency and their net impact beneficial to consumers, it would not seem bound by the repeal of the Miller-Tydings and McGuire Acts to refuse to give effect to that perception in modifying Sherman Act rules. If the Court regarded itself as so bound, it ought at a minimum give the argument for legality and state that only its reading of the congressional mood or intention prevented it from overruling *Dr. Miles*.

The inconsistency that Mr. Justice White pointed to in the majority's acceptance of vertical nonprice restraints and rejection of vertical price restraints is a real one, and no doubt it will continue to threaten the legality of vertical nonprice restraints so long as it is not faced. The law has difficulty living forever with inconsistencies; it has somewhat less difficulty removing them by producing the wrong consistency; and the strength of the unsophisticated, undifferentiated opposition to price fixing in any form may move a future Court or the Congress to produce the wrong consistent rule.

The trouble with the correct analysis of vertical restraints is that it appeared in the literature long after the law had to deal with the phenomenon, so that now the courts are asked to rethink and abandon an entire body of doctrine of many years standing. That would be difficult for courts to do in any event. It is probably doubly difficult since the new, correct doctrine would have to be supported by argument that some of the Court's most important constituencies would not understand. The rhetorical force of microeconomics is limited to a rather small audience. Distinctions between types of price fixing would not come easily to persons who have been trained to the slogan that all price fixing is evil and that persons who engage in it ought to go to jail. Still, the alternative is for the courts to proceed as they have, create and tolerate inconsistencies within the law, and destroy many socially valuable means of distribution. For the judge who understands the situation, the choice is probably not a comfortable one.

DOUGLAS LAYCOCK

FEDERAL INTERFERENCE WITH STATE PROSECUTIONS: THE NEED FOR PROSPECTIVE RELIEF

Six years ago, in *Younger v. Harris*[1] and *Samuels v. Mackell*,[2] the Supreme Court announced major restrictions on the power of federal courts to interfere with state prosecutions. These cases generally require dismissal of federal suits challenging state laws whenever there is a state prosecution pending against the federal plaintiff. Every subsequent Term has produced cases explicating these restrictions.[3]

Douglas Laycock is Assistant Professor of Law, The University of Chicago.

AUTHOR'S NOTE: My student research assistant, Paul Beach, was invaluable at every stage of this project. David Currie, Owen Fiss, and Joseph Kattan offered helpful comments on intermediate drafts.

[1] 401 U.S. 37 (1971).

[2] 401 U.S. 66 (1971).

[3] Trainor v. Hernandez, 97 S. Ct. 1911 (1977); Ohio Bureau of Empl. Servs. v. Hodory, 97 S. Ct. 1898, 1903–04 (1977); Wooley v. Maynard, 97 S. Ct. 1428 (1977); Juidice v. Vail, 97 S. Ct. 1211 (1977); Lockport v. Citizens for Community Action, 430 U.S. 259, 264 n.8 (1977); Colorado River Water Conservation Dist. v. United States, 424 U.S. 800, 816–17 (1976); Rizzo v. Goode, 423 U.S. 362 (1976); Doran v. Salem Inn, Inc., 422 U.S. 922 (1975); Hicks v. Miranda, 422 U.S. 332 (1975); Ellis v. Dyson, 421 U.S. 426 (1975); Kugler v. Helfant, 421 U.S. 117 (1975); McLucas v. DeChamplain, 421 U.S. 21, 33–34 (1975); Schlesinger v. Councilman, 420 U.S. 738, 753–61 (1975); Huffman v. Pursue, Ltd., 420 U.S. 592 (1975); Gerstein v. Pugh, 420 U.S. 103, 108 n.9

0-226-46429-6/78/1977-6000$03.47

A critical assumption underlying these cases is that defense of the pending prosecution usually furnishes an adequate remedy for any violation of the defendant's federal rights.[4] This assumption stands unjustified by the Court majority, unchallenged by the dissenters, and substantially unexamined by the commentators.[5] The major thesis of this article is that in many cases the criminal defense cannot provide an adequate remedy, because the criminal court cannot grant interlocutory, prospective, or class relief. These remedial limitations follow from the nature of the criminal process and are independent of conflicting views concerning the willingness of state judges to protect federal rights. Thus, even if one accepts the core of *Younger*—that federal relief should be withheld where the pending state remedy is adequate—a pending prosecution should not be a near automatic bar to a federal action. The federal court should consider whether the state remedy is actually adequate on each set of facts and provide supplemental relief where needed.

I. Younger and Its Progeny

Subject to a handful of narrow exceptions, which few federal plaintiffs have successfully invoked, *Younger* made federal relief unavailable to test the constitutionality of a state statute when there is pending a state criminal proceeding in which the constitutional challenge may be raised. It is this rule and its extensions which are now generally referred to as the *Younger* doctrine or as *Younger* "abstention."[6] Despite the abstention label, the rule requires dismis-

---

(1975); Sosna v. Iowa, 419 U.S. 393, 396–97 n.3 (1975); Allee v. Medrano, 416 U.S. U.S. 802 (1974); Village of Belle Terre v. Boraas, 416 U.S. 1, 3 n.1 (1974); Steffel v. Thompson, 415 U.S. 452 (1974); Speight v. Slaton, 415 U.S. 333 (1974); O'Shea v. Littleton, 414 U.S. 488 (1974); Gibson v. Berryhill, 411 U.S. 564 (1973); Braden v. 30th Jud. Circuit Court of Ky., 410 U.S. 484, 491–92 (1973); Roe v. Wade, 410 U.S. 113, 123–29 (1973); Fuentes v. Shevin, 407 U.S. 67, 71 n.3, 98 (1972); Lake Carriers' Ass'n v. MacMullan, 406 U.S. 498, 509–10 (1972); Lynch v. Household Finance Corp., 405 U.S. 538, 556, 560 (1972); see also McGautha v. California, 402 U.S. 183, 259 n.10 (1971); Byrne v. Karalexis, 401 U.S. 216 (1971); Dyson v. Stein, 401 U.S. 200 (1971); Perez v. Ledesma, 401 U.S. 82 (1971); Boyle v. Landry, 401 U.S. 77 (1971). (Hereinafter these cases will be identified in footnotes by the name of the first party.)

[4] See *Trainor*, 97 S. Ct. at 1916–17; *Kugler*, 421 U.S. at 124; *Huffman*, 420 U.S. at 600–03; *Steffel*, 415 U.S. at 460, 462; *Younger*, 401 U.S. at 43, 45–46.

[5] But see Fiss, *Dombrowski*, 86 Yale L. J. 1103, 1125 (1977); Gilbert, *Questions Unanswered by the February Sextet*, 1972 Utah L. Rev. 14, 15–17; Note, 90 Harv. L. Rev. 1133, 1305–08, 1321 (1977).

[6] For a more detailed review of the doctrine's development, see Fiss, note 5 *supra*.

sal rather than a stay pending the state proceedings.[7] *Younger* abstention applies to requests for injunctions against enforcement[8] and to requests for declaratory judgments that statutes are unconstitutional.[9] The federal courts must now abstain not only when there is a state criminal proceeding but also when there is a state civil proceeding in aid of the criminal law,[10] a state civil contempt proceeding,[11] or a civil enforcement action brought by a state in its sovereign capacity.[12] The doctrine requires deference not only to state proceedings pending when the federal case is commenced but to subsequent state proceedings commenced before "any proceedings of substance on the merits" in the federal case.[13] Once a state case is pending, the would-be federal plaintiff must pursue all state appellate remedies; he cannot end the state case by refusing to litigate it.[14] The doctrine is derived from "principles of equity, comity, and federalism,"[15] and the Court has said that those same principles preclude ongoing federal injunctive interference in the nonjudicial parts of the state criminal justice system, apparently without regard to whether a state case is pending in which a remedy could be had.[16]

There are, however, limits to the doctrine's expansion. After some initial uncertainty,[17] the Court held the doctrine inapplicable when no state proceeding is pending.[18] Thus *Younger* does not require that the would-be federal plaintiff initiate state proceedings which might provide a remedy,[19] and no one joined Chief Justice

---

[7] *Gibson*, 411 U.S. at 577; *cf.* Railroad Comm'n v. Pullman Co., 312 U.S. 496 (1941) (abstention to permit construction of ambiguous state law); England v. Louisiana State Bd. of Medical Exam'rs, 375 U.S. 411 (1964) (right to return to federal court after *Pullman* abstention); Reetz v. Bozanich, 397 U.S. 82, 85, 87 (1970) (federal court should retain jurisdiction pending *Pullman* abstention).

[8] *Younger*, 401 U.S. 37.

[9] *Samuels*, 401 U.S. 66.

[10] *Huffman*, 420 U.S. at 603–07.

[11] *Juidice*, 97 S. Ct. 1211.

[12] *Trainor*, 97 S. Ct. 1911.

[13] *Hicks*, 422 U.S. at 349 (alternative holding); accord, *Doran*, 422 U.S. 922.

[14] *Huffman*, 420 U.S. at 607–11.

[15] *Steffel*, 415 U.S. at 460.

[16] *Rizzo*, 423 U.S. at 380; *O'Shea*, 414 U.S. at 499–504; see Fiss, note 5 *supra*, at 1148–60.

[17] *Younger*, 401 U.S. at 45–47; Becker v. Thompson, 459 F.2d 919 (5th Cir. 1972), rev'd *Steffel*, 415 U.S. 452.

[18] *Steffel*, 415 U.S. 452; *Doran*, 422 U.S. 922.

[19] *Lake Carriers' Ass'n*, 406 U.S. at 510.

Burger last Term when he suggested that state administrative remedies be exhausted as a prerequisite to any federal relief, even direct review of a criminal conviction.[20] The Court has explicitly held open the question whether *Younger* abstention is required when state administrative proceedings are pending[21] or when ordinary civil litigation between private parties is pending.[22] The benefits of the doctrine may be waived by state officials.[23]

II. The Unexamined Question

Although the *Younger* doctrine does not apply when no prosecution is pending, it would be incorrect to say that the doctrine does not prevent injunctions against future prosecutions. Once the doctrine comes into play, it requires dismissal of the federal lawsuit.[24] *Younger* does not merely deny an injunction against the pending prosecution; it denies any relief that depends on resolution of the constitutional issue raised in the state case.[25] This result is based on a fear that federal resolution of the constitutional issue will indirectly interfere with the pending prosecution. But its effect has been to deny prospective relief—relief directed to future violations and future prosecutions—without attention to whether defense of a pending prosecution for a past violation can provide such relief.

The Court's opinions have not directly addressed the problem. The opinion in *Younger* offered one possible answer when it suggested that the standards there announced had historically been applied not only to requests to enjoin pending prosecutions but also to requests to enjoin threatened future prosecutions.[26] But that is quite misleading. As has been extensively documented,[27] the cases

---

[20] Moore v. City of East Cleveland, 97 S. Ct. 1932, 1947–52 (1977).

[21] *Gibson*, 411 U.S. at 574–75; *Ohio Bureau*, 97 S. Ct. at 1904 n.10.

[22] *Trainor*, 97 S. Ct. at 1919 n.8; *Juidice*, 97 S. Ct. at 1218 n.13; *Huffman*, 420 U.S. at 607.

[23] *Ohio Bureau*, 97 S. Ct. at 1904; *Sosna*, 419 U.S. at 396–97 n.3.

[24] *Doran*, 422 U.S. 922; *Samuels*, 401 U.S. 66.

[25] *Trainor*, 97 S. Ct. at 1920 (opinion of the Court); *id.* at 1923–24 (Brennan, J., dissenting); *Gerstein*, 420 U.S. at 108 n.9 (1975); see also cases cited in note 24 *supra*.

[26] 401 U.S. at 45.

[27] Wechsler, *Federal Courts, State Criminal Law, and the First Amendment*, 49 N.Y.U. L. Rev. 740 (1974); Whitten, *Federal Declaratory and Injunctive Interference with State Court Proceedings: The Supreme Court and the Limits of Judicial Discretion*, 53 N.C. L. Rev. 591, 629–39 (1975).

cited as to threatened future prosecutions were aberrations. Although a few prominent cases said that federal injunctions against future prosecutions should be hard to get,[28] in practice after *Ex parte Young*[29] in 1908 they became routine. They were the staple business of special district courts convened under the Three Judge Court Act,[30] and scores of these cases reached the Supreme Court.[31]

The reasons for such injunctions were repeatedly stated.[32] They were the same reasons relied on in *Steffel v. Thompson*, in which the Court reaffirmed the availability of declaratory relief in the absence of pending state proceedings. Unless some prospective remedy is available, a citizen can test the validity of a state law only by violating it and running the risk of criminal penalties. Describing this as "the Scylla of intentionally flouting state law and the Charybdis of forgoing what he believes to be constitutionally protected activity,"[33] the Court in *Steffel* held that *Younger* does not preclude prospective relief where no prosecution is pending. *Steffel* is the direct descendant of *Ex parte Young* and the many other cases given such short shrift in *Younger*.

This brief history frames the issue on which this article focuses. Given the citizen's long acknowledged need for prospective relief and the likelihood that such relief will interfere with any pending prosecution, what rules should govern claims for prospective relief when a prosecution for a past violation is pending?

The Court has handled this problem by assuming it away: it assumes that the pending prosecution eliminates the need for pros-

---

[28] Douglas v. City of Jeannette, 319 U.S. 157, 162–65 (1943); Williams v. Miller, 317 U.S. 599 (1942); Watson v. Buck, 313 U.S. 387, 400–01 (1941); Beal v. Missouri Pacific R. Co., 312 U.S. 45, 49–51 (1941); Spielman Motor Sales Co. v. Dodge, 295 U.S. 89, 95–97 (1935); Fenner v. Boykin, 271 U.S. 240, 243–44 (1926).

[29] 209 U.S. 123 (1908).

[30] Act of June 18, 1910, Chap. 309 § 17, 36 Stat. 539, 557, codified as 28 U.S.C. § 2281 (1970), repealed by Pub. L. No. 94–381, § 1, 90 Stat. 1119 (1976).

[31] See Wechsler, note 27 *supra*, at 779–93, 800–27 and n.376, 866–67 n.562.

[32] Toomer v. Witsell, 334 U.S. 385, 391–92 (1948); AFL v. Watson, 327 U.S. 582, 593–95 (1946); Gibbs v. Buck, 307 U.S. 66, 77–78 (1939); Grosjean v. American Press Co., 297 U.S. 233, 242 (1936); Lee v. Bickell, 292 U.S. 415, 421 (1934); Cline v. Frink Dairy Co., 274 U.S. 445, 451–52 (1927); Pierce v. Society of Sisters, 268 U.S. 510, 535–36 (1925); Terrace v. Thompson, 263 U.S. 197, 214–16 (1923); Dawson v. Kentucky Distilleries Co., 255 U.S. 288, 295–96 (1921); Rast v. Van Deman & Lewis, 240 U.S. 342, 355 (1916); Ohio Tax Cases, 232 U.S. 576, 587 (1914); Savage v. Jones, 225 U.S. 501, 520–21 (1912); Ex parte Young, 209 U.S. 123, 161–68 (1908).

[33] 415 U.S. at 462.

pective relief.[34] The Court has failed to consider the possibility of major remedial inadequacies in the criminal defense. Although it has acknowledged certain "extraordinary circumstances,"[35] they seem to get narrower each time the Court construes them. These circumstances have given rise to *Younger*'s limited exceptions.

One exception applies where the prosecution is brought in bad faith "without any hope of ultimate success."[36] But claims of bad faith have been almost impossible to prove.[37] Another exception applies if the state forum is "so biased by prejudgment and pecuniary interest that it could not constitutionally" decide the case.[38] A third possible exception arguably relevant to the analysis here, first suggested in dictum but ignored ever since, would apply where a series of prosecutions is threatened.[39] Another exception, which does not relate to the adequacy of the state remedy, is said to apply where the challenged statute is "flagrantly and patently violative of express constitutional prohibitions in every clause, sentence and paragraph, and in whatever manner and against whomever an effort might be made to apply it."[40] This exception has become meaningless since *Trainor v. Hernandez*.[41] The Court has also said that *Younger* does not apply where the constitutional issue cannot be raised in the state proceeding.[42] This may be characterized either as an exception,

---

[34] *Ibid.*

[35] *Kugler*, 421 U.S. at 124–25; *Younger*, 401 U.S. at 53.

[36] Dombrowski v. Pfister, 380 U.S. 479, 490 (1965); see also *Kugler*, 421 U.S. at 124; *Younger*, 401 U.S. at 47–49.

[37] *Juidice*, 97 S. Ct. at 1218–19; *Doran*, 422 U.S. at 929–30 n.3; *Allee*, 416 U.S. at 804–09, 811–21 (opinion of the Court); *id.* at 822–26, 833–46 (Burger, C.J., dissenting in part); *Perez*, 401 U.S. at 118 n.11 (Brennan, J., dissenting in part); Cameron v. Johnson, 390 U.S. 611, 619–22 (opinion of the Court); *id.* at 622–28 (Fortas, J., dissenting). For a review of lower court cases, see Fiss, note 5 *supra*, at 1115–16, n.36.

[38] *Gibson*, 411 U.S. at 578; see also *Trainor*, 97 S. Ct. at 1920 n.10 (opinion of the Court); *id.* at 1931 n.15 (Stevens, J., dissenting); *Juidice*, 97 S. Ct. 1211; *Kugler*, 421 U.S. at 127–29.

[39] *Younger*, 401 U.S. at 49; *cf. Wooley*, 97 S. Ct. at 1434 (multiple prosecutions justify injunction instead of declaratory judgment, where other reasoning justified federal intervention in the first place); *Doran*, 422 U.S. at 929–30 n.3 (multiple prosecution exception not mentioned in list of recognized exceptions).

[40] *Younger*, 401 U.S. at 53–54, quoting from Watson v. Buck, 313 U.S. 387, 402 (1941); see also *Kugler*, 421 U.S. at 125 n.4.

[41] 97 S. Ct. at 1920 (opinion of the Court); *id.* at 1928 (Stevens, J., dissenting); see also *id.* at 1925–26 (Brennan, J., dissenting).

[42] *Trainor*, 97 S. Ct. at 1920 (opinion of the Court); *id.* at 1923–24 (Brennan, J., dissenting); *Gerstein*, 420 U.S. at 108 n.9; *Fuentes*, 407 U.S. at 71 n.3.

based on the inadequacy of the state remedy, or as a situation outside the scope of the doctrine.

The inability of criminal courts to give prospective relief is a much more important remedial inadequacy. The analysis of that inadequacy that follows applies to federal plaintiffs who wish to repeat their violation and to pending criminal prosecutions. Where no repetition is contemplated, prospective relief is unnecessary. Where the pending state litigation is civil, prospective relief may be obtainable within it.[43]

The possibility of state civil relief suggests another question. Assuming a state criminal defendant needs relief unavailable from a criminal court, is he entitled to federal relief, or should he be sent to a state civil court? Careful analysis of that question must be reserved until the competing considerations have been more fully developed. But the presumptive answer is that the relevant jurisdictional statutes[44] give plaintiffs an unrestrained choice of forum, and the Court has always so construed them.[45] The *Younger* doctrine has so far been limited to situations where, in the Court's view, the federal claimant is not entitled to become a plaintiff at all, because he has an adequate remedy as a defendant. To require a federal claimant to initiate state litigation and submit his federal claim to a state court, without any prospect of returning to the federal district court, would be unprecedented, squarely inconsistent with the jurisdictional statutes, and only tenuously related to the policies *Younger* serves.

III. The Inadequacy of the Criminal Defense

Three important powers of equity courts are not available to criminal courts in Anglo-American jurisprudence: the power to give interlocutory relief, the power to give prospective relief, and the power to give class relief. Interlocutory relief is used here to mean relief available before the end of litigation, based on a tentative assessment of the law and facts, to minimize hardship pending

---

[43] *Cf.* Stainback v. Mo Hock Ke Lok Po, 336 U.S., 368, 381–84 (1949) (threatened civil enforcement action in court of equity).

[44] 28 U.S.C. § 1343 (1970); 28 U.S.C. § 1331 (1970).

[45] Douglas v. Seacoast Products, Inc., 97 S. Ct. 1740, 1744–45 n.4 (1977); *Doran*, 422 U.S. at 930; *Steffel*, 415 U.S. at 472–73; *Lake Carriers' Ass'n*, 406 U.S. at 510; Zwickler v. Koota, 389 U.S. 241, 248 (1967); McNeese v. Board of Educ., 373 U.S. 668, 671–74 (1963); Monroe v. Pape, 365 U.S. 167, 183 (1961).

final adjudication of the merits. Interlocutory relief is always future oriented; it is a special form of prospective relief. Class relief means relief given to a defined class of litigants, as under Federal Civil Rule of Procedure 23 or comparable state procedures. Although class relief may be retrospective, as in a class action for damages, the only form of class relief relevant here is prospective class relief.

Prospective relief in this context means relief directed to contemplated future violations of the challenged statute—an injunction against enforcement or a binding judgment that the statute cannot constitutionally be applied to the contemplated conduct. To be useful, prospective relief must be available in a pending proceeding or in a proceeding the citizen has power to initiate. In suits for prospective relief, the litigation is focused on future events, and a prospective judgment determines that the contemplated future conduct may or may not be punished. In contrast, a criminal judgment is retrospective. A criminal trial is focused on past events, and the judgment determines only that the alleged past conduct did or did not occur or may or may not be punished. An acquittal, dismissal, or conviction may give rise to inferences about the consequences of future conduct, but it does not determine those consequences of its own force. Some of the inferences that can be drawn from a criminal judgment are based on res judicata and stare decisis; these are indirect but binding consequences of the judgment. As a practical matter, there will often be additional, informal consequences. The Court's opinion may be persuasive even if not binding; the prosecutor may acquiesce, though he is not so bound. The Supreme Court's easy acceptance of the view that a pending prosecution furnishes an adequate remedy may rest on the belief that, if the first decision invalidates the statute, the prosecutor will give up.

It is easy, however, to overestimate the informal consequences of a criminal judgment. Many *Younger* cases involve bitter disputes. *Dombrowski v. Pfister*,[46] *Cameron v. Johnson*,[47] *O'Shea v. Littleton*,[48] and *Allee v. Medrano*[49] involved prolonged battles between entrenched local power structures and political activists seeking a share of that power. *Huffman v. Pursue, Ltd.*,[50] *Hicks v. Miranda*,[51]

[46] 380 U.S. 479 (1965).

[47] 390 U.S. 611 (1968).

[48] 414 U.S. 488 (1974).

[49] 416 U.S. 802 (1974).

[50] 420 U.S. 592 (1975).

[51] 422 U.S. 332 (1975).

and *Doran v. Salem Inn, Inc.*[52] pitted profitable businesses against officials determined to shut them down. In *Gibson v. Berryhill,*[53] a substantial portion of the income of every independent optometrist in Alabama was believed to be at stake. In such litigation, neither side is likely to give up until every legal possibility is exhausted or until the federal plaintiffs are financially unable to continue. *Dombrowski*[54] and *Cameron v. Johnson*[55] went to the Supreme Court twice. *Allee*[56] spent eight years getting there the first time, and there was a related state appeal.[57] After two opinions indicating the probable unconstitutionality of one ordinance regulating the Salem Inn,[58] the Town of North Hempstead enacted another.[59] After that was struck down,[60] the State of New York initiated liquor license revocation proceedings.[61] With nothing but principle at stake for either side, the plaintiff in *Wooley v. Maynard* was arrested three times in five weeks.[62]

When passengers sought to integrate the Jackson, Mississippi, bus terminal, more than 300 prosecutions were brought.[63] There were fifteen directed acquittals,[64] and the Supreme Court ordered a single judge to hold the statute unconstitutional, finding the state's contentions so frivolous that a three-judge court was not required.[65] But these developments did not cause the prosecutor to acquiesce, and due to standing problems the prosecutions were not enjoined.[66]

---

[52] 422 U.S. 922 (1975).

[53] 411 U.S. 564 (1973).

[54] Dombrowski v. Eastland, 387 U.S. 82 (1967); Dombrowski v. Pfister, 380 U.S. 479 (1965).

[55] 390 U.S. 611 (1968); 381 U.S. 741 (1965).

[56] 416 U.S. at 805–11.

[57] United Farm Wkrs. Organ. Comm. v. La Casita Farms, Inc., 439 S.W.2d 398 (Tex. Civ. App. 1968).

[58] Salem Inn, Inc. v. Frank, 501 F.2d 18 (2d Cir. 1974).

[59] Salem Inn, Inc. v. Frank, 522 F.2d 1045, 1046 (2d Cir. 1975).

[60] *Id.* at 1047.

[61] Salem Inn, Inc. v. Frank, 408 F. Supp. 852 (E.D.N.Y. 1976).

[62] 97 S. Ct. at 1434.

[63] Lusky, *Racial Discrimination and The Federal Law: A Problem in Nullification*, 63 Colum. L. Rev. 1163, 1179–80 (1963).

[64] *Id.* at 1180.

[65] Bailey v. Patterson, 369 U.S. 31, 33–34 (1962).

[66] *Id.* at 32–33.

There were 300 convictions. Many defendants gave up for lack of funds, and the appeals of the others dragged through the state courts[67] while various federal litigants made two more trips to the Court of Appeals.[68]

The Supreme Court's docket includes an unusually high percentage of such bitterly fought cases, but they exist throughout the system. The press reported recently that the United States attorney for the District of New Mexico pledged to prosecute violations of the Antiquities Act of 1906[69] "with vigor, wherever they occur,"[70] despite repeated rulings that the act was unconstitutionally vague.[71] Chicago's disorderly-house ordinance [72] is still enforced[73] after having been held unconstitutional.[74] Professor Amsterdam has collected his own set of examples.[75] Where a challenge is to a statute as applied, the prosecutor may find it especially easy to justify not acquiescing in an initial adverse decision. The point is not that judgments have no informal effects but that such effects cannot be relied on in place of judicial prospective relief.

A. INTERLOCUTORY RELIEF

The original articulation of the inadequacy of the criminal defense in *Ex parte Young* recognized the importance of both interlocutory and permanent prospective relief.[76] And in the post-*Younger* period the Court has reaffirmed the need for both types of relief where no prosecution is pending. *Steffel* made permanent

---

[67] Lusky, note 63 *supra*, at 1180.

[68] Bailey v. Patterson, 323 F.2d 201 (5th Cir. 1963); United States v. City of Jackson, 318 F.2d 1 (5th Cir. 1963).

[69] 16 U.S.C. § 433 (1970).

[70] "Warn artifact diggers on U.S. land despite court ruling," Chicago Sun-Times, 29 Aug. 1977, p. 26, col. 1, reporting United States v. Camazine (D.N.M. 1977).

[71] United States v. Diaz, 499 F.2d 113 (9th Cir. 1974); United States v. Camazine, Chicago Sun-Times, 29 Aug. 1977, p. 26, col. 1 (D.N.M. 1977).

[72] See Foster v. Zeeko, 540 F.2d 1310, 1311 (7th Cir. 1976).

[73] Counsel in *Foster v. Zeeko*, note 72 *supra*, stated in an interview that he has been retained by another client arrested in a situation substantially identical with the one there.

[74] Foster v. Zeeko, No. 73 C 891 (N.D. Ill. 1975), *rev'd in part, on other grounds*, 540 F.2d 1310 (7th Cir. 1976).

[75] Amsterdam, *Criminal Prosecution Affecting Federally Guaranteed Civil Rights: Federal Removal and Habeas Corpus Jurisdiction to Abort State Court Trial*, 113 U. PA. L. REV. 793, 841–42 (1965).

[76] 209 U.S. 123, 165 (1908).

prospective relief available in the form of a declaratory judgment.[77] *Doran* affirmed interlocutory relief: a preliminary injunction against enforcement pending a declaratory judgment proceeding, because "unless preliminary relief is available upon a proper showing, plaintiffs in some situations may suffer unnecessary and substantial irreparable harm."[78]

The Court did not feel obliged to cite authority for that proposition. In a wide variety of contexts, it has noted the need to protect against forfeiture of asserted constitutional rights during the pendency of litigation. Temporary losses of rights are important in themselves and may also entail serious consequences in some fact situations. Plaintiffs in *Doran* were tavern owners, threatened by "a substantial loss of business and perhaps even bankruptcy,"[79] if they had to comply with the challenged ordinance. Since states and state and local officials have total or partial immunity from suits for damages[80] and the liability of municipalities is unsettled,[81] there was no assurance that interim losses could be recovered in the event that the statute should ultimately be held unconstitutional. Thus, even easily measurable financial losses are irreparable in this context, as the pre-*Younger* Court explicitly recognized.[82]

Where the federal plaintiff is engaged in political speech, the effect of delay may be the collapse of his candidacy or movement. "A delay of even a day or two may be of crucial importance in some instances."[83] "[E]ach passing day may constitute a separate and cognizable infringement of the First Amendment . . . any First

---

77 415 U.S. at 462.

78 422 U.S. at 931.

79 *Id.* at 932.

80 Edelman v. Jordan, 415 U.S. 651 (1974) (states); Tenney v. Brandhove, 341 U.S. 367 (1951) (legislators); Pierson v. Ray, 386 U.S. 547 (1967) (judges); Imbler v. Pachtman, 424 U.S. 409 (1976) (prosecutors); Scheuer v. Rhodes, 416 U.S. 232 (1974) (other officials and employees of the executive branch); Wood v. Strickland, 420 U.S. 308 (1975) (same); Kattan, *Knocking on* Wood: *Some Thoughts on the Immunities of State Officials to Civil Rights Damage Actions*, 30 VAN. L. REV. 941 (1977).

81 *Compare* Monroe v. Pape, 365 U.S. 167, 187–92 (1961); *with* Bivens v. Six Unknown Fed. Narcotics Agents, 403 U.S. 388 (1971); City of Kenosha v. Bruno, 412 U.S. 507, 514 (1973); see Note, 89 HARV. L. REV. 922, 955–58 (1976).

82 *Compare* Toomer v. Witsell, 334 U.S. 385, 392 (1948); Youngstown Sheet & Tube Co. v. Sawyer, 343 U.S. 579, 584–85 (1952), *with Byrne*, 401 U.S. at 220; see also Sampson v. Murray, 415 U.S. 61, 90–91 (1974) (applying pre-*Younger* analysis to a suit against federal official).

83 Carroll v. Princess Anne, 393 U.S. 175, 182 (1968), quoting with approval A Quantity of Copies of Books v. Kansas, 378 U.S. 205, 224 (1964) (Harlan, J., dissenting).

Amendment infringement that occurs with each passing day is irreparable."[84]

The importance of temporary deprivations has also been recognized in other contexts, including property rights[85] and racial integration.[86] The preliminary injunction is one of the classic remedies where temporary deprivations impose hardship.[87]

Despite this well-settled law, the Court has ignored the inability of a pending prosecution to furnish interlocutory relief. As a result, it has failed to realize that, even if a pending prosecution is an adequate remedy for a completed violation, it is often no remedy at all for a contemplated future violation.

In *Roe v. Wade*,[88] where the issue was squarely presented, the Court failed to see that past and contemplated future violations can be present in the same case. In fact, both are present whenever, as is common in *Younger* cases, the plaintiff is engaged or desires to engage in a continuing course of conduct. In *Roe*, the Court denied relief to plaintiff Dr. Hallford because prosecutions for abortion were pending against him.[89] The doctor sought "to distinguish his status as a present state defendant from his status as a 'potential

---

[84] Nebraska Press Ass'n v. Stuart, 423 U.S. 1327, 1329 (1975) (Blackmun, J., in chambers). See also National Socialist Party v. Village of Skokie, 97 S. Ct. 2205, 2206 (1977); Nebraska Press Ass'n v. Stuart, 427 U.S. 539, 560–61 (1976); Walker v. City of Birmingham, 388 U.S. 307, 324–25; *id.* at 331 (Warren, C.J., dissenting); *id.* at 336 (Douglas, J., dissenting); *id.* at 348–49 (Brennan, J., dissenting) (1967).

[85] North Georgia Finishing, Inc. v. Di-Chem, Inc., 419 U.S. 601, 606, 608 (1975); Mitchell v. W. T. Grant Co., 416 U.S. 600, 608 (1974); *Fuentes*, 407 U.S. at 81–82, 84–86; Goldberg v. Kelly, 397 U.S. 254, 264 (1970); Sniadach v. Family Finance Corp., 395 U.S. 337, 339 (1969); Oklahoma Natural Gas Co. v. Russell, 261 U.S. 290, 293 (1923).

[86] Carter v. West Feliciana Parish School Bd., 396 U.S. 290 (1970); Alexander v. Holmes County Bd. of Educ., 396 U.S. 19 (1969); Rogers v. Paul, 382 U.S. 198, 199–200 (1965); Bradley v. School Bd., 382 U.S. 103, 105 (1965); Griffin v. County School Bd., 377 U.S. 218, 233–34 (1964); Watson v. City of Memphis, 373 U.S. 526, 532–33, 539 (1963).

[87] See *Doran*, 422 U.S. at 930–34; Brown v. Chote, 411 U.S. 452, 456–57 (1973); Carter v. West Feliciana Parish School Bd., 396 U.S. 226 (1969); Rogers v. Paul, 382 U.S. 198, 199–200 (1965); City of New Orleans v. Barthe, 376 U.S. 189 (1964), *aff'g* 219 F. Supp. 788 (E.D. La. 1963); Gremillion v. United States, 368 U.S. 11 (1961), *aff'g* Bush v. Orleans Parish School Bd., 194 F. Supp. 182 (E.D. La. 1961); Tugwell v. Bush, 367 U.S. 907 (1961), *aff'g* Bush v. Orleans Parish School Bd., 194 F. Supp. 182 (E.D. La. 1961); Louisiana ex rel. Gremillion v. NAACP, 366 U.S. 293 (1961); Youngstown Sheet & Tube Co. v. Sawyer, 343 U.S. 579, 584–85 (1952); Oklahoma Natural Gas Co. v. Russell, 261 U.S. 290, 293 (1923); Ex parte Young, 209 U.S. 123, 165 (1908).

[88] 410 U.S. 113 (1973).

[89] *Id.* at 125–27.

future defendant' and to assert only the latter for standing purposes" in federal court.[90] The Court rejected the argument in seven words with no analysis at all: "We see no merit in that distinction."[91]

The Court did not look very hard. If Hallford's constitutional claims had been vindicated, he would ultimately have been acquitted, and the prosecutions would have furnished a remedy with respect to the two completed abortions. But meanwhile, what was he to do with subsequent patients? As to them, he faced precisely the dilemma described in *Steffel:* he could perform the abortions, risking further indictments and consecutive sentences if his constitutional claims were rejected, or he could await the outcome of the pending litigation, forever forfeiting his asserted rights with respect to patients who reached term and delivered or sought abortions elsewhere during the pendency of the litigation. The pending prosecutions would furnish no remedy at all with respect to those patients.

An equity court confronted with Hallford's case may well have denied interlocutory relief. Motions for preliminary injunctions against enforcement of abortion laws presented extraordinarily difficult questions before the Supreme Court's decisions on the merits. But refusal to recognize the federal claimant's status as a potential future defendant keeps the case out of the equity court altogether and prevents those questions from even being explored. In the abortion litigation subsequent to the Supreme Court's landmark decisions, requests for interlocutory relief were much simpler, for the probabilities of success on the merits had dramatically shifted. But federal claimants who were prosecuted could not present such requests; they were barred from the equity court.

Another example is *Cameron v. Johnson.*[92] There, beginning in January 1964, civil rights organizations picketed the courthouse in Hattiesburg, Mississippi, staying within a "march route" designated by the sheriff to facilitate public access to the courthouse. On April 8, Mississippi passed a new Anti-picketing Law, and on April 9, the sheriff dispersed the Hattiesburg picketers. They reappeared on the morning of April 10 and were arrested. More arrests were made on the afternoon of April 10 and on April 11. The federal complaint was filed April 13; arrests resumed on May 18. Picketing then

[90] *Id.* at 126.

[91] *Ibid.*

[92] 390 U.S. 611 (1968).

stopped and had not been resumed when the Supreme Court denied relief four years later.

The arrests stopped the picketing, and the pending prosecutions were no remedy. Equity could have protected the picketers' rights by defining a nonobstructive march area and enjoining arrests as long as the picketers stayed within it. The remedy could have been implemented quickly, by temporary restraining order or preliminary injunction, and adjusted as necessary thereafter. The criminal courts could do none of these things, and ultimate acquittals may not revive a dead movement.

In *Doran v. Salem Inn*, where the Court affirmed a preliminary injunction, it denied relief to coplaintiff M & L Restaurant.[93] M & L was defendant in a pending prosecution filed after the federal complaint but before the district court issued the preliminary injunction. Salem Inn had avoided prosecution by complying with the new ordinance until the preliminary injunction was obtained; the two plaintiffs were otherwise similarly situated.

Why the delay that would irreparably injure Salem Inn would not injure M & L or how the state criminal court could alleviate such injury was not explained. The Court simply said that the case was controlled by *Younger* and *Samuels* and that M & L could not "complain that its constitutional contentions are being resolved in a state court," because it had "violated the ordinance, rather than awaiting the normal development of its federal lawsuit."[94]

The Court did leave open for consideration on remand M & L's claim "that it was the subject of 'repetitive harassing criminal prosecutions aimed at suppressing' " topless dancing, declining to consider the issue on the "spare record" before it.[95] That record showed that each day's violation was a separate offense and that M & L and its dancers had been criminally charged on four consecutive days after they resumed dancing.[96] No further proceedings are reported with respect to this aspect of the remand. It is not clear what additional showing the Court expected. Perhaps, given the wording of M & L's contention, the Court was thinking in terms of the prosecutor's motive or a claim of bad-faith harassment. What is clear is that every day M & L and its dancers had to decide whether to risk violating the statute, knowing that they could be arrested on the spot or charged later in a massive multicount indictment and that

[93] 422 U.S. at 924–25, 929.

[94] *Id.* at 929.

[95] *Id.* at 929–30 n.3.

[96] *Id.* at 925 & n.1.

their potential punishment at least equalled the maximum penalty times the number of days within the statute of limitations. The pending prosecutions furnished no remedy for their dilemma, and equitable relief should not depend on speculation about prosecutorial motive. Once one prosecution is filed, "even an accused relatively confident of the unlikelihood or impermissibility of conviction may well refuse to take the added risk of further criminal penalties that might obtain if he guesses wrong."[97]

These examples are not atypical; they illustrate a general principle.[98] If the challenged statute regulates a citizen's course of conduct, then immediately after his first indictment he faces the *Steffel* dilemma more acutely than ever before. He must now decide whether to repeat his violation, knowing that he could be prosecuted for each repetition and that the prosecutor's attention is focused on him. Under present law, he has forfeited any federal forum for the prospective relief he needs. To obtain relief, he had to obey the statute from its enactment (or from the time he first contemplated his course of conduct) until he got an injunction against enforcement or until substantial proceedings on the merits had occurred in federal court. It is possible to read *Wooley v. Maynard*[99] as substantially changing these requirements, but that is probably not what the Court intended.

The Court has decided sixteen major cases under *Younger* and the previous leading case, *Dombrowski v. Pfister*.[100] Eleven of these cases involved continuing courses of conduct to which the foregoing analysis is fully applicable.[101] Moreover, ten of the eleven were speech cases,[102] and seven of those involved political speech.[103]

---

[97] A Quantity of Copies of Books v. Kansas, 378 U.S. 205, 224 (1964) (Harlan, J., dissenting).

[98] For a similar but more limited analysis, see Note, note 5 *supra*, at 1305–08.

[99] 97 S. Ct. 1428 (1977); see text *infra* at 212–14.

[100] 380 U.S. 479 (1965).

[101] The five major cases not involving continuing courses of conduct are *Trainor*, 97 S. Ct. 1911 (due process challenge to state procedure); *Juidice*, 97 S. Ct. 1211 (same); *Kugler*, 421 U.S. 117 (same); *Rizzo*, 423 U.S. 362 (challenge to police brutality); *O'Shea*, 414 U.S. 488 (challenge to alleged racial discrimination in criminal justice system).

[102] *Wooley*, 97 S. Ct. 1428; *Doran*, 422 U.S. 922; *Hicks*, 422 U.S. 332; *Huffman*, 420 U.S. 592; *Allee*, 416 U.S. 802; *Steffel*, 415 U.S. 452; *Samuels*, 401 U.S. 66; *Younger*, 401 U.S. 37; *Cameron*, 390 U.S. 611; *Dombrowski*, 380 U.S. 479; the nonspeech case is *Gibson*, 411 U.S. 564.

[103] The three exceptions are *Doran*, *Hicks*, and *Huffman*.

There are hints in some of Mr. Justice Rehnquist's opinions that citizens should not be allowed to violate challenged statutes pending adjudication of their validity.[104] But it is not necessary that such violations be always permitted or always forbidden. The law relating to interlocutory injunctions is well developed and expressly designed to make individual determinations concerning such issues. The equity judge must consider the probable final result as well as the consequences to each side of an erroneous preliminary determination.[105] The injunction may be conditional if that is necessary to protect all the parties,[106] as it could have been, for example, in *Cameron v. Johnson*.[107]

In speech cases, the balance of hardships and probability of success will often tip decidedly in favor of the federal court plaintiff. Yet *Younger* has denied protection to speech for significant periods of time. Of course, it is not entirely fair to compare the promptness of a federal TRO with the delay of three appeals. To compare the potential timeliness of relief, one must assume that both courts will vindicate the constitutional claim at their first opportunity. Thus the comparison is between the federal TRO and the final judgment in the state trial court. How soon that judgment may be obtained depends on several factors: whether the constitutional issue requires factual development or can be resolved on the pleadings, whether state procedure allows the issue to be raised on the pleadings,[108] and whether the state docket is current. But it is clear that a criminal court can never responsibly reach final judgment as quickly as an equity court can grant preliminary relief. Even where the statute is "patently and flagrantly unconstitutional on its face," a criminal court judge should permit briefs before dismissing the indictment. An equity judge could immediately restrain enforcement pending final judgment. Moreover, in assessing the consequences of delay in any particular case, the equity judge must consider the possibility that one or more appeals might be required to vindicate the federal right in the criminal case.

---

[104] *Doran*, 422 U.S. at 929 (opinion of the Court by Rehnquist, J.); *Steffel*, 415 U.S. at 479–80 (Rehnquist, J., concurring).

[105] *Doran*, 422 U.S. at 931; Diversified Mortgage Investors v. U.S. Life Title Ins. Co., 544 F.2d 571, 576 (2d Cir. 1976); Fiss, Injunctions 168–69 (1972).

[106] Locomotive Eng'rs v. Missouri-Kan.-Tex. R. Co., 363 U.S. 528, 531–32 (1960).

[107] 390 U.S. 611 (1968); see text *supra*, at note 92.

[108] *Younger*, 401 U.S. at 57 n.* (Brennan, J., concurring).

This does no violence to the Supreme Court's assumption that the state courts will protect federal rights; it simply acknowledges the reality that errors occur in any system.

The interlocutory injunction is not a complete remedy. It does not forever prevent prosecution of violations committed under its protection; it temporarily prevents prosecution of all violations described in the order. If the final judgment holds the statute valid, dissolves the interlocutory injunction, and denies permanent relief, state officials would be free to prosecute any violation within the limitations period. To prevent that, the federal court would have to enjoin permanently prosecutions for any violations committed while the interlocutory injunction was in effect.

There are cases indicating that such injunctions should be issued,[109] but they do not squarely address the difficult questions involved. While the case for protecting litigants who relied in good faith on the interlocutory order of a federal court is strong, so is the argument that there is no federal power to enjoin enforcement of a constitutional state statute. One source of such authority may be the power to do complete equity in the case once jurisdiction is assumed, but that argument is clouded by recent decisions emphasizing that "federal remedial power may be exercised 'only on the basis of a constitutional violation.' "[110] Another possibility is to hold that the state denies due process when it imposes penalties in ways which deter access to normal judicial remedies.[111] As long as this issue remains unresolved or if it is resolved adversely to federal court plaintiffs, the risk of ultimate prosecution may have some chilling effect despite an interlocutory injunction.

The risk of ultimate prosecution does not make the interlocutory injunction unimportant. In political speech cases or cases where time

[109] Oklahoma Operating Co. v. Love, 252 U.S. 331, 338 (1920); Wadley Southern Ry. v. Georgia, 235 U.S. 651, 659 (1915); City of Marysville v. Standard Oil Co., 27 F.2d 478, 487 (8th Cir. 1928), *aff'd on other grounds*, 279 U.S. 582 (1929).

[110] Milliken v. Bradley, 418 U.S. 717, 738 (1974), quoting with approval from Swann v. Charlotte-Mecklenburg Bd. of Educ., 402 U.S. 1, 16 (1971); accord, Hills v. Gautreaux, 425 U.S. 284, 293 (1976).

[111] North Carolina v. Pearce, 395 U.S. 711, 723–26 (1969); St. Regis Paper Co. v. United States, 368 U.S. 208, 225–27 (1961); Natural Gas Pipeline Co. v. Slattery, 302 U.S. 300, 309–10 (1937); Life & Casualty Co. v. McCray, 291 U.S. 566, 574–75 (1934); Oklahoma Gin Co. v. Oklahoma, 252 U.S. 339 (1920); Wadley Southern Ry. v. Georgia, 235 U.S. 651 (1915); Missouri Pacific Ry. Co. v. Tucker, 230 U.S. 340 (1913); Ex parte Young, 209 U.S. 123, 145–48 (1908); Cotting v. Kansas City Stockyards Co., 183 U.S. 79, 99–102 (1901); *cf.* Bounds v. Smith, 97 S. Ct. 1491, 1495 (1977) (right of meaningful access to courts for prisoners); Wolff v. McDonnell, 418 U.S. 539, 579 (1974) (same); but see Yakus v. United States, 321 U.S. 414, 437–43 (1944).

is of the essence, litigants may be willing to risk prosecution at some indefinite future time, if they are free to speak or act at the critical moment without interruption by arrests, arraignments, and jailings. Their courage should get a further boost from a preliminary judicial determination that the statute is probably unconstitutional. In most cases, the preliminary determination will stand. In nonpolitical cases, if the statute is upheld and the federal plaintiff indicates an intention to comply, the primary dispute may be over. The prosecutor may choose not to bring multiple prosecutions for all the violations which took place under protection of the preliminary injunction or even any of them. Such violations do not show disrespect for law, and there is no reason to prosecute except vindictiveness. Of course, where the litigation is one battle in a larger underlying dispute, there may be multiple prosecutions simply to intimidate. If prosecutions are brought, reliance on the injunction may be a defense.[112] Where it is not a defense, the sentencing judge may take it into consideration.

These possibilities depend in part on the Court's assumption that state officials will act in good faith. Some will act in good faith even if all will not. And if major penalties are imposed for no apparent reason except retaliation for the federal lawsuit, the argument for federal intervention under the Due Process Clause is substantially strengthened.[113]

None of these considerations, individually or collectively, insures that a federal plaintiff can rely on an interlocutory injunction with complete safety. But they do suggest that an interlocutory injunction against enforcement significantly reduces the deterrent effect of an allegedly unconstitutional statute and thus significantly eases the dilemma described in *Steffel*. The remedy is thus far more practical and efficient, and more nearly complete, than the defense of a pending prosecution. That is the traditional test for determining the adequacy of a legal remedy.[114]

---

[112] United States v. Mancuso, 139 F.2d 90, 92 (3d Cir. 1943); City of Marysville v. Cities Service Oil Co., 133 Kan. 692 (1931); *cf.* United States v. Barker, 546 F.2d 940, 946–54 (D.C. Cir. 1976) (Wilkey, J., concurring); *id.* at 954–57 (Merhige, J., concurring) (mistake of law defense); A.L.I., MODEL PENAL CODE § 2.04(3)(b)(ii) (Prop. Off. Draft, 1962) (reliance on erroneous judicial opinion).

[113] *Cf.* North Carolina v. Pearce, 395 U.S. 711, 723–26 (1969) (increased sentence after retrial in retaliation for appealing first conviction denies due process).

[114] American Life Ins. Co. v. Stewart, 300 U.S. 203, 214–15 (1937); Terrace v. Thompson, 263 U.S. 197, 214 (1923); May v. LeClaire, 11 Wall. 217, 236 (1870); 30 C.J.S., *Equity* § 25 (1965) (collecting cases).

Of course there is some possibility that there will be no additional punishment for multiple violations pending a test case. But it would be foolhardy for defendants to assume that result and act on it and unreasonable for courts to expect them to do so. Reliance on one's own partisan view that a statute is unconstitutional is not nearly as persuasive an extenuating circumstance as reliance on an interlocutory injunction against enforcement. In *Steffel*, the Court referred to acting on one's own view of constitutionality as "intentionally flouting state law."[115]

The only informal solution worthy of serious consideration is a promise to bring only one test prosecution until the constitutional issue is resolved. The Court considered such a representation irrelevant in *Ex parte Young*[116] but relied on it in two of the deviant cases cited in *Younger*.[117]

A bare promise not to bring further prosecutions during the test case is inadequate. It includes no promise to refrain from prosecution of later violations committed during the pendency of the test case if the state wins it, no hope for permanent injunctive protection from such prosecutions, and no interlocutory determination of probable constitutionality to reduce the risk of reliance. Furthermore, it is not at all clear that such representations would be enforceable, either in state[118] or in federal court. Federal power to enjoin prosecutions in violation of such a representation must be based on an estoppel theory,[119] on a theory that due process requires that representations which induced the withholding of relief be enforced, or on the power to do complete equity in the case.[120] It

---

[115] 415 U.S. at 462; see text *supra*, at note 33; *Doran*, 422 U.S. at 934 (Douglas, J., dissenting in part).

[116] 209 U.S. at 171–72 (Harlan, J., dissenting).

[117] Beal v. Missouri Pacific R. Co., 312 U.S. 45, 50 (1941); Spielman Motor Sales Co. v. Dodge, 295 U.S. 89, 96 (1935).

[118] *Compare* United States v. Laub, 385 U.S. 475, 485–87 (1967); Raley v. Ohio, 360 U.S. 423, 437–42 (1959); *with* State v. Smith, 12 Wash. App. 514, 520 (1975); Giant of Md., Inc. v. State's Atty., 274 Md. 158, 179 (1975); Hopkins v. State, 193 Md. 489, 498 (1950), *appeal dismissed*, 339 U.S. 940 (1950). *Compare* State v. Rollins, 359 A.2d 315, 317–18 (R.I. 1976); *with* State v. Davis, 188 So.2d 24 (Fla. Ct. App. 1966); see also Santobello v. New York, 404 U.S. 257 (1971); Doyle v. State, 59 Tex. Cr. 39, 41 (1910).

[119] *Compare* Federal Crop Ins. Corp. v. Merrill, 332 U.S. 380 (1947); *with* Moser v. United States, 341 U.S. 41 (1951); Berger, *Estoppel against the Government*, 21 U. Chi. L. Rev. 680 (1954); Rapp, *Squaring Corners: A Proposal for Legislative Application of Equitable Estoppel against the Government*, 64 Ill. B. J. 688 (1976); *with* Comment, 46 U. Colo. L. Rev. 433 (1975); see also cases cited in note 118 *supra*.

[120] But see text *supra*, at note 110.

is not sufficient to hold out the possibility of subsequent action if the representation is dishonored, unless it is clear that there will be power to grant effective relief in that event.

The enforcement problem could be solved in either of two ways. The prosecutor could consent to an injunction. Alternatively, the Supreme Court could hold that a stipulation not to prosecute in these circumstances is enforceable by the federal court, which should retain jurisdiction for the purpose. Either a consent decree or an enforceable stipulation would be nearly the equivalent of a contested interlocutory injunction, but neither would include a judicial prediction concerning the merits. To avoid the additional deterrent effect created by that defect, the consent decree or stipulation should permanently preclude prosecution for additional violations committed before final resolution of the test case.

Such procedures could preserve both interlocutory rights and the primacy of the state criminal forum. There would be a cost to the state. Violations would be permitted in cases where the court would deny interlocutory relief. The state may be willing to pay that cost to keep out of federal court, and as long as we assume the fairness of the state forum, the would-be federal plaintiff should not be allowed to complain. But neither should the federal court plaintiff be required to rely on vague or unenforceable prosecutorial statements. In the absence of a consent decree or a clearly enforceable stipulation, an interlocutory injunction against any new prosecutions should be available where the normal requirements are met.

As noted, the post-*Younger* Court acknowledged the need for prospective relief in *Steffel* and temporary relief in *Doran*. The Court took another important step last term in *Wooley v. Maynard*. *Wooley* acknowledged the need for prospective relief where the federal plaintiff had been thrice convicted without appealing.[121] The defendant state officials argued that under *Huffman*[122] plaintiff was barred from federal court by his earlier failure to exhaust state appellate remedies. The Court quickly rejected this contention on the ground that "the relief sought is wholly prospective."[123] Plaintiff sought "only to be free from prosecutions for future violations" and did not seek to "annul" his earlier convictions or "any

[121] 97 S. Ct. at 1432–33.

[122] See text *supra*, at note 14.

[123] 97 S. Ct. at 1433.

collateral effects those convictions may have."[124] *Huffman* was distinguished because there the state court had closed the plaintiff's theater on account of past violations, and the relief sought had been to prevent enforcement of the state court judgment. In short, the Court accepted, at least in the context of unexhausted appeals, the distinction between past and future violations rejected in *Roe v. Wade*.[125] *Wooley*'s theoretical foundation can only be the inability of the criminal court to give prospective relief.

The intended scope of *Wooley* is unclear. The narrowest possible reading is that *Wooley* simply limits the application of *Huffman*'s requirement that appeals be exhausted and that *Wooley* does not apply where there is actually a pending prosecution. But that reading is untenable.[126] The requirement that appellate remedies be exhausted is not a supplemental requirement of less importance than the requirement that no prosecution be pending. Rather, it is an integral part of the *Younger* doctrine's basic rule that, once a state proceeding begins, the constitutional claims must be resolved there. Indeed, the Court quite plausibly suggested in *Huffman* that federal intervention is worse after the state trial than before.[127] This makes it impossible to limit *Wooley* to the appellate-exhaustion requirement.

Rather, *Wooley* is distinguishable from *Huffman* and from *Younger* itself only by the federal plaintiff's prayer for relief.[128] The plaintiff in *Wooley* sought only relief that could not have been obtained in the unexhausted appeals. If he had appealed, he would still have been subject to new prosecutions and to the dilemma of whether to comply pending the appeals. This would have been equally true if the time for appeal had not yet expired when the federal complaint was filed, if appeals had been taken and were still pending, if a fourth prosecution had been initiated, or even if the original prosecutions were still pending in the trial court. The result in *Wooley* should not have been different in any of these situations. In each, plaintiff should have been entitled to prospective

---

[124] *Ibid.*

[125] 410 U.S. at 126; see text *supra*, at notes 88–91.

[126] See Fiss, note 5 *supra*, at 1141–42.

[127] 420 U.S. at 608–09; see also Amsterdam, note 75 *supra*, at 835–36.

[128] *Cf.* Note, note 5 *supra*, at 1317–22 (other ways in which nature of plaintiff's claim affects applicability of *Younger*).

relief even if the pending prosecutions themselves could only be fought in state court.

Once this is recognized, there is no reason to make the pleading rule a trap for the unwary. If plaintiffs seeking only prospective relief are entitled to it, then plaintiffs seeking some prospective relief and some retrospective relief should be entitled to the prospective portion. It is not suggested that the Court intended all this in *Wooley*, but it is suggested that no rational line will be found between *Wooley* and a substantial retrenchment of the *Younger* doctrine.

B. PERMANENT PROSPECTIVE RELIEF

No order of the criminal court can have the effect of an interlocutory injunction. But its judgment may have predictable effects on future litigation, and some of these effects may be nearly as useful to litigants as a prospective final judgment. These effects are both formal and informal; they derive from res judicata, stare decisis, and the persuasive effect of court opinions.

Res judicata is a general term; it includes bar and merger, the rule that the same cause of action may not be relitigated, and collateral estoppel, the rule that issues determined adversely to a party in one litigation may not be relitigated by him in another cause of action.[129] If a final judgment of dismissal or acquittal is unambiguously based on the unconstitutionality of the statute and if that constitutional determination is given full collateral estoppel effect in subsequent prosecutions against the same defendant, then the defendant may rely on the criminal judgment to nearly the same extent that he would rely on a prospective judgment.

Whether or not collateral estoppel applies, the decision may be given stare decisis effect. In most states, this will occur only if the constitutional decision is made by an appellate court in a published opinion.[130] Stare decisis gives some prospective benefit to all potential defendants, although that effect is not as strong as collateral estoppel.

---

[129] See Sea-Land Services, Inc. v. Gaudet, 414 U.S. 573, 593 (1974); Ashe v. Swenson, 397 U.S. 436, 443 (1970); Larsen v. Northland Transp. Co., 292 U.S. 20, 25 (1934); LOUISELL & HAZARD, CASES AND MATERIALS ON PLEADING AND PROCEDURE: STATE AND FEDERAL 618–19 (3d ed. 1973).

[130] See cases collected in 21 C.J.S. *Courts* § 200 (1940); *id.* (1977 Supp.); 20 AM. JUR.2d *Courts* §§ 189, 201 (1965); *id.* (1977 Supp.)

Whether there is collateral estoppel in this context depends on each state's resolution of two subsidiary issues which have caused a good deal of confusion and disagreement. Does collateral estoppel apply to criminal judgments, and does it apply to issues of law? The federal rule that collateral estoppel does apply to criminal judgments has been made applicable to the states through the Double Jeopardy Clause.[131] But where the indictment is dismissed on motion before jeopardy attaches, the state remains free to apply its own law. The *Restatement* does not address the issue,[132] and at least some states have denied collateral estoppel effect to criminal judgments.[133]

As to issues of law, there is no governing federal rule. Instead, there are two competing lines of authority. Some cases suggest that estoppel applies to facts and to mixed law and fact, but not to pure law.[134] Others apply estoppel to all issues actually and necessarily determined without distinction between factual and legal issues.[135] One recent Supreme Court opinion denying estoppel effect to a legal conclusion gave no indication whether it was applying a general rule or a recognized exception which happened to fit the facts.[136] Elsewhere, there is a noticeable trend toward giving estoppel effect to legal determinations, subject to specified exceptions.[137]

Thus a criminal court may provide relief which is prospective in effect, if not in theory, in states which give collateral estoppel effect to issues of law decided in criminal cases, after defendant's

---

[131] Turner v. Arkansas, 407 U.S. 366 (1972); Harris v. Washington, 404 U.S. 55 (1971); Ashe v. Swenson, 397 U.S. 436, 443–45 (1970).

[132] A.L.I., Restatement of Judgments, Scope Note, at 2 (1942).

[133] State v. Ashe, 350 S.W.2d 768, 770–71 (Mo. 1961).

[134] See Ashe v. Swenson, 397 U.S. 436, 443 (1970); FPC v. Amerada Pet. Corp., 379 U.S. 687, 690 (1965); Yates v. United States, 354 U.S. 298, 336 (1957); Partmar Corp. v. Paramount Pictures Theatres Corp., 347 U.S. 89, 103 n.9 (1954); Commissioner v. Sunnen, 333 U.S. 591, 601–02 (1948); United States v. Moser, 266 U.S. 236, 242 (1924).

[135] See Emich Motors Corp. v. General Motors Corp., 340 U.S. 558, 569 (1951); State Farm Mut. Auto Ins. Co. v. Duel, 324 U.S. 154, 162 (1945); United States v. Stone & Downer Co., 274 U.S. 225, 230 (1927); Collins v. Loisel, 262 U.S. 426, 430 (1923); United States v. Oppenheimer, 242 U.S. 85 (1916); Frank v. Mangum, 237 U.S. 309, 334 (1915); Nalle v. Oyster, 230 U.S. 165, 181 (1913).

[136] Whitcomb v. Chavis, 403 U.S. 124, 162–63 (1971) (plurality opinion).

[137] *Compare* A.L.I., Restatement of Judgments § 70 (1942); *with* A.L.I., Restatement (Second) of Judgments §§ 68, 68.1(b), and Comment on Clause (b) at 29–35 (Tent. Draft No. 4, 1977); *compare* James, Civil Procedure § 11.22 (1965); *with* James & Hazard, Civil Procedure § 11.20 (2d ed. 1977).

constitutional claims are vindicated by the trial court and, in all states, after such claims are upheld on appeal.

The judgment has no prospective effect on the constitutional issue if that issue is not reached, and the state court may be obliged to avoid reaching it if possible.[138] Avoidance may be fairly easy in some cases, especially where the challenge is to the statute as applied. If the citizen wins in the trial court, the prosecutor may not be allowed to appeal.[139] Certainly he cannot be forced to appeal. The trial court judgment generally has no stare decisis effect, and its collateral estoppel effect may depend on quite unsettled state law or be denied by the state altogether. The *Restatement* suggests that the loser of the first case should not be bound by collateral estoppel if he could not appeal.[140] This rule cannot be applied where the Double Jeopardy Clause controls. But until the Supreme Court definitively decides that legal issues must be given collateral estoppel effect, the Double Jeopardy Clause does not control the situation under analysis. The limited prospective effect of trial court judgments is especially important, because the stronger the defendant's federal claim, the more likely he is to win in the trial court.

The prospective benefit of stare decisis is subject to the risk that the decision will be overruled. Similarly, the *Restatement* provision suggesting collateral estoppel effect for issues of law includes an exception for cases where "a new determination is warranted in order to take account of an intervening change in the applicable legal context or otherwise to avoid inequitable administration of the laws."[141] In either of these situations, prosecution for intervening violations should be precluded,[142] but that issue is also unsettled.[143]

In contrast, the injunction directly prevents future prosecution.

---

[138] *Cf.* Ashwander v. TVA, 297 U.S. 288, 346–48 (1936) (Brandeis, J., concurring) (federal courts).

[139] *Compare* United States v. Jenkins, 420 U.S. 358 (1975); *with* United States v. Wilson, 420 U.S. 332 (1975); and both with Tex. Code Crim. Proc. Ann. art. 44.01 (Vernon 1977) (no appeal by state under any circumstances).

[140] A.L.I., Restatement (Second) of Judgments § 68.1(a) (Tent. Draft No. 4, 1977).

[141] *Id.* at § 68.1(b)(ii).

[142] Bouie v. City of Columbia, 378 U.S. 347 (1964); State v. O'Neil, 147 Iowa 513 (1910).

[143] See State v. Hoover, 59 Ala. 57, 60 (1877); *cf.* Dobbert v. Florida, 97 S. Ct. 2290, 2300 (1977) (new death penalty statute applied to crime committed when former unconstitutional death penalty statute was in effect).

And whatever the general resolution of the question whether estoppel applies to issues of law, a federal declaratory judgment that a statute is unconstitutional must be given estoppel effect. Although the Court has treated the issue as open,[144] such judgments cannot fulfill the purpose for which the statute was enacted unless they are binding. The legislative history makes clear that Congress intended that declaratory judgments be available to test the constitutionality of state laws without risk of prosecution.[145] That purpose simply cannot be achieved if the resulting declaration of unconstitutionality is not binding. Moreover, if not binding, it would be only an unconstitutional advisory opinion.[146] Thus, the statutory provision that declaratory judgments "shall have the force and effect of a final judgment or decree,"[147] binding on the states under the Supremacy Clause, must be read as referring to res judicata.[148]

Of course even prospective judgments are not forever unchangeable. Injunctions may be modified,[149] and the collateral estoppel effect of a declaratory judgment may come to an end if there is a substantial change in controlling law. But this is better than a judgment with no collateral estoppel effect at all. In addition, the risk of prosecution for intervening violations is smaller. Allowing such prosecutions is inconsistent with the congressional purpose to create a risk-free remedy in the Declaratory Judgment Act. The burden of showing that an injunction should be modified is on the party seeking the modification,[150] and to modify a permanent injunction

---

[144] *Steffel*, 415 U.S. at 470–71 (opinion of the Court), quoting with approval from *Perez*, 401 U.S. at 125 (Brennan, J., concurring in part); 415 U.S. at 480–84 (Rehnquist, J., concurring).

[145] H.R. REP. No. 1264, 73d Cong., 2d Sess. (1934); S. REP. No. 1005, 73d Cong., 2d Sess. (1934). The history of this act is reviewed in *Steffel*, 415 U.S. at 465–68; *Perez*, 401 U.S. at 111–15, 125 n.16 (Brennan, J., concurring in part).

[146] Imperial Irrigation Dist. v. Nevada-Cal. Elec. Corp., 111 F.2d 319, 320–21 (9th Cir. 1940); but see Note, 46 U.S.C. L. REV. 803, 832–41 (1973).

[147] 28 U.S.C. § 2201 (1970).

[148] *Steffel*, 415 U.S. at 477 (White, J., concurring); A.L.I., RESTATEMENT OF JUDGMENTS § 77 (1942); A.L.I., RESTATEMENT (SECOND) OF JUDGMENTS § 76, and Reporter's Notes, Comment b at 29–31 (Tent. Draft No. 3, 1976); Note, note 146 *supra*, at 803.

[149] Pasadena City Bd. of Educ. v. Spangler, 427 U.S. 424, 437–38 (1976); Dombrowski v. Pfister, 380 U.S. 479, 492 (1965); System Federation v. Wright, 364 U.S. 642 (1961); Glenn v. Field Packing Co., 290 U.S. 177 (1933).

[150] United States v. United Shoe Machinery Corp., 391 U.S. 244, 248–49 (1968); United States v. Swift & Co., 286 U.S. 106 (1932).

in a way which would penalize past acts done in reliance on it would be seriously inconsistent with equitable doctrine.[151] Consideration of reliance on an injunction fits much more easily into equity doctrine than consideration of reliance on precedent fits into criminal law and its constitutional limitations.

The foregoing analysis of the legal effects of a favorable criminal judgment shows that they fall far short of assuring uninterrupted future exercise of the claimed federal right. But the prosecutor will not always take advantage of those defects. In some cases, he will give up after one acquittal or dismissal. Those cases are surely not negligible in number, but even more surely, they are nowhere near all. Nor is it possible to know in advance what the prosecutor will do. Thus, at the time the *Younger* doctrine requires dismissal of the federal case, it is often impossible to know whether the state remedy will be adequate even in effect.

In a case where interlocutory relief is denied or not sought, a federal court committed to maintaining the state criminal court as the primary forum might stay proceedings in its own case and await events or even dismiss without prejudice. If the state court reaches the federal issue and rules in favor of the federal plaintiff and the state accepts that decision, permanent prospective relief is unnecessary. But at the first clear sign that a second round of litigation will be required, all assumptions of adequacy must be rejected. At that point, the federal court must take as its premise that the state cannot permanently vindicate the federal right and proceed accordingly. Certainly it should not defer to a second pending proceeding in the same way it deferred to the first. And the delay caused by the initial stay should be taken into account if the plaintiff seeks interlocutory relief when the federal case resumes.

Given the limited prospective effects of a criminal judgment, the second prosecution may have some hope of success and thus be in good faith under present law.[152] Repeated prosecutions ending in repeated trial court invalidation of the statute might ultimately support a showing of bad-faith harassment. But that does not make the first criminal defense an adequate remedy. Nor are a series of such defenses followed by a federal lawsuit an adequate remedy;

---

[151] Dobbs, Handbook on the Law of Remedies § 2.4, at 52 (1973).

[152] See text *supra*, at notes 36–37.

remedies that require multiple litigation have always been held inadequate.[153]

The Supreme Court has not spoken to these considerations, even implicitly. They were not involved in *Wooley*,[154] because the state court rejected the constitutional claims. Had plaintiff pursued appeals, the state case would still have been pending, and plaintiff would have needed interlocutory relief. That is sufficient to explain not penalizing his failure to exhaust those appeals.

C. CLASS RELIEF

Even giving collateral estoppel effect to the legal conclusions underlying the state criminal judgment is inadequate if the federal case is properly brought as a class action. Theoretically, the criminal court's inability to give class relief may be overcome by abandoning the mutuality of estoppel rule[155] and holding the state bound as against any subsequent defendant who invokes the judgment. Although the majority view no longer requires mutuality of estoppel,[156] it is unlikely that any court will hold the state bound as against the world by one trial court judgment holding a statute unconstitutional, especially if the state could not appeal. The current draft of the *Second Restatement* suggests two exceptions which fit the situation nicely. The first is that a court may require mutuality of estoppel where "the issue is one of law and treating it as conclusively determined would inappropriately foreclose opportunity for obtaining reconsideration . . ."[157] The second is that relitigation is not precluded where the loser of the first case could not appeal.[158]

Whatever the reasoning, one can safely predict that other members of the federal plaintiff's class will not get collateral estoppel

---

[153] Graves v. Texas Co., 298 U.S. 393, 403 (1936); Lee v. Bickell, 292 U.S. 415, 421 (1934); DOBBS, note 151 *supra*, § 2.5 at 57; DOBBYN, INJUNCTIONS IN A NUTSHELL 45–46 (1974); *cf.* Toucey v. New York Life Ins. Co., 314 U.S. 118, 129 (1941) (no injunction to save litigant trouble of pleading res judicata in second suit); 28 U.S.C. § 2283 and Reviser's Note (1970) (statute amended to overrule *Toucey*).

[154] 97 S. Ct. 1428; see text *supra*, at notes 121–28.

[155] Blonder-Tongue v. University Foundation, 402 U.S. 313, 320–27 (1971).

[156] A.L.I., RESTATEMENT (SECOND) OF JUDGMENTS § 88, and cases collected in Reporter's Note, at 170–74 (Tent. Draft No. 3, 1976).

[157] *Id.* at § 88(7).

[158] *Id.* at § 68.1(a) (Tent. Draft No. 4, 1977).

benefits from the first state judgment. If it is appealed, they would get stare decisis benefit, but, as noted, appeal cannot be assured. The prosecutor will sometimes acquiesce, but he will probably refrain from prosecuting others because of nonbinding adverse decisions less often than he will refrain from reprosecuting the original defendant for a subsequent violation.

The class action can remedy this defect. The class action court can enjoin enforcement of the statute against any member of the class. Or it can declare the statute unconstitutional, and the collateral estoppel effect will extend to the whole class.[159]

The Court, however, appears to have held that a named plaintiff with an adequate remedy in a pending state proceeding may not represent a class which includes persons not yet sued or prosecuted.[160] This result is totally unexplained and may be based on nothing more than a desire to minimize the number of occasions on which federal relief will be available. It is not sufficient to say that such a named plaintiff is not a member of the class, for he may define the class to include both prosecuted and unprosecuted members. The issue is whether a class so defined and so represented meets the requirements of Rule 23. A respectable argument could be made in that situation that a named plaintiff's claim is atypical,[161] though that result is certainly not compelled by the weight of authority.[162]

Even if the Court's apparent restriction is accepted, however, once a named plaintiff is properly in federal court because his individual state remedy is inadequate, he should also be able to assert the inadequacy of the state remedy as to the class. Thus, if the named plaintiff seeks interlocutory or permanent prospective relief unavailable in the criminal case and the requirements of Rule 23 are met, he should be able to seek class relief.

More importantly, there are situations in First Amendment cases in which the named plaintiff's remedy is not adequate even for him-

---

159 Fed. R. Civ. P. Rule 23(c)(3); Supreme Tribe of Ben-Hur v. Cauble, 255 U.S. 356, 366–67 (1921); A.L.I., RESTATEMENT (SECOND) OF JUDGMENTS §§ 85(1)(e), 85(2) and Reporter's Note, Comments e, f at 68–70 (Tent. Draft No. 2, 1975).

160 *Trainor*, 97 S. Ct. at 1920 (semble); *cf. Allee*, 416 U.S. at 828–29 (Burger, C.J., dissenting in part) (plaintiff not threatened with prosecution cannot acquire standing by representing those who are); *O'Shea*, 414 U.S. at 494 (same).

161 Fed. R. Civ. P. Rule 23(a)(3); Blankner v. City of Chicago, 504 F.2d 1037, 1043 (7th Cir. 1974); Koos v. First Nat'l Bank, 496 F.2d 1162, 1164–65 (7th Cir. 1974).

162 3B MOORE'S FEDERAL PRACTICE ¶ 23.06–2 (2d ed. 1948; 1976–77 Supp.)

self unless it extends to a class. In cases where groups are campaigning for a common goal, like *Allee* and *Cameron*,[163] the individual speaker is much more likely to be successful if his class is free to speak with him.[164] For similar reasons, it has been held that candidates suffer legally cognizable injury when their supporters are coerced into working for opponents.[165] The right at issue may be conceived of as the plaintiff's right to associate with others for the advancement of his ideas[166] or as a right to "effective advocacy"[167]—a right to speak free of improper or unequal state-created obstacles to persuasion. Whatever the legal theory, an injunction against prosecution for political speech is not adequate unless it protects the named plaintiff's associates, and he should have standing so to assert.

There are also situations where special substantive considerations suggest a need for class relief. Speakers are allowed to raise claims of overbreadth and vagueness on the theory that, otherwise, nonparties would be deterred from speaking.[168] It would be anomalous, though not technically inconsistent, if the named plaintiff in these cases could raise the substantive rights of absent class members but not the procedural rights. Thus, in overbreadth and vagueness cases, the plaintiff should also be able to rely on the lack of class relief in the criminal case to show the inadequacy of the criminal defense.

The criminal court's inability to give class relief is partly alleviated by the possibility that, even if one suit is dismissed because a prosecution is pending against the named plaintiff, others may bring a federal suit[169] and may bring it as a class action. But the possibility that someone else may sue later is no reason to deny a needed remedy now to a litigant before the court. Nor does such reasoning prove the criminal defense to be an adequate remedy; rather, it

---

[163] See text *supra*, at note 92.

[164] NAACP v. Alabama ex rel. Patterson, 357 U.S. 449, 460 (1958).

[165] Shakman v. Democratic Organization, 435 F.2d 267, 269 (7th Cir. 1970).

[166] See Williams v. Rhodes, 393 U.S. 23, 30–32 (1968) (opinion of the Court); *id.* at 38–39 (Douglas, J., concurring); *id.* at 41–42 (Harlan, J., concurring); NAACP v. Button, 371 U.S. 415, 428–38 (1963); Bates v. City of Little Rock, 361 U.S. 516, 522–24 (1960); NAACP v. Alabama ex rel. Patterson, 357 U.S. 449, 460–63 (1958).

[167] See NAACP v. Alabama ex rel. Patterson, 357 U.S. 449, 460 (1958); *cf.* Williams v. Rhodes, 393 U.S. 23, 30 (1968) ("right . . . to cast . . . votes effectively").

[168] Gooding v. Wilson, 405 U.S. 518, 521 (1972).

[169] *Doran*, 422 U.S. at 928–29; *Steffel*, 415 U.S. 452; *Roe*, 410 U.S. at 120–29; Fiss, note 5 *supra*, at 1130–33.

admits the inadequacy of the criminal defense and offers to cure it in another class action instead of in the one filed.

Moreover, there is no assurance under present law that the second suit can or will be brought. If the class is loosely knit and disorganized, no second named plaintiff may step forward, especially if the prosecutor is careful quickly to indict and thus disqualify potential leaders. Many may be willing to engage in legal protest but unwilling to violate the law or commence litigation. On the other hand, if the class is well organized and can easily arrange for another plaintiff, there are indications that the second plaintiff may be barred because his "interest" is "intertwined" with the defendant in the pending criminal prosecution,[170] and he may be able to "see to it" that his federal claims are presented there.[171] *Steffel*, *Allee*, and *Doran* suggest some limits to that astounding holding, but they are not well defined. Certainly the present jurisprudence of the Court does not assure that class relief will be available when needed.

D. THE IMMINENCE ARGUMENT

One other possible objection to prospective relief is that there is no sufficiently imminent threat of a subsequent prosecution to support a claim for relief which has as its justification the prevention of subsequent prosecutions. In part of the *Younger* opinion dealing with unprosecuted coplaintiffs, the Court imposed an apparently stringent requirement that prosecution be imminently threatened before federal relief is granted.[172] This requirement was based partly on case or controversy considerations and partly on traditional conditions for equitable relief. In practice, the Court's treatment of the imminence requirement has been quite varied. Most opinions again seem willing to assume that states will enforce their statutes unless there are reasons for believing otherwise.[173] Yet opinions in

[170] *Hicks*, 422 U.S. at 348 (alternative holding); *Allee*, 416 U.S. at 826–33 (Burger. C.J., dissenting in part).

[171] *Hicks*, 422 U.S. at 349 (alternative holding).

[172] *Younger*, 401 U.S. at 41–42; *Steffel*, 415 U.S. at 476 (Stewart, J., concurring).

[173] *Ellis*, 421 U.S. at 434 (opinion of the Court); *id.* at 447 (Powell, J., dissenting); Doe v. Bolton, 410 U.S. 179, 188–89 (1973); *Lake Carriers' Ass'n*, 406 U.S. at 506–09; see also Hunt v. Washington State Apple Advertising Comm'n, 97 S. Ct. 2434 (1977); Douglas v. Seacoast Products, Inc., 97 S. Ct. 1740 (1977); Dixon v. Love, 97 S. Ct. 1723 (1977); Linmark Assoc., Inc. v. Township of Willingboro, 97 S. Ct. 1614 (1977); *cf.* Carey v. Population Services Int'l, 97 S. Ct. 2010, 2015–16 n.3 (1977) (standard unclear); *Steffel*, 415 U.S. at 459–60 (same).

slightly different contexts treat the imminence requirement stringently.[174]

In the prototype *Younger* situation, a case filed while the first prosecution is pending, the imminence argument is entitled to little weight. Indeed, it is really the adequacy argument in disguise. There is clearly a case or controversy between the parties as to whether the federal plaintiff is entitled to continue his course of conduct; the pending prosecution proves that. The prayers for a declaratory judgment of unconstitutionality and for an interlocutory injunction against enforcement are as ripe as they will ever be. If there is an acquittal in the pending case and if the prosecutor acquiesces, then there may no longer be a continuing controversy.[175] But that possibility is precisely the possibility that the prosecution may furnish a practically adequate remedy; it does not negate the existence of a ripe controversy prior to judgment.

Similarly, under the pressure of a threatened interlocutory injunction, the prosecutor may promise to bring only one test case. But such promises are not likely to be made without such pressure, and federal plaintiffs should not be expected to rely on them in any event. Prosecuting one violation implies a threat to prosecute others. The deterrent effect of the criminal law is based on that implied threat,[176] and the deterrent effect of a pending prosecution on the defendant is real, immediate, and entitled to judicial attention under any reasonable construction of the imminence requirement.[177]

Nor is there any imminence problem with respect to potential class members—persons not yet prosecuted who also are violating or desire to violate the statute. As the Court has recognized, prosecuting one violator implies a threat to prosecute others and thus supports a finding that there is a ripe controversy as to those others.[178]

---

[174] *Juidice*, 97 S. Ct. at 1216 n.9; *Rizzo*, 423 U.S. at 370–73; *O'Shea*, 414 U.S. at 493–98.

[175] *Cf. Steffel*, 415 U.S. at 459–60 (no continuing controversy if federal plaintiff abandons desire to continue course of conduct).

[176] Zimring & Hawkins, Deterrence 163 (1973).

[177] A Quantity of Copies of Books v. Kansas (Harlan, J., dissenting), quoted note 97 *supra*; *cf.* cases cited in note 178 *infra*; see also Zimring & Hawkins, note 176 *supra*, at 217–24, 246.

[178] Carey v. Population Services Int'l, 97 S. Ct. 2010, 2015–16 n.3 (1977) (prosecution twelve years before); *Steffel*, 415 U.S. at 459 (ongoing prosecution).

IV. Implications of the Need for Prospective Relief

A. EQUITY, COMITY, AND FEDERALISM

The *Younger* doctrine is based on "relevant principles of equity, comity, and federalism."[179] If the phrase is only a slogan for unreasoned deference to claims of states' rights in an ever growing number of contexts, as some have charged,[180] then careful analysis is futile. But if the Court has accurately stated the interests which the *Younger* doctrine serves, then careful study of its opinions is essential to any effort to accommodate those interests with the need for prospective relief.

Although comity and federalism are distinguishable,[181] *Younger* used them as two names for the same idea,[182] and the Court has never attempted to separate them in *Younger* cases involving state courts. Moreover, all of *Younger's* teeth came from its view of federalism. Equity's contribution was limited to the basic idea that an injunction should issue only if the plaintiff has no adequate remedy at law, *i.e.*, if he will suffer irreparable injury without the injunction. "Irreparable injury" and "no adequate remedy at law" are two formulations of the same requirement; injury is reparable if, and only if, there is an adequate legal remedy.[183] There is no support for the Court's unexplained treatment of these two formulations as separate requirements in *Trainor*.[184] Fortunately, nothing was made to turn on it.

The normal equity rule had been implicitly modified when the Court first considered whether defense of a state prosecution might be an adequate remedy. In other contexts, it is settled that only a federal legal remedy will cause a federal court to withhold an injunction.[185]

In the name of federalism, *Younger* and *Samuels* extended the old equity rule in much more dramatic fashion. A legal remedy is not adequate unless it is "as complete, practical and efficient as that

---

[179] *Huffman*, 420 U.S. at 602–03; *Steffel*, 415 U.S. at 462.

[180] Francis v. Henderson, 425 U.S. 536, 551 (Brennan, J., dissenting) (1976).

[181] *Schlesinger*, 420 U.S. at 753–61 (deference to court martial).

[182] 401 U.S. at 44.

[183] See Fiss, note 105 *supra*, at 9; Dobbs, note 151 *supra*, § 2.10, at 108.

[184] 97 S. Ct. at 1917.

[185] *Ibid.*; AFL v. Watson, 327 U.S. 582, 594 n.9 (1946); City Bank Farmers Trust Co. v. Schnader, 291 U.S. 24, 29 (1934).

which equity could afford."[186] But the Court made no effort to evaluate the remedy it posited in *Younger*. Moreover, it said that plaintiff's injury must be not only irreparable but "great and immediate."[187] These last two adjectives have never been given any content, except that we have been repeatedly told that the "cost, anxiety, and inconvenience of having to defend against a single criminal prosecution" is not great, immediate, and irreparable injury.[188] Second, the Court deferred to a pending prosecution even when the equity case was filed first.[189] The settled equity rule had been that legal remedies which first became available after the equity suit was filed were irrelevant.[190] Finally, the Court extended the equity rule to declaratory judgments,[191] despite the explicit provision of Rule 57 that the "existence of another adequate remedy does not preclude" a declaratory judgment[192] and the statutory provision that a declaratory judgment is available "whether or not further relief is or could be sought."[193]

These extensions of the equity rule must draw their support from the Court's view of federalism. The initial statement of that view in *Younger* was broad and vague,[194] and there are echoes of that initial sweep in applications of the doctrine outside the context of challenges to the constitutionality of statutes.[195] But in that context, the Court's view of federalism was given content in *Steffel*, and the content turned out to be rather narrow. The Court's view of federalism would not overturn the Supremacy Clause or *Cohens v. Virginia*.[196] The federal courts are still to be the final arbiters of the constitutionality of state statutes. Additional deference to state judiciaries and executives is required, but not to state legislatures.[197]

---

[186] Terrace v. Thompson, 263 U.S. 197, 214 (1923); accord, other authorities cited in note 114 *supra*.

[187] 401 U.S. at 46.

[188] *Huffman*, 420 U.S. at 601–02; *Younger*, 401 U.S. at 46.

[189] *Hicks*, 422 U.S. at 349 (alternative holding).

[190] American Life Ins. Co. v. Stewart, 300 U.S. 203, 215 (1937); Dawson v. Kentucky Distilleries Co., 255 U.S. 288, 296 (1921).

[191] *Samuels*, 401 U.S. 66.

[192] Fed. R. Civ. P. Rule 57.

[193] 28 U.S.C. § 2201 (1970).

[194] 401 U.S. at 44–45.

[195] Francis v. Henderson, 425 U.S. 536, 541–42 (1976); *Rizzo*, 423 U.S. at 380.

[196] 6 Wheat. 264 (1821).

[197] See Fiss, note 5 *supra*, at 1107.

Younger federalism defers only to the state's interests in completing its own proceeding once begun. The Court identified three such interests in *Steffel*:[198]

> When no state criminal proceeding is pending at the time the federal complaint is filed, federal intervention does not result in duplicative legal proceedings or disruption of the state criminal justice system; nor can federal intervention, in that circumstance, be interpreted as reflecting negatively upon the state court's ability to enforce constitutional principles.

It is reasonably clear what the Court meant by duplicative proceedings and negative reflection on state courts. "Disruption of the state criminal justice system" is more ambiguous. In *Steffel,* the phrase could only mean disruption of a pending prosecution filed before the federal suit was filed. So construed, it is not clear how any of these three interests support the "reverse removal power"[199] conferred on state prosecutors in *Hicks v. Miranda,*[200] and the opinion makes no effort to tell us. Where the federal case is filed first, under normal usage it is the state case that results in duplication. Similarly, it does not reflect negatively on state courts for a federal court to finish a case already commenced. And there is no disruption of the state criminal justice system as that phrase was used in *Steffel. Hicks* must rest on a broader view of what it means to disrupt the state criminal justice system and possibly on the view that the federal court causes duplication and negative reflection when it insists on retaining without strong cause a case barely begun. *Hicks* implicitly expands the meaning of "disruption of the state criminal justice system" to include interruption of any pending case, without regard to when it was filed. But, still implicitly, *Hicks* suggests that there comes a time in the progress of the first-filed federal case when the interest in avoiding such disruption is no longer strong enough to require dismissal.[201]

A fourth interest was suggested by the Court in *Trainor v. Hernandez:* giving the state court an opportunity "to construe the

---

[198] *Steffel,* 415 U.S. at 462, quoted in *Huffman,* 420 U.S. at 603; see also Note, note 5 *supra,* at 1282–90.

[199] See Fiss, note 5 *supra,* at 1134–36.

[200] 422 U.S. at 349–50 (alternative holding); accord, *Doran,* 422 U.S. 922; see text *supra,* at note 13.

[201] For a somewhat different analysis, see Note, note 5 *supra,* at 1303–04.

challenged statute in the face of the actual federal constitutional challenges."[202] But that interest carries equal weight whether or not a state case is pending and, in any event, is fully served by *Pullman* abstention.[203]

No one of the three interests taken alone is sufficient to support the Court's results. All but the interest in avoiding duplicative litigation can be served by letting the state and federal cases proceed simultaneously. Duplicative litigation can be avoided by enjoining the state proceeding as well as by dismissing the federal proceeding. One of the other interests must be invoked to choose between those two options. The desire to avoid disrupting the state system does not necessarily determine that choice, because *Younger* abstention disrupts the federal judicial system in ways parallel to the proscribed disruption of the state system. Federal cases are dismissed, or never filed, because of the state proceedings.

This suggestion focuses attention on another implicit component of the Court's views. The state's interest in maintaining its own judicial proceeding is proportionate to the strength of the state's substantive interests at issue in the litigation. Put less neutrally, the Court gives important weight to the state's interest in being the judge of its own case. This appears most clearly in the Court's extension of *Younger* to civil cases to which the state is a party in its sovereign capacity.[204] Similarly, in extending *Younger* to civil contempt proceedings, the Court ignored the normal distinction between civil contempt as benefiting litigants and criminal contempt as vindicating the court's authority.[205] It relied on the state's interest in vindicating "the regular operation of its judicial system."[206]

Thus, the phrase "disruption of state judicial proceedings in which the state seeks to vindicate its own interests" should probably be substituted for *Steffel's* "disruption of the state criminal justice system." In the Court's view, disruption of such a proceeding is apparently more objectionable than disruption of federal judicial proceedings to which the United States is not a party and in which federal substantive policies would be vindicated only for the benefit

---

[202] 97 S. Ct. at 1919.

[203] Railroad Comm'n v. Pullman Co., 312 U.S. 496 (1941); see note 7 *supra*.

[204] *Trainor*, 97 S. Ct. at 1917–19; *Huffman*, 420 U.S. at 603–05.

[205] United States v. United Mine Workers, 330 U.S. 258, 302–04 (1947).

[206] *Juidice*, 97 S. Ct. at 1217.

of private litigants. But if the Court extends *Younger* to all civil proceedings, then disruption of the federal case will become equal in importance to disruption of the state case. At that point, only fears of negative reflection on state courts would be available to support the Court's preference for dismissing the federal case rather than interfering with the state case.

B. THE IMPACT OF PROSPECTIVE RELIEF

Equitable intervention in the situations heretofore identified does not reflect negatively on state courts. The inability of criminal courts to give interlocutory, permanent prospective, or class relief is general in Anglo-American jurisprudence. Federal criminal courts could do no better. And there are strong reasons for maintaining the clear distinctions between civil and criminal procedure. Similarly, recognition of the limited effect of a state's res judicata rules is not stigmatizing. These limitations are independent of any views on the ability of state judges to decide constitutional claims fairly and intelligently. The need for different forms of relief justifies the partial duplication caused by equitable intervention in these situations.

Analysis becomes more difficult when one considers disruption of the pending state proceeding. As long as we assume the good faith and competence of the state courts, the state remedy is not inadequate because the state court is harming the federal court plaintiff, but only because it cannot do enough to help. That problem is solved by making additional relief available in the federal court. It is not necessary to prevent the state court from acting. This suggests the result in *Cline v. Frink Dairy Co.*,[207] where, for purely formal reasons and without analysis, the Court affirmed injunctions of future prosecutions but vacated injunctions of pending prosecutions against the same plaintiffs. But that does not completely solve the problem. If the federal judgment is given collateral estoppel effect in the state court, then the state proceeding would still be disrupted. Instead of deciding the constitutional issue, the state court would decide the res judicata issue.

It is important to specify the degree of disruption that possibility entails. The *Cline* solution would permit no interlocutory injunction against the pending prosecutions; that prosecution could proceed

---

[207] 274 U.S. 445, 452–53, 466 (1927); Transcript of Record, at 10; Beatrice Creamery Co. v. Cline, 9 F.2d 176, 177 (D. Colo. 1925).

in normal course at least until the federal judgment. If the federal court upholds the challenged statute, the pending prosecution need not be disrupted at all. Conviction could come as soon as if there had been no federal litigation. Moreover, even if collateral estoppel may be invoked against a criminal defendant, the state can waive the benefits of the doctrine if it wants its own courts to decide the constitutional issue.

Second, there would be no disruption where the state case is decided before the federal case. This would not be unusual and would be routine if the federal courts stay proceedings when interlocutory and class relief are either denied or not sought.

Third, where the statute is challenged as applied, the state court would decide whether the prosecuted conduct is distinguishable from the contemplated conduct adjudicated in the federal action. If so, collateral estoppel would not apply, and the state case would proceed undisrupted except for the injection of one additional issue. If pending prosecutions are enjoined, this issue would be determined in federal court.

Thus, the disruptive effects of granting prospective relief are not nearly so severe as the disruptive effects of enjoining a pending prosecution. This degree of disruption, though far from trivial, should be accepted in order to meet the need for prospective relief.

If the Court is not willing to permit even this degree of indirect disruption of state proceedings, then it should create an exception to the collateral estoppel doctrine, permitting the state court to ignore the federal judgment in this narrow situation. It may be anomalous to envision a litigant protected from future prosecution by a federal injunction suffering punishment for a past violation of the same statute, but that is better for the litigant than being punished and without future protection. Moreover, since the Court assumes that state courts are as capable of deciding constitutional issues as federal courts, it must also assume that such anomalies would be infrequent. Presumably, the state and federal court would normally agree. Where they disagree, both judgments would not necessarily be carried out. The Supreme Court could resolve the conflict on appeal or writ of certiorari. And where custodial punishment is imposed, habeas corpus would lie,[208] generally to the

[208] Wainwright v. Sykes, 97 S. Ct. 2497, 2502 (1977); Ex parte Siebold, 100 U.S. 371, 376–77 (1879).

same federal court which granted prospective relief,[209] a result not forbidden by the *Younger* doctrine.[210]

There is no insuperable legislative bar to such an exception to collateral estoppel doctrine. The Full Faith and Credit Clause and its implementing statute[211] do not refer to federal judgments. As long as the federal judgment is binding as to future violations, it is not reduced to a mere advisory opinion, and it fulfills the congressional intention to create a risk-free remedy in the Declaratory Judgment Act. The last sentence of § 2201[212] presents a problem, but the federal plaintiff could be required partially to waive its benefits as a condition of prospective relief, and the waiver could be made binding by inclusion in the judgment.

It still remains briefly to apply this analysis to the three forms of prospective relief. The federal plaintiff's claim is strongest if he shows a right to interlocutory relief, whether for himself alone or for a class. There will be a need for such relief in a large percentage of cases;[213] the right to it will turn on the probability of success and the balance of hardships.[214] If an interlocutory injunction is issued, the federal court should proceed expeditiously to final judgment, to minimize the injury to the parties if the injunction is ultimately held erroneous.

The federal plaintiff's claim is weakest when he is entitled only to permanent individual relief. If the court decides that plaintiff is not entitled to interlocutory relief and not entitled to represent a class, then it might consider retaining jurisdiction but staying further proceedings pending resolution of the state prosecution. Such a stay is inappropriate unless the state law clearly accords collateral estoppel effect to legal issues decided in criminal cases, the pending state case fairly presents the constitutional issue, and there is no substantial chance of an acquittal on nonconstitutional grounds. Federal plaintiffs should not be denied permanent prospective relief because of speculation that state prosecutors will voluntarily honor a judgment without collateral estoppel effect.

Where the federal plaintiff seeks permanent class relief, his claim is stronger. There is much less possibility that the state judgment

---

209 *Compare* 28 U.S.C. § 1391(b) (1970); *with* 28 U.S.C. § 2241(a) (1970).

210 *Huffman*, 420 U.S. at 605–07.

211 28 U.S.C. § 1738 (1970).

212 See text *supra*, at note 147.

213 See text *supra*, at notes 98–103.

214 See authorities cited in note 105 *supra*.

will give prospective benefits. There is no possibility of collateral estoppel. The only hope is that there will be an appeal and stare decisis effect or voluntary prosecutorial compliance. The arguments for a stay of the federal case are parallel to but substantially weaker than the arguments for a stay in an individual case. In no event should there be a dismissal with prejudice until the criminal case is completed and is seen at least to have informal prospective and class effects.

These suggested results may not take full account of the Court's view that ordinary irreparable injury is not enough to justify federal intervention.[215] But that view is hard to analyze because, as noted,[216] it has never been given any content. It seems more responsive to a general disposition against federal intervention than to the specific state interests identified by the Court. Rigid insistence that only great and immediate injury to the federal plaintiff offsets the state's interests ignores the extent to which the inadequacy of the state remedy directly eliminates some of the state's interests from the balance. The desire to avoid negative reflection on the state courts simply drops out of the equation when the federal intervention is to grant relief unavailable there. If the Court insists, however, on an especially great showing of irreparable injury, then it might conclude that uncertainy over the permanent prospective effect of a state judgment is insufficient. In that event, stays or dismissals without prejudice might be routinely granted, subject to the conditions suggested earlier.[217]

C. RES JUDICATA AND CONGRESSIONAL INTENT

Permitting two actions to proceed simultaneously raises the question whether the first judgment becomes res judicata in the other case. This gives increased prominence to an issue that has been lurking unresolved in federal jurisprudence for some time: Should a state constitutional judgment be given collateral estoppel effect in a federal action under § 1983?[218] Because the issue can arise in many

[215] *Younger*, 401 U.S. at 46.

[216] See text *supra*, at notes 187–88.

[217] See text *infra*, at note 218.

[218] Theis, *Res Judicata in Civil Rights Act Cases: An Introduction to the Problem*, 70 Nw. L. Rev. 859 (1976); Note, note 5 *supra*, at 1330–54; see *Ellis*, 421 U.S. at 435 (opinion of the Court); *id.* at 439–43 (Powell, J., dissenting); *Huffman*, 420 U.S. at

contexts,[219] full examination of it is beyond the scope of this paper. But some tentative exploration is necessary to assess the workability and likely effect of the foregoing conclusions concerning federal equity power. The only court to face the issue squarely in this context was divided but held the state conviction binding.[220]

By statute, a state court judgment has the same effect in federal court as in courts of the rendering state.[221] The issue is whether § 1983, like the Habeas Corpus Act,[222] creates an exception to that rule. There are substantial parallels between the two statutes. Both date from Reconstruction, and both provide for relief against public officials. Both acts provide a broad range of protection for all rights secured by the Constitution and federal laws.

Most importantly, the legislative history of both reflects a profound mistrust of state courts and a desire to provide a federal remedy for their abuses.[223] Reconstruction legislation was premised on Congress's belief that state governments, including state courts, could not or would not enforce federal rights and would in some cases work affirmatively to deny them.[224] The legislative history

---

607–08 n.19; Preiser v. Rodriguez, 411 U.S. 475, 497 (1973) (opinion of the Court); *id.* at 509 n.14 (Brennan, J., dissenting); Florida State Bd. of Dentistry v. Mack, 401 U.S. 960, 960–62 (1971) (White, J., dissenting from denial of certiorari); *cf. Wooley*, 97 S. Ct. 1428 (issue not raised).

[219] See cases and commentaries collected at Theis, note 218 *supra*, at 865–66 n.35.

[220] Thistlethwaite v. City of New York, 497 F.2d 339 (2d Cir. 1974).

[221] 28 U.S.C. § 1738 (1970); but see Parker v. McKeithen, 488 F.2d 553, 558 n.7 (5th Cir. 1974); American Mannex Corp. v. Rozands, 462 F.2d 688, 689–90 (5th Cir. 1972); Vestal, *Res Judicata/Preclusion by Judgment: The Law Applied in Federal Courts*, 66 MICH. L. REV. 1723, 1734, 1736–39, 1746 (1968); Note, note 5 *supra*, at 1334.

[222] 28 U.S.C. § 2241 (1970).

[223] As to § 1983, see notes 224–27, 232 *infra*. As to habeas corpus, see CONG. GLOBE 4229 39th Cong., 1st Sess. (1866) (Sen. Trumbull); see generally *id.* at 4228–30, 4150–51; *id.* at 729, 730, 790, 903, 945 39th Cong., 2d Sess. (1867); see also debates on related bills considered earlier and at greater length, *id.* at 1983 39th Cong., 1st Sess. (1866) (Sen. Clark, Sen. Trumbull); *id.* at 2021 (Sen. Clark); *id.* at 2023 (Sen. Howard); *id.* at 2054 (Sen. Clark, Sen. Wilson); *id.* at 2055 (Sen. Trumbull); *id.* at 2058 (Sen. Cowan); *id.* at 2061–62 (Sen. Johnson); *id.* at 2063 (Sen. Clark, Sen. Stewart); *id.* at 2065 (Sen. Sherman); *id.* at 4096 (Rep. Wilson).

[224] CONG. GLOBE 374 42d Cong., 1st Sess. (1871) (Rep. Lowe); *id.* at 653 (Sen. Osborn); *id.* at 807 (Rep. Garfield); *id.* at App. 216–17 (Sen. Thurman) (1871); see generally *id.* at 43–44, 113, 116–18, 123–31, 134–35, 144–45, 152–67, 172–76, 179–82, 189–92, 194–211, 219–27, 231–33, 236–40, 244–49, 317–22, 329–41, 343–58, 361–401, 408–63, 475–93, 498–506, 508–24, 534–38, 566–82, 599–610, 645–66, 686–709, 754–66, 769–79, 787–95, 798–801, 804–08, 819–31, 833, App. 14–39, App. 46–50, App. 67–316. Much of this legislative history is reprinted in 1 SCHWARTZ, STATUTORY HISTORY OF THE UNITED STATES: CIVIL RIGHTS 591–653 (1970). Much of that which relates to mis-

contains repeated statements that state courts would not enforce the rights of blacks and Republicans.[225] Representative Perry said that one of the "most dangerous things an injured party can do is to appeal to justice."[226] The congressional remedy for the failings of state courts included § 1983[227] and four important grants of federal jurisdiction: general federal question jurisdiction,[228] original civil rights jurisdiction,[229] civil rights removal jurisdiction,[230] and modern habeas corpus jurisdiction.[231]

The Reconstruction Congresses believed that federal courts were more independent than state courts and more likely to rise above or resist local "influence . . . , sympathies . . . , prejudices . . . , passions or terror."[232] No subsequent Congress has taken away any substantial portion of the jurisdiction they granted. Modern commentators have argued persuasively that federal judges are still more receptive to federal claims than their state counterparts.[233] There are important institutional factors suggesting that this should be so,[234] even assuming complete good faith and integrity on the

---

trust of state courts is excerpted and summarized in Mitchum v. Foster, 407 U.S. 225, 238–42 (1972); Pierson v. Ray, 386 U.S. 547, 559–62 (1967) (Douglas, J., dissenting); Monroe v. Pape, 365 U.S. 167, 172–83 (1961).

225 CONG. GLOBE 334–35 42d Cong., 1st Sess. (1871) (Rep. Hoar); *id.* at 345 (Sen. Sherman); *id.* at 505 (Sen. Pratt); *id.* at App. 166–67 (Rep. W. Williams); *id.* at App. 277 (Rep. Porter).

226 *Id.* at App. 78.

227 Act of April 20, 1871, Chap. XXII, § 1, 17 Stat. 13, now 42 U.S.C. § 1983 (1970).

228 Act of March 3, 1875, Chap. 137, § 1, 18 Stat. 470, now 28 U.S.C. § 1331 (1970).

229 Act of April 20, 1871, Chap. XXII, § 2, 17 Stat. 13, now 28 U.S.C. § 1343 (1970).

230 Act of April 9, 1866, Chap. XXXI, § 3, 14 Stat. 27, now 28 U.S.C. § 1443 (1970).

231 Act of Feb. 5, 1867, Chap. XXVIII, § 1, 14 Stat. 385, now 28 U.S.C. § 2241(c)(3) (1970).

232 Remarks of Rep. Coburn, CONG. GLOBE 460 42d Cong., 1st Sess. (1871).

233 Dombrowski v. Pfister, 227 F. Supp. 556, 571 (E.D. La. 1964) (Wisdom, J., dissenting); Neuborne, *The Myth of Parity*, 90 HARV. L. REV. 1105, 1106, 1115–31 (1977); Kanowitz, *Deciding Federal Law Issues in Civil Proceedings: State versus Federal Trial Courts*, 3 HAST. CONST. L. Q. 141, 158 (1976); Schneider, *State Court Evasion of United States Supreme Court Mandates: A Reconsideration of the Evidence*, 7 VAL. U. L. REV. 191 (1973); Beatty, *State Court Evasion of United States Supreme Court Mandates during the Last Decade of the Warren Court*, 6 VAL. U. L. REV. 260 (1972); Gilbert, note 5 *supra*, at 19–21; Manwaring, *The Impact of Mapp v. Ohio*, in EVERSON, ED., THE SUPREME COURT AS POLICY MAKER: THREE STUDIES ON THE IMPACT OF JUDICIAL DECISIONS 1 (1968); Vines, *Southern State Supreme Courts and Race Relations*, 18 WEST. POL. Q. 5, 8–18 (1965); Amsterdam, note 75 *supra*, at 793–802; Lusky, note 63 *supra*, at 1163; Note, 21 U. FLA. L. REV. 346 (1969).

234 FEDERALIST No. 10 (Madison).

part of state judges.[235] The large volume of *Younger* litigation gives rise to its own inferences: with so many prosecutors fighting to stay in state court and so many defense lawyers fighting to get into federal court, one must wonder if they are all wrong about where their clients' interests lie. But it is not necessary to resolve this as an empirical question; the congressional determination should be conclusive.

The Court's treatment of this legislative history has been quite inconsistent. The *Younger* cases have ignored it. In them, the Court has insisted that state courts are as able as federal courts and has refused to grant relief which might suggest otherwise. But the Court has also repeatedly recognized that the purpose and effect of the Reconstruction legislation was to make the federal courts "the *primary* and powerful reliances for vindicating every right given by the Constitution, the laws and treaties of the United States."[236] Outside the *Younger* context, the Court has held that federal review of state judgments is an inadequate substitute for plaintiffs' right to federal fact finding.[237] More recently, in *Mitchum v. Foster*,[238] the Court relied heavily on the congressional view that state courts were hostile to federal rights and concluded that the Reconstruction legislation was part of "a vast transformation" from earlier concepts of federalism.[239]

One can only guess whether the Court will consider the res judicata issue another appropriate occasion to ignore the congressional assessment of the reliability of state courts. But that assessment should be relevant. It would be strange if the prospective relief authorized by § 1983 could be defeated by a prior state determination of the federal issue in a different cause of action, when the original reason for granting federal jurisdiction was mistrust of the state courts.

The issue requires further study. The failure to enact removal jurisdiction over all cases in which federal defenses are raised, together with the omission from § 1983 of any express reference to

---

[235] Neuborne, note 233 *supra*, at 1118–28; Amsterdam, note 75 *supra*, at 800–02.

[236] *Steffel*, 415 U.S. at 464; Zwickler v. Koota, 389 U.S. 241, 247 (1967); both quoting FRANKFURTER & LANDIS, THE BUSINESS OF THE SUPREME COURT: A STUDY IN THE FEDERAL JUDICIAL SYSTEM 65 (1927); accord, McNeese v. Board of Educ., 373 U.S. 668, 672 (1963).

[237] England v. Louisiana Bd. of Medical Exam'rs, 375 U.S. 411, 416–17 (1964).

[238] 407 U.S. 225 (1972).

[239] *Id.* at 242.

state judgments,[240] supports an argument that Congress intended state judgments to have at least bar and merger effect except on habeas corpus. But those considerations carry little weight with respect to collateral estoppel and prospective relief, since enforcement of the first judgment would not be prevented. Additionally, a collateral estoppel exception is much more important to the effectuation of § 1983 than a bar and merger exception.

Even if § 1983 does not create an exception to collateral estoppel doctrine, suits for prospective relief of the type here proposed would not be made unworkable or superfluous. Interlocutory relief is needed before the state judgment. Permanent prospective relief is most needed in those states that deny collateral estoppel effect to legal determinations in criminal judgments. But in those states, the legal determination should also be denied collateral estoppel effect in federal court.[241]

D. STATE CIVIL REMEDIES

It is now possible to return to the question why the state criminal defendant who needs prospective relief should not be required to go to state civil courts. As noted earlier, *Younger* and its progeny require only that, once a citizen becomes a defendant in certain kinds of state proceedings, he must pursue the remedies which defense of those proceedings offers. But the Court has not wavered from the rule that, when the citizen is free to become a civil rights plaintiff, he has a right to file in federal court.[242] Just last Term, the Court unanimously rejected a contention that constitutional claims first be presented to state courts, reaffirming that "it is the 'solemn responsibility' of 'all levels of the federal judiciary to give due respect to a suitor's choice of a federal forum for the hearing and decision of his federal constitutional claims.' "[243]

---

[240] *Cf.* 28 U.S.C. § 2254(a) (1970) ("in custody pursuant to the judgment of a State court"); Act of Feb. 5, 1867, Chap. XXVIII, § 1, 14 Stat. 385, 386 ("pending such proceeding . . . and after . . . discharge . . . any proceeding . . . in any State court . . . shall be deemed null and void"); but *cf.* Mitchum v. Foster, 407 U.S. 225, 236–38, 242–43 (1972) (§ 1983 expressly authorizes injunctions against pending state proceedings because to construe it otherwise would deprive it of its intended scope).

[241] 28 U.S.C. § 1738 (1970); but see note 221 *supra.*

[242] Douglas v. Seacoast Products, Inc., 97 S. Ct. 1740, 1744–45 n.4 (1977); *Doran*, 422 U.S. at 930; *Steffel*, 415 U.S. at 472–73; *Lake Carriers' Ass'n*, 406 U.S. at 510.

[243] Douglas v. Seacoast Products, Inc., 97 S. Ct. 1740, 1744–45 n.4 (1977), quoting with approval from Zwickler v. Koota, 389 U.S. 241, 248 (1967).

This rule follows directly from the cause of action created by § 1983 and the implementing grant of jurisdiction in 28 U.S.C. § 1343. To require § 1983 plaintiffs to initiate state litigation would be totally inconsistent with the congressional intention to create a federal remedy, independent of any remedies in the state courts that Congress so mistrusted and available at the plaintiff's choice.[244] To require a litigant to file a state suit is a much more direct denial of his choice of forum than to require him to defend a pending case. Requiring him to defend may be reconcilable with the statutory scheme as a way of preserving the choice not to enact removal for federal defenses, though the Court has not made this argument.

Moreover, requiring state criminal defendants entitled to equitable relief to initiate state litigation would not serve *Younger's* policies. Any argument in support of such a special rule would have to start from the premise that the civil and criminal cases were related and that related cases within the same system are somehow more desirable than related cases in different systems. The problem of related cases is not new. There are a variety of devices for bringing such cases together—joinder, counterclaim, consolidation, res judicata. Modern procedural rules neither permit nor require counterclaims in criminal cases. They do not provide for joinder or consolidation of civil and criminal cases. They provide different rules for civil and criminal cases.[245] The long-term judgment of our jurisprudence is that civil and criminal cases do not mix; a contrary judgment would be inconsistent with the special protections given criminal defendants. The pendency of a criminal case is irrelevant to choice of forum in a civil case, because the two cases cannot be brought together even if they are in the same system.

Thus the effect of a separate civil proceeding on the state criminal process does not depend on where the civil case is filed. Having a federal judge take jurisdiction over a related dispute raising the same constitutional issue is no more duplicative, disruptive, or insulting to the criminal judge than having a second state judge with different powers do so. The considerations of equity and comity are identical. As to federalism, if the plaintiff's choice of forum

---

[244] Zwickler v. Koota, 389 U.S. 241, 248 (1967); McNeese v. Board of Educ., 373 U.S. 668, 671–74 (1963); Monroe v. Pape, 365 U.S. 167, 183 (1961).

[245] Fed. R. Civ. Proc. and Fed. R. Crim. Proc.; see generally Helvering v. Mitchell, 303 U.S. 391, 402 (1938); CATALDO, KEMPIN, STOCKTON, & WEBER, INTRODUCTION TO LAW AND THE LEGAL PROCESS 115–16 (2d ed. 1973).

makes any invidious comparison, it is not between the federal court and the criminal court where the first case is pending but between the federal court and the state civil court where the new case would be filed. That is precisely the comparison that the plaintiff's choice of forum always makes and which is required by § 1983 and the jurisdictional statutes.

V. Conclusion

This article has considered not only the criminal remedy and the normal forms of prospective relief but also potential substitutes such as enforceable stipulations, consent decrees, voluntary stays, and dismissals without prejudice. Such possibilities are not unimportant, but they should not obscure the basic reality. Criminal courts do not have sufficient powers to assure prospective relief. A citizen undertaking a forbidden but constitutionally protected course of conduct needs one resolution of his constitutional claim which will be binding in the future, both for himself and his class. He needs a preliminary resolution of the issue and immediate interlocutory protection. Not every citizen claiming such relief is entitled to it, but he is entitled to have his claim examined free of the erroneous assumption that a criminal court can furnish the relief he seeks.

Adjusting the *Younger* doctrine to incorporate the need for prospective relief will require careful assessment and balancing of competing interests in particular cases. In striking such balances, the Court should give weight to the fact that important First Amendment interests are at stake in many *Younger* cases. And it must give weight to the fact that Congress provided for prospective federal relief. Congress gave the civil rights litigant his own cause of action, at law or in equity, not merely a right to defend at law. And not trusting the state courts, it gave him the right to file that cause of action in the forum of his choice.

There are three paths now open to the Supreme Court. It can narrowly construe *Wooley*, substantially ignore the defects in the criminal remedy, and continue to send litigants away without the prospective relief they need. Alternatively, it can vigorously develop a system of stipulations, stays, and other devices to encourage or coerce informal solutions and "voluntary" acquiescence. In this way, it may manage to provide near substitutes for the various forms of prospective relief while usually leaving the primary adjudication of the constitutional issue to the state criminal court. This is the minimum required of the Court under its own articulated premises. But there is no reason for it to work so hard to keep federal claims out of federal court.

The third alternative is freely to entertain claims for prospective relief and to decide the issues raised by such claims. Even though they refuse to enjoin the first prosecution, federal courts should not deny relief with respect to contemplated future violations. Certainly they should not do so in defiance of congressional intent. At most, *Younger*'s deference to state courts should be limited to cases in which the state court has power to grant full relief. *Younger*'s premises require no more.

Stare decisis should not bar this course. *Younger* is a recent innovation, resting shakily on a view of prior law which, at least with respect to prospective relief, is seriously misleading. Not until *Wooley v. Maynard* did the Court begin to think about a need for prospective relief unmet by state prosecutions. *Wooley* should point the way to a reassessment of all the cases that expound on *Younger* without considering that need.

FRED L. MORRISON

THE RIGHT TO FISH FOR SEACOAST PRODUCTS: GIBBONS v. OGDEN RESURRECTED

The steamboat *United States* entered New York in triumph, with streamers flying, after the Supreme Court under Chief Justice Marshall had broken the Livingston-Fulton steamboat monopoly by its decision in *Gibbons v. Ogden*[1] in 1824.[2] Celebration was more muted, probably limited to a single corporate boardroom, when Mr. Justice Thurgood Marshall applied the same statute that John Marshall had invoked to render ineffectual the protectionist fishing legislation of many Atlantic coastal states in *Douglas v. Seacoast Products, Inc.*[3] With that decision, the latest in a long series of state efforts to preserve coastal fisheries for local fishermen fell into constitutional oblivion. The earlier cases had turned on questions of equal protection,[4] privileges and immunities,[5] or the application of the Commerce Clause.[6] In contrast, *Douglas* appeared on

---

Fred L. Morrison is Professor of Law, University of Minnesota.

[1] 9 Wheat. 1 (1824).

[2] 1 Warren, The Supreme Court in United States History 615–17 (rev. ed. 1926).

[3] 97 S.Ct. 1740 (1977).

[4] Takahashi v. Fish and Game Comm'n., 334 U.S. 410 (1948).

[5] Toomer v. Witsell, 334 U.S. 385 (1948).

[6] Foster-Fountain Packing Co. v. Haydel, 278 U.S. 1 (1928).

0-226-46429-6/78/1977-8000$01.51

its face to be a mere instance of statutory interpretation, but that statutory interpretation necessarily invoked constitutional criteria.

Paradoxically, the decision permitted a British-owned fishing fleet to catch menhaden, an inedible fish used in animal foods and fertilizer, within the three-mile limit, while Congress was concurrently prohibiting fishing by foreign-flag vessels for 200 miles offshore.[7] The new congressional legislation did not, however, affect the respondent corporation in the *Douglas* case, because while it was British owned, its fishing fleet consisted of American-flag vessels.

I

Two cases were before the Court. The principal case, *Douglas* v. *Seacoast Products, Inc.*, involved two provisions of Virginia law which gave preferred or exclusive access to domestic commercial fishermen in certain coastal waters within three miles of that State's coast. One provision excluded all aliens and alien-controlled firms and corporations from holding state commercial fishing licenses.[8] The second provision permitted only Virginia residents to fish in the Virginia portion of Chesapeake Bay.[9] It thus excluded both aliens and the citizens of other states. This second provision did not, however, exclude licensed nonresident American fishermen from fishing in Virginia waters outside of Chesapeake Bay.

Seacoast Products is a Delaware corporation. Formerly owned by American interests, it was acquired in 1973 by a British holding company. The operations of Seacoast remained essentially unchanged. Its fishermen, captains, and ships were the same; only the ownership interest was transferred to foreign hands. Seacoast thus became subject to the alien prohibition, which appears to have been enacted principally to suppress its activity.[10] Its competitors

---

[7] Fishery Conservation and Management Act of 1976, § 201; 90 Stat. 337, 16 U.S.C. § 1821(a). The federal act does not, however, prohibit such fishing within the three-mile zone, since the statute defines the coastal protection zone as that portion lying seaward of the limits of state jurisdiction.

[8] Va. Code § 28.1—81.1.

[9] Va. Code § 28.1—60.

[10] Hanson Trust acquired Seacoast in 1973. The Virginia legislature first prohibited alien operations in 1975. The record before the district court, 432 F. Supp. 1 (E.D.Va. 1975), indicated a strong involvement of one of Seacoast's competitors in the promotion of this legislation.

failed in their efforts to oppose transfer of vessel licenses but succeeded in convincing the Virginia legislature to pass the anti-alien provisions attacked in the case. Seacoast had previously closed some of its Virginia shore stations in an effort to rationalize its activities and thus lost the resident status which it had once enjoyed.

Seacoast sought an injunction against Douglas, the chief Virginia fisheries officer, to restrain enforcement of both laws. A three-judge federal district court concurred in Seacoast's claim on two grounds. It found that the federal Bartlett Act[11]—since repealed—preempted state regulation of commercial fishing by aliens. The Bartlett Act prohibited fishing from foreign-flag vessels within the territorial waters of the United States. Unlike Virginia law, the Bartlett Act looked principally to the nominal nationality of a corporation and its management rather than to the nationality of its ultimate owners. For the purposes of the federal act, Seacoast was a citizen of Delaware, since it was chartered there. The Virginia law, on the other hand, pierced the corporate veil and excluded on the basis of ultimate foreign ownership. The three-judge court also held the exclusion of nonresidents from the Chesapeake Bay territorial waters to be invalid as a violation of the Equal Protection Clause of the Fourteenth Amendment. Its opinion on this point merely asserted the conclusion of unconstitutionality without substantial explanation. The State appealed.

The second case was *Massachusetts v. Westcott.*[12] Westcott, a resident of Rhode Island, attempted to use certain prohibited implements to fish commercially within the three-mile limit of Massachusetts off Martha's Vineyard. A statutory prohibition enacted by Massachusetts in the 1920s permitted residents, but not nonresidents, to employ "beam or otter trawls" in fishing in this area during three summer months.[13] The Supreme Judicial Court of Massachusetts held the state statute to be an unconstitutional violation of the Privileges and Immunities Clause of Article IV of the United States Constitution and reversed Westcott's conviction.[14] The privileges

[11] 16 U.S.C. § 1081 *et seq*. The Bartlett Act was enacted in 1964, primarily in response to Japanese fishing off the Pacific coast. It was repealed by the Fishery Conservation and Management Act of 1976, note 7 *supra*.

[12] 97 S.Ct. 1755 (1977).

[13] 1923 Mass. Acts 17, c. 35, and 1962 Mass. Acts 107, c. 219.

[14] 344 N.E.2d 411 (Mass. 1976).

and immunities argument had been unavailable to Seacoast, because it was a corporation.[15] The State appealed.

Thus, the issues as framed and decided below were based on a wide variety of constitutional and other doctrines: equal protection, privileges and immunities, and the preemptive effect of the Bartlett Act. Additionally, a number of other issues were briefed and argued, including interference with interstate commerce generally and the exclusivity of federal authority over foreign relations. The initial briefing before the Court centered on the issues decided in the courts below. The first substantial discussion of the application of the decisive *Gibbons v. Ogden* rationale appeared in respondent's brief for Seacoast Products. Indeed, in *Westcott*, the record on appeal did not reveal the license status of the vessel. The Court had to take judicial notice of the fishing license.[16]

The Supreme Court brushed aside all of the constitutional arguments, deciding both cases on the "statutory" ground of the fishery licenses granted under the old federal shipping laws, applying the doctrine first articulated in *Gibbons*.

The disposition of the cases was simple and direct. The boats of Seacoast, like that of Gibbons, were federally enrolled and licensed. Since the license granted the right to engage in the "mackerel fishery,"[17] Virginia could not restrict it, either by its exclusion of alien owners or by its exclusion of nonresident fishermen.[18] The exclusivity of the federal licensing power was based on the judicial dicta in *Gibbons*, reaffirmed by subsequent reenactment of the legislation.[19] Westcott's case was remanded to the Massachusetts court for reconsideration in light of *Douglas*.[20]

---

[15] Bank of Augusta v. Earle, 13 Pet. 519 (1839), Paul v. Virginia, 8 Wall. 168 (1869).

[16] 97 S. Ct. at 1756 n.2.

[17] Menhaden are "statutory mackerel." The licensing system once differentiated between species of fish, with separate licenses for mackerel, cod, whales, etc. While the separate licenses still exist, they permit the holder to catch "fish of any other description whatever," including shellfish. 46 U.S.C. §§ 263, 325.

[18] Since the decision is articulated in preemptive terms, it should not preclude application of the Virginia statutes to fishing vessels which do not possess federal licenses. This hypothetical validity of the statutes is, however, illusory, since virtually any commercial fisherman could secure a federal license.

[19] 97 S. Ct. at 1748–49.

[20] *Id.* at 1756. The Massachusetts court summarily entered a rescript again reversing Westcott's conviction.

II

The Court's application of the *Gibbons* rule to these cases was somewhat of a surprise. Other cases involving restrictive fisheries laws have been decided on Commerce Clause or equal protection bases. Indeed, the Attorney-General of Massachusetts, in his last papers filed in the case, indicated that he had no objection to the Court taking judicial notice of the federal license status of Mr. Westcott's boat but could not fathom why they were interested in this question in light of the issues briefed.[21]

Gibbons v. *Ogden* ambiguously involved two different, but related, grounds of decision. One of them, touched on by Chief Justice Marshall early in his opinion, is the exclusiveness of the federal commerce power. The narrower rationale for the case is a simple assertion of the supremacy of federal law coupled with an early form of the preemption doctrine.

The doctrine of exclusive federal power over interstate commerce is indicated by such statements as:[22]

> It has been contended by the counsel for the appellant, that, as the word "to regulate" implies in its nature, full power over the thing to be regulated, it excludes, necessarily, the action of all others that would perform the same operation on the same thing. . . . There is great force in this argument, and the court is not satisfied that it has been refuted.

The Chief Justice expressed doubts about the universal application of an absolute rule of exclusive national power. He recognized the applicability of state law to commercial transactions both before and after they entered commerce among the states.[23] In *Douglas*, Mr. Justice Marshall clearly rejected such exclusive national power in reaffirming the validity of nondiscriminatory state regulations.[24]

The narrower rationale of *Gibbons* is expressed as a rule of supremacy. It is actually a precursor of preemption. Congress had created a vessel identification and licensing system, which, pursuant to the Supremacy Clause, overrode any conflicting state regulation. The federal registration and licensing machinery, then as now,

---

[21] Supplemental brief for the Attorney-General for Massachusetts, p. 2.

[22] 9 Wheat. at 209.

[23] *Id.* at 194–95.

[24] 97 S. Ct. at 1747–48.

was a two-step process. First, a vessel is registered or enrolled, which provides a system of identification. Then, based on that registration or enrollment, it is granted a "license" to engage in certain activities, the coasting trade or mackerel fishery being most significant.

All vessels over twenty tons must be enrolled (or registered) and licensed. Vessels over five tons may obtain licenses without enrollment. Virtually all commercial fishing vessels exceed five tons; many exceed twenty tons. Gibbons had a coasting license, Seacoast a mackerel license. Did this license indicate merely that there was no federal impediment to coastal trade or fishing, or was it an affirmative grant of the right to engage in this trade or fishing? Both in *Gibbons* and in *Douglas* the Supreme Court opted for the latter interpretation, but the *Douglas* opinion indicates that this affirmative grant of power is still subject to "reasonable," nondiscriminatory state regulation.

In *Gibbons*, the New York courts had seen the federal license merely as an indication that the vessel could engage in the particular trade without clearing customs at every port. Chancellor Kent upheld the New York law which granted a franchise on the state's waterways to the Livingston-Fulton consortium and was affirmed in this view by the highest state court.[25] In light of the early history of the United States, this may have been a realistic interpretation. Since customs agents were not available at all seacoast villages, unlicensed boats were required to "clear" at customs ports before going to their ultimate destinations.[26] A vessel licensed for the coastal trade could proceed from one seacoast village to another without clearing customs before every stop. A licensed fishing vessel could also return from the fisheries without first seeking out a customs collector for clearance. The form of the license, which still emphasizes the ship captain's oath not to defraud the revenue of the United States,[27] exemplifies this limited purpose. The New York courts thus viewed the federal regulation as supplemental to, not exclusive

[25] 4 Johnson's Chanc. 150 (N.Y. 1819); 17 Johns. 488 (N.Y. 1820).

[26] Act of 31 July, 1789, c. 5, § 3, 1 Stat. 29, at 36 (1789); Act of 1 Sept. 1789, c. 11, § 22, 1 Stat. 55, at 60–61 (1789).

[27] The quaint form of the license is prescribed at 46 U.S.C. § 262. The captain must swear that the license shall not be used "in any trade or business whereby the revenue of the United States may be defrauded." It makes no mention of fishery regulation, save to grant the license.

of, the right of the state to franchise the commercial use of its waterways.

Chief Justice John Marshall saw the matter otherwise. The Supreme Court held that states could not constitutionally preclude the federally licensed interstate trade from their waterways. Subsequent commentators have more frequently concurred with Chancellor Kent's construction than with that of Chief Justice Marshall.[28] The Great Chief Justice's statutory arguments may have been contrived, but the franchise system in question did strike at the very heart of interstate commerce, prohibiting traffic between the states without the approval of all concerned legislatures. The franchise system was a last gasp of a dying mercantilism. *Gibbons* ushered in a system of *laissez-faire* interstate shipping, since federal enrollment and licensing were freely available. There was little supplementary national law to regulate the carriers for more than a half century. For John Marshall, there was no effective difference between constitutional exclusion and statutory preemption—both wholly precluded state legislation.[29]

The national monopoly over coastal shipping, adumbrated if not defined in *Gibbons*, soon waned. States were gradually permitted to require pilots,[30] to prohibit excessive smoke emissions,[31] or to prohibit racial segregation of passengers[32] on federally licensed ships, because of their "legitimate interest." This legitimating state interest was found largely in the residual state police power. The police power is plenary but must, of course, give way to conflicting federal law, which may be found either in statute or in the "negative implications" of the Commerce Clause. In *Douglas*, the interpretation of the potentially conflicting federal law presented the question for examination. Since there is little basis for establishment of the legislative intent of Congress in the 1793 licensing laws, Mr. Justice Marshall in *Douglas* looked to Chief Justice Marshall's in-

---

[28] As Mr. Justice Thurgood Marshall expressly notes. 97 S. Ct. at 1748 n. 13.

[29] The decree issued in *Gibbons* stated: " . . . this court is of opinion, that the several licenses . . . gave full authority to those vessels to navigate the waters of the United States, by steam or otherwise, for the purpose of carrying on the coasting trade, any law of the state of New York to the contrary notwithstanding; . . . " 9 Wheat. at 239–40.

[30] Cooley v. Board of Wardens, 12 How. 299 (1851).

[31] Huron Portland Cement Co. v. Detroit, 362 U.S. 440 (1960).

[32] Bob-Lo Excursion Co. v. Michigan, 333 U.S. 28 (1948) (license not mentioned in opinion).

terpretation in *Gibbons* and transferred the reasoning from coastal shipping to fishing.[33] He saw in the repeated reenactment of the licensing provisions Congressional affirmation of the *Gibbons* interpretation.[34] The 1977 Court could also invoke specific Congressional language authorizing the "taking of fish."[35]

Seen as an interpretation of the licensing law, the case would have little import beyond its immediate facts, but it went further. Concealed in the statutory interpretation is a disapproval of protectionist legislation, even in those fields in which special state interests have heretofore been recognized.

III

Traditionally, the Court emphasized three general factors in determining preemption by federal law: the degree of conflict with federal regulation, the comprehensiveness of federal law, and the dominance of the federal interest.[36] In *Douglas*, the Court recognized that the federal license grants an affirmative right to fish but found that this right prevails over only some state statutes, not all.[37] Only indirectly did it reveal the criterion by which it differentiates these.

A differentiation based on the extent or nature of conflict with federal law does not supply an answer. The comprehensiveness of the federal law likewise provided little foundation for the distinction drawn. There is a comprehensive system of federal fisheries law, but the *Gibbons* licensing acts are not part of it. They are rather an appendage to the registration and enrollment laws.[38] They

[33] 97 S. Ct. at 1749.

[34] The licensing provisions have repeatedly been reenacted in successive codifications of the maritime laws.

[35] 97 S. Ct. at 1750–51 n.19.

[36] Hines v. Davidowitz, 312 U.S. 52 (1941); Pennsylvania v. Nelson, 350 U.S. 497 (1956). The Court cited more recent opinions: De Canas v. Bica, 424 U.S. 351 (1976); Jones v. Rath Packing Co., 97 S. Ct. 1305 (1977). *Hines* emphasized the "nature of the power exerted by Congress, the object sought to be attained, and the character of the obligations imposed by the law," 312 U.S. at 70. *Nelson* enumerated three factors: the pervasiveness of the scheme of regulation, the dominance of the federal interest, and the danger of conflict with federal law. 350 U.S. at 502, 504, 505.

[37] 97 S. Ct. at 1753.

[38] The registration, enrollment, and licensing laws are contained in Title 46 of the United States Code, which deals with Shipping; the fisheries regulations are contained in Title 16, Conservation. The distribution of sections among code titles which have not been enacted into positive law is not formal evidence of purpose, yet with the increasing reliance on the codes, it is of more than passing importance.

make no provision for conservation, catch limitations, net size, or any of the other elements that a comprehensive modern law would include. If the licensing act itself is evidence of a comprehensive scheme of regulation, it is one of *laissez faire*, which may have been acceptable to John Marshall but hardly bespeaks contemporary concerns about national resources.

A dominant federal interest is also missing from the preemption calculation. Not only have the states traditionally claimed authority over national resources, Congress has recently affirmed state jurisdiction over their own territorial waters.[39] State efforts to maintain exclusivity of fishing rights have been litigated for decades, on equal protection, commerce, privileges and immunities, and other grounds, with little reference to the licensing scheme as an indication of federal intent.[40]

In its 1976 legislation extending the American claim to regulate fisheries to the now-common 200-mile limit, Congress expressly recognized a continuing role for the states in regulating fishing in their own waters. Congress should not be presumed to have been engaging in a futile exercise of perpetuating that which did not exist. Far from indicating dominance or requiring uniformity, the federal law supports the proposition that state regulation is permissible.[41]

If the core concepts of preemption do not provide an adequate criterion for discerning which state regulations are unconstitutional, one must look elsewhere. The Court appears to look not so much to the federal legislative purpose as to the legitimating interests in support of the state statute. It is a kind of inverted preemption test,

---

[39] Fishery Conservation and Management Act of 1976, § 306, 90 Stat. 355, 16 U.S.C. § 1856. The provision not only asserts state jurisdiction but also provides a regulatory mechanism for imposing federal standards on the state territorial waters, if the Secretary of Commerce finds that the state regulation impedes federal regulation of the fisheries beyond the three-mile limit.

[40] McCready v. Virginia, 94 U.S. 391 (1876) (privileges and immunities); Takahashi v. Fish and Game Comm'n, 334 U.S. 410 (1948) (equal protection); Toomer v. Witsell, 334 U.S. 385 (1948) (privileges and immunities). Only in Manchester v. Massachusetts, 139 U.S. 240 (1891), was the license status raised. The Court there, however, found the state statute valid.

[41] 16 U.S.C. § 1856. The Fisheries Act does not expressly confer upon the states any jurisdiction but merely reaffirms that jurisdiction which Congress assumed they already possessed. The section stands, not as an independent grant, but as evidence that Congress believed that it had never preempted this regulation. Except for the provisions mentioned note 39 *supra*, the remainder of the act regulates only fishing seaward of the three-mile or other state jurisdictional limit.

in which it is not the dominance of the federal interest, but the weakness of the state interest, which becomes the decisive factor.

The classic modern regulatory case involving licensed vessels is *Huron Portland Cement Co. v. Detroit.*[42] The Court allowed Detroit to apply its smoke abatement ordinances to a federally licensed vessel engaged in "coastal" shipping on the Great Lakes. The ship was required to comply with the local ordinance, although it already complied with all of the applicable federal regulations directly governing smoke discharges.

Such acquiescence in state regulation has not been a peculiarity of the coastal shipping laws. The Court has allowed state regulation of race relations for crews of interstate airliners[43] and the passengers of boats which move in interstate commerce[44] pursuant to federal licenses. It has permitted states to impose a wide range of safety regulations on forms of motor transport,[45] absent a clear federal mandate to the contrary. In short, absent an express federal preemption, a "legitimate" state regulatory interest can be enforced.

In determining the legitimacy of a state interest, those cases have stressed that evenhandedness or nondiscrimination is part of the test.[46] What discrimination tests was the Court applying in these cases? The district court in *Douglas* held one of the Virginia laws invalid under the Equal Protection Clause, citing *Takahashi v. Fish and Game Comm'n.*[47] But *Takahashi* was based largely upon the racist element in the California discrimination against resident Japanese fishermen.

Under modern equal protection tests, fishing rights would not be sufficiently "fundamental" to demand "strict scrutiny,"[48] nor would the classifications against aliens and nonresidents be themselves constitutionally "suspect." A discrimination against resident aliens might have fallen under this test[49] but not one against nonresidents

[42] 362 U.S. 440 (1960).

[43] Colorado Anti-Discrimination Commission v. Continental Airlines, 372 U.S. 714 (1963).

[44] Bob-Lo Excursion Co. v. Michigan, 333 U.S. 28 (1948); *cf.* Boynton v. Virginia, 364 U.S. 454 (1960).

[45] Bibb v. Navajo Freight Lines, 359 U.S. 520, 524 (1959).

[46] 97 S. Ct. at 1747–48.

[47] 334 U.S. 410 (1948).

[48] Dandridge v. Williams, 397 U.S. 471 (1970).

[49] Graham v. Richardson, 403 U.S. 365 (1971); Sugarman v. Dougall, 413 U.S. 634 (1973); In re Griffiths, 413 U.S. 717 (1973).

like the owners of Seacoast. If strict scrutiny is not applied and the case is deemed one of mere economic regulation, virtually any state law would be upheld.[50] Putting aside privileges and immunities arguments, which were unavailable to Seacoast because of its corporate status, the only remaining antidiscrimination test is found in the negative implications of the Commerce Clause. It was on this basis, disguised as a preemption argument, that the Virginia laws fell.

Put differently, *Douglas* was like those cases in which states have attempted to protect their local dairies[51] or fruit packers[52] or consumers[53] from the effects of interstate competition. The Court appears to apply the same standards. Local regulations that affect interstate commerce may be sustained if they have a legitimate local purpose, capable of articulation in noneconomic terms. It must be for the protection of the "health, safety, or welfare" of the community.[54] Thus, regulations for environmental protection (smoke abatement),[55] or the protection of human rights (racial equal protection)[56] are permissible, but those which overtly or covertly are designed to protect local producers (exclusion of imported commodities)[57] or consumers (limitation on export of needed commodities)[58] will fall. Virginia had asserted a conservationist purpose for its legislation. Conservation measures may be permissible, even though they have an economic objective and an adverse impact on interstate commerce, so long as they are nondiscriminatory,[59] just as regulations of "commercial integrity" are permissible despite

[50] Village of Belle Terre v. Boraas, 416 U.S. 1 (1974).

[51] Baldwin v. G. A. F. Seelig, Inc., 294 U.S. 511 (1935); Dean Milk Co. v. Madison, 340 U.S. 349 (1951); Polar Ice Cream Co. v. Andrews, 375 U.S. 361 (1964).

[52] Pike v. Bruce Church, Inc., 397 U.S. 137 (1970).

[53] Pennsylvania v. West Virginia, 262 U.S. 553 (1923) (reservation of natural gas for local users unconstitutional).

[54] This standard was once applied as a test of state legislation under the Due Process Clause. Since Nebbia v. New York, 291 U.S. 502 (1934), it no longer has a role in that context but has found continuing vitality in the Commerce Clause context.

[55] Huron Portland Cement Co. v. Detroit, 362 U.S. 440 (1960).

[56] Colorado Anti-Discrimination Commission v. Continental Airlines, 372 U.S. 714 (1963); Bob-Lo Excursion Co. v. Michigan, 333 U.S. 28 (1948).

[57] Baldwin v. G. A. F. Seelig, Inc., 294 U.S. 511 (1935); Dean Milk Co. v. Madison, 340 U.S. 349 (1951).

[58] Pennsylvania v. West Virginia, 262 U.S. 553 (1923).

[59] Railroad Commission v. Rowan & Nichols Oil Co., 310 U.S. 573 (1940).

their economic impact, so long as they are evenhanded.[60] But conservation may not be used to effectuate a disguised discrimination. As the Court noted, reducing the number of fishermen does not necessarily reduce the number of fish caught.[61]

Mr. Justice Marshall's warning that states may not use the Court's express acceptance of conservationist or environmental purposes as a pretext for discrimination against interstate competitors is an application of Commerce Clause standards. Although legislatures are commonly afforded deference when challenged on Fourteenth Amendment grounds, they have no claim for special consideration when discrimination against commerce is alleged.[62]

The doctrine enunciated is thus not new. It is only the old negative implications of the Commerce Clause in a new guise of statutory preemption. It is a peculiar form of preemption, for it is dependent, not so much on the nature of the preempting federal law, but on that of the preempted state statute.

IV

Virginia's claims, however, went beyond mere regulatory authority. They also included assertion of a special right to regulate the offshore fisheries, not paralleling other forms of regulation. It sought to perpetuate a series of proprietary claims which have been successfully asserted by states and also to rely upon a Congressional reconveyance of marine resources and regulatory power to the states in the 1950s.

Fisheries, like other "public goods," present particular regulatory problems. The utilization of other resources is restrained primarily by the economic choices of their owners and only secondarily by public regulation. The taking of wildlife is a peculiar situation in which ordinarily there is no private owner. Some of the older case law suggests that wildlife is therefore in the "common ownership" of the citizens of the state.[63] Other cases more

[60] Sligh v. Kirkwood, 237 U.S. 52 (1915); *cf.* Pike v. Bruce Church, Inc., 397 U.S. 137 (1970), limiting the application of this doctrine.

[61] 97 S. Ct. at 1752 n.21.

[62] Even though there is a strong presumption of validity, the courts measure such cases by their impact on commerce, not whether there was a "rational basis." Bibb v. Navajo Freight Lines, 359 U.S. 520, 529 (1959).

[63] Geer v. Connecticut, 161 U.S. 519 (1896); Manchester v. Massachusetts, 139 U.S. 240 (1891).

bluntly assert that, as part of the state's *ius privatum* or private rights, it is immune from the operation of constitutional doctrine.[64] The Court, in *Douglas*, rejected this view. Ownership begins, according to Mr. Justice Marshall, with possession, and without reducing "these creatures" to possession the state had no proprietary right.[65] He discarded, in a single paragraph, a line of constitutional cases founded upon the peculiar status of fisheries.[66] Justices Rehnquist and Powell, dissenting in part, saw the problem as far more complex than the simple Marshall analysis suggests.[67] The fact that the state does not "own" the fish in the normal sense does not obviate the fact that additional regulatory measures may be both needed and justified. The state has interests of "substantial legal moment" in regulating its collective natural resources.

The constitutional history of claims of special state interests immune from mandates of interstate equality can be traced to the decision of Justice Washington in *Corfield* v. *Coryell*.[68] The decision of a single Justice on circuit, *Corfield* has acquired a constitutional stature few lower court cases enjoy. *Corfield* has a special claim to authoritative status in conjunction with *Gibbons*. The case was argued before Justice Washington in 1824. He took it under advisement, proceeded to the capitol, and participated in the decision of *Gibbons*. He then returned to circuit and decided *Corfield*, relying heavily on the *Gibbons* decision. In upholding a New Jersey statute which excluded nonresidents from oyster fisheries in the Delaware River, he passed both on Commerce Clause[69] and privileges and immunities arguments. He distinguished between privileges and immunities, "which are, in their nature, fundamental; which belong, of right, to the citizens of all free governments; and which have, at all times, been enjoyed by the citizens of the several states which compose this Union, from the time of their becoming free, independent, and sovereign,"[70] and less significant rights. For

---

[64] Corfield v. Coryell, 6 Fed.Cas. 546, 551 (Case No. 3,230) (C.C.E.D.Pa. 1825).

[65] 97 S. Ct. at 1751.

[66] Corfield v. Coryell, 6 Fed.Cas. 546 (Case No. 3,230) (C.C.E.D.Pa. 1825); McCready v. Virginia, 94 U.S. 391 (1876); Manchester v. Massachusetts, 139 U.S. 240 (1891). Mr. Justice Marshall purports to be following *Manchester*, since he views the regulation affirmed there as "evenhanded."

[67] 97 S. Ct. at 1753.

[68] 6 Fed.Cas. 546 (Case No. 3,230) (C.C.E.D.Pa. 1825).

[69] *Id.* at 550–51.

[70] *Id.* at 551.

the former category, of which he provided a long list of examples, a state could not discriminate against nonresidents. He finally rejected the notion that this doctrine of equality controlled a state in the disposition of its "common property" such as fishing rights.[71] The other fish and game cases which have upheld state regulation have largely followed the same rationale, whether argued on privileges and immunities or Commerce Clause grounds.[72] but their number has waned in recent years.

Douglas adds to the evidence that the *Corfield* category of special interests has become a derelict on the sea of legal history. The doctrine has been hard put to survive the demise of the right-privilege dichotomy in other branches of constitutional law.[73] Thus far the process has been one of erosion, rather than eradication. The right of states to exclude nonresidents from institutions of higher learning, or to charge them higher tuition, may survive, but it has been severely limited by the abolition of irrebuttable presumptions.[74] Their right to create corporations once carried with it a right to exclude "foreign" corporations from their courts, but in some cases this is now seen as a violation of the Commerce Clause.[75] Other erstwhile special interests, like welfare benefits,[76] which were once perceived as provision by the community corporate for its members, or public employment, once a private-law relationship between state and officer,[77] have become fully protected constitutional rights.

The Massachusetts court had faced this question squarely in the

---

[71] *Ibid.*

[72] McCready v. Virginia, 94 U.S. 391 (1876); Manchester v. Massachusetts, 139 U.S. 240 (1891); Geer v. Connecticut, 161 U.S. 519 (1896). The decision in Skiriotes v. Florida, 313 U.S. 69 (1941), does not fall into this pattern, because it was decided on the question of the extent of the state's regulatory jurisdiction over its own citizens.

[73] Van Alstyne, *The Demise of the Right-Privilege Distinction in Constitutional Law*, 81 Harv.L.Rev. 1439 (1968).

[74] Starns v. Malkerson, 401 U.S. 985 (1971), *aff'g*, 326 F.Supp. 234 (D.Minn. 1970); *cf.* Vlandis v. Kline, 412 U.S. 441 (1973).

[75] Allenberg Cotton Co. v. Pittman, 419 U.S. 20 (1974).

[76] Shapiro v. Thompson, 394 U.S. 618 (1969), is only one of the many modern cases on this point.

[77] Contrast the application of constitutional doctrines in any of the modern cases, *e.g.*, Board of Regents v. Roth, 408 U.S. 564 (1972), with older decisions like McAuliffe v. New Bedford, 115 Mass. 216, 220 (1892). Although these cases do not deal with discrimination against nonresidents, they are based on the absence (in *Roth*) and presence (in *McAuliffe*) of arguments on the same type of "special interest" or "private law relationship" basis.

Westcott case,[78] invalidating the state statute as a violation of the Privileges and Immunities Clause in a carefully reasoned opinion by Justice Braucher. By deciding the issue on a preemption-discrimination ground, the Supreme Court succeeded in avoiding formal decision of the issue.

The special interest doctrine is hard to support. Despite their formal denomination as commonwealths, Virginia and Massachusetts are not giant partnerships which pay dividends in kind; they are states which exercise governmental functions like all others. The European notion of the state or municipality as a closed corporation, which, in addition to exercising governmental functions, also operates essentially as a business enterprise, is alien to modern American government. Modern mobility of population makes such proprietary claims unrealistic at best. Virginia is not a fishmonger. Added regulation may be justified, but it can be accomplished within restraints of equality.

Virginia's claim was supposedly further butttressed by a transfer of jurisdiction over the submerged lands which Congress had made through the Submerged Lands Act of 1953.[79] It thus revived one of the constitutional conflicts of that period, the tidelands controversy. Prior to the 1940s, concurrent state and federal jurisdiction over the offshore waters of the United States was merely assumed, and property rights over the underlying lands were of little significance. With the development of technology for the exploitation of undersea resources, these rights became critical. Both the federal government and the coastal states claimed the property rights and the consequent oil royalties. The federal government prevailed in litigation,[80] which gave it exclusive proprietary rights over the offshore lands, but lost in the political process. Congress granted to the states the proprietary rights, as well as regulatory authority, within the three-mile limit[81] but retained for the federal domain all of the rights over the newly claimed continental shelf.

The interpretation of these provisions produced the second of

---

78 344 N.E.2d 411 (Mass. 1976).

79 67 Stat. 29, 43 U.S.C. § 1301 *et seq.*

80 United States v. California, 332 U.S. 19 (1947), United States v. Louisiana, 339 U.S. 699 (1950); United States v. Texas, 339 U.S. 707 (1950).

81 The conveyance was of the submerged lands within the territory of the state, which is defined as three miles seaward from the coastal boundary unless Congress had approved some other dimension for a particular state. 43 U.S.C. §§ 1311, 1312.

the two points of divergence among members of the Court. Mr. Justice Marshall, speaking for the majority, saw the conveyance as possibly transferring to the states the right to control fishing but assumed that Congress had taken it back in the same statute. Mr. Justice Rehnquist thought it had never been transferred.

Marshall's interpretation grants the states regulatory power by a chain of dubious inferences and then denies them authority to exercise that jurisdiction by an equally tenuous line of deductions. The statute had given the states ownership of resources "within such lands and waters"[82] and had extended regulatory authority over these subjects to the states in a subsequent provision.[83] Only if fish were resources in the demised waters, and were previously owned by the United States,[84] was the statute applicable at all. There was minimal legislative history in support of this proposition, since primary legislative consideration of the bill was focused on the lucrative oil royalties, not on fishing rights. Mr. Justice Marshall accepts this as a grant of authority but then effectively revokes it on the basis of the federal reservation of regulatory power.[85] Since the mackerel licenses were issued pursuant to a statute and that statute was enacted pursuant to the commerce power, the mackerel licenses were issued pursuant to the reserved federal powers and overrode state authority. Justices Rehnquist and Powell reached a similar result by a less tortuous route: They viewed the Submerged Lands Act primarily as conveying mineral, not animal, resources and thus found it wholly inapplicable.[86]

The Marshall chain of reasoning on this point seems unnecessary. Even assuming that Congress ceded the three-mile belt to the states and granted them regulatory jurisdiction over it, there is no reason to presume it also ceded unusual and extraordinary legislative powers to the states. The states' authority should be presumed to be no greater than their authority over the public domain on dry land. Such regulation would be subject to the same negative implications of the Commerce Clause, whether of its own force or disguised as

[82] 43 U.S.C. § 1311 (a) (1).

[83] 43 U.S.C. § 1311 (a) (2).

[84] The conveyance is a quitclaim, not a warranty. See 43 U.S.C. § 1311 (b) (1), conveying the United States' rights "if any it has."

[85] 97 S. Ct. at 1751.

[86] *Id.* at 1754.

a statute, which are the heart of the case. In short, although Congress can permit the states to impose burdens on interstate commerce,[87] it should not be presumed to have done so by a mere recognition of regulatory authority.

V

Because it purports to be based on statutory interpretation, *Douglas* leaves two major constitutional questions open. One relates to the continued vitality of the distinction between "fundamental" and other privileges and immunities first enunciated in *Corfield*. The Massachusetts court based its original decision in *Westcott* on this point. Its carefully reasoned decision would undermine many of the preferences accorded to local residents. The Supreme Court may have only temporarily avoided ruling on this issue since another case, involving nonresident elk hunting licenses in Montana, will be before the Court in the 1977 Term.[88] As increased personal mobility renders state citizenship even less significant than at the founding of the nation, special local rights such as lower tuition at public universities, preference in hunting and fishing licenses, and greater access to local parks may seem even less consistent with orderly government. The decisions in forthcoming cases may be articulated in privileges and immunities terms, providing a revival of that disused constitutional doctrine, or they may take on more fashionable Equal Protection Clause or Commerce Clause coloring. The latter is more likely because of the limited applicability of privileges and immunities decisions. Or the process may involve only the continuing slow erosion of the special interest doctrine through the application of yet other limitations. Other preemption decisions, paralleling *Douglas*, may be part of this process.

A second series of questions involves the right of alien-owned businesses to operate in states which seek to exclude them. Under present law, resident aliens are entitled to equal protection, and many nonresident aliens have treaty rights to engage in certain commercial activities. But this provides only incomplete protection.

---

[87] In re Rahrer, 140 U.S. 545 (1891); Kentucky Whip & Collar Co. v. Illinois Central Railroad, 299 U.S. 334 (1937).

[88] Baldwin v. Fish & Game Comm'n, *prob. jurisdiction noted*, 429 U.S. 1089 (1977).

Some nonresident aliens have little or no treaty protection.[89] Such claimants may seek to expand the scope of equal protection or to rely on the exclusivity of federal power over foreign relations to invalidate state legislation.[90] The scope of their rights and the nature of state interests necessary to legitimate action against them will be a recurring problem.[91]

By framing the decision in statutory terms, the Court clearly reserved to Congress the option of permitting the states to reassert their licensing authority.[92] Yet the language of the Court seems to advise against this course of action because of its inconsistencies with "sound policy considerations of federalism."[93] Congress has already prohibited discrimination on the basis of residence outside of the three-mile limit and has regulated fishing there.[94]

The *Douglas* decision does not necessarily mean a total nationalization of offshore fishery regulation. The states still may make legitimate, "evenhanded" conservation regulations; only those which are discriminatory will be struck down. Within the narrow band of the three-mile limit, this still leaves the states with some choice, if the Court approves that choice.

---

89 For a discussion of the treaty rights of aliens, see Note, 72 MICH.L.REV. 551, 568–77 (1974). Strangely, the citizens of Britain and Canada have fairly weak treaty protection, presumably because they have not suffered discrimination in recent years.

90 See the cases cited note 49 *supra*, for equal protection arguments. See also Zschernig v. Miller, 389 U.S. 429 (1968).

91 It may arise particularly in the context of operations like Seacoast, in which an identifiable American entity is retained, but aliens assume ownership for investment, not management, purposes. Can the states pierce the corporate veils?

92 It expressly says so. 97 S. Ct. at 1745 n.6. Preemption is clearly a "preferred ground" for constitutional decision making. Even a decision on Commerce Clause grounds could have been overturned by Congress, however, by a declaration that the state activity was not a burden. See Prudential Insurance Co. v. Benjamin, 328 U.S. 408 (1946). Congress may have been unable to overturn a decision on privileges and immunities or equal protection grounds quite so simply.

93 97 S. Ct. at 1752.

94 16 U.S.C. § 1851 (a)(4).

RICHARD DANZIG

HOW QUESTIONS BEGOT ANSWERS IN FELIX FRANKFURTER'S FIRST FLAG SALUTE OPINION

Lawyers who draft briefs, bureaucrats who compose issue papers, and surveyors assessing popular opinion all know that the way they pose questions powerfully affects—if it does not determine—the answers they will receive. Appellate judges know, or ought to know, that a lawyer's shrewdness, imagination, and forensic skill will be as much manifested in an articulation of the "questions presented" in a case as it will be in the arguments advanced about the resolution of those questions. The wise judge also knows that at the stage of opinion writing, the advantage of framing the questions passes to the bench. Probably no other factor operates so strongly in favor of securing approval for an opinion of the courts as the willingness of readers to accept the question put by the opinion writer.

Richard Danzig is Associate Professor of Law, Stanford University.

AUTHOR'S NOTE: Parts of this essay are drawn from a larger work on the *Flag Salute* cases and *Martin v. Struthers*. Portions of that larger work have been presented at Stanford, Harvard, Yale, and The University of Chicago Law Schools. These portions have been supported by grants from the American Bar Foundation and the Rockefeller Foundation. I am grateful for the assistance. Beyond this, the contributions of Jay Casper, Fred Konefsky, and Jan Vetter to the larger project have been so substantial that I think they must be specifically reflected even in this short essay. I owe particular thanks to them.

0-226-46429-6/78/1977-9000$01.58

The first of my propositions here is that the opinions of Justice Frankfurter often benefited from his understanding this fact. I offer two pairs of cases by way of illustration. In both *Wolf v. Colorado*[1] and *Rochin v. California*,[2] the petitioners contended that their state criminal convictions were constitutionally infirm because they rested on evidence which had been illegally obtained. In *Wolf*, Justice Frankfurter sided with the state; in *Rochin*, with the petitioner. He did not do this by invoking different constitutional doctrines. Nor did he contrast the facts to which the constitutional standard was applied.[3] Justice Frankfurter produced contradictory opinions in these cases by a technique that might be called "differential focusing." He directed attention to different questions in each case. In *Wolf* he focused on remedies. Was it compatible with basic notions of "ordered liberty" to restrict Wolf to a tort suit as the method of redressing the effects of an illegal search? In *Rochin* the focus was on rights. The question Justice Frankfurter saw in the case was whether the challenged search itself was so repelling as to be contrary to the concept of "ordered liberty." Presumably Rochin, too, could invoke the remedy of a tort suit. But this point was ignored.

A similar ploy characterizes my second pair of examples, *Francis v. Resweber*[4] and *Solesbee v. Balkcom*,[5] two cases roughly contemporaneous to *Wolf*. The lawyers for Willie Francis argued that it was contrary to basic notions of "ordered liberty" to attempt again to electrocute him after a first electrocution had miscarried. Justice Frankfurter focused only on the remedy. He did not ask whether a second electrocution attempt would be contrary to "ordered liberty." Instead he put a more beguiling question. Did it contravene fundamental notions of liberty to leave this question to the decision of a state governor? It did not. Three years later Solesbee's lawyers pressed the claim that it contravened the Constitution to execute an insane man. Justice Frankfurter agreed. He did not ask

[1] 338 U.S. 25 (1949).

[2] 342 U.S. 165 (1952).

[3] To the contrary, the facts in *Wolf* were stated in so scanty a fashion that it is only by consulting the record and briefs that one can determine the nature and circumstances of the search in question.

[4] 329 U.S. 459 (1947).

[5] 339 U.S. 9 (1950).

whether it was adequate to leave such a matter to the decision of a state governor who might grant a reprieve. Instead he focused on the right. Did an insane person have a constitutional right not to be executed? With the question phrased in this manner, Justice Frankfurter decided for the petitioner.

The tendency to ask a question about remedies in some cases and about rights in others is so frequently exhibited in Justice Frankfurter's opinions that differential focusing might fairly be said to be a process central to the functioning of his jurisprudence. When he was self-abnegating about the use of judicial power he tended to focus on remedy. He would build an argument for restraint in the use of federal constitutional power by noting the existence of alternative remedies by resort to the common law, to legislation, or to the executive authority. Conversely, when moved to intervene and exercise judicial power, Justice Frankfurter would phrase the issue at hand in terms of rights.

In this essay, rather than dwell on this point, however, I should like to make some observations stemming from the fact that "differential focusing" is part of a larger phenomenon. It is an aspect of asking questions, and Justice Frankfurter had other modes of asking questions that are worthy of attention. I propose here to examine in some detail one of these other modes but in the context of a single case. I call this technique "inflation" and show how it not only shaped an important opinion, but served to dispose of a precedent that might otherwise have undermined that opinion. Beyond this, by a detailed review of a single case, I hope to cast some light on a larger problem: Why was it that Justice Frankfurter's questions were frequently loaded? I suggest that contemporary circumstances were very important factors in the case discussed here, and that it was at the point of question framing that these factors were most readily absorbed in the Justice's opinion. In general, I suggest, the technique of loading questions, whether by means of inflation or by differential focusing, permits simultaneous deference to two conflicting but greatly valued imperatives. It gives play to a judge's sense of what is right and necessary in the everyday world, while it preserves the purity of an opinion's legal logic. The judge refrains from smuggling things personal and expedient into the analysis. Instead, they are made part of the premise from which the analysis proceeds.

I

In June of 1940, in *Minersville School District v. Gobitis*,[6] the Supreme Court of the United States held by a vote of eight to one that it was constitutionally tolerable to expel children of Jehovah's Witnesses from public schools if they refuse to salute the flag. Felix Frankfurter wrote the majority opinion; Harlan Fiske Stone wrote the lone dissent. Near the beginning of his opinion, Justice Frankfurter sketched the facts of the case in the barest detail:[7]

> Lillian Gobitis, aged twelve, and her brother William, aged ten, were expelled from the public schools of Minersville, Pennsylvania, for refusing to salute the national flag as part of a daily school exercise. . . . The Gobitis family are affiliated with "Jehovah's Witnesses," for whom the Bible as the Word of God is the supreme authority.

He then went through a series of permutations of statements of the issue. First the Justice said: "We must decide whether the requirement of participation in such a ceremony, exacted from a child who refuses upon sincere religious grounds, infringes without due process of law the liberty guaranteed by the Fourteenth Amendment."[8] Shortly thereafter, the question was put again in a somewhat different form:[9] "When does the constitutional guarantee [of free exercise of religion] compel exemption from doing what society thinks necessary for the promotion of some great common end, or from a penalty for conduct which appears dangerous to the general good?" Two pages later the question recurred: "the question remains whether school children, like the Gobitis children, must be excused from conduct required of all the other children in the promotion of national cohesion."[10]

Finally, in a fourth version, Justice Frankfurter articulated "the question" of the case in its ultimate form:[11]

> The case before us must be viewed as though the legislature of Pennsylvania had itself formally directed the flag-salute for the children of Minersville; [and] had made no exemption for children whose parents were possessed of conscientious scru-

---

6 310 U.S. 586 (1940).

7 *Id.* at 591.

8 *Id.* at 592–93.

9 *Id.* at 593.

10 *Id.* at 595.

11 *Id.* at 597.

> ples like those of the Gobitis family. . . . The precise issue, then, for us to decide is whether the legislatures of the various states and the authorities in a thousand counties and school districts of this country are barred from determining the appropriateness of various means to evoke that unifying sentiment without which there can ultimately be no liberties, civil or religious.

Thus phrased, Justice Frankfurter was sure of the resolution of the issue in the case. The Court, he said, should not "stigmatize legislative judgment in providing for this universal gesture of respect for the symbol of our national life . . . ,"[12] and it ought not to "exercise censorship over the conviction of legislatures that a particular program or exercise will best promote in the minds of children who attend the common schools an attachment to the institutions of their country."[13] To exempt children on grounds of religion, the Court would have to "maintain that there is no basis for a legislative judgment"[14] that they ought not to be exempted. Since exemption of some might undermine the program for all, there was a basis for the legislative judgment, and the claim of unconstitutionality had to fail.

II

At crucial points in its analysis this opinion was dependent on acts of "inflation." The magnitude of the inflation is most apparent when one realizes that, though Justice Frankfurter spoke of "stigmatiz[ing]" the "legislative judgment" and of "exercis[ing] censorship over the conviction of legislatures," in fact no decision to mandate a flag salute had ever been made by the Pennsylvania legislature, much less had that legislature ever considered whether religious scruples might warrant exemption from a general requirement. The state legislature had merely established school districts, set procedures for electing school boards, and specified subjects these boards might require. Beginning in 1919, that authority explicitly extended to supervising work in "civics, including loyalty to the State and National Government."[15]

---

[12] *Ibid.* [13] *Id.* at 599. [14] *Id.* at 600.

[15] 1921 Pa. Laws 983. For this information, as well as for the details of events in Minersville, I have relied on MANWARING, RENDER UNTO CAESAR 76, 81 ff. (1962), and on STEVENS, SALUTE 32 ff (1973), both of whom interviewed participants in the town, on the school board, and in the litigation.

When the Gobitis children refused to conform, no statute or regulation, not even one of the Minersville School District, required them to salute. A pledge of allegiance occurred in the Minersville school merely by custom; no regulation mandated it. The Gobitis's insubordination" provoked the school board to inquire of the State Department of Public Instruction whether it could coerce a salute. A Department opinion declared that it could. At this time, also, the state attorney-general ruled to the same effect. The Minersville Board then met and established a salute requirement. "Immediately following this vote,"[16] the school superintendent rose and declared the Gobitis children expelled.

It required a substantial inflation for Justice Frankfurter to draw from the events in the small town of Minersville, in Schuylkill County, Pennsylvania, an assertion that the "case before us must be viewed as though the legislature of Pennsylvania had itself formally directed the flag-salute."[17] Yet more inflation was required to replace the Minersville school board by "the legislatures of the various states and the authorities in a thousand counties and school districts,"[18] and to argue that the Court should not strike down the salute requirement because to do so would be to "exercise censorship over the conviction of legislatures that a particular program or exercise will best promote in the minds of children who attend the common schools an attachment to the institutions of their country."[19] By stating, working, reworking, and then again reworking the question in the case, Justice Frankfurter eventually brought the matter to a point where the decision pivoted on an inflated rather than a real concern. The question became not how the *ex post facto* act of a single small-town school board was to be assessed against the challenge of the Gobitis children, but whether the "conviction" of countless "legislatures" was to be honored.

An argument could have been made to justify this act of inflation. It might have been said that any effort to distinguish between a school board and a legislative judgment would chill the tendency of legislatures to delegate decisions to agencies. Surely President Roosevelt's Justices did not want to discourage such delegation. Moreover, they might well have wanted to foreclose any thought of federal

[16] Manwaring, note 15 *supra*, at 83. Stevens, note 15 *supra*, at 34, says "Minutes after the vote [the Superintendent] expelled the Witnesses' Children."

[17] 310 U.S. at 597.

[18] *Ibid.*

[19] *Id.* at 599.

courts piercing the veil of state relationships by passing on such a delicate intrastate question as whether a school board had the authority to do as it did.[20]

But the doctrine underlying this approach was not debated. The logic behind Justice Frankfurter's policy of judicial deference, and thus restraint, was open to challenge. It had to be premised at least in part on notions about legislatures: their representativeness, their responsiveness, and their capacity for making constitutional judgments. Were the same notions equally relevant to the decision of the Minersville School Board? This question was never asked because the question that was asked masked the issue.

Authority lay directly at hand that could have been used to support a holding that judgments of the legislature were unique in their claim to deference, and that challenged actions which could not be directly traced to legislative intent should be reviewed without the benefit of a favorable presumption. In the very month that *Gobitis* was being written, Justice Roberts had advanced this thought for a unanimous Court in *Cantwell v. Connecticut.*[21] There, one count of the conviction of a Jehovah's Witness for playing a virulently anti-Catholic phonograph record on a street corner rested on "the common law offense of inciting a breach of the peace."[22] Justice Roberts held that the Court would not defer to the state interest in criminalizing such conduct "in the absence of a statute narrowly drawn to define and punish specific conduct."[23] In words whose logic could have been made relevant to *Gobitis*, Justice Roberts said:[24]

---

[20] There was even precedent at hand which proscribed such inquiry in a case involving an economic regulation. In Pacific States Co. v. White, 296 U.S. 176 (1935), Justice Brandeis, for a unanimous Court, upheld an order of Oregon's Department of Agriculture. There it was "urged that this rebuttable presumption of the existence of a state of facts sufficient to justify the exertion of the police power attaches only to acts of legislature; and that where the regulation is the act of an administrative body, no such presumption exists, so that the burden of proving the justifying facts is upon him who seeks to sustain the validity of the regulation." *Id.* at 185. To this, Justice Brandeis replied: "The question of law may, of course, always be raised whether the legislature had power to delegate the authority exerted. Compare *Panama Refining Co.* v. *Ryan*, 293 U.S. 388 and *A.L.A. Schechter Poultry Corp.* v. *United States*, 295 U.S. 495. But where the regulation is within the scope of authority legally delegated, the presumption of the existence of facts justifying its specific exercise attaches alike to statutes, to municipal ordinances, and to orders of administrative bodies." *Id.* at 186.

[21] 310 U.S. 296 (1940).

[22] *Id.* at 300.

[23] *Id.* at 311.

[24] *Id.* at 307–08.

Conviction on the fifth count was not pursuant to a statute evincing a legislative judgment that street discussion of religious affairs, because of its tendency to provoke disorder, should be regulated, or a judgment that the playing of a phonograph on the streets should in the interest of comfort or privacy be limited or prevented. Violation of an Act exhibiting such a legislative judgment and narrowly drawn to prevent the supposed evil, would pose a question differing from that we must here answer. Such a declaration of the State's policy would weigh heavily in any challenge of the law as infringing constitutional limitations. Here, however, the judgment is based on a common law concept of the most general and undefined nature.

Justice Frankfurter, however, avoided *Cantwell* and the whole of the issue of the appropriate deference to be given the state action by the way in which he phrased the question before him. In declaring that in this case he weighed a legislative judgment against an individual right, he advanced a proposition for which he cited neither authority nor reason. But because the proposition was buried in the phrasing of the question it garnered no attention from either the dissent or from the numerous critics of the opinion.

III

There was another precedent besides *Cantwell v. Connecticut* which Justice Frankfurter had to overcome in order to reach the result in *Gobitis*. *Schneider v. State*,[25] decided by nearly a unanimous Court earlier that very Term, ran counter to the simple rationality test Frankfurter advanced in *Gobitis*. In *Schneider* the Court held that four cities' undeniably rational statutes that prohibited leafletting because it tended to lead to littering were consitutionally invalid as invasions of the rights of free speech. In an opinion which Frankfurter joined, Justice Roberts put the Court on the record this way:[26]

We are of opinion that the purpose to keep the streets clean and of good appearance is insufficient to justify an ordinance which prohibits a person rightfully on a public street from handing literature to one willing to receive it. Any burden imposed upon the city authorities in cleaning and caring for the streets as an indirect consequence of such distribution re-

[25] 308 U.S. 147 (1939).

[26] *Id.* at 162.

sults from the constitutional protection of the freedom of speech and press. This constitutional protection does not deprive a city of all power to prevent street littering. There are obvious methods of preventing littering. Amongst these is the punishment of those who actually throw papers on the streets.

Here is how Frankfurter distinguished *Schneider* in *Gobitis*:[27]

> We are dealing with an interest inferior to none in the hierarchy of legal values. National unity is the basis of national security. To deny the legislature the right to select appropriate means for its attainment presents a totally different order of problem from that of the propriety of subordinating the possible ugliness of littered streets to the free expression of opinion through distribution of handbills. Compare *Schneider* v. *State*, 308 U.S. 147.

Frankfurter put this view yet more clearly in a private letter to Justice Stone:[28]

> It is not a case where conformity is exacted for something you and I regard as foolish—namely a gesture of respect for the symbol of our national being—even though we deem it foolish to exact it from Jehovah's Witnesses. It is not a case, for instance, of compelling children to partake in a school dance or other scholastic exercise that may run counter to this or that faith.

On its own terms, this view was indisputable. "National security" indeed might so commonly be thought to rank higher than the public interest in avoiding littering, that any judge at all alive to the world would think *Gobitis* a different case from *Schneider*. But such an analysis compared incommensurate concerns. "National security" was not self-evidently at stake in *Gobitis*. One might as well say that "public health" was at issue in *Schneider* and argue, as Frankfurter once argued in defense of a statute, "Health is the foundation of the state."[29]

---

[27] 310 U.S. at 595.

[28] Frankfurter to Stone, 27 May 1940. The original of this letter may be found in the Stone Papers, Library of Congress, Box 65, File 690. Copies are extant in the Frankfurter Papers, Library of Congress, Box 105, File 2197, and in the Murphy Papers (University of Michigan, Ann Arbor), Box 60, File 690.

[29] Adkins v. Children's Hospital, 261 U.S. 525 (1923), Brief for the Appellants, at 1053.

On their face, the government actions questioned in *Gobitis* and *Schneider* prescribed flag saluting and proscribed littering. If judges and other observers saw larger issues at play it was through individual acts of inflation. The facts presented by these controversies were like flaccid balloons waiting to be pumped up by those who interested themselves in the matter. The size the cases would reach when full blown, the heights of abstraction to which they would be lifted, would be determined by the heat of the principles with which they were injected and by the energy and intensity with which Justices pumped them.

What Felix Frankfurter was doing in comparing *Schneider* and *Gobitis* was to take the former case in its uninflated, flaccidly factual state and compare it with a fully inflated *Gobitis*. There is no reason to believe that the comparison was duplicitous. Rather, it seems simply that for Frankfurter, the state interest in *Schneider* consistently appeared limp—nothing in his thought or experience gave it buoyancy. In contrast, he invested the flag-salute controversy with issues of such great intensity that for him it always loomed full blown.

When acts of inflation precede and determine much of the logic of an opinion, when, as I have suggested, such acts obfuscate issues and swap relevant precedent, then it is imperative for an analysis of an opinion to inquire into the causes of inflation. Toward this end, I would suggest that Felix Frankfurter was encouraged in his inflation of *Gobitis* by his present and past concerns. *Gobitis* was written against the backdrop of his perceptions of the need to mobilize America for war and of the psychological problems in doing so. Harold Ickes recorded this sense of Felix Frankfurter on the eve of the announcement of *Gobitis*:[30]

> The discussion at Archibald MacLeish's on Sunday night [the *Gobitis* decision was announced on Monday morning] ran until well after twelve o'clock, I hear, with Felix Frankfurter holding the center of the stage. Apparently there was a good deal of feeling between Bob Jackson and Felix. The latter is really not rational these days on the European situation.

To Frankfurter it was apparent that America would have to fight Germany. But in May of 1940 Americans were neither united

[30] 3 The Secret Diary of Harold Ickes 199 (1954).

nor prepared to fight. As Frankfurter put it to the President in a suggestive metaphor, it was necessary that the country be "taken to school"[31] and educated about the struggle ahead. His input into a Roosevelt speech the following autumn was largely devoted to "emphasizing that the indispensable defenses—those without which tanks and flames even are of no avail—are the defenses of the mind . . . [I]f recent history teaches us anything, it is that those who are hostile to the democratic way of life count most on disorganizing the moral forces of democracy."[32]

"Mobilization" in every sense of the word was an intense and pervasive concern for Frankfurter while he wrote *Gobitis.* On May 3, he brought with him to lunch at the White House with the President his former mentor, Henry Stimson, once Secretary of State and Secretary of War. Stimson's diary records that the three "talked quite openly . . . about a number of confidential foreign policy developments."[33] Frankfurter left some hint of his mood by recording his gratitude to Roosevelt as thanks for "taking me out of my marble prison."[34]

In March, 1939, Hitler had swallowed Czechoslovakia; in September he had moved into Poland. The Russians had invaded Finland in December of that year. On April 9, 1940, sixteen days before *Gobitis* was argued, the supposedly "phony" wars of the North had become more chillingly real as the Germans stormed and quickly subdued Denmark and Norway. On the tenth of May, as Frankfurter was assembling his opinion, Luxembourg, Holland, and Bel-

[31] Quoted in FREEDMAN, ROOSEVELT AND FRANKFURTER: THEIR CORRESPONDENCE, 1928–1945 512 (1967). See also Frankfurter to Stimson, 27 June 1940, Frankfurter Papers, Library of Congress, Box 104, File "Stimson Correspondence" (appearance before a Senate Committee should be made "a first rate opportunity for educating the American people to an understanding of what national defense really means . . . an informed and vigorous public opinion is indispensable to the realization of an effective program of national defense").

[32] Frankfurter to Sam Rosenman, 7 Oct. 1940, Frankfurter Papers, Library of Congress, Box 246, File 4329. (The carbon is unsigned, but clearly from Frankfurter.)

[33] Stimson Diary, Henry L. Stimson Papers, Library *Wf* Congress.

[34] Frankfurter to Roosevelt, 3 May 1940, reprinted in FREEDMAN, note 31 *supra*, at 521. See also JOHNSON, THE BATTLE AGAINST ISOLATION 72 (1944), quoting a letter from Frankfurter to William Allen White which "came on May 26, 1940": "The bench is partly prison; but not even the stuffiest notions of propriety preclude my expressing my gratitude to you for mobilizing our opinion so that our action may become effective in the challenge that mad brute force is hurling against the accumulated gains—oh! so painfully accumulated—of civilization."

gium were invaded.[35] That night Roosevelt delivered "one of the greatest speeches of his career,"[36] saying, among other things, that if the "dictator states" were successful in dominating Europe, "they will, we know down in our hearts, enlarge their wild dream to encompass every human being and every mile of the earth's surface."[37] Frankfurter immediately telegraphed the President, "Our gratitude for . . . [you] at your best."[38]

The month was studded with bad news from Europe, militant Roosevelt speeches, and highly evocative letters from Frankfurter to the President. On May 16 the Justice sat in the House of Representatives as the President spoke. An hour later he wrote:[39]

> These are days when one realizes the importance of things unseen, and is sure of things not susceptible of ordinary proof. . . . [You inspire] all who are determined that the precious achievements of man's spiritual nature shall not perish from the earth. . . .
>
> Your message was just right. You can count on Lincoln's "common people."

On May 26, a day after another presidential speech, Frankfurter summed up the feelings of the moment and the month:[40]

> Dear Frank–
>
> This is Sunday morning and I humbly believe that not the most pious church attendant has his thought more outside himself and on the ultimate destiny of mankind than I have this forenoon here in my study. It is in that mood that I am venturing to break in on you. My one excuse is that I cannot resist doing so.
>
> You don't have to be told what thoughts you stirred in me yesterday morning about our country and your relation to it at this juncture. And these thoughts have been with me for all these weeks–hardly anything else has been.

---

[35] On the events of this period and the reaction to them in Washington, see Langer & Gleason, The Challenge to Isolation, 1937–1940 (1952), esp. pp. 436–96.

[36] The judgment is Max Freedman's note 31 *supra*, at 521.

[37] *Ibid.*

[38] Frankfurter to Roosevelt, 10 May 1940. *Id.* at 522.

[39] Frankfurter to Roosevelt, 16 May 1940. *Ibid.*

[40] Frankfurter to Roosevelt, 26 May 1940. *Id.* at 523.

Indeed, since Frankfurter sent a carefully worded five-page confidential letter about *Gobitis* to Stone on Monday, May 27, it seems highly likely that the work on which his war thoughts intruded, as he sat in his study that Sunday morning, was his flag salute opinion. Writing to Stone as "his thought . . . [was] outside himself and on the ultimate destiny of mankind," Frankfurter clearly made the link between his judicial and his extrajudicial lives, between his correspondence with the President and his correspondence with Stone:[41]

> For time and circumstances are surely not irrelevant in resolving . . . this particular case. . . . I had so many talks with Holmes about his espionage opinions and he always recognized that he had a right to take into account the things that he did take into account when he wrote Debs and the others [during the spring of 1919] and the different emphasis he gave the matter in the Abrams case [in the fall of 1919].

Frankfurter was not merely reflecting abstractly on war-related questions at the time he wrote these words. The letter of May 26 urged Roosevelt to solicit the resignation of his cabinet so that a new cabinet especially committed to and suited for the war effort could be formed.[42] In pressing this suggestion, Frankfurter reflected a plan he had evolved around this time with a law school classmate and close friend, Grenville Clark. Their aim was to replace the incompetent and uncommitted Secretary of War, Woodring, with someone more capable and inclined toward preparedness. By the end of the month, during a lunch in Frankfurter's Supreme Court chambers, Frankfurter and Clark agreed on a candidate: Henry Stimson.[43]

---

[41] Frankfurter to Stone, 28 May 1940, note 27 *supra*.

[42] Frankfurter to Roosevelt, 26 May 1940, in FREEDMAN, note 31 *supra*, at 523.

[43] SPENCER, A HISTORY OF THE SELECTIVE TRAINING AND SERVICE ACT OF 1940 (Ph.D. Diss. Harvard University 1951). Spencer, drawing on separate interviews with Clark and Frankfurter, says that, at this luncheon, "[T]hey pondered several possibilities . . . but in a matter of minutes they suddenly seized by common consent on the perfect candidate: Henry L. Stimson." *Id.* at 113. Freedman, writing while apparently unaware of Spencer's thesis and with no apparent authority for a contrary conclusion, dates Frankfurter's campaign for Stimson at least as far back as the May 3 White House luncheon. FREEDMAN, note 31 *supra*, at 521. A letter from Clark to McGeorge Bundy, detailing these events as background for Bundy's biography of Stimson, supports Spencer's view. See Clark to Bundy, 18 July 1947 in Frankfurter Papers, Library of Congress, Box 44, File 789 (copy).

On June 1, the day that *Gobitis* was handed down, Frankfurter visited the President and urged Stimson's candidacy on him.[44] On June 20 the Frankfurter-Clark idea was implemented. Stimson was appointed Secretary of War and Judge Patterson, a former law partner of Clark's and a protege of Frankfurter's,[45] was named Assistant Secretary of War.[46]

Simultaneously, over the period beginning in late May, Frankfurter privately reviewed and encouraged a plan devised by Clark and others to have the United States conduct its first peacetime draft. During the following September this plan also matured. Despite an initial total lack of support from professional politicians, Congress passed and the President signed the Selective Service Act.[47]

The natural—one is tempted to say inevitable—overlap between Frankfurter's war-related concerns and his thinking about the flag salute case was probably enhanced by a fact which may seem surprising to one who focuses only on Justice Frankfurter's passionate assertions about the dispassionate, insulated nature of the judicial process. The Justice's partner in these lobbying efforts, Grenville Clark, was not only an old friend and preparedness activist, but was a former legal associate of FDR's and the man who had introduced Roosevelt to Frankfurter.[48] He was also the leading signer and the responsible principal behind an American Bar Association Committee on the Bill of Rights amicus brief in support of the Witnesses in *Gobitis*. He had organized the committee, suggested the brief, and then supervised its drafting.[49]

Efforts to prepare the country for war and efforts at writing the

---

[44] Spencer, note 43 *supra*, at 115 ff. (Spencer's account of the conversation is based on an interview with Frankfurter.) See also Frankfurter to Roosevelt, 4 June 1940, reprinted in Freedman, note 31 *supra*, at 524, recapitulating arguments for Stimson and Patterson.

[45] Frankfurter to Patterson, 5 July 1932: "You will always remain my prize baby student—favorite editor-in-chief of the *Law Review*. . . ." Quoted in Baker, Felix Frankfurter 240 (1969).

[46] In his placement of Patterson as Stimson's second, Frankfurter replicated a service he had performed for Stimson several decades earlier when Stimson was Secretary of State and needed advice on the appointment of an undersecretary. At that time Frankfurter's nominee was Joseph P. Cotton.

[47] See, generally, Spencer, note 43 *supra*.

[48] Baker, note 45 *supra*, at 24.

[49] "Most of the actual writing seems to have been done by the Chairman, Grenville Clark," Manwaring, note 15 *supra*, at 126, citing a letter to this effect from Walter Fennell, an ACLU lawyer active in the case.

salute opinion involved some of the same people and many of the same days. The psychological effect of this conjunction of people and events was to abet an inflated perception of the state's interests in *Gobitis*. It was as if the littering question in *Schneider* had arisen in the midst of an epidemic endangering the health of a nation, and as though a chief (albeit behind the scenes) medical officer was called on to write the opinion in that case.[50]

Nor were assessments of the relevant variables in *Gobitis* conducted only against the backdrop of contemporary events. Frankfurter saw the judicial role in this crisis in the context of his impressions of the judicial role in prior crises.[51] During the Great Depression, legislative action had been paralyzed by judicial reaction. Even before that, indeed for the whole of his adult lifetime, Felix Frankfurter had seen the Supreme Court cut down legislative initiatives dealing with what he viewed as pressing problems. As an academic, as a publicist,[52] and as a litigator[53] he had bitterly fought this tendency toward legislative emasculation by constitutionalization. He was not about to succumb to it now.

Here an argument advanced by the Witnesses was probably counterproductive. The Witnesses' lawyer attacked the salute requirement as an ill-advised experiment, indeed a "cruel experiment":[54]

> The modern-day compulsory flag saluting as a daily exercise or ceremony in the public schools is clearly an experiment. The nation has existed for more than a century without any such enforced rule or even the thought thereof.

[50] "I should think you historians fail, as much as you fail in anything, in recapturing that impalpable thing, what was in the air." FELIX FRANKFURTER REMINISCES 57 (Phillips, ed., 1960).

[51] In this, as in other respects, Frankfurter was not unique in his thoughts. See, *e.g.*, JACKSON, THE STRUGGLE FOR JUDICIAL SUPREMACY xv (1941): "The preservation of democracy on this continent may well depend on an effective government through which it may function. If we are now able to organize our economy effectively to support national defense against totalitarianism, it will be because it no longer can be slowed up by the obstacles to effective government which were interposed in the path of our national defense against depression."

[52] See, most notably, for example, Frankfurter's unsigned editorial, *Can The Supreme Court Guarantee Toleration?*, in KURLAND, ED., FELIX FRANKFURTER ON THE SUPREME COURT 175 (1970), decrying the fact that the "inclination of a single Justice, the tip of his mind—or his fears—determines the opportunity of a much-needed social experiment to survive, or frustrates, at least for a long time, intelligent attempt to deal with a social evil."

[53] See Brief for the Appellants, note 29 *supra*, at lxvi.

[54] Brief for the Respondents, p. 20.

This could not but have struck sparks from Justice Frankfurter. He seemed determined to make the *Gobitis* case—even if it was marginal to the war effort—an occasion for giving a clear signal to legislatures that their attempts to prepare the nation for war would not be hampered as efforts at dealing with past problems had been. Though the message came through in the opinion, the motive, and the context which generated it, were more starkly revealed in private correspondence. I return to the letter Frankfurter wrote to Stone, and quote from it more fully:[55]

> . . . it seems to me that we do not trench on an undebatable territory of libertarian immunity to permit the school authorities a judgment as to the effect of this exemption in the particular setting of our time and circumstances.
> For time and circumstances are surely not irrelevant considerations in resolving the conflicts that we do have to resolve in this particular case. Contingencies that may determine the fate of the constitutionality of a rent act (Chastleton Corp v Sinclair 264 US 543) may also be operative in the adjustment between legislatively allowable pursuit of national security and the right to stand on individual idiosyncracies. . . . I had many talks with Holmes about his espionage opinions and he always recognized that he had a right to take into account the things that he did take into account when he wrote Debs and others, and the different emphasis he gave the matter in the Abrams case.
> After all, despite some of the jurisprudential "realists" a decision decides not merely the particular case. Just as *Adkins v. Children's Hospital* had consequences not merely as to the minimum wage laws but in its radiations and in its psychological effects, so this case would have a tail of implications as to legislative power that is certainly debatable and might easily be invoked far beyond the size of the immediate kite. . . .

Frankfurter's reference to the *Adkins* case underscores two causes of his acts of inflation in this case. At one level *Adkins* stood for the debilitating effects Frankfurter saw as "radiations" from an adverse decision on the constitutionality of a particular statute.[56]

---

[55] Frankfurter to Stone, 27 May 1940, note 28 *supra*.

[56] See also FELIX FRANKFURTER REMINISCES, note 50 *supra*, at 103–4: "[S]econdly, a decision like the Adkins decision doesn't merely bring about the result in that case, but has very serious inhibiting influences on kindred legislation. . . . [A]ny other social

There, by striking down a women's minimum wage law, an activist Court had chilled progressive initiatives throughout the country. *Adkins* was an especially significant example of paralyzing negativism, because it was in sustaining this precedent and thus striking down a New York minimum wage law that the Court, in Frankfurter's judgment, reached its nadir during the New Deal years,[57] and it was in reversing *Adkins*, in *West Coast Hotel v. Parrish*,[58] that the Court began its climb back to respectability through restraint.

At another level the citation to *Adkins* reinforced the earlier reference to *Chastleton*. For in *Adkins* counsel attempted, through the medium of an 1106-page, heavily factual "Brandeis brief," to show that contemporary circumstances justified the questioned legislative action. But in *Adkins*, as contrasted with *Chastleton* (which a year later also dealt with a District of Columbia statute), the Court refused to consider anything other than juridical fact.[59] Reasoning from that vantage point, Justice Sutherland, for the majority, concluded that the Nineteenth Amendment and collateral "great changes" in the status of women brought "contractual, political and civil" inequalities between men and women, "almost, if not quite, to the vanishing point."[60] Thus, in the opinion of the Court, a legislature had no basis for specially regulating the wages of women.

---

legislation would encounter the argument that it's unconstitutional within the principle, or the meaning, or implication of the Adkins case. And so, while there might be only one bomb, as it were, the radiation from it did lethal damage to kindred legislation." On Frankfurter's largely futile efforts to limit "radiation" from *Adkins*, see Vose, *The National Consumers' League and the Brandeis Brief*, 1 Midwest J. Pol. Sci. 267, 275, 281–82 (1957).

[57] Morehead v. New York ex rel. Tipaldo, 298 U.S. 587 (1936). And in the judgment of more objective observers as well, see Jacobs, Law Writers and the Courts 95 (1954): "With the decision in the *Adkins* case the apparent trend away from substantive due process, from liberty of contract, and from laissez faire was abruptly halted. In a very real sense the majority opinion delivered by Justice Sutherland . . . constitutes the high-water mark in the application of laissez faire principles by the Supreme Court."

[58] 300 U.S. 379 (1937).

[59] "We have also been furnished with a large number of printed opinions approving the policy of the minimum wage, and our own reading has disclosed a large number to the contrary. These are all proper enough for the consideration of the lawmaking bodies, since their tendency is to establish the desirability or undesirability of the legislation; but they reflect no legitimate light upon the question of its validity, and that is what we are called upon to decide." 261 U.S. at 559–60.

[60] 261 U.S. at 553.

The force of the recollection of this case at the time of *Gobitis* had to be great for Felix Frankfurter. For the counsel who wrote the "Brandeis brief" in *Adkins* and who argued that "On all these questions we appeal from 'judgment by speculation' to 'judgment by experience,' "[61] and who lost the case, was Frankfurter himself. The assertion of the relevance of circumstances was no thought of the moment inspired by the events of 1940. It was part and parcel of the complex attitude which Frankfurter brought to the *Gobitis* case.

IV

This essay is not intended as a complete analysis of the content or causes of Felix Frankfurter's position in the first flag salute case. Such an analysis needs to dwell, among other things, on Frankfurter's own assimilation as an immigrant Jew into American life and the relationship between that experience and the issues provoked by the conduct and the arguments of the Jehovah's Witnesses. The point here is a modest one which puts this complex of issues aside. It is that significant concepts were smuggled into the *Gobitis* opinion by the act of inflating one side of the question at hand. The question in *Gobitis* was made to seem different in kind from the question in *Schneider*, and it was made to pivot on a question of deference to a legislative judgment which had never been made. Though Justice Stone dissented from Frankfurter's opinion and a great Associate Justice later wrote an opinion reversing the holding in this case, though a generation of academics and others have criticized Justice Frankfurter's performance, the inflation in the *Gobitis* opinion has been largely unnoticed. In this, as in other cases, readers and writers of judicial opinions would do well to focus more on the questions asked before turning to the intellectual operation which generates the answers given.[62] As the point has been put in quite another context, "In our ends shall be our beginnings."

---

[61] Brief for the Appellants, note 29 *supra*, at lxvi; 261 U.S. at 535.

[62] I have tried to do this in the larger work described in the author's note at the beginning of this essay.

GERALD M. ROSBERG

THE PROTECTION OF ALIENS FROM DISCRIMINATORY TREATMENT BY THE NATIONAL GOVERNMENT

The conferral of the "suspect classification" mantle on aliens in *Graham v. Richardson*[1] in 1971 signaled a fundamental change in the Supreme Court's treatment of the constitutional rights of aliens. Prior to that time aliens had, to be sure, enjoyed some important victories in the Supreme Court.[2] But for each such victory there had been three or four stinging defeats.[3] What emerged in 1971, in explanation of a holding that states could not discriminate against resident aliens in providing welfare benefits, was the proposition that classifications based on alienage, because suspect, require the strictest possible judicial scrutiny and can be upheld only if justified by some compelling state interest. Under that approach aliens were sure to go on winning, for no state seems able to meet that burden.[4]

Gerald M. Rosberg is Associate Professor of Law, University of Michigan.

[1] Graham v. Richardson, 403 U.S. 365 (1971).

[2] Takahashi v. Fish and Game Comm'n, 334 U.S. 410 (1948); Truax v. Raich, 239 U.S. 33 (1915); The Japanese Immigrant Case (Yamataya v. Fisher) 189 U.S. 86 (1903).

[3] Shaughnessy v. United States *ex rel.* Mezei, 345 U.S. 206 (1953); Harisiades v. Shaughnessy, 342 U.S. 580 (1952); Terrace v. Thompson, 263 U.S. 197 (1923); Patsone v. Pennsylvania, 232 U.S. 138 (1914); Fong Yue Ting v. United States, 149 U.S. 698 (1893).

[4] During the 1976 Term the Supreme Court upheld the aliens' claim in what was in many respects the hardest case to date. Nyquist v. Mauclet, 97 S. Ct. 2120 (1977). The

0-226-46429-6/78/1977-1100$04.80

Since *Graham*, the state and federal courts have indeed struck down a wide variety of state statutes disadvantaging aliens as a class.

But what of discrimination against aliens at the hands of the national government? Does the seemingly irresistible force of suspect classification analysis require the same purging of federal statutes classifying on the basis of alienage as it has required of comparable state statutes?[5] From the outset there were two reasons to doubt that it could have that effect, even though there is nothing on the face of the suspect classification doctrine to warrant its nonapplication to the federal government. In the first place, federal statutes distinguish between citizens and aliens in an extraordinary number of ways.[6] The use of the suspect classification doctrine could require invalidation of many more federal statutes than all those struck down over the past 200 years.[7] Moreover, the federal government has its peculiar interest to throw onto the scales. It has long been said that the federal government has plenary power to control the admission and exclusion of aliens and to dictate the terms and conditions under which they may live in the United States. This past Term the Supreme Court provided a reminder of the potency of the latter proposition when it upheld, under an extremely relaxed standard of review, a federal immigration provision that classified noncitizens on the basis of legitimacy and gender.[8]

The Court had an opportunity to work through the problem of federal government discrimination against aliens in two cases decided at the close of the 1975 Term. What it appeared to do, however, was to choose between competing slogans, preferring the

"right" that the state would have denied aliens—higher education assistance benefits—was not in any sense fundamental, see text and note *infra* at note 48, and the class was defined so as to minimize the "immutability" of the status on which the classification was based. See text and note *infra* at note 112.

[5] But see CARLINER, THE RIGHTS OF ALIENS 205–55 (1977), listing state statutes restricting alien employment. The great majority of these provisions have not yet been repealed or declared unconstitutional.

[6] In an appendix to its brief in Hampton v. Mow Sun Wong, 426 U.S. 88 (1976), the Government provided a list of 243 statutory provisions drawn from thirty-one different titles of the United States Code, all of which drew distinctions between citizens and aliens. And this list did not include Title 8, Aliens and Nationality, nearly every provision of which is premised on such a distinction.

[7] FREUND, SUTHERLAND, HOWE, BROWN, CONSTITUTIONAL LAW 18–20 (4th ed. 1977) describes the instances, barely more than 100, in which the Court has held an Act of Congress unconstitutional.

[8] Fiallo v. Bell, 97 S. Ct. 1473 (1977).

proposition that the federal government has plenary power to the proposition that alienage classifications are suspect. The apparent result is that all or nearly all challenged state statutes must fall, but all federal statutes will apparently survive.[9] The Court has not, however, formulated an adequate doctrinal basis for this double standard, nor has it come to grips with the hardest questions raised by federal government discrimination against aliens.

It may be helpful at the outset to clarify the difference between the two major classes of aliens in the United States. In each of the state alienage cases decided by the Supreme Court since 1971, plaintiffs were resident aliens. As defined in the federal immigration laws, a resident—or immigrant—alien is a person admitted for permanent residence, entitled to work and live anywhere in the country and eligible for naturalization after five years of residence. A nonresident—or nonimmigrant—alien is a person admitted for a fixed period of time determined prior to entry. Included in the nonresident category are officials of foreign governments, temporary visitors for business or pleasure, foreign students, temporary workers and trainees, foreign journalists, and others who are not authorized to remain in the country indefinitely.[10] No amount of residence will make a nonimmigrant eligible for naturalization. Whereas the number of immigrant or resident aliens admitted to the United States each year is in the neighborhood of 400,000, the number of nonimmigrants admitted for temporary periods each year exceeds 3 million.[11]

I. The Challenge to Federal Discrimination against Aliens

As it reached the Supreme Court, the challenge to federal government discrimination against aliens came in the form of two cases that had a special charm because each was a nearly perfect replica of an earlier case in which aliens had prevailed against a

[9] Hampton v. Mow Sun Wong, 426 U.S. 88 (1976); Mathews v. Diaz, 426 U.S. 67 (1976).

[10] An alien who is a nonresident for federal immigration purposes may under some circumstances be considered a state resident under state law. Unless otherwise specified, however, the term "nonresident alien" is used in this article to describe an alien who is a nonimmigrant under the immigration laws, whatever his residence status under state law.

[11] Harper, Immigration Laws of the United States 668 (3d ed. 1975). The total number of resident aliens in the United States is in excess of 4 million. INS, Annual Report for 1975, p. 21 (1975).

state government. *Hampton v. Mow Sun Wong*[12] called into question the validity of a Civil Service Commission rule excluding aliens from federal civil service employment. Its counterpart was a case holding invalid a New York statute barring aliens from that state's competitive civil service.[13] The second case was *Mathews v. Diaz*,[14] which involved a challenge to a federal statute denying aliens certain benefits under the Medicare program. Its twin was the *Graham* case, in which the Court first announced the proposition that alienage classifications are suspect, and held unconstitutional the efforts of Pennsylvania and Arizona to deny welfare benefits to aliens. In each of the cases the plaintiffs insisted that the federal government should not be permitted to discriminate in ways foreclosed to the states by the Fourteenth Amendment.

The aliens prevailed in the Civil Service case, but on grounds much narrower than they would have liked. The Supreme Court held the Civil Service Commission rule invalid on a very intriguing theory neither presented below nor argued to the Court. Writing for five Justices, Mr. Justice Stevens identified three interests of the national government that might be served by a policy of excluding aliens from the civil service: facilitating the President's ability to negotiate treaties by giving him a bargaining chip that could be used to obtain reciprocal concessions for American citizens in other countries; maintaining an incentive for resident aliens to obtain naturalization as soon as possible; and avoiding the administratively cumbersome process of screening alien job applicants for loyalty on a case-by-case basis. After noting that aliens are "subject to disadvantages not shared by the remainder of the community," and in particular are largely without political power, the Court went on to say that "[w]hen the Federal Government asserts an overriding national interest as justification for a discriminatory rule which would violate the Equal Protection Clause if adopted by a State, due process requires that there be a legitimate basis for presuming that the rule was actually intended to serve that interest."[15] The Court could find no basis for such a presumption in this case. "[I]f the rule were expressly mandated by the Congress or the

---

[12] 426 U.S. 88 (1976).

[13] Sugarman v. Dougall, 413 U.S. 634 (1973).

[14] 426 U.S. 67 (1976).

[15] 426 U.S. at 102–03.

President, we might presume that any interest which might rationally be served by the rule did in fact give rise to its adoption."[16] But the rule in question was promulgated by the Civil Service Commission, whose "only concern . . . is the promotion of an efficient federal service."[17] The interest in enhancing the President's bargaining power and the interest in encouraging aliens to seek naturalization are "so far removed from [the] normal responsibilities" of the Civil Service Commission that the Court could not presume it was seeking through the rule to foster these interests.[18] The desire to avoid case-by-case screening could be termed an interest in the efficiency of the service and therefore germane to the appropriate concerns of the Commission, but the Court could find no evidence that the Commission had promulgated the rule with this consideration in mind. In any case, the Court maintained, "[a]ny fair balancing of the public interest in avoiding the wholesale deprivation of employment opportunities caused by the Commission's indiscriminate policy, as opposed to what may be nothing more than a hypothetical justification, requires rejection of the argument of administrative convenience in this case."[19]

This is no ordinary holding that an agency has exceeded its authority by promulgating a rule that goes beyond its statutory mandate. The Court conceded that Congress had, after all, acquiesced in the Commission's rule.[20] But it found in the Due Process Clause a requirement that the decision to enforce the policy, given its heavy impact on an already disadvantaged group, must be made by an appropriate agency of the national government—that is, an agency having responsibility for the enhancement of the governmental interests purportedly served by that policy. The Court's emphasis on the process of policymaking, as opposed to the substance of the policy, is especially appealing in this context because the rule in question is a direct descendant of one originated in 1883, when there was a "greater inclination than we can now accept to regard 'foreigners' as a somewhat less desirable class of persons than

[16] *Id.* at 103.

[17] *Id.* at 114.

[18] *Id.* at 105.

[19] *Id.* at 115–16.

[20] *Id.* at 105. Noting that the Civil Service Commission had maintained its alien ineligibility policy from the time the agency was created in 1883, the Court found it "fair to infer that both the Legislature and the Executive have been aware of the policy and have acquiesced in it."

American citizens."[21] The Court seemed to be saying that where liberty was involved it would be little inclined to defer to the policy of the political branches of the government if there was no reason to believe that those branches had formulated the policy in the open and with full political accountability. On this sensitive matter Congress and the President would not be permitted to hide behind the Civil Service Commission. On the other hand, if the executive or legislative branch would think the problem through on the merits, making their decision openly and informed by contemporary views on the appropriate treatment of aliens, the Court would be much more willing to defer to their judgment.

Perhaps the Court doubted that the government could reenact the rule under those conditions. In fact, within a few months of the Court's decision President Ford issued an executive order barring aliens from employment in the civil service except "when necessary to promote the efficiency of the service in specific cases or for temporary appointments."[22] If the Court's goal in *Mow Sun Wong* was, indeed, to force either the executive or legislative branch to face up to the underlying policy questions and accept political responsibility for the rule, the goal was plainly not achieved. The President indicated in a letter accompanying the executive order that he believed it is in the "national interest" to preserve the general prohibition on the employment of aliens, but he did not make even a token effort to explain why.[23] The whole point of his order, as the letter makes clear, was to preserve the status quo pending congressional rethinking of the problem. Congress, the President asserted, "has the primary responsibility with respect to the admission of aliens into, and the regulation of the conduct of aliens within, the United States."[24] But Congress may well prefer to stay clear of the issue and allow the present policy to remain in operation by default.[25] The public, to the extent it has heard about the question at all, probably supposes that the President's order had something to do with the much-publicized problem of illegal aliens and the count-

---

[21] *Id.* at 107.

[22] Exec. Order # 11,935, 41 FED. REG. 37,301 (1976).

[23] 41 FED. REG. 37,303 (1976).

[24] *Id.* at 37,304.

[25] 426 U.S. at 100. Several bills were introduced in the 95th Congress to exclude aliens expressly from the Civil Service, but none of these seems to have any significant chance of passage.

less jobs they are so often said to be taking from American workers. In short, we are left precisely where we were before the decision in *Mow Sun Wong:* Aliens are still barred from employment in the civil service, although neither of the political branches has taken clear responsibility for the formulation of the policy.

The Court did not expressly say how it would handle a rule barring aliens from the civil service if enacted in the appropriate manner. There is language in the opinion suggesting that the Court might view with sympathy a claim that the rule, however promulgated, is inconsistent with the guarantees of the Due Process Clause. The Court termed the aliens' interest in federal employment a liberty interest for purposes of analysis under the Fifth Amendment. And although it grounded its decision on a finding of noncompliance with what it called a "procedural" aspect of the Due Process Clause, the Court acknowledged that the Clause has a "substantive" aspect as well. It indicated that, in this respect, the Clause limits the policy choices open to the federal government in much the same way as the Equal Protection Clause of the Fourteenth Amendment limits state action. The Court suggested that the federal government might have interests that would justify a particular rule even though an identical state rule could not pass scrutiny under the Fourteenth Amendment. But the Court was careful to speak in terms of "overriding national interests,"[26] suggesting that the standard applicable to the federal government might be similar to the "compelling interest" standard applicable to the states. Moreover, the Court was obviously not prepared to accept uncritically any interest that the federal government could dredge up in support of its policy choice.

Thus, after noting that the government had dropped its argument that the rule could be upheld as rationally serving the interest in "enhancing the economic security of United States citizens," the Court hinted broadly that the argument might have no force in any

[26] The Court used the phrase three times: "[T]here may be overriding national interests which justify selective federal legislation that would be unacceptable for an individual State." *Id.* at 100. "We agree with the petitioners' position that overriding national interests may provide a justification for a citizenship requirement in the federal service even though an identical requirement may not be enforced by a State." *Id.* at 100–01. "When the Federal Government asserts an overriding national interest as justification for a discriminatory rule which would violate the Equal Protection Clause if adopted by a State . . . ." *Id.* at 103. One might infer that a national interest which is less than "overriding" will not suffice to justify a federal statute discriminating against aliens.

event in light of the earlier holding that the state classifications based on alienage could not be upheld on such a "citizens first" rationale.[27] And in a manner reminiscent of cases applying an unusually rigorous version of the rational basis test,[28] the Court dismissed out of hand the government's asserted interest in administrative convenience.[29]

Still, the Court did not show any eagerness to look behind the asserted interest in encouraging the naturalization of aliens or enhancing the President's ability to bargain for treaties. If Congress or the President had formulated the bar to alien employment the Court would evidently have presumed that the policy was designed with one or both of these interests in mind. The Court gave no indication that it was prepared to weigh these interests against the interest of the aliens denied employment. Nor did it consider whether some less restrictive means might accomplish the same objective. Justices Brennan and Marshall, concerned about the inferences that might be drawn from the Court's opinion, concurred on "the understanding that there are reserved the equal protection questions that would be raised by congressional or Presidential enactment" of a rule excluding aliens from the civil service.[30]

The second case raising a challenge to federal government discrimination against aliens was *Mathews v. Diaz*,[31] decided the same day as *Mow Sun Wong* and again with Mr. Justice Stevens writing for the Court. Whereas in *Mow Sun Wong* the Court was reluctant to attempt a precise definition of the extent of federal power over aliens, apparently recognizing the difficulty of the ultimate question and preferring to rest its decision on a "procedural" matter, the Court stepped right up to the ultimate question in *Diaz* and resolved it as if the answer were too obvious to warrant serious discussion. Mysteriously, Justices Brennan and Marshall joined in the opinion of the Court, apparently acquiescing in the resolution of the very questions they were at pains to see left open in *Mow Sun Wong*.

---

[27] *Id.* at 104 n.24.

[28] Craig v. Boren, 429 U.S. 190, 198 (1976); Frontiero v. Richardson, 411 U.S. 677, 690 (1973); Stanley v. Illinois, 405 U.S. 645, 656 (1972).

[29] See text at note 19 *supra*.

[30] 426 U.S. at 117 (Brennan, J., concurring).

[31] 426 U.S. 67 (1976).

At issue in *Diaz* was the validity of a federal statutory provision controlling participation in the Medicare supplementary insurance program. The provision permits the enrollment of all citizens who are at least sixty-five years old. Aliens of the same age may be enrolled only if they have been admitted to the United States for permanent residence and if they have resided in the United States continuously for five years.[32] The program, which insures participants against certain medical expenses,[33] is financed partly out of premiums paid by the participants and partly out of general federal revenues.[34] The Supreme Court emphatically rebuffed the challenge to the constitutionality of the provision limiting alien participation in the program.

The starting point for analysis of the Court's opinion must be the realization that no comparable state law provision could possibly have passed scrutiny under the Fourteenth Amendment. If a state were to allow aliens to participate in such a program only on satisfying certain conditions that were inapplicable to citizens, like a durational residency requirement, the Supreme Court would subject the state classification to strict scrutiny. And while a state might in theory persuade the Court that it had a compelling interest to justify the different treatment of citizens and aliens, no state has

---

[32] 42 U.S.C. § 1395*o* (Supp. V, 1975): "Every individual who—(1) is entitled to hospital insurance benefits under part A, or (2) has attained age 65 and is a resident of the United States, and is either (A) a citizen or (B) an alien lawfully admitted for permanent residence who has resided in the United States continuously during the 5 years immediately preceding the month in which he applies for enrollment under this part, is eligible to enroll in the insurance program established by this part."

It may be possible for an alien unable to qualify under subsection (2)(b) to qualify under subsection (1) as an individual "entitled to hospital insurance benefits under part A." Any person, without regard to citizenship, who qualifies for old-age and survivors insurance benefit payments, 42 U.S.C. § 402 (1970 and Supp. V, 1975), is eligible for participation in the Part A insurance program. 42 U.S.C. § 426 (1970 and Supp. V, 1975). But to qualify for old-age and survivors insurance benefit payments under § 402 it is in general necessary to be a "fully insured individual" as defined in § 414(a), and that ordinarily requires forty calendar quarters of employment "within the United States." 42 U.S.C. § 410(a)(A)(i) (1970). An alien who can qualify for participation in the Part A program should have no difficulty qualifying directly for Part B under § 1395*o*(2)(B)—that is, as an alien who has resided in the United States for five years.

[33] The Part A Medicare insurance program generally covers hospital expenses. Part B, the program at issue in *Diaz*, "covers a part of the cost of certain physicians' services, home health care, outpatient physical therapy, and other medical and health care." 426 U.S. at 70 n.1; 42 U.S.C. § 1395k (1970 and Supp. V, 1975).

[34] 42 U.S.C. § 1395r(b) (1970 and Supp. V, 1975).

managed to put forward an interest that was sufficiently compelling to save a statute of this kind.[35]

Had the Supreme Court found some "compelling" or "overriding" federal interest in distinguishing between citizens and aliens in this context, one might readily explain why the federal provision could survive when a comparable state provision could not. And since the federal government has responsibilities not shared by any state, it may well have interests, compelling or otherwise, that no state can assert. Thus, the upholding of the federal provision would not necessarily indicate that the Court had tested it under a standard different from that applicable to the states. But the Court left no doubt that it had, in fact, applied a different standard. Far from insisting upon the demonstration of a compelling interest, the Court upheld the provision under an astonishingly lenient version of the rational-basis test. The Court likened the statutory provision to classifications used in the federal tax laws, and it explained that "[w]hen this kind of policy choice must be made, we are especially reluctant to question the exercise of congressional judgment."[36] In marked contrast, "a State which adopts a suspect classification [such as alienage] 'bears a heavy burden of justification.' . . . In order to justify the use of a suspect classification, a State must show that its purpose or interest is both constitutionally permissible and substantial, and that its use of the classification is 'necessary . . . to the accomplishment' of its purpose or the safeguarding of its interest."[37]

The federal provision at issue in *Diaz* was undeniably spared that kind of scrutiny. The Court assumed that the durational residence requirement was "longer than necessary to protect the fiscal integrity of the program."[38] And in apparent explanation of that assumption it described without critical comment the district court's find-

---

[35] The Supreme Court has summarily affirmed a three judge district court decision that state and federal statutes imposing a citizenship requirement for service on grand and petit juries are justified by a compelling governmental interest. Perkins v. Smith, 426 U.S. 913 (1976), *aff'g* 370 F. Supp. 134 (D. Md. 1974). And the Court has also dismissed for want of a substantial federal question an appeal from a state court decision that aliens have no constitutional right to vote. Skafte v. Rorex, 553 P.2d 830 (Colo. 1976), *app. dismissed*, 97 S. Ct. 1638 (1977). See Rosberg, *Aliens and Equal Protection: Why Not the Right to Vote?* 75 MICH. L. REV. 1092 (1977).

[36] 426 U.S. at 84.

[37] In re Griffiths, 413 U.S. 717, 721–22 (1973), *quoting* McLaughlin v. Florida, 379 U.S. 184, 196 (1964).

[38] 426 U.S. at 83.

ing that the durational residence requirement for aliens was not even rationally related to the program's fiscal integrity.[39] The Court also assumed that "unnecessary hardship is incurred by [aliens] just short of qualifying" for the program.[40]

The only rationale offered for the program was that "those who qualify under the test Congress has chosen may reasonably be presumed to have a greater affinity with the United States than those who do not."[41] The strongest claim one can make for the statutory provision, if it must be justified on the basis of this supposed government interest, is the one in fact made for it by the Court–it is not "wholly irrational."[42] The Court never explained what was meant by "greater affinity with the United States" or why the alien's degree of affinity is relevant to his right to participate in the insurance program. Affinity with the United States surely does not correlate with need for the benefits of the program. And it seems impossible to explain the residence requirement as a device to encourage some kinds of behavior or to discourage others.[43] The Court pointed to no other feature of the Medicare program that could be said to reflect an interest in limiting benefits to those with the greatest affinity with the United States, and it made no effort to show that the durational residence requirement for aliens was actually designed to identify those with the greatest affinity with the country. Indeed, the requirement has the bizarre effect of limiting participation to the very aliens who are aliens by choice. Naturalization ordinarily requires five years of residence in the United States.[44] An alien who has satisfied that residence requirement but chooses nonetheless to forego the opportunity for citizenship is eligible for participation in the program. The alien who has not yet resided in the United States for five years–the one for whom alienage is an involuntary and, for the time being at least, immutable characteristic–

---

[39] *Id.* at 83 n.22; Diaz v. Weinberger, 361 F. Supp. 1, 10–12 (S.D. Fla. 1973).

[40] 426 U.S. at 83.

[41] *Ibid.*

[42] *Ibid.*

[43] *Cf.* Dandridge v. Williams, 397 U.S. 471, 486 (1970), which upheld a state welfare provision as rationally related to "the State's legitimate interest in encouraging employment and in avoiding discrimination between welfare families and the families of the working poor."

[44] 8 U.S.C. §1427(a)(1) (1970).

is barred from the program no matter how great his "affinity" with the United States.[45]

The Court has used so many different standards of review under the name of the "rational basis" test[46] that it is never easy to dispute the application of the test in a particular case. The finding that the classification at issue in *Diaz* was sufficiently "rational" to pass muster under the test should probably come as no surprise. But what is perplexing, given the Court's sensitivity to the rights of aliens in other cases—not only state cases but *Mow Sun Wong* as well—is the Court's insistence on using the rational basis test at all (and an extremely lenient version of the test at that).[47]

It might be that restrained review is appropriate in *Diaz* because of the relative unimportance of the right or opportunity denied to aliens by virtue of the statutory classification.[48] The government provides insurance coverage against medical expenses for those who elect to participate. It is not designed to guarantee medical care for those who cannot otherwise afford it. The case does not involve, in other words, anything that could reasonably be called a "right to medical services." Nevertheless, the program does have important

---

[45] To be sure, not every alien eligible for participation in the program is also eligible for citizenship. Aliens may participate in the program if they are admitted to permanent residence and have resided in the United States for five years. The provision does not require that the alien have lived in the United States for five years as a permanent resident, whereas naturalization does require five years' residence as a permanent resident. 8 U.S.C. § 1427(a)(1)(1970). In other words, an alien who has lived in the United States for five years as a nonimmigrant and then adjusts his status to become a permanent resident will be eligible for the program immediately. He will not be eligible for naturalization until he has resided in the country for an additional five years.

[46] Trimble v. Gordon, 97 S. Ct. 1459, 1463–64 (1977); Eisenstadt v. Baird, 405 U.S. 438 (1972); Reed. v. Reed, 404 U.S. 71 (1971).

[47] Parts II and III of this article are concerned with the two principal justifications for a lenient standard of review in cases of federal government discrimination.

[48] In the 1976 Term, the Supreme Court considered the constitutionality of a New York statute denying resident aliens financial assistance for higher education. Dissenting from the Court's conclusion that the statute was invalid under the Fourteenth Amendment, Chief Justice Burger pointed out that "[i]n this case the State is not seeking to deprive aliens of the essential means of economic survival." *Mauclet*, 97 S. Ct. at 2128. By contrast, he suggested statutes denying aliens the right to engage in certain occupations could be said to impair "their ability to earn a livelihood," and statutes denying them welfare benefits could leave them without "means to obtain essential food, clothing, housing, and medical care." *Id.* at 2127, 2128. The Court rejected the Chief Justice's conclusion that "[w]here a *fundamental* personal interest is not at stake—and higher education is hardly that—the State must be free to exercise its largesse in any reasonable manner." *Id.* at 2128. It declared, quoting *Graham*, 403 U.S. at 376, that alienage classifications require strict scrutiny "whether or not a fundamental right is impaired." *Id.* at 2125 n.9.

welfare features. It is financed in equal proportions out of the premiums paid by participants and out of general federal revenues.[49] Those who would otherwise be eligible but cannot afford the monthly premiums may be able, as the district court pointed out, to have the premiums paid "by state public assistance programs, . . . which are funded in substantial part by the federal government."[50] In view of the potentially ruinous cost of medical care for the aged, the alien who is denied the opportunity to participate in the program is left to face on his own substantial risks from which the participants in the program are largely protected.

In any case, the Court made no effort to disparage the plaintiffs' interest as too trivial to warrant serious judicial concern. And there is simply no reason why the standard of review should depend on the fundamentality of the right at issue. The need for strict scrutiny in *Diaz* or any other alienage case arises, not from "the relative importance of the subject with respect to which equality is sought," but rather from "the relative invidiousness of the particular differentiation."[51] If the state alienage cases are any guide, the use of an alienage classification is suspect, and therefore requires strict scrutiny, irrespective of the nature of the right (or privilege) denied to the members of the class.

One could argue, of course, that the reliance on a finding of suspect classification to justify strict scrutiny, whatever the nature of the right denied, is uniquely a feature of equal protection analysis under the Fourteenth Amendment. The Court has often said that the Due Process Clause of the Fifth Amendment imposes limits on the federal government that are much the same as those imposed on the states by the Equal Protection Clause of the Fourteenth Amendment,[52] but it has been careful to add that the operation of the two clauses is not necessarily identical.[53] Although the Court has not spelled out precisely how the operation of the two Clauses

---

[49] 42 U.S.C. § 1395r(b) (1970 and Supp. V, 1975); 426 U.S. at 70 n.1.

[50] 361 F. Supp. 1, 11 (S.D. Fla. 1973), citing 42 U.S.C. §§ 1395v(d)(1), 1396b(a)(1) (1970).

[51] Cox, *Constitutional Adjudication and the Promotion of Human Rights*, 80 Harv. L. Rev. 91, 95 (1966); *cf.* Michelman, *On Protecting the Poor through the Fourteenth Amendment*, 83 Harv. L. Rev. 7, 33–34 (1969).

[52] Buckley v. Valeo, 424 U.S. 1, 93 (1976); Johnson v. Robison, 415 U.S. 361, 364 n.4 (1974); Bolling v. Sharpe, 347 U.S. 497, 499–500 (1954).

[53] *Mow Sun Wong*, 426 U.S. at 100; *Bolling*, 347 U.S. at 499.

might differ, it would not be unreasonable to suggest that the difference should arise from the very different wording of the two Clauses. Whereas the Fourteenth Amendment speaks of "equal protection" in the abstract, the Fifth guarantees due process only where the federal government would deny some person life, liberty, or property. Assuming that the concept of due process subsumes some limitation on the power of the federal government to classify persons for purposes of awarding benefits or imposing burdens, a literal reading of the Clause would suggest that the limitation could apply only where the classification is the means of denying some person life, liberty, or property. Under this view, it is possible for the use of an invidious classification—race, nationality, or alienage, for example—itself to trigger strict scrutiny in cases arising under the Equal Protection Clause, but that is precisely because of the absence from that Clause of the "life, liberty, or property" language. Since it would be very difficult to describe the aliens' interest in participating in the Medicare program as an interest in life, liberty, or property, at least as the Court has construed those terms in recent cases,[54] the use of a relaxed standard of review in *Diaz* would seem to follow logically. And this analysis may also explain why in *Mow Sun Wong* the Court was so much more solicitous of the aliens' claim. Viewed in this light, the crucial finding in *Mow Sun Wong* was that the exclusion of aliens from the civil service constituted an infringement of liberty for purposes of analysis under the Fifth Amendment.[55]

Still, the Court gave no hint in *Diaz* that its use of restrained review was actually predicated on any such literal reading of the Due Process Clause. Nor, so far as I am aware, has the Court approached any other federal equal protection problem in these terms. The very fact that the Court has dwelt on the need for a literal reading of the Clause in recent "right to a hearing" cases[56] suggests that its failure to apply the analysis expressly in the present context is significant. Besides, can there be any doubt that the Court would reject this kind of argument if offered in support of restrained re-

[54] Meachum v. Fano, 427 U.S. 215 (1976) (liberty); Bishop v. Wood, 426 U.S. 341 (1976) (property); Board of Regents v. Roth, 408 U.S. 564 (1972) (liberty and property). Van Alstyne, *Cracks in "The New Property": Adjudicative Due Process in the Administrative State*, 62 CORNELL L. REV. 445 (1977).

[55] 426 U.S. at 102 & n.23. See text at note 25 *supra*.

[56] *See* at note 54 *supra*.

view of a statute limiting the right of blacks to participate in the Medicare insurance program? Relying on the equal protection component of the due process guarantee, the Court has invalidated statutes denying rights no more obviously connected with life, liberty, or property than the right at issue in *Diaz*.[57] And it has accomplished these results on the understanding that the right to be free of unreasonable classification—in particular, classification based on one of the suspect criteria—is a liberty right which the Court will protect under the authority of the Fifth Amendment.[58] Except on that understanding it is impossible to make any sense out of the federal equal protection cases.

The Court's opinion in *Diaz* suggests another possible explanation for the use of restrained review. The statutory provision at issue excluded from the program some but not all aliens. Those admitted to the United States for permanent residence who had resided in this country for the five years immediately preceding their attempted enrollment were accorded the same benefits as citizens. "The real question," the Court maintained, "is not whether discrimination between citizens and aliens is permissible; rather, it is whether the statutory discrimination *within* the class of aliens—allowing benefits to some aliens but not to others—is permissible."[59] And the Court evidently assumed that this question could be answered under a relaxed standard of review.

The Court's analysis appears to be that because aliens are a discrete and insular minority and have little political power, the Court

---

[57] *See* Weinberger v. Wiesenfeld, 420 U.S. 636 (1975) (survivors' benefits under Social Security Act); Jimenez v. Weinberger, 417 U.S. 628 (1974) (childrens' benefits under Social Security Act); U.S. Dept. of Agriculture v. Moreno, 413 U.S. 528 (1973) (food stamps); Frontiero v. Richardson, 411 U.S. 677 (1973) (increased quarters allowances and medical and dental benefits); Shapiro v. Thompson, 394 U.S. 618 (1969) (Aid to Families with Dependent Children); Bolling v. Sharpe, 347 U.S. 497 (1954) (school desegregation).

[58] *Cf. Bolling*, 347 U.S. at 499–500: "Although the Court has not assumed to define 'liberty' with any great precision, that term is not confined to mere freedom from bodily restraint. Liberty under law extends to the full range of conduct which the individual is free to pursue, and it cannot be restricted except for a proper governmental objective. Segregation in public education is not reasonably related to any proper governmental objective, and thus it imposes on Negro children of the District of Columbia a burden that constitutes an arbitrary deprivation of their liberty in violation of the Due Process Clause." Significantly, the Court did not say that plaintiffs had a right to attend an integrated school. The liberty right is the right to be free of the arbitrary classification that had compelled them to attend segregated schools.

[59] 426 U.S. at 80.

will view with suspicion any line drawn by the majority between aliens and citizens. Where, however, the line is between long-term alien residents and short-term alien residents, there is no obvious reason for suspicion about the proper functioning of the majoritarian political process in drawing this line. The argument does not, in the end, provide an adequate basis for the use of restrained review. It is simply not correct to say that the discrimination is within the class of aliens rather than between citizens and aliens. The statute imposes on all aliens a qualification for admission to the program that is applicable to no citizen, a requirement that they demonstrate their "affinity" with the United States by proving that they have been admitted to the United States for permanent residence and have resided here for five years. Even though some aliens can satisfy the additional qualification, the fact remains that all aliens are judged under a distinct standard. If the statute governing eligibility in the insurance program imposed a durational residence requirement on blacks but not on whites, the Court could not avoid strict scrutiny on the theory that, since some blacks will satisfy the extra requirement, the discrimination is really within the class of blacks. The Court had previously considered and rejected just this kind of argument in cases involving state classifications based on alienage.[60] The argument has no greater force when it is the federal government that would impose an additional qualification on aliens.

In explaining why the discrimination within the class of aliens would not require strict scrutiny, the Court asserted: "Since it is obvious that Congress has no constitutional duty to provide *all aliens* with the welfare benefits provided to citizens, the party challenging the constitutionality of the particular line Congress has drawn has the burden" of demonstrating that the line is invalid.[61] The preliminary finding that Congress had no obligation to open the program to all aliens is said to convert the case into one involving discrimination within the class of aliens, rather than discrimination between aliens and citizens. Even with that proviso, however, rational basis review is inappropriate. It hardly follows

---

[60] *Mauclet*, 97 S. Ct. at 2125–26 n.12. The Court has rejected the same argument in other contexts as well. Mathews v. Lucas, 427 U.S. 495, 504–05 and n.11 (1976).

[61] 426 U.S. at 82.

from the fact that Congress need not open the program to every alien that it need not include any alien.

The plaintiffs' claim was that some aliens are situated so much like citizens with respect to the purposes of this program that it is unreasonable to treat them differently from citizens. The cases holding alienage a suspect classification rest on the finding that aliens admitted to the United States for permanent residence are, indeed, situated very much like citizens, and strict scrutiny is required of any statute that treats them differently from citizens. Yet the Court upheld the statutory classification in *Diaz* without requiring the government to show that it needed to draw a distinction between citizens and the aliens who are most like citizens. It pointed out instead that the disadvantaged class also included some aliens whose position is, on the whole, very different from that of citizens. The observation is correct but beside the point. One could have said precisely the same thing in each of the cases involving state discrimination against resident aliens.[62] It was not thought to make any difference to the standard of review in any of those cases, and it should not have made any difference in *Diaz*.[63]

As in the state cases, the plaintiffs in *Diaz* asked the Court to strike down a provision discriminating against resident aliens—

[62] In each of the recent state alienage cases the statute at issue was challenged by resident aliens, who sued on behalf of themselves or all resident aliens. But the statutes denied the benefit not only to resident aliens, but to nonimmigrants as well.

[63] This is not to say that a situation could never arise where the Court might properly use the rational basis test to review the subdividing of a suspect classification. But the threshold question must be very different from the one asked in *Diaz*. Instead of inquiring whether the legislature has an obligation to treat all members of the class as well as it treats nonmembers, the Court should ask whether the legislature must treat any member of the class as well as it treats nonmembers. Once it is decided that the legislature can deny a benefit to or impose a burden on every member of the class, the legislative decision to subdivide the class and treat some members differently from others need not occasion strict scrutiny (assuming, of course, that the class is not subdivided according to race or some other suspect criterion that would independently warrant strict scrutiny). The point is well illustrated by the Japanese curfew and relocation cases. Korematsu v. United States, 323 U.S. 214 (1944); Hirabayashi v. United States, 320 U.S. 81 (1943). The government's classification of persons according to ancestry was obviously suspect, but the Court concluded that the classification was justified by a compelling governmental interest. That is, the Court upheld the government's power to detain every person of Japanese ancestry. Unless the Court could find that the subdivision of the class was made on grounds that were independently suspect, it could properly uphold under the rational basis test the lines drawn within the class. But all of this proceeds from the premise that the government had a compelling interest that would permit it to act against any member of the class. (The very fact that the government did not detain every member of the class could be seen as evidence that the government's interest in classifying according to ancestry was not really compelling, but that is another matter.)

namely, the five-year durational residence test that was applied to them but not to citizens. But unlike any of the state cases, they also asked the Court to hold that certain nonimmigrant aliens were constitutionally entitled to the benefits of the programs. They had no choice in the matter. Several of the plaintiffs were nonimmigrants, and that alone was enough to make them ineligible under the statute even if they could have satisfied the durational residence requirement. They argued that the government must show a compelling need to exclude them from the program. By refusing to acknowledge the legitimacy of the line between immigrant and nonimmigrant aliens, they encouraged the Court to think of aliens as ranging across a spectrum from those very much like citizens to those having almost no resemblance to citizens.[64] They did not make clear at what point along this spectrum the government's obligation to demonstrate a compelling interest would end. Perhaps they believed that the government should have to show a compelling interest to justify the denial of benefits to any alien. The Court's response was not surprising:[65]

> [T]he differences between the eligible and the ineligible are differences in degree rather than differences in the character of their respective claims. When this kind of policy choice must be made, we are especially reluctant to question the exercise of congressional judgment. In this case, since [plaintiffs] have not identified a principled basis for prescribing a different standard than the one selected by Congress, they have, in effect, merely invited us to substitute our judgment for that of Congress in deciding which aliens shall be eligible to participate in the supplementary insurance program on the same conditions as citizens. We decline the invitation.

Although the challenge to the line between immigrants and nonimmigrants may help to explain the Court's eagerness to use a rational basis standard of review, it does not justify the use of that standard. In prior cases the Court had spoken of aliens as constituting a group that needed extraordinary judicial protection, but it never had to identify precisely the aliens who were entitled to this protection. The state cases were easier than *Diaz* insofar as the plaintiffs in all of them were resident aliens, and resident aliens

[64] 426 U.S. at 78–79 and n.13.

[65] *Id.* at 83–84.

plainly have the strongest claim to protection under the suspect classification doctrine. *Diaz* raised a very difficult question, since the nonimmigrant plaintiffs there were situated, in a number of important respects, very much like resident aliens and citizens.[66] The Court might have canvassed the reasons for holding alienage a suspect classification in order to determine whether this particular group of nonimmigrants should enjoy the protection of that doctrine. That inquiry might have persuaded the Court that the position of the nonimmigrant plaintiffs was so different from that of resident aliens that they were not entitled to extraordinary protection under the suspect classification doctrine. On the basis of that finding, the Court could then have upheld their exclusion from the program as rationally related to a legitimate governmental interest, even though the government would have to show a compelling interest to justify the exclusion of resident aliens. Alternatively, the Court might have extended to these nonimmigrants the protection of suspect classification analysis and applied strict scrutiny across the board. What the Court did instead was hold that the entire scheme could be upheld under the most lenient standard of review, thus denying strict scrutiny to the immigrant plaintiffs as well as to the nonimmigrants. In this way the Court neatly disposed of the problem of distinguishing between the immigrant and nonimmigrant plaintiffs. But it did not explain why the immigrant plaintiffs should lose the protection of strict scrutiny merely because the classification also disadvantaged nonimmigrants.

II. Alienage as a Suspect Classification

The Court pointed out in *Diaz* that the federal government has interests with respect to aliens that are not shared by any state.

---

[66] The nonimmigrant plaintiffs in *Diaz* were Cuban refugees admitted on parole into the United States at the discretion of the Attorney General. *See* 8 U.S.C. § 1182(d)(5) (1970). The Cuban refugees were brought into the United States outside the system of numerical limitations because the number of visas available was a tiny fraction of the number needed. Unlike most nonimmigrants, they were admitted with the expectation that they would stay in this country indefinitely. The Act of Nov. 2, 1966, Pub. L. No. 89-732, 80 Stat. 1161, made them eligible for adjustment of status to permanent residence after two years of residence in the United States and as soon as a visa number became available. Under subsequent legislation, their adjustment of status does not use up a visa number that would otherwise be available to a more conventional immigrant. P.L. 94-571, § 8, 90 Stat. 2706 (1976). In *Diaz*, the Government stipulated that the nonimmigrant plantiffs were bona fide residents of the United States even though they had not yet been admitted for permanent residence under the immigration laws.

Article I, § 8, clause 4 of the Constitution itself confers on the federal government the power to make "an uniform Rule of Naturalization," and the power to regulate immigration to the United States has long been thought to rest exclusively in the federal government.[67] The existence of these special federal interests may explain why the federal government can demonstrate a compelling need for a particular classification even though a state could not. But it does not in any obvious way explain why the burden of justification on the federal government should be different from the burden on a state. Put another way, if alienage is a suspect classification when made the basis of state legislation, should it not remain suspect when it is used by the federal government? The answer to that question depends on the reasons for considering alienage a suspect classification in the first place.

In *Graham*, the landmark case, the extension to aliens of suspect classification analysis was accomplished in these terms.[68]

> Under traditional equal protection principles, a State retains broad discretion to classify as long as its classification has a reasonable basis . . . . This is so in "the area of economics and social welfare." . . . But the Court's decisions have established that classifications based on alienage, like those based on nationality or race, are inherently suspect and subject to close judicial scrutiny. Aliens as a class are a prime example of a "discrete and insular" minority [citing *United States v. Carolene Products*][69] for whom such heightened judicial solicitude is appropriate. Accordingly, it was said in [*Takahashi v. Fish and Game Comm'n*][70] that "the power of a state to apply its laws exclusively to its alien inhabitants as a class is confined within narrow limits."

Just a few years earlier, Justice Harlan, in dissent, had reached a very different conclusion about what it was that the Court's prior decisions had established. In the course of arguing that equal protection requires nothing more than rationality except in the special case of racial discrimination, he maintained that "[m]ore

[67] Hines v. Davidowitz, 312 U.S. 52 (1941); Takahashi v. Fish and Game Comm'n, 334 U.S. 410 (1948).

[68] 403 U.S. at 371–72.

[69] 304 U.S. at 144, 152–53 n.4 (1938).

[70] 334 U.S. at 420.

explicit attempts to infuse 'Equal Protection' with specific values have been unavailing,"[71] and he illustrated his point by citing one of the Court's many prior decisions upholding discrimination against aliens under a very relaxed standard of review.[72] Only a handful of cases could be said to support the view that classifications based on alienage are inherently suspect, and their significance in this context is by no means clear.

Yick Wo v. Hopkins,[73] often cited as the bedrock of the constitutional protection of aliens, held that an alien is a "person" within the meaning of the Equal Protection Clause. But the case was plainly concerned with discrimination on the grounds of race, not on the grounds of citizenship. Yick Wo was disadvantaged because he was a person of Chinese origin, not because he was an alien. The holding that he was a "person" for purposes of analysis under the Equal Protection Clause was necessary to make clear that the Fourteenth Amendment barred racial discrimination whether its victims were citizens or aliens.

Carolene Products, cited by the Court for its famous language on the need for special judicial protection of certain minorities, offers no direct support for the Court's conclusion that alienage classifications are inherently suspect. To illustrate its point about discrimination against discrete and insular minorities, the Court in *Carolene Products* cited cases involving discrimination against religious, national, and racial minorities.[74] It made no mention of aliens as a group in need of special judicial protection.

The hardest cases to evaluate are *Truax v. Raich*[75] and *Takahashi v. Fish and Game Comm'n*.[76] In *Truax* the Court struck down a statutory classification based unmistakably on alienage, but the decision's support for the use of suspect classification analysis is problematic. At issue was an Arizona statute requiring any employer of at least five persons to have no less than 80% citizen employees. The Court held the statute invalid both as an interference with the supremacy of federal law on the admission of aliens and as a denial

---

[71] Harper v. Virginia Bd. of Elections, 383 U.S. 663, 682 n.3 (1966).

[72] Patsone v. Pennsylvania, 232 U.S. 138 (1914) (Holmes, J.) (upholding statute that barred aliens from killing wildlife or owning or possessing a gun). See also Porterfield v. Webb, 263 U.S. 225 (1923); Blythe v. Hinckley, 180 U.S. 333 (1901); McCready v. Virginia, 94 U.S. 391 (1877).

[73] 118 U.S. 356 (1886).

[74] 304 U.S. at 152–53 n.4.

[75] 239 U.S. 33 (1915).

[76] 334 U.S. 410 (1948).

of equal protection under the Fourteenth Amendment. Some of the analysis in connection with the equal protection claim is consistent with the view that classifications based on alienage warrant special scrutiny. Several times the Court spoke of discrimination based on "race or nationality,"[77] as if the two were essentially interchangeable. And its comment that a classification based on alienage could be upheld if designed to serve a "special public interest"[78] might be viewed as an anticipation of the compelling interest standard of review. But the Court did not say that its standard of review was unusually high. The only justification offered for the statute was the state's interest in promoting the economic security of its citizens at the expense of aliens. In the Court's view, this amounted to making discrimination against aliens "an end in itself."[79] With no legitimate interest cited in support of the statute, the Court held it invalid. But as if to make clear how little justification was needed for a statute discriminating against aliens, less than a month later the Court unanimously upheld a New York statute barring aliens from employment on public works construction projects.[80]

Perhaps *Truax* is best explained in terms of then-fashionable principles of freedom of contract. Whereas New York, in its role as public works employer, could hire anyone it wanted without interference from the Constitution, the Constitution would bar Arizona from interfering with the right of employers in the private sector to hire anyone they wanted. In any case, in the years after *Truax* the Court upheld under a very relaxed standard of review statutes discriminating between resident aliens and citizens with respect to such things as ownership of land,[81] state employment,[82] and licensing to operate billiard rooms.[83] No one suggested that *Truax* required a higher standard.

Takahashi v. Fish and Game Comm'n laid the groundwork for extending suspect classification analysis to aliens, but it stopped significantly short of the position reached by the Court in *Graham*.

---

[77] 239 U.S. at 41.

[78] *Id.* at 43.

[79] *Id.* at 41.

[80] Heim v. McCall, 239 U.S. 175 (1915); Crane v. New York, 239 U.S. 195 (1915).

[81] Terrace v. Thompson, 263 U.S. 197 (1923). But *cf.* Oyama v. California, 332 U.S. 633 (1948).

[82] Heim v. McCall, 239 U.S. 175 (1915).

[83] Ohio *ex rel.* Clarke v. Deckebach, 274 U.S. 392 (1927).

In explanation of its holding that a California statute denying commercial fishing licenses to certain aliens was unconstitutional, the Court used language suggesting that classifications based on alienage warrant special scrutiny. The power of the states to classify on the basis of alienage was said to be "confined within narrow limits."[84] But in explaining that conclusion, the Court dwelt at least as much on the supremacy of federal law concerning the admission of aliens as it did on the equal protection problems involved in state discrimination against aliens. The Court rejected California's argument that it had a "specific public interest" in regulating the catching of fish it "owned" in its territorial waters, and in doing so it cast doubt on the validity of earlier cases upholding discrimination against aliens on the basis of "specific public interests" no more substantial than the one asserted by California. But what makes it very difficult to evaluate *Takahashi* is that it can reasonably be viewed as concerned with discrimination on the grounds of race rather than alienage. That, at any rate, is how Justice Harlan characterized it in explaining his view that racial discrimination is the only area where equal protection requires more than rationality.[85] The statute denied fishing licenses to aliens "ineligible to citizenship." At the time, persons of Japanese origin (and virtually no other persons)[86] were barred from naturalization under federal law,[87] and it was at this racially defined group that the California statute was aimed.[88] As a transparent piece of racial discrimination,

[84] 334 U.S. at 420.

[85] 383 U.S. at 682 n.3.

[86] 334 U.S. at 412 n.1.

[87] At the time, federal statutes made naturalization available only to "free white persons," "persons of African descent," and several other specially designated groups. The Supreme Court had earlier held that a person of Japanese origin did not fall within the statutory definition of "free white person." Ozawa v. United States, 260 U.S. 178 (1922). In 1952 all racial restrictions on eligibility for naturalization were finally eliminated by statute. 8 U.S.C. § 1422 (1970).

[88] 334 U.S. at 422 (Murphy, J., concurring): "Even the most cursory examination of the background of the statute demonstrates that it was designed solely to discriminate against [persons of Japanese origin] . . . . The statute in question is but one more manifestation of the anti-Japanese fever which has been evident in California in varying degrees since the turn of the century." Mr. Justice Black, the author of the Court's opinion in *Takahashi*, concurred in the Court's opinion in an earlier case striking down portions of California's alien land law. Like the statute at issue in *Takahashi*, the land law applied only to aliens ineligible for citizenship. Justice Black, concurring, argued that the Court should strike down the law under the Equal Protection Clause since it "single[d] out aliens of Japanese ancestry" and therefore amounted to discrimination on the grounds of "race or color." Oyama v. California, 332 U.S. 633, 647, 649 (1948).

the statute had to fall whatever one's views on the constitutionality of drawing lines on the basis of alienage.

There can be no doubt that *Takahashi* used a stricter standard of review than had the earlier cases upholding discrimination against aliens. But it very carefully avoided reliance on the extremely strict standard of review that the Court was already using in cases involving racial discrimination against citizens.[89] In short, *Takahashi* falls somewhere between a race case and an alienage case. Although it implicitly called into question much of the Court's reasoning in prior alienage cases, it took almost twenty-five years before the Court was prepared to take the additional step of equating alienage cases and race cases, applying to both an extremely strict standard of review.

In almost every conceivable way 1971 was an unlikely time for the Court to take that additional step. The Court had two new members who had not participated in the equal protection revolution of the 1960s, and it was showing signs of diminished interest in the marvels of suspect classification analysis.[90] There seemed to be no significant political pressure to give aliens increased constitutional protection.[91] And the Court was already having difficulty fixing on an appropriate standard of review in cases involving discrimination on the basis of gender[92] and legitimacy.[93] Yet, without any dissent,[94] the Court upheld the aliens' constitutional claims in *Graham* and brought aliens under the protection of the strict scrutiny doctrine.[95] In subsequent cases the Court has not wavered in its commitment to the view that alienage classifications are inher-

---

[89] *Oyama*, 332 U.S. at 646; *Korematsu*, 323 U.S. at 216.

[90] See *Dandridge*, 397 U.S. at 485; see also Lindsey v. Normet, 405 U.S. 56, 73–74 (1972).

[91] But *cf.* Landes & Posner, *The Independent Judiciary in an Interest-Group Perspective*, 18 J. L. & Econ. 875, 893 (1975) (the Constitution protects "groups sufficiently powerful to obtain constitutional protection for their interests").

[92] Reed v. Reed, 404 U.S. 71 (1971).

[93] *Compare* Weber v. Aetna Casualty & Surety Co., 406 U.S. 164 (1972), *with* Labine v. Vincent, 401 U.S. 532 (1971).

[94] Justice Harlan concurred in the result on Supremacy Clause grounds and did not reach the equal protection issues. 403 U.S. at 383.

[95] The California Supreme Court had anticipated the development two years earlier. Purdy & Fitzpatrick v. State, 71 Cal. 2d 566 (1969).

ently suspect, notwithstanding the strong objections of Mr. Justice Rehnquist.[96]

Apart from its comment that "aliens as a class are a prime example of a 'discrete and insular' minority,"[97] the Court has offered no theoretical explanation for bringing aliens within the suspect classification doctrine. The appropriate place to begin is with an understanding of the consequences of finding a classification suspect. The ordinary legislative classification will be upheld as long as it bears some rational relationship to a legitimate governmental interest.[98] A suspect classification, by contrast, requires a showing that the state's "purpose or interest is both constitutionally permissible and substantial, and that its use of the classification is 'necessary . . . to the accomplishment' of its purpose or the safeguarding of its interest."[99] There would seem to be two reasons for concluding that certain classifications require this very unusual showing. The first relates to the seriousness of the injury inflicted by the classification. The second is concerned with the integrity of the political process that chose this particular classification instead of others that might have accomplished the same ultimate objective.

Every legislative classification benefits some persons more than others or burdens some persons less than others. But certain classifications have a tendency to cause an injury to the members of the disadvantaged group that goes substantially beyond the denial of whatever benefit is at issue and raises problems of fundamental fairness. Thus, a classification may carry with it a badge of inferiority, stigmatizing members of the disadvantaged class as inherently less worthy than members of the advantaged class. A classification that

---

[96] *Mauclet*, 97 S. Ct. at 2129; *Sugarman*, 413 U.S. at 649. Mr. Justice Blackmun has played the leading role in formulating the Court's approach. He wrote the opinion for the Court in all but one of the five principal cases decided by the end of the 1976 Term: *Mauclet, supra*; Examining Bd. of Engineers v. Flores de Otero, 426 U.S. 572 (1976); *Sugarman*; and *Graham*. Mr. Justice Powell wrote for the Court in *Griffiths*. Of the Justices now sitting, only Mr. Justice Rehnquist has objected unequivocally to the conclusion that alienage classifications are suspect. Chief Justice Burger dissented in two of the five cases on grounds suggesting that he had some doubts about the underlying theory. *Mauclet*, 97 S. Ct. at 2127; *Griffiths*, 413 U.S. at 730. But he joined the opinion for the Court in the other cases, all of which stated clearly that the decision rested on suspect classification analysis.

[97] 403 U.S. at 372.

[98] *Dandridge*, 397 U.S. at 485; McGowan v. Maryland, 366 U.S. 420, 425–26 (1961).

[99] *Griffiths*, 413 U.S. at 721–22, quoting from *McLaughlin*, 379 U.S. at 196.

has this effect is not necessarily impermissible. But it may be considered suspect on the grounds that it offends deeply held views about the dignity of each individual and the danger of labeling some persons as inferior to others.[100] Similarly, to classify persons on the basis of a status over which they have no control seems "to violate some shared sense of fairness."[101] That is not to say that the Equal Protection Clause or any other part of the Constitution establishes a fundamental right to be immune from this kind of classification. Nevertheless, "[t]he principle that classification by involuntary characteristics counts against the validity of a classification . . . rests upon values that are central to our conception of the good society and . . . of the proper role of government."[102] Recognizing the serious injury caused by classifications that stigmatize or that rest on involuntary characteristics, the Court may bar their use except where they are necessary to achieve an end that is sufficiently important to warrant such costly means. In that sense the classifications are considered suspect.

The seriousness of the injury is not the only reason for treating a classification as suspect. In one of its clearer statements of the principle underlying suspect classification analysis, the Court identified the "traditional indicia of suspectness" in these terms: the class must be "saddled with such disabilities, or subjected to such a history of purposeful unequal treatment, or relegated to such a position of political powerlessness as to command extraordinary protection from the majoritarian political process."[103] The relaxed standard of review generally applicable to state legislation rests on the presumption of its constitutionality. And that presumption rests in turn on the expectation that all groups potentially affected by the legislation have had an opportunity to express their views and pursue their interests in the legislative forum. That is not to say, of course, that the Court will scrutinize every piece of legislation to see who the losers are and then determine whether the losers'

[100] Brown v. Board of Educ., 347 U.S. 483, 494 (1954); Strauder v. West Virginia, 100 U.S. 303, 308 (1879); *cf. Lucas*, 427 U.S. at 506.

[101] Sandalow, *Racial Preferences in Higher Education: Political Responsibility and the Judicial Role*, 42 U. Chi. L. Rev. 653, 668 (1975).

[102] *Id.* at 672. *Cf. Frontiero*, 411 U.S. at 686–87 (plurality opinion); *Aetna Casualty & Surety Co.*, 406 U.S. at 175–76.

[103] San Antonio School Dist. v. Rodriguez, 411 U.S. 1, 28 (1973).

legislative representation was proportional to their numbers.[104] One assumes that every group will lose on some issue from time to time. So long as the group has had an opportunity to form alliances with other groups, trade support on one issue for support on another, make a strategic concession on a less important point in order to gain a bargaining advantage on a more important one, there is little reason to doubt the integrity of the process that produced the political decision.[105]

Where a group is systematically shut out of the political process, however, and is denied an opportunity to form alliances with any other group, it may well lose on every issue. At that point the proper functioning of the majoritarian political process is very much in question.[106] In such case, the Court begins to fear that the injury to the members of the disadvantaged class, far from being an unintended by-product of the state's effort to serve a legitimate interest, was in fact the very purpose of the classification. And the likelihood increases that the classification was based on a stereotypical and erroneous view of the characteristics of the members of the group.[107] Where persons are essentially without political power and where history gives evidence of the majority's willingness to stereotype them unfairly or to take advantage of them precisely because they are weak, the Court will declare suspect a classification that singles them out for adverse and unequal treatment. As a result, the state must show that the classification is more than just one possible way of serving the legitimate purpose ascribed to it. It must be the only way (or at any rate the least restrictive way) of serving that particular interest.

With respect to aliens, then, one has to know whether there is something about the class that makes treating them unequally especially severe or that raises doubts about the proper working of the political process insofar as it singles them out for special treatment. It would seem very difficult to explain the conclusion that alienage is an inherently suspect classification on the grounds that the

---

[104] See Note, 82 HARV. L. REV. 1065, 1126 (1969).

[105] See generally BUCHANAN & TULLOCK, THE CALCULUS OF CONSENT (1962).

[106] Note, note 104 *supra* at 1125.

[107] *Cf.* Califano v. Goldfarb, 430 U.S. 199, 223, (1977) (Stevens, J., concurring); *Lucas*, 427 U.S. at 520–21 (1976) (Stevens, J., dissenting); *Frontiero*, 411 U.S. at 684–85 (plurality opinion).

status is involuntary or immutable. Although an immigrant to the United States is necessarily an alien for some period of time, the fact of alienage is simply not immutable. After five years of residence—even less in the case of certain aliens[108]—virtually every permanent resident alien is eligible for citizenship.[109] If an alien chooses to retain that status even when naturalization is possible, one can reasonably say that the status is voluntary. Of course, the decision to become a citizen may be a difficult one for the alien to make. It requires him to cast off whatever nationality he has previously had[110] and thereby close a door to the past. No one suggests that aliens should be under an obligation to make that choice and accept naturalization as soon as it is offered. On the contrary, an alien can remain in this country indefinitely without accepting citizenship. Nevertheless, it is an acknowledged and important part of our immigration policy to encourage immigrants to commit themselves to our society. The country's naturalization requirements are among the most lenient in the world. Even before immigrants acquire American citizenship, their children born in this country are automatically citizens at birth. If an alien declines the opportunity to become a citizen, it would appear that he has made a knowing and intelligent choice between his interest in retaining a tie to the country of his birth and his interest in enjoying the benefits that are made available exclusively to citizens. The special injury associated with classifying persons on the basis of an involuntary characteristic does not seem to be a problem here.

It remains true, however, that during the first five years of residence alienage is ordinarily an involuntary characteristic. But not every classification defined in terms of an involuntary or immutable characteristic is suspect,[111] and it is not clear why a five-year waiting period is so burdensome as to warrant strict scrutiny on the grounds of "immutability" alone. Besides, if the immutability of the

---

[108] 8 U.S.C. § 1430 (1970) (three years' residence required for naturalization of alien whose spouse is a citizen of the United States).

[109] With all racial restrictions on naturalization now repealed, see note 87 *supra*, the principal requirements in addition to residence are an understanding of the English language, knowledge of the history and form of government of the country, good moral character, and attachment to the principles of the Constitution. 8 U.S.C. §§ 1423, 1427 (1970).

[110] 8 U.S.C. § 1448 (1970).

[111] Sandalow, note 101 *supra*, at 667.

status were the real reason for bringing aliens within the protection of the suspect classification doctrine, the class entitled to this protection would have to be defined much more narrowly than all permanent resident aliens in the United States.[112] After all, the aliens who have the least power to change their status are those admitted to the United States as nonimmigrants. For them the five-year waiting period does not even begin until they have adjusted their status to permanent residence,[113] and that adjustment is in most cases very difficult to accomplish. Yet the Court has never suggested that nonresident aliens even fall within the specially protected class, much less that they are the ones most deserving of protection.

With regard to the possible stigmatizing effect of the classification, the aliens' claim is a good deal stronger. The very word, "alien," calls to mind someone strange and out of place, and it has often been used in a distinctly pejorative way. Moreover, discrimination against aliens has traditionally taken a form that tends to increase the likelihood of stigma. In this area one rarely finds a statute that injures aliens indirectly—a statute, harmless on its face, that has the purpose or effect of disadvantaging large numbers of aliens. When a state decides to impose some special burden on aliens or to deny them some benefit, ordinarily it will do so explicitly, making no effort to camouflage the discrimination by classifying on the basis of some apparently neutral characteristic that tends to correlate with alienage. By its own terms the statute will single out aliens for special treatment. The explicitness of the discrimination can only add to the injury.

Still, I doubt that stigma alone can be enough to make alienage classification suspect. The very fact that an alien can give up his status and become a citizen mitigates the seriousness of the problem. And however the Court treats statutory classifications based on alienage, much of the stigmatizing effect will remain so long as the

---

[112] A New York statute awarded certain education assistance benefits to citizens and to those aliens who were taking steps to become citizens or who would affirm an intent to apply for citizenship as soon as they were eligible. The class of persons denied benefits was defined, in other words, to keep problems of immutability to a minimum. And yet the Court, over the dissent of four Justices, concluded that the classification was suspect. *Mauclet*, 97 S. Ct. at 2125–26 n.11. The Court specifically declined to narrow the definition of the specially protected class "to include at most only those who have resided in this country for less than five years." *Id.* at 2125 n.11.

[113] 8 U.S.C. § 1427 (a) (1970) (naturalization requires five years' residence in the United States "after being lawfully admitted for permanent residence").

Constitution itself denies aliens certain benefits.[114] One could also argue that the greatest stigma is experienced, not by aliens as such, but rather by "foreigners"—a category that can include citizens and aliens.[115] Many aliens are indistinguishable from citizens, and discrimination against them may involve little stigma. By contrast, discrimination against the foreign-born or against persons perceived as foreign because of their ethnic or racial background will inevitably produce much greater stigma. But at this point one has moved from discrimination on the grounds of alienage to discrimination on the grounds of race or national origin, and there strict scrutiny is obviously required.

If classifications based on alienage are to be held suspect, that conclusion must ultimately be derived from the political powerlessness of aliens. The exclusion of aliens from the political process goes far beyond the denial of the right to vote[116] and the right to hold high political or elective office.[117] Many aliens have come to the United States from countries where active political participation is not encouraged, and they may have no taste for the kinds of activity—joining political groups, sending letters to government officials, dramatizing grievances, and the like—that often play a more important role than voting in shaping governmental policy. In addition the eagerness of aliens to engage in these activities may well be affected by their experience with the power of the national government.

Aliens must register with the government whenever they change

---

[114] The Constitution makes aliens ineligible for the Presidency, the Senate, and the House of Representatives. Moreover, the denial to aliens of the right to vote will evidently survive the finding that alienage classifications are suspect. Skafte v. Rorex, 97 S. Ct. 1638 (1977), dismissing appeal from 553 P.2d 830 (Colo. 1976).

[115] Higham, Strangers in the Land (2d ed. 1963); Franklin, The Legislative History of Naturalization in the United States 184–300 (1906). To take just one of many examples of discrimination against foreigners (as opposed to aliens), it was fear of their impact at the polls that first prompted English literacy tests for voters and proposals for special residence requirements for voting applicable only to naturalized citizens. See Porter, A History of Suffrage in the United States 102–03, 114–17, 229 (1969).

[116] *Cf.* Skafte v. Rorex, 553 P.2d 830 (Colo. 1976), *appeal dismissed*, 97 S. Ct. 1638 (1977). An alien who declines the opportunity for naturalization is, in effect, disenfranchised by choice. But that is not a reason for withholding special judicial protection. The Court's proper concern is the powerlessness of aliens as a group. And as a group their lack of political power is not in any sense voluntary.

[117] *Cf. Sugarman*, 413 U.S. at 647–49.

their address, and once each year in any event.[118] They may be aware of their vulnerability to deportation on any one of several hundred possible grounds,[119] which include engaging in conduct that is not in any sense illegal.[120] In order to gain entry to the United States in the first place they have had to deal with three or four different government agencies—the Immigration and Naturalization Service, the State Department, the Labor Department, the Public Health Service—and in an area where legal standards are frequently indistinct, agency discretion is substantial, and official high-handedness is not at all unknown. In many instances the possibility of judicial review is nonexistent.[121] Because they may "look like aliens" they may frequently be stopped and questioned by government officials who want to see some evidence that their presence in the United States is lawful.[122] These experiences are more likely to bring out fear of governmental authority than a desire to participate actively in political affairs so as to influence the exercise of that authority.

But what follows from the powerlessness of aliens? As I indicated earlier, the Court has suggested that the total exclusion of a group from the political process warrants concern about the integrity of the political process that generated the unequal treatment. And there would seem to be good cause for such concern in this context. Take, for example, a classic variety of discrimination against aliens: a state statute that bars them from owning land.[123] A statute of this sort might be said to serve an interest in insuring that landowners

---

[118] 8 U.S.C. § 1305 (1970).

[119] See 8 U.S.C. § 1251 (1970). One writer indicates that there were more than 700 possible grounds for deportation as of 1960. CARLINER, note 5 *supra* at 61 and n.2.

[120] Harisiades v. Shaughnessy, 342 U.S. 580 (1952); 1 GORDON & ROSENFIELD, IMMIGRATION LAW AND PROCEDURE § 4.3c (rev. ed. 1977).

[121] Burrafato v. United States Dept. of State, 523 F.2d 554, 557 (2d Cir. 1975) (district court had no power "to review what happened to [the alien] in Italy or what he claims the Department of State did to him here"); De Pena v. Kissinger, 409 F. Supp. 1182 (S.D. N.Y. 1976).

[122] 8 U.S.C. § 1357(a)(1) (1970). United States v. Martinez-Fuerte, 428 U.S. 543, 563 (1976); Cheung Tin Wong v. INS, 468 F.2d 1123, 1127–28 (D.C. Cir. 1972); *cf.* United States v. Brignoni-Ponce, 422 U.S. 873, 884 n.9, 885–87 (1975). *But cf.* Illinois Migrant Council v. Pilliod, 398 F. Supp. 882, 899 (N.D. Ill. 1975), *aff'd*, 540 F.2d 1062 (7th Cir.), *modified on rehearing in banc*, 548 F.2d 715 (1977).

[123] 1 POWELL, THE LAW OF REAL PROPERTY 374–414 (rev. ed. 1977); Sullivan, *Alien Land Laws: A Reevaluation*, 36 TEMP. L.Q. 15 (1962). The Supreme Court has upheld the constitutionality of statutes restricting the right of aliens to own land. Terrace v. Thompson, 263 U.S. 197 (1923).

are loyal to the United States and knowledgeable about the laws, language, and customs of the country. In this view, alienage is a proxy for other characteristics—lack of loyalty and knowledge—that are the state's real concern. It is the assumed correlation between alienage and these other qualities that prompts the classification, not any sense that aliens as aliens are undesirable landowners. But why does the state have an interest in insuring a higher-than-average degree of loyalty and knowledgeability on the part of landowners? In all likelihood the state can point to no other aspect of its land ownership laws that gives evidence of such an interest. How important can the state's interest be if it is prepared to separate the loyal from the disloyal by means of a technique as haphazard as classifying on the basis of alienage? The classification is seriously under- and overinclusive, and even without strict scrutiny a court might well hold that the connection between means and end is too slight to support the classification.[124]

But this would certainly seem a situation where strict scrutiny is warranted. Given the lack of fit between the classification and its asserted purpose, there is good reason to believe that the legislature acted on the basis of a very inaccurate stereotype, or that the real purpose of the classification was different from the one asserted. Since the group disadvantaged by the classification was totally excluded from the process of deciding who should be allowed to own land and who should not, why should the Court close its eyes to the obvious and presume that the asserted purpose was in fact the real one? Aliens have unquestionably suffered a "history of purposeful unequal treatment" in this country, and that history should generate some skepticism of a state's claim that alien land laws are a reasonable response to the interest in having loyal and knowledgeable landowners. The strict scrutiny test affords an appropriate means of giving expression to that skepticism. If the state can show that its ultimate goal is important and that classifying on the basis of alienage is the only way, or at least the most effective way, of achieving that goal, then the classification can be upheld. For that showing gives some assurance that the majority has not deliberately inflicted an injury on a minority that lacks the political power to protect itself.

A statute that denies aliens the right to own land is so ineffective

---

[124] *Cf.* Eisenstadt v. Baird, 405 U.S. 438 (1972).

a means of identifying loyal and knowledgeable landowners that its real purpose must lie elsewhere. A statute of this sort rests—as, in the end, does almost every other classification based on alienage—on a judgment that land (or whatever other benefit is at issue) is an item in short supply and should be rationed so that a disfavored group (aliens) gets none in order that more will be available for a favored group (citizens). It is tempting to say that the goal of enhancing the economic well-being of citizens at the expense of aliens makes discrimination "an end in itself"[125] and is inherently illegitimate.[126] If it is illegitimate, then strict scrutiny should eliminate all classifications based on alienage. There is simply no other state goal whose accomplishment requires the use of a classification based on alienage. But what is it that makes the interest illegitimate? The state may bear no grudge against aliens. But it has a special feeling of affection for and responsibility to the members of its polity. And that polity does not include aliens, not even resident aliens, any more than it includes residents of another state. If a state has two licenses to distribute and three persons apply—one a native-born citizen, one a naturalized citizen, and one a resident alien who has so far declined the opportunity for naturalization—and if the three are identically qualified in every respect other than citizenship, is it unfair to seize on citizenship as an appropriate basis of distinction?

The Supreme Court has clearly indicated that it is, indeed, unfair and impermissible. In *Graham* the Court held that "a State's desire to preserve limited welfare benefits for its own citizens is inadequate to justify Pennsylvania's making noncitizens ineligible for public assistance."[127] The state "may legitimately attempt to limit its expenditures," but not by means of an "invidious classification."[128] This particular classification is invidious because it violates "a general policy" embodied in "[t]he Fourteenth Amendment and the laws adopted under its authority . . . that all persons lawfully in this country shall abide 'in any state' on an equality of legal privi-

---

[125] *Truax*, 239 U.S. at 41.

[126] *Examining Bd. of Engineers*, 426 U.S. at 605–06 ("To uphold the statute on the basis of broad economic justification of this kind would permit any State to bar the employment of aliens in any or all lawful occupations").

[127] 403 U.S. at 374.

[128] *Id.* at 374–75, quoting from *Shapiro*, 394 U.S. at 633.

leges with all citizens under non-discriminatory laws."[129] Without that principle aliens cannot defeat legislative classifications based on alienage. But the source of the principle is not apparent. It certainly cannot be derived from the holding in *Yick Wo v. Hopkins* that an alien is a "person" within the meaning of the Fourteenth Amendment.[130] For that holding indicates only that a state must treat an alien as well as it treats others who are similarly situated. And the question here is whether or not an alien and a citizen are similarly situated with respect to the state's interest in giving a preference to the members of its polity.

It is not a sufficient answer to apply the suspect classification label and dismiss the state's interest as less than compelling. If one looks behind the label one should be able to find something about the situation of aliens that explains why a distinction of this kind is unacceptable. One gets no help from the "history of purposeful unequal treatment" that aliens have suffered, since that history could be viewed as persuasive evidence that we have always recognized a difference between aliens and citizens and acted on the assumption that it was permissible to deny them certain benefits.[131] Nevertheless, the political powerlessness of aliens does furnish an adequate basis for rejecting the state's effort to give citizens a preference in awarding public benefits.

When a state denies benefits to aliens so as to enhance the position of citizens, it is still using alienage as a proxy for some other characteristic, although that characteristic is difficult to describe. The state evidently feels a greater responsibilty to its citizens because it assumes they all share a common past and hold certain basic values, including an appreciation of the community's real worth, a sense of identification with its other members, and a commitment to its long-range well-being. Aliens, it is assumed, do not share

[129] 403 U.S. at 374, quoting from *Takahashi*, 334 U.S. at 420.

[130] 118 U.S. at 369.

[131] In his opinion for the Court in *Diaz*, Mr. Justice Stevens recited a long list of federal statutes discriminating against aliens, and he suggested that the list counted in favor of the classification, not against it as one might have supposed from the Court's ordinary concern in equal protection cases with the "history of purposeful unequal treatment." 426 U.S. at 78 n.12. It should also be noted that discrimination against aliens is not an aberrational phenomenon found only in a small number of states. Every state has discriminated against aliens in a substantial number of ways. Does that indicate that everyone understands the difference between citizens and aliens, or that everyone is prejudiced against aliens?

these values. But viewed in these terms, the classfication is extremely imprecise. Many aliens will have the characteristics that the state associates with membership in its polity, and by the same token many citizens will not. Besides, why is it so important for the state to draw a line between a person having these characteristics and a person lacking them, even assuming that an alienage classification accurately separates the two? It warrants emphasis that in every state aliens are obligated to pay taxes whether or not they share the basic values of the community.[132] They help to create the fund out of which the state would provide benefits for citizens alone.[133] Is the state's interest in enhancing the economic position of those who share the basic values of the community sufficiently important to justify making aliens bear all the burdens but receive less than all of the benefits? Where an alien and a citizen are competing for a benefit and the two are indistinguishable in every respect except their appreciation for the values of the community, it may be reasonable to prefer the citizen (assuming the citizen is the one who has this special quality). But it will surely be the rare case where the two applicants are indistinguishable in every respect except this one. When a state makes alienage an automatic bar to the awarding of the benefit, it is effectively saying that as between the least qualified citizen and the most qualified alien, it would rather give the benefit to the citizen. Again, why is it so important to put this much emphasis on the one characteristic?

Classification on the basis of membership in the polity seems to be an extremely crude way of serving a state interest whose importance is very hard to explain. But many state classifications are imprecise and many state interests are a good deal less than compelling. Given the exclusion of aliens from the political process, it is nevertheless reasonable for the Court to demand a special showing from the state if it is to classify on the basis of alienage. The state has presumably weighed its interest in giving a preference to the members of its polity against the aliens' interest in enjoying the benefits at issue. But aliens have had no opportunity to participate

[132] This is a point the Court has emphasized again and again. *Graham*, 403 U.S. at 376 (1971) ("There can be no 'special public interest' in tax revenues to which aliens have contributed on an equal basis with the residents of the State."). See also *Mauclet*, 97 S. Ct. at 2127; *Griffiths*, 413 U.S. at 722.

[133] The Court has also emphasized that resident aliens are subject, like citizens, to the selective service laws. *Griffiths*, 413 U.S. at 722; *Graham*, 403 U.S. at 376.

in the process of measuring the relative weight of these two interests. Since the legislature has denied aliens any chance to assert their own interests in the political forum, it cannot expect the courts to maintain their usual deference to the legislature's balancing of the interests.[134] The risk is simply too great that the legislature has capriciously (or perhaps malevolently) undervalued the aliens' interest. The demand for a showing that the legislature's goal is an exceptionally important one and that a classification on the basis of alienage is necessary to the accomplishment of that goal is both a moderate and appropriate judicial response to the problem.

But if it is presumptively impermissible for a state to define aliens as falling outside its polity, it might be said that the definition of nonresident citizens as falling outside the polity is equally suspect. Nonresidents of the state, even though citizens of the United States, are as effectively excluded from the state's political process as resident aliens. Thus, the reasoning that requires the state to show a special need to deny benefits to aliens might be thought to require a comparable showing to justify the denial of benefits to anyone in the world. Surely the state must have some freedom to define membership in its polity. Why, then, does the Constitution require strict scrutiny of the decision to leave aliens out of the definition, when the exclusion of nonresidents occasions no comparable scrutiny?

A line drawn on the basis of geographic boundaries does not present all of the difficulties of a line drawn on the basis of citizenship. Suppose New York denies a benefit to two persons: to one because he is a resident of another state, and to the other because he is an alien. Both lack political rights in New York. But the nonresident has access to the political process in New Jersey or Connecticut or wherever he lives, and he may be able to persuade his state to bring its influence to bear on New York.[135] He also has access to the political process at the national level and may gain some relief there. The alien resident of New York has nowhere to turn.[136] Besides, the same line that separates residents from nonresi-

---

[134] Rostow, *The Democratic Character of Judicial Review*, 66 HARV. L. REV. 193, 202 (1952).

[135] *Cf.* Austin v. New Hampshire, 420 U.S. 656, 662 (1975).

[136] The alien does in theory have an opportunity to seek the assistance of the country whose nationality he holds. But the opportunity exists in theory only. *See* Rosberg, note 35 *supra*, at 1114–15.

dents also tends to separate those who bear the burdens of living in the state from those who do not. A line drawn between those who pay taxes in the state and those who do not is a good deal easier to understand than a line drawn between those taxpayers who share the basic values of the state and those who do not. Because the purpose behind the line is more easily understood, it is much less likely to involve stigma for those who fail to qualify. I conceded earlier that stigma alone may not be enough to warrant strict scrutiny of every classification based on alienage. But there is surely some reason for concern on this account. Where a state denies benefits to aliens, the lack of congruence between burdens and benefits almost inevitably creates the impression that aliens must be in some way inferior to citizens or less worthy of public assistance. Of course, the line between residents and nonresidents is by no means perfect. Some nonresidents do pay taxes[137]—perhaps a larger amount than many residents. But the correlation between residence and taxpaying is ordinarily very close, and there is little reason to fear that the state has lumped all nonresidents together according to an inaccurate stereotype. Imprecision of the geographic line is less troublesome than imprecision of the citizenship line because of the lesser chance for stigma, the greater opportunity for political participation at some level, and the greater importance of the state's ultimate goal (awarding benefits only to those who bear the burdens). The Court can reasonably hold a state to a higher standard of precision when it draws lines on the basis of citizenship than when it draws lines on the basis of residence. And the geographic line, in any case, has constitutional difficulties of its own.[138]

---

[137] In another context, Professor Bittker has suggested the ultimate example of "a French businessman who was a passenger on a plane that, while en route from Paris to Montreal, was forced by engine trouble to land at Kennedy International Airport. Having spent the night in New York City, where he made several long distance telephone calls that were subject to federal excise tax," he brought a taxpayer's suit against the United States challenging the constitutionality of the Louisiana Purchase. Bittker, *The Case of the Fictitious Taxpayer: The Federal Taxpayer's Suit Twenty Years after Flast v. Cohen*, 36 U. CHI. L. REV. 364, 365 (1969).

[138] A state statute that grants preferences to residents at the expense of nonresidents can run afoul of the Commerce Clause, H. P. Hood & Sons v. DuMond, 336 U.S. 525 (1949), and Pennsylvania v. West Virginia, 262 U.S. 553 (1923); the Privileges and Immunities Clause of Article IV, Doe v. Bolton, 410 U.S. 179, 200 (1973), and Toomer v. Witsell, 334 U.S. 385 (1948); and, to the extent the statute classifies on the basis of duration of residence, it may interfere with the constitutionally protected right to travel. Memorial Hospital v. Maricopa County, 415 U.S. 250 (1974); Dunn v. Blumstein, 405 U.S. 330 (1972); Shapiro v. Thompson, 394 U.S. 618 (1969). But more to the point, discrimination against nonresidents can raise serious questions of equal protection. *See*

Assuming that classifications denying benefits to resident aliens require strict scrutiny, how should the Court handle the nonresident aliens' claim for equal treatment? In terms of the "traditional indicia of suspectness,"[139] the class of nonimmigrants is very much like the class of immigrants. Their status is, if anything, less mutable than the status of resident aliens. The stigmatizing effect of the classification is the same. And they are just as effectively excluded from the political process. Yet one has an intuitive sense that the denial of benefits to nonimmigrant aliens rests on a real difference between their position, on the one hand, and the position of both resident aliens and citizens on the other. The Supreme Court, at any rate, has not held it unconstitutional to discriminate against nonimmigrant aliens. It has not even suggested that such aliens are within the class protected under the suspect classification doctrine.[140]

Immigrant aliens are admitted to the United States with the expectation that they will remain here indefinitely and will eventually become citizens. Nonimmigrants, by contrast, cannot have an intention of remaining here indefinitely, since they are admitted for a limited purpose and for a limited period of time.[141] They do not share all the burdens that are imposed on residents of the country.[142] In many respects their position is similar to that of nonresident citi-

---

WHYY v. Borough of Glassboro, 393 U.S. 117 (1968); *cf.* Hughes v. Alexandria Scrap Corp., 426 U.S. 794, 810–14 (1976); Aronson v. Ambrose, 479 F.2d 75 (3d Cir. 1973); Clarke v. Redeker, 259 F. Supp. 117 (S.D. Ia. 1966). Where a classification on the basis of residence is reasonable, the courts will nevertheless police the drawing of the line between residents and nonresidents to insure that it is done with a good deal of precision. Vlandis v. Kline, 412 U.S. 441 (1973); Ramey v. Rockefeller, 348 F. Supp. 780 (E.D. N.Y. 1972); Newburger v. Peterson, 344 F. Supp. 559 (D. N.H. 1972). But *cf.* Sosna v. Iowa, 419 U.S. 393, 409 (1975).

[139] *Rodriguez*, 411 U.S. at 28.

[140] The Court has taken pains in each of the recent cases to make clear that the plaintiffs were resident aliens, and in explaining why alienage classifications are suspect it has referred pointedly to the position of resident aliens. *Mauclet*, 97 S. Ct. at 2122, 2123.

[141] Included within the statutory definition of nonimmigrants are tourists, students, trainees, diplomatic personnel, and journalists. 8 U.S.C. § 1101(a)(15) (A)–(L) (1970). For most nonimmigrants, the statute expressly requires as a precondition to entry that they have "a residence in a foreign country which [they have] no intention of abandoning." *Id.* at § 1101(a)(15)(B) (temporary visitors for business or pleasure); (F) (students); (H) (temporary workers); and (J) (exchange visitors). For all aliens in this category, an intention to reside permanently in the United States is ordinarily inconsistent with bona fide nonimmigrant status. HARPER, note 11 *supra*, at 228.

[142] With respect to taxes and the obligation of military service Congress has generally drawn no distinction between citizens and resident aliens, but at the same time has provided for different treatment of nonimmigrants. GORDON & ROSENFIELD, note 120 *supra*, at §§ 1.41, 1.42, 2.49.

zens who are temporarily present in the state. It may be perfectly rational to deny them benefits that are made available to the state's permanent residents. If strict scrutiny is required, however, a flat rule denying benefits to nonresident aliens would presumably have to fall. It seems unlikely that the state could show either that its purpose was important enough to warrant the classification or that the classification was necessary to accomplish the purpose.

In considering whether strict scrutiny is appropriate, one has to distinguish between two different types of statute: one that disadvantages nonresident aliens as part of a general policy of denying a benefit to all aliens, and another that confers a benefit on residents (alien and citizen) but denies the benefit to nonresidents (alien and citizen). With regard to a statute of the second type, I would argue that strict scrutiny is not appropriate. Although nonresident aliens are disadvantaged, it is clear on the face of the statute that the basis of the classification is their nonresidence rather than their alienage. Of course, an alien who is a nonresident for purposes of the federal immigration laws is not necessarily a nonresident as the state understands that term. Treating all nonresident aliens as nonresidents for state purposes involves some overinclusiveness. But the legislature's willingness to treat resident aliens as well as it treats citizens strongly suggests that the classification did not arise out of ill will or a stereotyped view of aliens or a desire to exploit a weak minority by imposing burdens on them while giving them few benefits. The classification does tend, to be sure, to ignore the real differences that exist among the various classes of nonimmigrants. The state is essentially saying that the costs of working out a more precise screening mechanism are great enough to outweigh the problems caused by mechanically relying on the alien's status under the federal immigration laws. That approach can raise serious problems of unfairness,[143] but the Court has made clear that it can deal with the most troublesome cases of this type under the rubric of the rational basis test.[144] As long as the state has keyed the statutory scheme to

---

[143] Moreno v. University of Maryland, 420 F. Supp. 541 (D. Md. 1976), *cert. granted sub. nom.* Elkins v. Moreno, 98 S. Ct. 260 (1977).

[144] Jimenez v. Weinberger, 417 U.S. 628 (1974); Cleveland Bd. of Educ. v. LaFleur, 414 U.S. 632 (1974); Vlandis v. Kline, 412 U.S. 441 (1973); Stanley v. Illinois, 405 U.S. 645 (1972). Where the state awards benefits on the basis of case-by-case screening, a court should presumably give less weight to the claim that reliance on the federal definition of nonresidence is required by considerations of administrative convenience. *Cf. Griffiths*, 413 U.S. at 725–27.

residence rather than alienage, I see no reason to bring out the strict scrutiny doctrine and obliterate the classification.

The situation is very different where a state denies a benefit to all aliens, immigrant and nonimmigrant alike. Although there might be good reason to deny the benefit to some aliens, or even to rule ineligible the entire category of nonimmigrants, the very fact that the state has based the classification on alienage is enough to call into question the validity of the statute as a whole. By its own terms the statute disadvantages the nonresident alien because he is an alien, not because he is a nonresident. Of course, if the statutory scheme includes other requirements that the nonimmigrant cannot satisfy, including a requirement of bona fide residence, the benefit may be withheld on those grounds. But the Court has no warrant to search for reasons why the legislature might have wanted to deny him the benefit as a nonresident. If the nonimmigrant would be eligible for the benefit but for his alienage, the Court should declare such a statute unconstitutional on its face.

The purpose of this inquiry into the reasons for treating alienage as a suspect classification was to see if these reasons should prove equally applicable to the federal government. Aliens stand in the same position with respect to the federal government as they do with respect to the states. The same problem of stigma is involved. They are as effectively excluded from the political process at the national level. Indeed, given their greater vulnerability to hostile federal action, especially deportation, they are even less likely to adopt an overtly political role. And aliens have suffered as long a history of purposeful unequal treatment at the hands of the federal government as they have at the hands of the states.[145] The federal government may seek to justify an alienage classification on the basis of several interests that a state cannot assert—for example, an interest in creating a bargaining chip for use in negotiating with other countries or an interest in preserving an incentive for aliens to seek naturalization. But a statute disadvantaging all or almost all aliens is a remarkably imprecise, if not irrational, way to go about serving these interests.[146] Most federal classifications based on alienage, like

[145] The so-called Palmer Raids of 1920, named for the Attorney General who carried them out, represent one of many possible examples. CHAFEE, FREE SPEECH IN THE UNITED STATES 196–240 (1948).

[146] To encourage naturalization one hardly needs to deny the benefit to aliens within their first five years of residence in the United States. Yet the statute at issue in

most such state classifications, are ultimately designed to enhance the economic well-being of members of the national polity at the expense of outsiders. Surely that is what the government was conceding in *Mathews v. Diaz* when it sought to justify the classification at issue there as a preference for persons with the greatest affinity to the United States. As a test of affinity, an alienage classification is seriously over- and underinclusive. But to hold the statute invalid the Court must find a principle that makes alienage classifications disfavored. In connection with state cases the Court has derived the necessary principle from the fact that aliens lack the political power to protect themselves from exploitation by the majority. By the same reasoning the principle must apply to the federal government.

The Court's description of aliens as a discrete and insular group lacking power could be said, however, to obscure rather than explain the real source of the principle. In *Takahashi*, which announced the "general policy" that all persons lawfully in the country shall enjoy "an equality of legal privileges with all citizens under non-discriminatory laws,"[147] the Court interwove arguments based on equal protection and the supremacy of federal law on the subject of aliens and immigration. Perhaps the principle of equal privileges for citizens and aliens is a creature of federal law and is imposed on the states by the Supremacy Clause. Calling alienage a suspect classification may be just another way of saying that federal law implicitly requires the states, except in cases of special need, to accord resident aliens the same treatment as citizens. On that assumption, it plainly makes no sense to say that a federal classification based on alienage is suspect.

Diaz, far from allowing such aliens to participate in the program, made them the only group of aliens unable to participate. *See* text at note 45 *supra*. Besides, if one can justify any particular act of discrimination against aliens on this theory, one can presumably also justify on this theory any (and every) imaginable act of discrimination against them. *Cf. Mauclet*, 97 S. Ct. at 2127. As for the interest in creating a bargaining chip, the use of resident aliens as hostages certainly involves a good deal of overkill. Some countries, perhaps the one from which the alien seeking the benefit comes, will already extend the particular benefit to American citizens when the situation is reversed. More commonly, the alien's country, operating under different constitutional norms, will withhold the benefit from Americans. But in all likelihood there are no negotiations on the subject under way or even remotely foreseeable, and few if any Americans are actually injured by the other country's policy. The nexus between the alienage classification and the desire to increase bargaining power seems, to say the least, remote. HENKIN, FOREIGN AFFAIRS AND THE CONSTITUTION 254 (1972).

[147] 334 U.S. at 420.

In many ways the Supremacy Clause argument is the strongest one that can be made against a state statute that draws lines on the basis of alienage. Indeed, it may be the only argument that the Court should have offered.[148] But in *Graham* the Court very pointedly distinguished the supremacy and equal protection arguments, indicating that either was sufficient to invalidate the statute.[149] In subsequent cases the Court has continued to differentiate the two arguments. Several times it has even declined to reach the supremacy issue because it has found the equal protection claim fatal to the statute.[150] Since the equal protection argument is not logically dependent on the Supremacy Clause argument, its rationale must be as fully applicable to the federal government as it is to the states.

III. The Plenary Federal Power over Aliens

The Court did not require the Government to show a compelling need to draw lines on the basis of alienage in determining eligibility for the supplementary Medicare insurance program. On the contrary, finding that the classification concerned "the relationship between the United States and our alien visitors,"[151] the Court held it immune from all but the most perfunctory judicial scrutiny:[152]

> Since decisions in these matters may implicate our relations with foreign powers, and since a wide variety of classifications must be defined in the light of changing political and economic circumstances, such decisions are frequently of a character more appropriate to either the Legislature or the Executive than to the Judiciary. . . . The reasons that preclude judicial review of political questions also dictate a narrow standard of review of decisions made by the Congress or the President in the area of immigration and naturalization.

---

[148] In *Graham*, Justice Harlan concurred in the Court's opinion insofar as it held the state statute invalid on supremacy grounds, and he did not reach the equal protection questions. 403 U.S. at 383. As long ago as *Truax v. Raich* the Court recognized the independence of the equal protection claim from the argument based on the Supremacy Clause. 239 U.S. 33 (1915).

[149] 403 U.S. at 376–77.

[150] *Sugarman*, 413 U.S. at 646; *Griffiths*, 413 U.S. at 718 n.3.

[151] 426 U.S. at 81.

[152] *Id.* at 81–82.

In the classic statement, the plenary power thesis requires judicial deference to "[t]he power of Congress to exclude aliens altogether from the United States, or to prescribe the terms and conditions upon which they may come to this country."[153] The Court's reliance on the plenary power thesis to explain the use of restrained review in *Diaz* is disappointing in two respects. First, the proposition that the federal government has nearly limitless power in this area is open to serious question on constitutional, historical, and logical grounds.[154] Even in the situations to which it was plainly intended to apply, it furnishes a dubious basis of decision. Second, it is by no means obvious that the situation presented in *Diaz* falls within the intended reach of the proposition. Yet without discussing the reasons for and against its application in this context, the Court relied on the proposition to defeat the aliens' equal protection claims.

The Court has consistently refused to question the judgment of Congress on which classes of aliens should be admitted to the United States. Even when Congress decided to make race a test of admissibility—in the laws barring entry of Chinese aliens on the basis of ancestry alone—the Court upheld the legislative judgment.[155] Indeed, it was in the *Chinese Exclusion Cases* that the Court first articulated the plenary power thesis. The Court's deferential attitude with respect to admission and exclusion questions was carried over into related areas. Thus, the Court declared that "[t]he right of a nation to expel or deport foreigners, who have not been naturalized or taken any steps towards becoming citizens of the country, rests upon the same grounds [as the power to exclude], and is as absolute and unqualified."[156] Congress has also enjoyed virtually unrestricted discretion in determining the classes of aliens that should be eligible for naturalization.[157] In all three areas—exclusion,

---

[153] Lem Moon Sing v. United States, 158 U.S. 538, 547 (1895). *See also* Nishimura Ekiu v. United States, 142 U.S. 651, 659 (1892).

[154] *See* Gordon & Rosenfield, note 120 *supra*, at § 4.3a, at 4–13 and n.6, and articles cited therein.

[155] *See, e.g.*, Fong Yue Ting v. United States, 149 U.S. 698 (1893); The Chinese Exclusion Case (Chae Chan Ping v. United States), 130 U.S. 581 (1889).

[156] *Fong Yue Ting*, 149 U.S. at 707. *See* Guan Chow Tok v. INS, 538 F.2d 36, 38 (2d Cir. 1976).

[157] *See* United States v. MacIntosh, 283 U.S. 605 (1931); Hein v. INS, 456 F.2d 1239 (5th Cir. 1972). *See generally*, Hertz, *Limits to the Naturalization Power*, 64 GEO. L. J. 1007 (1976); Note, 80 YALE L. J. 769 (1971).

deportation, and naturalization—the Court has refused to enforce the constitutional standards that control the exercise of other powers of the national government.

Just this past Term the Court reaffirmed its reluctance to scrutinize federal statutes dealing with immigration. In *Fiallo v. Bell*,[158] plaintiffs challenged an immigration provision on the grounds that it classified persons in a manner inconsistent with the equal protection requirements of the Fifth Amendment's Due Process Clause. But the injury alleged was not to the prospective immigrants whose position was affected by the provision. Given the Court's repeated insistence that no alien has a constitutionally protected right to enter the United States, plaintiffs undoubtedly assumed that the Court would dismiss out of hand any claim presented on behalf of the aliens seeking entry. To avoid the plenary power argument, plaintiffs attacked the statute on the grounds that it unconstitutionally discriminated among citizens and resident aliens with respect to their right to bring relatives to the United States from overseas.

Central to the immigration scheme is the goal of family reunification. Indeed, Congress has placed so much emphasis on this one value at the expense of all others that our immigration scheme can reasonably be said to reflect a "national policy of nepotism."[159] To the end of family reunification, Congress accords preferential treatment to persons who can establish certain family relationships to citizens and resident aliens. But the statute confers no privilege on aliens seeking entry. The privilege belongs to the citizen or resident alien who seeks to bring the overseas relative to the United States. Unless the citizen or resident alien seeks the preference on behalf of the prospective immigrant, no preference is available.[160]

One of the preferred relationships is that of parent and child. But as the statute defines the term, an illegitimate child is not the "child" of its father but only of its mother.[161] Neither the illegitimate child nor the father can give or receive a preference by virtue of the parent-child relationship. The effect of the definition is to discriminate among citizens and resident aliens according to legiti-

---

[158] 97 S. Ct. 1473 (1977).

[159] North & Houstoun, *The Characteristics and Role of Illegal Aliens in the U.S. Labor Market*, U.S. Dep't. of Labor Research and Development Contract No. 20-11-74-21, at 8 (1976).

[160] Gordon & Rosenfield, note 120 *supra*, at §3.5a.

[161] 8 U.S.C. § 1101(b)(1)(D) (1970).

macy and gender. A legitimate child who is a citizen or resident alien can confer an immigration preference on his alien father, but an identically situated illegitimate child cannot. By the same token, a woman can confer an immigration preference on her illegitimate alien child, but a man cannot obtain the same benefit for his. Had the statute discriminated between men and women or between legitimate and illegitimate children with respect to any other privilege or benefit—for example, welfare—I have little doubt that the Court would have held it invalid.[162] But because the benefit was paid out in the form of immigration preferences rather than dollars, the Court felt constrained to hold that ordinary standards of judicial scrutiny simply do not apply.

Plainly, the Court was not saying that the power to regulate immigration overrides all constitutional limitations. Although the Court has repeatedly described the power as plenary, the use of that term does not in itself suggest that the power is without limits under the Constitution. The Court recently declared that "the plenary power of Congress in matters of Indian affairs 'does not mean that all federal legislation concerning Indians is . . . immune from judicial scrutiny.'"[163] The Court has also said that "regulations of commerce which do not infringe some constitutional prohibition are within the plenary power conferred on Congress by the Commerce Clause."[164] And the Court has described the President's "delicate, plenary and exclusive power . . . as the sole organ of the federal government in the field of international relations" as a power that "like every other governmental power, must be exercised in subordination to the applicable provisions of the Constitution."[165]

In a number of cases the Court has emphasized the political nature of immigration policy questions, conveying the impression that the constitutional challenge to the policy might be nonjusticiable under the political question doctrine.[166] In fact, the Court has not

[162] Although the Court has not brought classifications based on gender or legitimacy within the suspect classification doctrine, it does scrutinize these classifications with unusual care. Trimble v. Gordon, 97 S. Ct. 1459 (1977), decided on the same day as *Fiallo*, and Craig v. Boren, 429 U.S. 190 (1976).

[163] Delaware Tribal Business Comm. v. Weeks, 430 U.S. 73, 83–84 (1977).

[164] United States v. Darby, 312 U.S. 100, 115 (1941).

[165] United States v. Curtiss-Wright Export Corp., 299 U.S. 304, 320 (1936).

[166] Harisiades v. Shaughnessy, 342 U.S. 580 (1952).

refrained from giving immigration statutes at least some minimal scrutiny.[167] And, at least as the Court has recently described it,[168] the political question doctrine does not seem applicable in this context.[169] *Fiallo*, in any event, specifically disclaimed reliance on the political question doctrine. As the Court correctly stated, "Our cases reflect acceptance of a limited judicial responsibility under the Constitution even with respect to the power of Congress to regulate the admission and exclusion of aliens."[170]

But why should the Court's responsibility be especially limited? The Constitution itself offers no textual support for the view that the Court's responsibility in this area is more narrowly confined than in any other area. Indeed, the Constitution does not even expressly grant the federal government the power to regulate immigration, much less to regulate it without regard to the dictates of the Constitution.[171] And one gets no help from analysis of the early congressional understanding of the breadth of federal immigration power. For more than three quarters of a century Congress imposed no significant restrictions on immigration. Of course, "[i]t is an accepted maxim of international law, that every sovereign nation has the power, as inherent in sovereignty, and essential to self-preservation, to forbid the entrance of foreigners within its dominions, or to admit them only in such cases and upon such conditions as it may see fit to prescribe."[172] But one can accept the validity of the maxim without conceding that congressional power in this area knows no limits.

The maxim indicates, in the first place, that the federal government has the power, as a matter of international law, to exclude or expel an alien over the objections of the alien's native country.[173] As a principle of international law, it speaks to the relations be-

---

[167] HENKIN, note 146 *supra*, at 213.

[168] Powell v. McCormack, 395 U.S. 486 (1969); *cf.* Baker v. Carr, 369 U.S. 186 (1962).

[169] Jalil v. Hampton, 460 F.2d 923, 925 n.1 (D.C. Cir. 1972); Note, 85 HARV. L. REV. 1130, 1155–56 (1972). *Cf. Delaware Tribal Business Comm.*, 430 U.S. at 83–85.

[170] 97 S. Ct. at 1478 n.5.

[171] The closest the Constitution comes to granting such a power is in Article I, § 8, cl. 4, which empowers Congress to "establish an uniform Rule of Naturalization."

[172] Nishimura Ekiu v. United States, 142 U.S. 651, 659 (1892).

[173] Hesse, *The Constitutional Status of the Lawfully Admitted Permanent Resident Alien: The Pre-1917 Cases*, 68 YALE L. J. 1578, 1586–87 (1959).

tween countries. The relations between the nation and the individuals with which it deals are still subject to regulation under domestic law, including in this case the Constitution. The maxim also has relevance to the allocation of power between the national and state governments. Preserving national sovereignty, carrying on international relations, and safeguarding the country from foreign dangers are all significant responsibilities of the national government. The fact that immigration inherently relates to these responsiblities is an appropriate reason for rejecting the view that the power to regulate immigration is "reserved to the states" for want of its enumeration in Article I of the Constitution.[174] But it is not in itself a reason for concluding that the standard of judicial review must be extraordinarily lenient. As Professor Henkin has pointed out, "[n]othing in the Constitution suggests that the rights of individuals in respect of foreign affairs are different from what they are in relation to other exercises of governmental power."[175]

The Court has carefully scrutinized congressional legislation bearing directly on foreign relations and national sovereignty. In *Perez v. Brownell*,[176] where the Court upheld a provision expatriating certain citizens, the Court declared that "[t]he restrictions confining Congress in the exercise of any of the powers expressly delegated to it in the Constitution apply with equal vigor when that body seeks to regulate our relations with other nations." Subsequently, the Court held invalid a statute providing for the denaturalization of certain naturalized citizens who take up residence outside the United States, notwithstanding the government's interest in avoiding "embarrassment in the conduct of our foreign relations."[177] The Court eventually concluded that congressional power to expatriate citizens is narrowly limited by the Constitution, and it will scrutinize with care a statute that purports to turn a citizen into an alien.[178]

In a case involving national security wiretapping, the Court re-

---

[174] U.S. Const., Amend. X; *cf.* Henderson v. Mayor of New York, 92 U.S. 259 (1876); The Passenger Cases (Smith v. Turner), 7 How. 283 (1849).

[175] Henkin, note 146 *supra*, at 252.

[176] 356 U.S. 44, 58 (1958).

[177] Schneider v. Rusk, 377 U.S. 163, 166 (1964).

[178] Afroyim v. Rusk, 387 U.S. 253 (1967). But *cf.* Rogers v. Bellei, 401 U.S. 815 (1971).

jected the government's claim that "internal security matters are too subtle and complex for judicial evaluation." Balancing "the duty of Government to protect the domestic security [against] the potential danger posed by unreasonable surveillance to individual privacy and free expression,"[179] the Court came out on the side of the individuals and against the government. Notwithstanding Justice Harlan's dissenting argument that "the scope of the judicial function in passing upon the activities of the Executive Branch of the Government in the field of foreign affairs is very narrowly restricted,"[180] the Court denied the government an injunction against publication of the Pentagon Papers, rejecting the government's "good-faith claims . . . that publication [would] work serious damage to the country."[181] And it has enforced Fourth Amendment limitations on the government's right to interrogate and search persons even where the search and interrogation were part of the government's overall strategy to identify illegal immigrants and protect the integrity of the immigration scheme.[182]

It is no answer to say that each of these cases involved an interference with the rights of citizens. The whole point of the plaintiffs' claim in *Fiallo* was that the government had denied equal protection to citizens by classifying them (not the aliens seeking entry) according to gender and legitimacy. Besides, the Court has not suggested that the Bill of Rights is unavailable to aliens when they are victimized by action of the federal government. Although the Court has never upset a deportation provision on the grounds that it classified aliens unfairly, it has at least recognized the government's constitutional obligation to give an alien a hearing before expelling him from the country.[183] The government cannot seize the property of a nonenemy alien without complying with the requirements of the Fifth Amendment.[184] Nor can it impose criminal

---

[179] United States v. U.S. District Court, 407 U.S. 297, 314–15, 320 (1972).

[180] New York Times Co. v. United States, 403 U.S. 713, 756 (1971).

[181] *Id.* at 733 (White, J., concurring).

[182] United States v. Brignoni-Ponce, 422 U.S. 873 (1975); Almeida-Sanchez v. United States, 413 U.S. 266 (1973). But *cf.* United States v. Martinez-Fuerte, 428 U.S. 543 (1976).

[183] Woodby v. INS, 385 U.S. 276 (1966); Kwong Hai Chew v. Colding, 344 U.S. 590 (1953); The Japanese Immigrant Case (Yamataya v. Fisher), 189 U.S. 86 (1903).

[184] Russian Volunteer Fleet v. United States, 282 U.S. 481 (1931).

penalties on an alien—even one who entered the country unlawfully—without observing the limitations of the Bill of Rights.[185]

In recent years the Supreme Court has edged away from its most extreme statements concerning the limited scope of judicial review in this context.[186] A number of lower federal courts have gone even further.[187] But despite some apparent misgivings about the self-imposed limitation on its role in this area, the Court is unwilling to abandon the plenary power thesis. In *Fiallo* the Court referred to an often-quoted statement of Justice Frankfurter's in a 1954 opinion for the Court:[188]

> In light of the expansion of the concept of substantive due process as a limitation upon all powers of Congress, even the war power, . . . much could be said for the view, were we writing on a clean slate, that the Due Process Clause qualifies the scope of political discretion heretofore recognized as belonging to Congress in regulating the entry and deportation of aliens. . . .
>
> But the slate is not clean. As to the extent of the power of Congress under review, there is not merely "a page of history," . . . but a whole volume . . . .
>
> We are not prepared to deem ourselves wiser or more sensitive to human rights than our predecessors, especially those who have been most zealous in protecting civil liberties under the Constitution.

In *Fiallo* the Court indicated that it was still not "inclined to reconsider this line of cases."[189]

The irony of it all is that in the years since Justice Frankfurter wrote those words, the members of the Court have shown little reluctance to "deem [themselves] wiser or more sensitive to human rights than [their] predecessors." The modern chapter in the volume of history to which Justice Frankfurter referred was written by the Court in the early 1950s—a time when it was much more

185 Wong Wing v. United States, 163 U.S. 228 (1896).

186 Gordon & Rosenfield, note 120 *supra*, at § 4.3a, at 4–13.

187 Francis v. INS, 532 F.2d 268 (2d Cir. 1976); *cf.* Vissian v. INS, 548 F.2d 325 (2d Cir. 1975); De Pena v. Kissinger, 409 F. Supp. 1182 (S.D. N.Y. 1976); Chinese American Civic Council v. Attorney General, 396 F. Supp. 1250, 1252–53 (D.D.C. 1975).

188 Galvan v. Press, 347 U.S. 522, 530–32 (1954).

189 97 S. Ct. at 1478 n.4. The Court pointed out that it had declined to reconsider this line of cases just a few years earlier in Kleindienst v. Mandel, 408 U.S. 753, 767 (1972).

prepared than now to defer to the federal government in a wide range of matters involving internal security and foreign affairs. Since then the Court has wiped the slate clean in a number of different contexts, imposing constitutional obligations on the federal government and the states in ways that Justice Frankfurter could hardly have foreseen in 1954. In particular, the Court's understanding of the constitutional position of aliens has changed dramatically. Moreover, just one week before Justice Frankfurter made the statement, the Court overruled *Plessy v. Ferguson*,[190] a decision of the same vintage as the cases upholding the Chinese exclusion laws and reflecting the same general attitude toward discrimination on the basis of race. It was also in 1954 that the Court first put real teeth into the equal protection component of the Fifth Amendment's Due Process Clause.[191]

Nevertheless, the Court remains committed to a narrow standard of review in the area of immigration and naturalization because it believes, as it said in *Mathews v. Diaz*,[192] that "[t]he reasons that preclude judicial review of political questions" dictate that narrow standard. The Court did not elaborate on those reasons. But it almost certainly had in mind what Professor Bickel has described as the basis of the political question doctrine:[193]

> [T]he court's sense of lack of capacity, compounded in unequal parts of the strangeness of the issue and the suspicion that it will have to yield more often and more substantially to expediency than to principle; the sheer momentousness of it, which unbalances judgment and prevents one from subsuming the normal calculations of probabilities; the anxiety not so much that judicial judgment will be ignored, as that perhaps it should be, but won't.

The formulation of an immigration policy requires the drawing of an extraordinary number of lines, many of them necessarily arbitrary. As long as the country hopes to impose a limitation on the number of immigrants who can enter, the decision to give priority to one class of immigrants will come at the expense of other poten-

---

190 163 U.S. 537 (1896).

191 Bolling v. Sharpe, 347 U.S. 497 (1954).

192 426 U.S. at 81–82.

193 Bickel, *The Passive Virtues*, 75 Harv. L. Rev. 40, 75 (1961).

tial immigrants. Thus, the invalidation of any one rule could have ramifications throughout the entire system. The rules are very detailed, because we are determined to keep some limit on the discretionary authority of the government officials who administer the system. Applicants with similar qualifications are often treated differently, because we cannot admit all who would like to come. And because the policy is designed in considerable part to serve this country's selfish interest in admitting those who can contribute most, the rules often appear cynical and harsh. Moreover, immigration rules must be drawn with diplomatic considerations in mind; other countries are likely to view with great displeasure any provision that tends to disadvantage their citizens.[194] The Court is undoubtedly fearful of becoming enmeshed in the process of formulating immigration policy. Too much judicial scrutiny could bring down the entire system of intricate and interconnected rules, reducing it all to a shambles.

The Court's fear is certainly reasonable. Indeed, it is hard to see how the government could ever show that it had a compelling need to give an immigration preference to one alien rather than another. But the government's legitimate interest in flexibility does not require immunity from careful judicial scrutiny for every piece of federal legislation that has some bearing on aliens or immigration.

It is in the area of admission and exclusion of aliens that the government's need for flexibility is greatest. But the Court can accommodate that need within the ordinary standards of judicial review. Our immigration rules disadvantage a great many aliens by making it difficult or impossible for them to settle in this country. Some of the distinctions drawn among competing applicants for admission are harsh, arbitrary, and perhaps unfair. But how much fairness does the United States owe to aliens who reside in other countries and whose only contact with the United States is that they have decided they want to live here? A person who is physically outside the United States and who has neither a stake in the country nor any legal tie to it cannot make the same demands on the government as the citizen or resident alien. That is not to say that the Constitution does not apply at all when the federal government acts against

---

[194] Konvitz, Civil Rights in Immigration 6-7 (1953), describing the very negative reaction of the government and people of Japan to this country's decision in 1924 to exclude the Japanese from entry.

aliens overseas.[195] But where the alien's only complaint is that the classifications of the immigration laws are unreasonable—for example, because they give too much priority to relatives of American citizens or to persons with certain skills or to persons fleeing persecution—the Court should have no difficulty holding that the classifications are reasonable enough to satisfy whatever obligation this country owes to those who would like to settle here.[196] The Court does not have to concede the government plenary power to justify the result.

The situation is very different, however, when an immigration provision disadvantages a citizen of the United States. The government must have the same obligation to treat its citizens fairly in connection with the immigration laws as it does in connection with the welfare, selective service, or tax laws. Not every injury to a citizen should require the invalidation of an immigration provision. For the most part, if the injury results from a classification that is reasonably related to a legitimate governmental interest, the Court can uphold the classification. But a classification that distinguishes among citizens on grounds that are disfavored or suspect must receive special scrutiny. Thus, if Congress were to decree that white citizens can confer an immigration preference on their alien relatives but black citizens cannot, one can hardly believe that the Court would uphold the classification.[197] Absent a compelling interest, the government cannot inflict that kind of injury on a class of citizens defined in terms of race. The immigration provision at issue in *Fiallo* classified citizens in terms of gender and legitimacy. While these classifications do not require scrutiny as strict as that applied to a

---

[195] Hart, *The Power of Congress to Limit the Jurisdiction of Federal Courts: An Exercise in Dialectic*, 66 HARV. L. REV. 1362 (1953); *cf.* Reid v. Covert, 354 U.S. 1, 5–14 (1957).

[196] HENKIN, note 146 *supra*, at 267: "In the United States virtually all the safeguards of the Constitution apply to all who are here—citizens, alien residents, even those sojourning temporarily or in transit. Abroad, constitutional protection for the individual against governmental action is enjoyed by American citizens, perhaps also by alien residents of the United States who are temporarily abroad. But an inhabitant of a foreign country presumably cannot invoke the Constitution when he is aggrieved, say, by discrimination in American trade or immigration policy . . . ." It is not clear that an alien with no tie to the United States would even have standing to challenge a statutory classification that made his admission as an immigrant difficult or impossible. *Cf.* Brownell v. Tom We Shung, 352 U.S. 180, 184 n.3 (1956); Johnson v. Eisentrager, 339 U.S. 763, 771 (1950); Chinese American Civic Council v. Attorney General, 396 F. Supp. 1250, 1251 (D.D.C. 1975).

[197] Fiallo v. Levi, 406 F. Supp. 162, 170 (E.D. N.Y. 1975) (Weinstein, J., dissenting).

racial classification, they certainly need more than the token review carried out by the Court in *Fiallo*.[198]

It is not always easy, of course, to distinguish between the injury to a citizen and the injury to a prospective immigrant. For example, Congress might conclude that persons of a particular race or national origin make undesirable residents of the United States. To prevent citizens of that race or national origin from concentrating in certain parts of the country, Congress might order their dispersal. Obviously, the Court would insist upon a showing of compelling interest to justify the order.[199] But what if Congress were instead to order the exclusion from the United States of any alien of that race or national origin? In my view, such a classification would also require strict scrutiny, not because of the injury to the aliens denied admission, but rather because of the injury to American citizens of the same race or national origin who are stigmatized by the classification. When Congress declares that aliens of Chinese or Irish or Polish origin are excludable on the grounds of ancestry alone, it fixes a badge of opprobrium on citizens of the same ancestry. The point is not that aliens have a right to enter the United States or to have their eligibility for admission determined without regard to race. But Congress does have a duty to its own citizens. Except when necessary to protect a compelling interest, Congress cannot implement a policy that has the effect of labeling some group of citizens as inferior to others because of their race or national origin.

In any event, the situation presented in *Mathews v. Diaz*—discrimination against aliens with respect to eligibility for the Medicare insurance program—seems to present a very different problem. The classification inflicts an injury on lawful residents of the United States—on members of the American community. While

---

[198] Of course, citizens may often believe that they are injured by the immigration scheme because they cannot secure admission for someone whose presence they desire. For example, the immigration laws accord no preference to nieces or nephews of American citizens, and, to the extent that he finds it more difficult to bring his favorite niece or nephew to this country, an American citizen is injured. But no one has suggested that uncles as a class are in need of special judicial protection, and the provision should be upheld as long as it has a rational basis, which it surely has. On the other hand, if Congress were to draw lines among uncles on the basis of race or national origin, allowing some to bring in their nieces and nephews but not others, the provision would require much more rigorous judicial scrutiny.

[199] Korematsu v. United States, 323 U.S. 214 (1944).

the United States may owe little in the way of fairness to aliens who have never lived in this country, it certainly has an obligation to deal fairly with aliens who make this country their home and who bear all the burdens of citizenship, including the obligation to pay taxes and serve in the armed forces. As residents of the country they develop ties and loyalties that may be every bit as strong as those of a citizen. Moreover, the reasons for extraordinary deference to the political branches on immigration matters do not seem to have any force here. When the government distinguishes between citizens and aliens with respect to welfare benefits or federal employment, the Court can scrutinize the legislation without fear of enmeshing itself in the complex process of formulating immigration policy. Although the Court may fear that it lacks the capacity to handle problems involving the admission and exclusion of aliens because of the "strangeness of the issue and the suspicion that it will have to yield more often and more substantially to expediency than to principle,"[200] that is no reason to shy away from the question presented in *Diaz.* The issue was no more strange than the routine question of equal protection. Nor was there any reason to fear that a principled basis of decision would be more elusive than in other areas. The government policy at issue was not "vitally and intricately interwoven with contemporaneous policies in regard to the conduct of foreign relations, the war power, and the maintenance of a republican form of government."[201] And there was no danger that a judicial decision in favor of the aliens' claim could disrupt the interlocking set of rules that constitute the nation's immigration policy.

But the nub of the problem is that at some level the equal protection issue presented in *Diaz* does run together with the admission and exclusion issue presented in *Fiallo.* If aliens have no right to enter the United States and the federal government can exclude them on any remotely reasonable basis, can it not condition their admission on acceptance of any terms it dictates?[202] In fact, conditions are commonly imposed on entering aliens. In the

---

[200] Bickel, note 193 *supra*, at 75.

[201] *Harisiades*, 342 U.S. at 588–89.

[202] The Supreme Court has expressly indicated that Congress can impose such conditions as it deems appropriate. *Lem Moon Sing*, 158 U.S. at 547, quoted in text *supra*, at note 153.

best-known example, most nonimmigrants—including foreign students and tourists—are admitted without the right to work in this country.[203] Unless they accept that condition they cannot enter. And if they do obtain employment without government approval, they can be deported for violating the terms of their admission. No comparable rules apply to citizens or resident aliens. If a foreign student or tourist were to challenge this discriminatory treatment, one could reasonably respond that the bar to employment was a condition of entry. If the term was unacceptable to the nonimmigrant, he should not have come.[204] Is it not also possible to say, then, that aliens admitted for permanent residence are admitted subject to certain conditions? And one of these conditions may be that they have no right to participate in the Medicare supplementary insurance program. On that assumption, the Court should decline to give strict scrutiny to the provision denying resident aliens an opportunity to participate in the program, because the provision does not, properly understood, discriminate against resident aliens. Its real impact is against prospective immigrants to the United States, who have no right to enter and must come on whatever conditions Congress imposes.

But calling the Medicare rule a condition on entry cannot change the essential nature of the inquiry. If the government can enforce this condition, it is not because the entering alien agreed to it, but rather because the restriction itself is, according to some as yet undetermined standard, inherently reasonable. Otherwise, the government could impose the most appalling restrictions on aliens by inducing them to "accept" these restrictions as the price of admission to the United States. In a decision that Professor Hart has called "one of the bulwarks of the Constitution,"[205] the Court denied the federal government the power to impose criminal punishment on aliens without a judicial trial.[206] The decision would have to be the same even if the alien had agreed, as a condition on entry, that he could be punished without the safeguards of a

[203] Gordon & Rosenfield, note 120 *supra*, at § 2.6b, at 2–48.

[204] In fact the restriction has been upheld in the face of an attack on constitutional grounds. Pilapil v. INS, 424 F.2d 6 (10th Cir. 1970); *cf.* Silverman v. Rogers, 437 F.2d 102 (1st Cir. 1970).

[205] Hart, note 195 *supra*, at 1387.

[206] Wong Wing v. United States, 163 U.S. 228 (1896).

criminal trial.[207] Calling immigration a privilege rather than a right does not help at all.[208]

To determine what conditions are reasonable, one has to make the same kind of inquiry as is needed to determine whether a classification is reasonable for purposes of equal protection analysis. It is no easier to choose the appropriate standard of review or to find some neutral principle that dictates the correct result. The same "political" issues are necessarily involved. The Court has suggested that for a state to deny benefits to aliens because of an interest in enhancing the economic position of citizens is to make discrimination "an end in itself."[209] The interest has no logical stopping point; if it furnishes a sufficient reason to deny aliens any particular benefit, it presumably can also justify the denial of every possible benefit.[210] Even in the context of federal government discrimination against aliens, the Court has cast some doubt on the legitimacy of this government interest.[211] Surely it does not suddenly become more legitimate when made the basis of an implicit condition on entry than it was when made the basis of a classification among persons already here.

But the condition-on-entry argument does have some significance. In cases involving state discrimination against aliens, the Court has found a material principle, extrinsic to the Equal Protection Clause itself,[212] that makes it presumptively unreasonable to draw lines between citizens and aliens. The principle was identified by the Court as the "general policy that all persons lawfully in this country shall abide 'in any state' on an equality of legal privileges with all citizens under non-discriminatory laws."[213] A

---

[207] By the same token, the alien's right to a hearing before deportation, *see* note 183 *supra*, cannot be withdrawn by making the waiver of that right a condition on entry to the United States.

One of the ironic aspects of a condition-on-entry argument is that it requires a special effort to show that the alien who enters the United States surreptitiously is not better off than the alien who enters lawfully and accepts, implicitly or explicitly, the conditions of entry. *Cf.* Hess v. Pawloski, 274 U.S. 352 (1927).

[208] Van Alstyne, *The Demise of the Right-Privilege Distinction in Constitutional Law*, 81 HARV. L. REV. 1439 (1968).

[209] Truax v. Raich, 239 U.S. 33, 41 (1915). *See* text *supra* at note 125.

[210] *See* Examining Bd. of Engineers v. Flores de Otero, 426 U.S. 572, 605–06 (1976).

[211] *See* text *supra* at note 27.

[212] *Cf.* Sandalow, note 101 *supra*, at 656.

[213] Takahashi v. Fish & Game Comm'n, 334 U.S. 410, 420 (1948), *quoted in* Graham v. Richardson, 403 U.S. 365, 374 (1971).

restriction imposed on aliens by the federal government—whether called an alienage classification or a condition on entry—undermines that general policy. But the critical question is whether the policy has any application to the federal government. Calling the restriction a condition on entry drives home the fact that federal law is what created the category of "resident alien." Why can't the federal government define the category any way it wants?

To answer that question one has to know the source of the material principle applied in the state alienage cases. If aliens are entitled to an "equality of legal privileges" only because federal law says they are, then surely the federal government can exempt itself from the operation of the general principle. But if the material principle is only the creation of federal law, why did the Court go beyond the Supremacy Clause issue in the state cases and hold that the discrimination against aliens was also a violation of the Equal Protection Clause? For 200 years the United States has welcomed immigrants and permitted them to live and work here on essentially the same terms as citizens.[214] The expectation that aliens and citizens will be treated alike, at least with respect to civil and economic matters, is to a large extent the creation of federal immigration policy. But perhaps we have reached the point where that expectation has become so much a part of our thinking about the rights of aliens that it limits the immigration policy that created it. In the state cases the Court has implicitly held that it violates our fundamental sense of fairness for a state to establish two classes of residents within its borders, both classes bearing the same burdens but one class receiving disproportionate benefits. It can only trivialize that conclusion for the Court to turn around and say that the federal government is free to discriminate against aliens in the very ways that the states cannot.

If the Court is to give strict scrutiny to federal provisions that discriminate against aliens, it must find in the Constitution itself, as opposed to the federal immigration laws, the proposition that resident aliens are presumptively entitled to the same treatment as citizens. That presumption would not forbid the imposition of all conditions or restrictions on immigration. The federal government could still require, for example, that at the time of entry aliens have skills or qualifications that make them desirable as immigrants. And

---

[214] *Cf.* Bickel, The Morality of Consent 33–54 (1975).

the Court could review these requirements under a very lenient standard of review. What would be disfavored are conditions or restrictions that linger on after the immigrant has taken up permanent residence. For it is these continuing restrictions that divide the community in a manner inconsistent with the material principle.

The question, in other words, is whether the Court can draw a distinction between an immigration rule that operates as a condition subsequent and one that operates as a condition precedent.[215] The fundamental difference between the two becomes apparent if one reformulates any of the present immigration rules as conditions subsequent. Take, for example, the labor certification requirement. Because of congressional concern that immigration to the United States could have an adverse effect on the economic position of American workers, Congress has required prospective immigrants falling into certain categories to obtain certification by the Department of Labor that no Americans are able, willing, qualified, and available to do the work that the alien has been hired to do.[216] The purpose and effect of the requirement is to discriminate among prospective immigrants, giving preference to those with skills

---

[215] In considering the rights of naturalized citizens, the Court has implicitly recognized the difference between the two types of conditions. The conditions precedent to naturalization—residence, good moral character, and the rest—are all within the constitutional power of Congress. But a condition subsequent would not be constitutional, because it would create a "second-class citizenship." Schneider v. Rusk, 377 U.S. 163, 169 (1964). In analyzing a restriction on the rights of naturalized citizens that operated as a condition subsequent, the Court started from the "premise that the rights of citizenship of the native born and of the naturalized person are of the same dignity and are coextensive." *Id.* at 165. The condition subsequent infringed this material principle, and in the absence of some compelling governmental interest it had to be struck down under the Due Process Clause of the Fifth Amendment.

In a related context, however, the Court has refused to acknowledge a difference between the operation of a condition precedent and a condition subsequent. Congress has generally conferred citizenship at birth on some children born to American parents overseas, even though these children have no constitutional right to citizenship. In some situations a child who obtains this *ius sanguinis* citizenship at birth will forfeit it unless he takes up residence in the United States as required by statute. 8 U.S.C. § 1401 (b) (1970 and Supp. V, 1975). A person who had lost American citizenship for failure to comply with the condition subsequent brought a challenge to its constitutionality, arguing that the condition subsequent was impermissible because it created two classes of citizens, one more easily expatriated than the other. The Court saw no reason to allow Congress less room to impose conditions subsequent than precedent, and it held the expatriation provision constitutional. Rogers v. Bellei, 401 U.S. 815 (1971). What the Court was really saying was that it could discern no material principle requiring Congress to treat the two classes of citizens (persons born to American parents overseas, on the one hand, and all other citizens, on the other) alike. The classification was not, in the Court's view, unreasonable, and Congress could create two classes of citizens if it so desired.

[216] 8 U.S.C. § 1182 (a)(14) (1970).

needed in the United States. But the consequences of this discrimination are visited upon persons who are not residents of the United States and who have no significant tie to the country. Congress certainly has constitutional power to sort out prospective immigrants according to this standard.

It is important to note, however, that the effects of the condition are spent before the alien establishes permanent residence in the United States. The alien can leave the job for which he was certified and compete on an equal basis with American workers for any job that he would like to hold. To prevent that competition, Congress might decide that the labor certification requirement should operate on a continuing basis even after the alien establishes "permanent" residence. All immigrants might be required, for example, to renew their labor certification each year. Whenever it develops that American workers are able, willing, qualified, and available to do the work that the alien is doing, the alien would have to leave the country.

This condition subsequent on entry would effectively eliminate the category of "resident alien." The terms of admission would resemble those imposed on agricultural workers brought in from Mexico for many years after World War II.[217] All aliens admitted to the United States would be, in effect, braceros. The bracero program produced an extraordinary amount of controversy, in part because the whole point of it—bringing workers into the United States when their skills were needed but forcing them out when their skills were no longer needed—was so plainly inconsistent with the traditional premises of the country's immigration policy.[218] If Congress were to eliminate the category of resident alien and allow aliens to enter as nonimmigrants or not at all, there would be literally nothing left of those traditional premises. But the premises are not established in the Constitution, and it is hard to see why Con-

[217] *See generally* Subcomm. No. 1 of the House Comm. on the Judiciary, Study of Population and Immigration Problems, Special Series No. 11, at 27–48 (1963); Report of Select Comm'n on Western Hemisphere Immigration 91–93 (1968); GALARZA, MERCHANTS OF LABOR (1964).

[218] North and Houstoun, the authors of a very instructive study on illegal immigration, have pointed out that "[a]t bottom, a decision to use aliens—nonimmigrants [such as braceros] or illegals—as a supply of cheap, low-skill labor is an attempt to acquire that labor and to adjure its economic and social costs." NORTH & HOUSTOUN, note 159 *supra*, at 169. *Cf.* Berger, *Those Convenient Migrants: Europe's Expendable Work Force*, 221 NATION 369 (1975).

gress would lack the power to destroy them. After all, until the early 1920s all entering aliens were immigrants. The category of nonimmigrant aliens came into existence as an essential part of the scheme of numerical limitation on immigration. The goal was not to limit the number of aliens coming to the United States for any purpose, but to limit the number coming to establish permanent residence. In return for an exemption from the numerical limitation, nonimmigrants were denied many of the rights of the immigrant alien, including the right to reside in this country permanently.

To resolve the equal protection issue presented in *Mathews v. Diaz*, the Court did not have to explore the ultimate limits of federal power to reshape the fundamental precepts of the nation's immigration policy. The provision restricting alien participation in the Medicare insurance program was not in any obvious way concerned with immigration. It did not operate as an express condition on the right of resident aliens to enter the United States or to make this country their home. There are two reasons why this should make a difference. The first concerns the question of fair notice. The United States discriminates against aliens in a great many different ways. Aliens who enter the United States as permanent residents are not formally advised of any of these restrictions, and they are doubtless unaware of most of them. They are not asked to enter into any formal agreement with the United States, renouncing all claim to certain privileges in return for the chance to enter. If every one of these restrictions is to be considered a condition on entry, surely we have some obligation to give prospective immigrants adequate notice of the terms they are accepting when they take advantage of the opportunity to immigrate. Still, the problems of inadequate notice are not all that serious here since most prospective immigrants probably assume that they will be subject to some restrictions, even if they cannot anticipate the precise terms.[219] Moreover, the terms are probably not the sort that would, if known, persuade prospective immigrants that the bargain is a bad one and that they should therefore stay home. In this sense, the failure to give adequate notice is certainly an error, but perhaps it is a harmless one.

---

[219] For one thing, the countries from which most aliens come will, in all likelihood, impose on their alien residents the same kinds of restrictions that the United States has imposed on aliens living here. Note, 8 U. CALIF. DAVIS L. REV. 1, 21 (1975).

There is, however, a second reason for concern about the failure to make the condition formal and explicit. And this concern is a good deal more troublesome than the problem of notice. Some conditions on admission—for example, the restriction against foreign students' working in the United States—are open and notorious. The existence of the restriction is known not only to the alien seeking entry, but also to all Americans concerned about the formulation of immigration policy. The restriction is plainly an integral part of the immigration scheme, and it is debated in terms of its impact on immigration policy: How many aliens can the country reasonably admit? What impact would foreign students have on the labor market? How important to the students' educational program is the opportunity to take employment? What impact will the restriction have on the students' attitude toward the United States? What will be its impact on our relations with other countries? The very fact that the issue is debated in these terms and in the open suggests that there is political accountability for the decision. The students themselves do not, of course, participate in the decision. But the Court can reasonably presume that the political branches have made the decision on the basis of the fairest possible balancing of the students' interests against the interests of the United States in protecting itself from the impact of unrestricted immigration. Indeed, considering that several million nonimmigrants enter the United States each year, the need for a rule imposing some limit on the right of these nonimmigrants to work could well be described as compelling. And while nonimmigrant students do not enjoy the benefits of citizenship, they are at least spared many of the burdens (military service, for example) that fall on citizens and resident aliens alike. That in itself is evidence that the political process has acted fairly in balancing their interests against the interests of the United States.

Unlike the rules that prevent nonimmigrants from accepting employment, the great majority of the statutory provisions discriminating against resident aliens, certainly including the provision at issue in *Diaz*, have no explicit connection with immigration. They are not codified in the immigration laws. For the most part they did not originate in immigration legislation and were not acted upon by the congressional committees primarily concerned with immigration. They are not part of any bargain between the government and the aliens who enter. While it is doubtless true that most immigrants would come to the United States even if informed of all the implicit conditions, it is no less true that we would admit them anyway even if the conditions could not be enforced. The restrictions are simply not a part of the congressional judgment about the classes of aliens that should be admitted to the United States. Aliens are subject to discriminatory treatment because Congress, in the course of deciding who should receive the benefits of a particular program, decides to leave them out. Some members of Congress may believe that the economic integrity of the program will be enhanced by denying participation to a group of taxpayers who lack the political power to make sure that they are included. Others may want to leave aliens out because they see aliens in stereotyped terms and believe they are all undeserving of the benefit. Still others, recognizing that aliens are often excluded from government programs, may act out of habit. There may, to be sure, be good reasons for excluding aliens from the program, including reasons intimately connected with immigration policy. But the state governments also may have good reasons for distinguishing between citizens and aliens. The point of treating alienage as a suspect classification is to make clear that the legislature must have more than just a good reason for treating them differently from citizens, because resident aliens cannot protect their own interests. Given their political powerlessness, courts cannot presume that the legislature has evaluated their interests fairly. In the absence of a strong and legitimate government interest that requires the drawing of lines on the basis of alienage, federal government discrimination against resident aliens should meet the same fate as comparable discrimination against aliens by the state governments.

IV. Conclusion

Plainly, the federal government's powers in dealing with alien residents of the country are broader than the powers of the states. But it hardly follows that all federal statutes dealing with aliens are constitutional or that federal power in this area is limitless. In *Mathews v. Diaz* the Court refused to acknowledge the tension between two basic facts: first, the reasons for treating alienage as a suspect classification apply as forcefully to the federal government as to the states, and second, the power to determine the standards for admission of aliens must inevitably give rise to some power to regulate what aliens can and cannot do in this country. The Court disposed of the problem by turning its back on the proposition that alienage is a suspect classification, and it left the federal government with extraordinary latitude to legislate in this area. That is no more satisfying a solution to the problem than prohibiting all conditions on entry the effects of which linger on after the alien establishes permanent residence. What the Court should have recognized is that conditions of this type must be disfavored because they undermine the traditional premise of the country's immigration policy—that resident aliens are virtually full-fledged members of the American community, sharing the burdens of membership as well as the benefits. At some point the Court may have to recognize that the political branches of the federal government have decided to nullify that basic premise. But that issue was not presented in *Diaz*. The statute was not on its face concerned with immigration and it reflected no judgment—express or implied—about the classes of aliens that should be admitted to the United States. The Court must scrutinize a statute of this type with care, because it carries precisely the same risk of impermissible injury to aliens as the state statutes struck down in the years since alienage was first declared a suspect classification under the Equal Protection Clause. The need for careful scrutiny is especially great where the statute withholds benefits from aliens, like welfare or the opportunity to work for the federal government, that resident aliens have helped to pay for with their taxes.

I cannot pretend that the line between immigration matters and nonimmigration matters is easily marked.[220] But the difficulty of drawing the line is no reason to abandon the effort altogether. Alienage is not a run-of-the-mill suspect classification, and it presents problems of analysis not associated with other suspect classifications. For example, the line between civil rights and political rights is also obscure, and yet the Court has suggested that it will try to draw such a line in state alienage cases.[221] Besides, what makes it seem so difficult to draw the line between immigration matters and

[220] *Id.* at 18–22.

[221] *See* Perkins v. Smith, 370 F. Supp. 134 (D. Md. 1974), *aff'd mem.*, 426 U.S. 913 (1976) (service on grand and petit juries); Skafte v. Rorex, 553 P.2d 830 (Colo. 1976), *app. dismissed*, 97 S. Ct. 1638 (1977).

nonimmigration matters is the assumption that all statutes falling on one side of the line must be constitutional, whereas all statutes on the other side must be unconstitutional. But that assumption is unwarranted. There may be situations where the federal government, like a state, has a compelling reason to classify on the basis of alienage even though it is not purporting to make a judgment about immigration policy. And even where the federal government is exercising its undeniable power to establish immigration policy and determine the classes of persons that can enter the United States, its power must still be confined within constitutional limits. A condition subsequent on entry is very different from a condition precedent precisely because its impact is felt by residents of the United States, to whom the government has an obligation of fair dealing. When the government acts against residents of the country pursuant to the immigration power, just as when it acts against them pursuant to any other constitutional source of authority, it must act in compliance with the standards of the Constitution.

Because the Court would not try to accommodate federal power to regulate immigration to the need of aliens for special judicial protection, it concluded, in effect, that there cannot even be a reasonable doubt about the constitutionality of federal legislation in this area.[222] This is in many ways the most distressing aspect of the Court's opinion. I am not suggesting that the Court use "doubts" about the constitutionality of federal immigration legislation to rewrite the immigration laws. But the Court can and should play the role that it plays in other contexts—asking questions about the purposes of a statutory provision, pointing out the lack of fit between the effect of a provision and the purpose it was designed to serve, and generally making Congress aware of the constitutional norms that must limit legislative action. The Court has traditionally declined to play that role whenever it believed that immigration was even remotely involved. Worse, it has gone to the opposite extreme and insisted that the immigration power is as nearly limitless as any power of the national government. Whatever the Court's intention, its repeated insistence that Congress has plenary power to act against aliens in any way it wants must be seen as an invitation to Congress to act capriciously and without significant concern for the legitimate interests of resident aliens.

---

[222] *Cf.* Hart, note 195 *supra*, at 1395.

In marked contrast to its opinion in *Mathews v. Diaz*, the Court's opinion in *Hampton v. Mow Sun Wong* implicitly acknowledged that federal discrimination against resident aliens raises difficult constitutional questions. The invalidation of the Civil Service Commission rule, not for want of federal power but rather because of the manner in which the rule was enacted, represents exactly the sort of imaginative and moderate judicial approach that could enhance the process of policymaking in the immigration area. Yet *Diaz*, decided on the same day as *Mow Sun Wong* and in an opinion by the same author, was a great deal less solicitous of the aliens' constitutional claims. And the Court's analysis in that case apparently resolved the issues said to have been left open in *Mow Sun Wong*, and in a way that immunizes all federal legislation bearing on aliens from any significant constitutional scrutiny. It remains to be seen whether in subsequent cases the Court will follow the approach of *Mow Sun Wong*, acknowledging at least some doubt about the power of the federal government to discriminate against aliens, or instead the road of judicial abdication marked out in *Mathews v. Diaz*.